FIGHTERS OF THE DYING SUN

THE MOST ADVANCED JAPANESE FIGHTERS OF THE SECOND WORLD WAR

JUSTO MIRANDA

FONTHILL

Fonthill Media Language Policy

Fonthill Media publishes in the international English language market. One language edition is published worldwide. As there are minor differences in spelling and presentation, especially with regard to American English and British English, a policy is necessary to define which form of English to use. The Fonthill Policy is to use the form of English native to the author. Justo Miranda was born and educated in Spain; therefore, British English has been adopted in this publication.

Fonthill Media Limited
Fonthill Media LLC
www.fonthillmedia.com
office@fonthillmedia.com

First published in the United Kingdom and the United States of America 2021

British Library Cataloguing in Publication Data:
A catalogue record for this book is available from the British Library

Typeset in 10.5 pt on 13 pt Minion Pro
Printed and bound in England

Contents

1
The Japanese Aggressor
(28 January 1932–15 August 1945)

After the abolition of feudalism in 1871, Japan hastened to create an industrial monster that quickly exceeded the very few natural resources of the country. The inertia generated by the machines dragged the Japanese into a militaristic spiral that only a major defeat could stop.

In 1895, they annexed Taiwan; in 1905, they defeated Russia; and in 1910, they invaded Korea to seize large amounts of coal. To save Japan from the effects of the Great Depression, the Imperial Japanese Army occupied Manchuria in 1931, giving the Japanese industry access to its numerous natural resources of iron, aluminium, coking coal, soybeans, and salt.

In 1933, Japan occupied the Chinese province of Jehol and initiated a type of large-scale warfare in 1937 that alarmed the international community. Following the clash with the Soviets in Nomonhan, Japan lost access to oil concessions from Northern Sakhalin.

When France capitulated in June 1940, Japan moved into Northern French Indochina, and the US Administration reacted by banning the export of essential defence materials: aviation motors, high-octane aviation fuel, lubricants, iron, and steel scrap. The embargo was expanded in July 1941 to all grades of oil, and the British and the Dutch followed suit, embargoing exports of copper, tin, bauxite, rubber, and petroleum to Japan from their colonies in southern Asia. The Allies were putting Japan in an untenable position that would force oil-starved Japan to seize the of the Dutch East Indies.

To do this, the Imperial Japanese Army (IJA) needed to neutralise the powerful British defences in Singapore and the Imperial Japanese Navy (IJN) had to make landings in the Philippines defended by the Americans. The war would be inevitable, the Allies knew, but they did not expect the attack to succeed and were surprised when only seventeen Mitsubishi G4M bombers from the IJN *Genzan Kōkūtai* managed to sink two of the most modern British battlecruisers in a few minutes.

Shortly thereafter, eighty-seven Nakajima Ki.27b and fifty-nine Nakajima Ki.43-Ia from the IJA exterminated the 114 Brewster Buffaloes and fifty-one Hawker Hurricanes defending Malaya, pushing the Brits back to Sumatra and Burma initially, then to Ceylon and Australia. At Pearl Harbor, the Philippines, Java, and Ceylon, the Mitsubishi A6M2 Zero-Sen showed terror by annihilating most of the P-35, P-36, P-40, Hurricane Mk II, Curtiss CW.21B, and Fairey Fulmar fighters that opposed them.

The exceptional dogfight capabilities of the Japanese fighters and the ferocity and experience of their pilots had been virtually ignored by Allied intelligence officers—how did that happen?

The Nakajima Ki.27 Nate had been operating in China since March 1938, and several specimens had been captured and tested by the Chinese and Soviets. His performances were well-known in the West, but the archaic aspect of his airframe with a fixed undercarriage (inspired by that of the 1934 Northrop XFT) made the Allies think that it was a technologically outdated design.

In fact, under the protection of 600 Ki.27 fighters, the IJA conquered 90 per cent of the territories occupied during the Second World War. The aeroplane was not examined by Allied experts until the capture of a Ki.27-Otsu of the 77th *Sentai* in Burma in April 1942.

The Zero was also unknown. In the spring of 1941, the Chinese managed to shoot down an A6M2 Type 11 over Chengdu. A very accurate datasheet and three-view drawings were delivered to the US Navy Department and the US War Department, but experts did not consider the data to be credible and the report was ignored.

The Zero was designed to meet the IJN specification of 19 May 1937 that required a fighter capable of flying at more than 500 kph, with an exceptional range, to escort the bombers under the specific conditions of the war in China. Its construction was only possible by adopting a retractable landing gear, based on that of the prototype Chance Vought V-143 acquired by the Japanese in 1937. The armour and all the auxiliary equipment of a naval fighter were detached, until obtaining an aircraft that weighed 25 per cent less than the Grumman F4F, though retaining its powerful weaponry.

No one in the West believed that a fighter with these characteristics could exist until the attacks of Pearl Harbor, the Philippines, and Java. In July 1942, American experts were able to examine a Zero that had been captured in Akutan Island, managing to identify the weak points of their construction—vital information that saved US airmen's lives and that was used to design the Grumman Hellcat.

On the other hand, the Nakajima Ki.43 Hayabusa was completely unknown outside Japan. The success of the Ki.27 had delayed the start of its production until April 1941, and only forty units had entered service in December. A complete surprise to the Allies, which initially mistook it for the Zero, the Japanese Army decided to reveal its existence in April 1942. Equipped with butterfly combat flaps and weighting 33 per cent less than the P-40B, the Ki.43 was able to outmanoeuvre the Buffaloes, Hurricanes, and Tomahawks. The first unit was captured at Chittagong in the spring of 1942. Tested by the Australians, the Chinese, and the Americans, it revealed weaknesses in combat—its lack of pilot armour and self-sealing fuel tanks. The Allies soon developed 'hit and run' tactics that could be used successfully against it.

The Japanese R/T devices never worked air-to-air; the pilots used to uninstall them to save weight and communicated with movements of the wings. Their obsolete telescopic gunsights restricted the environment vision, and many Ki.27 and Ki.43 pilots were surprised by 'hit and run' attacks during the strafing of an airfield. Following initial successes achieved through attacks with local numerical superiority against second-line Allied fighters, the Japanese sword blunted in Midway, Guadalcanal, and New Guinea.

The Allies reacted by designing and building thousands of Hellcats, Seafires, Corsairs, Mustangs, Thunderbolts, and Lightings in record time, while the same 1941 models continued to be manufactured in Japan. The effective blockade by the US Navy submarine force prevented the Japanese industry from accessing China's coal; the sugarcane of the Philippines; the petroleum from Sumatra, Celebes, and Burma; the tin and bauxite from Malaya; and the rice from Thailand and Cochinchina that so much blood had cost to get. The defeat of Japan was a matter of industrial production and resources. Without them, Japanese aviation was forced to retreat to the mother islands, eventually losing air superiority over them and sacrificing themselves in pointless suicide attacks.

Nakajima Ki.27 Nate

The main effort of the IJA in late 1941 took place in Malaya, Burma, and the Philippines. At that time, Japan had fewer than 400 Zeros and over forty Hayabusas.

Its main fighters force consisted of over 600 Nates that were distributed in twenty-eight *Sentais* and manned by highly skilled pilots, most of them veterans with combat experience over China.

Under the protection of the Nates, along with small amounts of Hayabusas and Shokis, the IJA conquered 90 per cent of the territories occupied by Japanese forces during the Second World War. The IJA fighters crushed the Hurricanes, Buffaloes, Demons, and Hawks of the Allies with very aggressive tactics, often including ramming, according to the experience acquired during the aerial warfare against Soviet forces in 1939.

The first documented case was the destruction of a Blenheim bomber from the 60th Sqn RAF over Mingaladon, rammed by a Ki.27-Otsu of the 77th *Sentai*, in February 1942. On 25 February, in the same area, an aeroplane from the 50th *Sentai* that was piloted by Lt Masao Mihara rammed a Hawker Hurricane Mk II of the 135th Sqn, piloted by Squadron Leader Sutton, over Mingaladon. On 19 December 1944, the B-29 42-24715 of the 794th BS was rammed by a Ki.27-Otsu of the *Mukden Hikko Gakko*, piloted by Lt Sono-o Kasuga, over Mukden.

With the arrival of Spitfires, Hellcats, Corsairs, Thunderbolts, and Mustangs to the Far East, the surviving Nates were assigned to the Akeno, Kumagaya, and Tachiarai Army Flying Schools. Not a single Nate survived the Second World War.

Nakajima Ki.43 Hayabusa

The excellent results obtained by the Nate during the early years of the Second World War delayed the decision to replace it with a more modern, more expensive aircraft, which was ultimately more difficult to maintain. Therefore, when the manufacturing of the Ki.43 started, all Oerlikon FFL cannons, produced under license in Japan, had already been assigned to the IJN as standard weapons for the Zero fighters. Throughout its whole operational life, the Hayabusa was armed with only two machine guns.

In the course of combat against American planes, the Japanese aircraft exhausted all its small-calibre ammunition without obtaining an appreciable effect on the target. The armour and robust construction of the airframe of Airacobras, Tomahawks, Fortresses, and Liberators operating in the Far East were responsible for the minimal success of the Japanese units. The IJA pilots—veterans of the China and Khalkin-Gol conflicts against the Soviet fighters using 'Taran' tactics—were forced to perform ramming attacks to achieve results, especially when fighting the four-engined bombers.

On 26 March 1943, a Beaufighter of the 27th Sqn RAF was rammed by a Hayabusa of the 64th *Sentai*, piloted by Lt Sanae Ishii, over Shwebandaw-Burma. On 1 May, a B-24 of 492nd BS was rammed by a Ki.43 of the 64th *Sentai* piloted by Sgt Miyoshi Watanabe over Rangoon. On 8 May, B-17 41-24520, *The Fighting Swede*, was rammed by a Ki.43-II of the 24th *Sentai*, piloted by Sgt Tadao Oda, near Madang. On the 19th of that month, the Liberator 41-24269 was rammed by one Hayabusa of the 24th *Sentai*, piloted by Sgt Hikoto Sato, over Karkar Island. On 8 October, Sgt Satoshi Anabuki, of the 50th Sentai based in Mingaladon, shot down a B-24 near Rangoon using a ramming attack. On the 26th, another Liberator of the 436th BS was rammed by a Ki.43 of the 64th *Sentai* piloted by Capt. Tomio Kamiguchi, over Rangoon. On 27 December, a Ki.43 of the 25th *Sentai* piloted by Capt. Nakazaku Ozaki rammed a P-40 of the 14th AF on Suichan-China. On 6 June 1944, a Hayabusa of the 50th *Sentai*, piloted by Sgt Tomesaku Igarashi, rammed a P-38 of 459th FS over Burma. On 4 August 1944, a Ki.43 of the 25th *Sentai* rammed a B-25 over Hengyang, China.

On 2 November, the IJA ordered all air defence *Sentais* to form a *Shinten Seiku Tai* unit to be specialised in ramming tactics, with the objective to confront the American heavy bombers. A group of selected pilots received special training in the Army Flying Schools of Akatsuki (1st *Hakko Tai*), Hitachi (2nd and 10th *Hakko Tai*), and the 244th *Sentai* (4th *Hakko Tai*), mainly using Ki.43 and Ki.44 fighters.

On 7 December, B-29 42-63356, *Georgia Peach*, was rammed over Manshū by a Ki.43 of the 4th Training *Sentai*, piloted by Lt Fumiro Sou. On 21 December, another Superfortress, the *Old Campaigner* (42-24715), was rammed by one Hayabusa of the Manchurian Air Force, piloted by WO Takei Matsumoto over the same area.

The emphasis placed by the Japanese designers in the lightness of the airframes of their fighters, to save weight and gain manoeuvrability, acted against all attempts by Nakajima to equip the Ki.43 with a more powerful armament. The wing structure simply could not resist the vibrations produced by the recoil of the 20-mm cannon.

By mid-1944, some launch tests were conducted at the Army Aero Test Department using 10-cm Ro-San Dan Ro.3 air-to-air rockets mounted beneath the wings of a Ki.43-III-Ko. The Ro.3 was a scaled-down version of the 12-cm AA naval spin-stabilised rocket barrage fired from a wire basket made of welded wires or from an iron tube. As happened with their German counterparts *Föhn* and W Gr.21, the launch tests from aeroplanes showed that this type of rocket, without fins, lacked the precision necessary to be effective in air-to-air combat.

In the summer of 1945, tests were made with two prototypes of the Ki.43-III-Otsu with extensive modifications on wing and fuselage structure and two nose-mounted Ho-5 cannons, theoretically suitable for propeller synchronisation, without obtaining good results. To improve the destructiveness of the Hayabusa, they also tried to use *Ta-Dan* bombs. They were submunition containers, originally designed to bomb airfields, produced for the IJA in two versions (HE and hollow charge) that were widely used in air-to-air bombing tactics by the Ki.43, Ki.44, Ki.45, Ki.46, and Ki.84.

On 14 February 1944, a Ki.43-II of the 59th *Sentai*, piloted by WO Kazuo Shimizu, destroyed three Mitchell bombers over New Guinea, using *Ta-Dan* bombs. He repeated the attack on a Thunderbolt that was also destroyed the next day.

Mitsubishi A6M Zero

Designed in 1938 to defend the Imperial Fleet against the low-level attacks of the torpedo-bombers and against the dive bombers at medium-altitude, the Zero did not need to have good performances above 8,000 m.

The IJN did not consider the American B-17, conceived as a strategic bomber at high altitude, to be a threat to the warships in the open sea, although the great range of the Fortress would allow it to attack Japanese naval bases on the periphery of the empire. The answer seemed to be the Raiden, a high-altitude point defence interceptor with high climb rate. Yet it proved to be so complex and difficult to maintain that it finally went into service too late and in small numbers.

When the B-17 and B-24 heavy bombers began to operate against areas of Japanese influence, there were only three types of available fighters to intercept them—the Hayabusa, the Shoki, and the Zero. However, neither of them had enough firepower to effectively fight against the American aeroplanes, a task considered difficult even for the *Sturm* German fighters equipped with heavy armour and 30-mm cannons.

After many experiments and losses, the Japanese learned to fight these giants using air-to-air bombing tactics. The IJA used the Type 2, No. 6, Mk 21 bomb of 52.5 kg—basically, a breakaway canister of a hexagonal section containing thirty-six HE submunition Model II of 1 kg, with an impact fuse, or forty hollow-charge 0.4-kg baby bombs that had originally been designed to attack airfields. The naval model was very similar but with a circular section. This type of bomb, known as a *Ta-Dan* bomb, was first used in 1944 together with the 3-Go aerial burst bombs of 33.7, 56.6, and 251.8 kg. The 3-Go tailfins had offset tailfins that rotated at 1,000 rpm after release as well as a clockwork tail fuse. When the bomb detonated, explosive charges blew out steel pellets filled with white phosphorus in a circular area of 70 m in diameter, causing fires in the engines and upper surfaces of the bombers.

In September 1944, some A6M2 Model 21 fighters of the 381st *Kōkūtai* were equipped with ten 3-Go bombs mounted beneath the wings. The IJN recommended to launch them at 1,300 m from the target and 150 m over the flight level of the bomber 'box' formation.

On 26 April 1944, six Ki.43 fighters of the IJA 204th *Sentai* had a worrying first contact with a B-29, which was shot twelve times without apparent results. The giant plane, heavily loaded with supplies and the tail gun off service, just ascended until the Hayabusas were forced to abandon the pursuit by lack of oxygen. It was known that the B-29 could fly at high altitudes thanks to its turbocharged engines, but when it first appeared 10,000 m above Tokyo on a reconnaissance mission, it was flying so fast that the Ki.44 interceptors of the 47th *Sentai* could not reach it. By contrast, the J2M4, J2M5, and N1K5-J fighters that had been designed to face it had not even begun to be manufactured.

The problem was the technology of the turbochargers, whose manufacturing methods were kept so secret that the Americans refused to share them even with the Allies.

In 1937, Japan acquired a turbocharger to the Swiss company Brown, Boveri & Cie; the Hitachi, Nakajima, and Mitsubishi engineers received the assignment to develop their own turbocharger based on the Swiss model. One experimental three-stage Mitsubishi turbocharger was installed in Raiden prototypes J2M4 and J2M5, with such poor results that its series production was dismissed. The Hitachi turbo was manufactured with the best alloys of chrome-molybdenum steel, but its development was too slow and was still being tested, installed in a Saiun night fighter by the end of the Second World War.

The Nakajima team tried to modify an A6M2 by installing a Sakae turbocharged engine without an intercooler. The prototype was named A6M4 and started its flight test in Yokosuka Arsenal in 1943, experiencing fires and multiple ruptures in the compressor and ducting. The origin of these failures was that the imported turbo was actually a design for diesel 500-hp engines with an operating temperature that was 200 degrees Celsius lower than that of petrol Japanese engines. Despite all these problems, the Mitsubishi engineers managed to build the A6M3 model in 1942, powered by a Sakae 21 that was able to climb up to 11,000 m thanks to a modest two-speed supercharger.

In 1943, the A6M5 already had an absolute ceiling of 11,740 m, but it took nearly thirty minutes to reach that altitude. For lack of a better weapon, the IJN was forced to use the Zero to defend its bases, its fleet and the imperial capital. On 21 November 1944, the B-29 42-93848 was rammed by an A6M5 of the 352nd *Kōkutai*, piloted by Lt Mikihiko Sakamoto over Omura. On 3 December, some A6M3 night fighters of the 302nd *Kōkutai* managed to destroy two B-29s (42-63461 and 42-24656) over Tokyo using *Ta-Dan* bombs and 20-mm cannons installed in *Schräge Musik* configuration.

In 1945, some A6M5 from 302nd *Kōkutai* began using the Type 3, Mk 27 rocket-propelled burst bombs that could be launched from the altitude of the bomber formation without flying over it. The air-to-air bombing used to be complemented by a *tai-atari* (ramming attack) against the bombers that had been hit. On 3 January 1945, one A6M5-Ko of the 302nd *Kōkutai* based in Atsugi shot down the 42-24785 over Nagoya. It was the first B-29 destroyed by the Mk 27 60-kg rocket bombs. Another suicide method used by the Zero pilots was to position themselves at the centre of the 'box' and manually detonating a 250-kg bomb kg carried under the belly of the plane.

Although the ramming concept was not new to the Japanese, they were concerned about the high structural strength of the US aircraft and its great capacity to withstand battle damage. When on 20 December 1943, the Bulgarian pilot of a Messerschmitt Bf 109 G-2 destroyed a B-24 by ramming, the Japanese Embassy in Sofia requested details of the attack.

IJA JAPANESE FIGHTERS 1937-1942

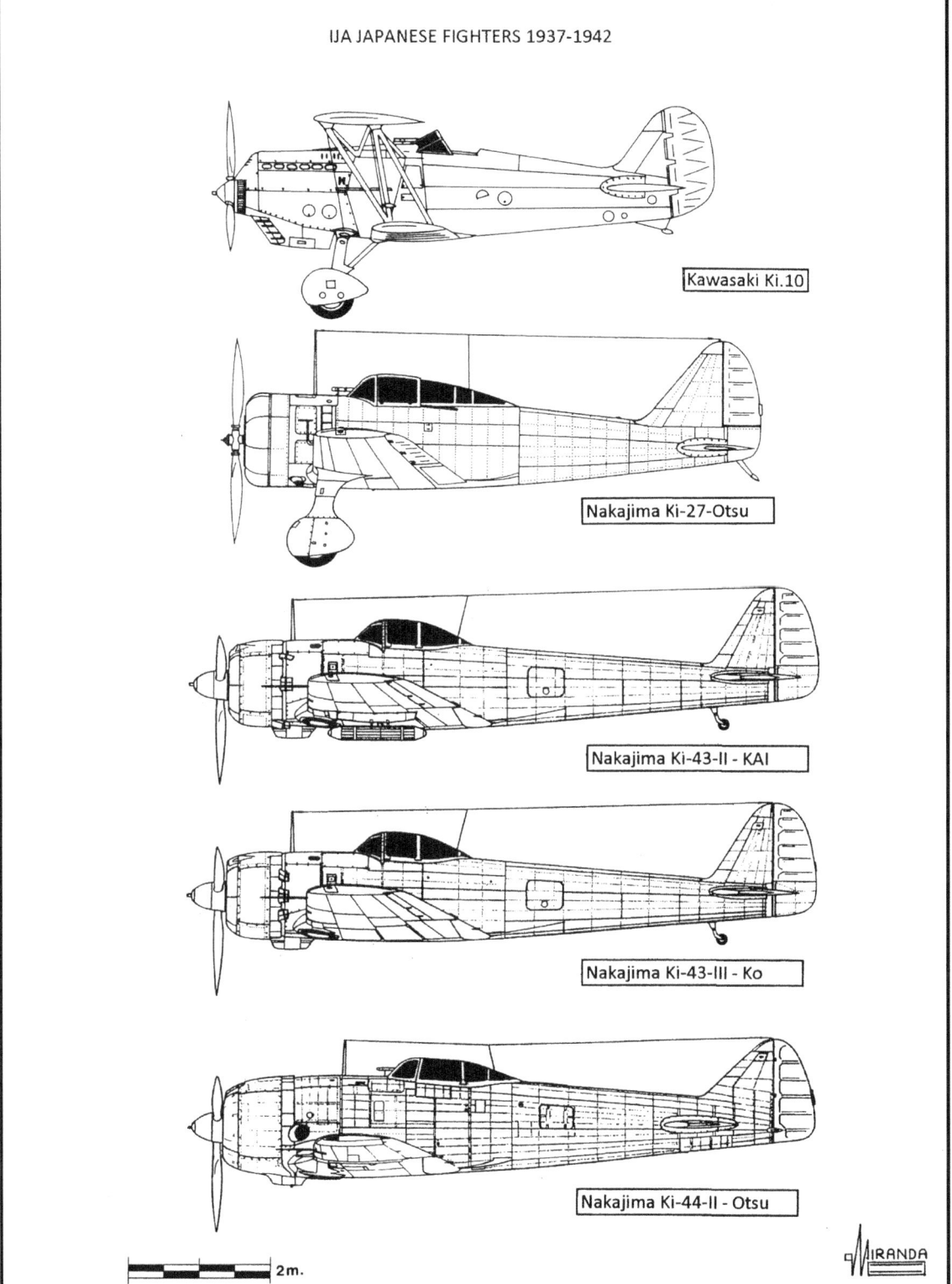

Kawasaki Ki.10

Nakajima Ki-27-Otsu

Nakajima Ki-43-II - KAI

Nakajima Ki-43-III - Ko

Nakajima Ki-44-II - Otsu

2m.

MIRANDA

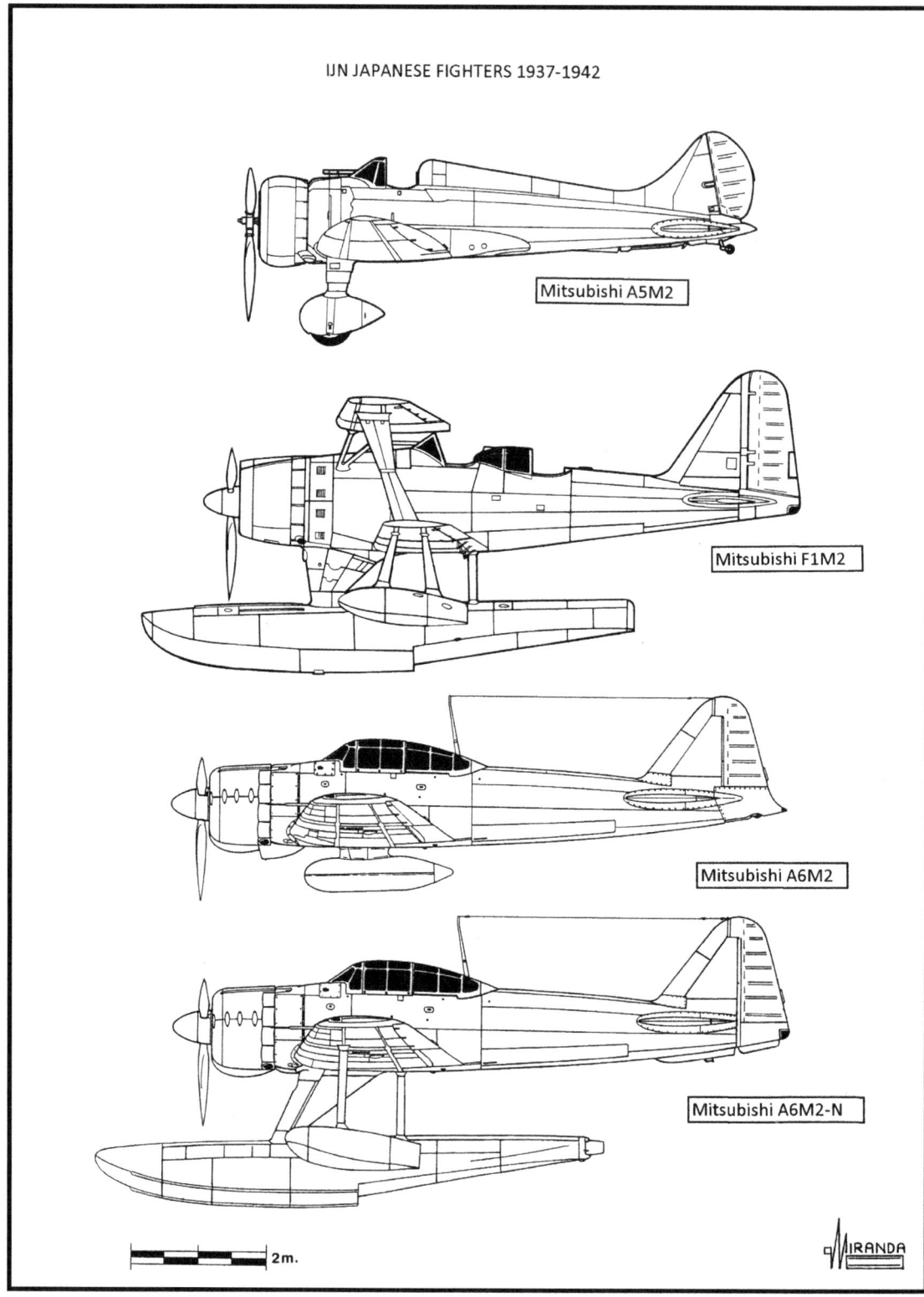

IJN JAPANESE FIGHTERS 1937-1942

Mitsubishi A5M2

Mitsubishi F1M2

Mitsubishi A6M2

Mitsubishi A6M2-N

2 m.

MIRANDA

Imperial Japanese Army Aircraft and Projects

Nakajima Ki.44 Shoki

During the 1930s, the Western powers that constrained the Japanese territorial expansion were developing four-engined heavy bombers. The Tupolev TB-3, capable of reaching Tokyo taking off from Soviet territory, flew for the first time in 1930. In 1932, the French Farman 222 also performed its first flight; although ugly as all its kind, it was very effective to control navigation in the area to the south of Formosa, operating from Saigon. The Boeing B-17 prototype was on the air in 1935, and the British Sunderland and Stirling prototypes, capable of transatlantic flights, followed in 1938 and 1939. Even the Dutch worked on a four-engined version of the Fokker T-IX, named T-VI /115.

The B-17 had a 2,000-mile range, turbocharged engines, and such a powerful armament that allowed this aircraft autonomous defence. When the Imperial Japanese Army (IJA) was aware of these excellent performances, they realised that the American bomber was above the interception capabilities of the standard fighter Ki.27 and possibly exceeded its successor Ki.43, which had not yet entered service.

Given the potential threat that the B-17s based in the Philippines could represent, the IJA *Kaigun Koku Hombu* (Army's Air Headquarters) requested Nakajima design the Ki.44, a point-defence interceptor with a high climb rate and twice the armament of the Ki.43. Realities of war showed that this effort would not be enough since the US industry was able to design, test, and mass-produce a new aircraft in a third of the time than the Japanese.

On 1 November 1944, the first American bomber flew over Tokyo; it was not the expected B-17 but a giant B-29 F-13 42-93852, of the 3rd Photo Recon Sqn, ironically named 'Tokyo Rose'. When the Ki.44-II-Otsu of the 47th *Sentai* tried to intercept it, they discovered that the Superfortress flew so high and fast that they could not reach it. It turned out that the Japanese plane used for the intended interception, equivalent to the Starfighter of the time and with an astonishing climb rate of 5,000 m in four minutes, was not good enough to do the work for which it had been designed.

The psychological impact caused by this realisation on the Japanese pilots had important consequences. The IJA needed interceptors equipped with turbosuperchargers, but the Japanese industry was unable to build them or even replicate those of the enemy bombers that had been shot down. They also needed more powerful weapons with a wider range, whose usefulness was not foreseen until it was too late.

In 1944, the German Luftwaffe had two types of 30-mm cannons to fight against the B-17 and B-24. The MK 103, a potent and heavy weapon, with a great effective range and a low rate of fire, difficult to install in single-engined fighters given its powerful recoil that damaged the airframes and the MK 108, light and with a high rate of fire, but with a low effective range that forced the *Sturm* assault fighters to come dangerously close to the self-defence formations of American bombers.

Across the world, the Japanese interceptors fighting against the B-29 had similar problems. The IJA 37-mm Ho-203 cannon weighed 89 kg, with a rate of fire of 120 rpm and an effective range of 1,000 m. As was the case with the German Mk 103, this gun was difficult to integrate into the fragile airframes of the Japanese fighters because of their excessive recoil. The alternative seemed to be the new 40-mm Ho-301, weighing about half of the Ho-203; it had a moderate recoil and an increased rate of fire of 450 rpm, although their range was 150 m only because the ammunition was propelled by small spin-stabilised rockets.

During its design, it was determined that the warhead should at least contain 65 g of high explosive (HE) to be effective against the B-29s, but this could only be achieved by reducing the amount of rocket propellant and thus the range of the weapon. The manufacturing of the Venturi nozzles at the base of this type of rocket, which generated both propulsion and spin, required an accuracy that the Japanese industry could not achieve for large production runs. Therefore, the trajectory of the rockets was not accurate enough for air-to-air combat.

Under pressure from the bombings and the proven futility of the 12.7- and 20-mm weapons, the IJA decided to carry out a series of operational tests with two Ho-203 guns (with twenty-five-round drum magazines) installed in the wings of some Ki.44-II-Hei of the 70th *Sentai*, based in Manchuria.

On 8 September 1944, ninety B-29s from the 58th BW made an attack on the Showa Steel Works at Anshan. The aircraft of the 70th *Sentai* attempted interception, but the extra weight of the guns prevented them from reaching the flight altitude of the bombers in time. Meanwhile, the aircraft of the 59th and 104th *Sentais*, equipped with standard armament, could only manage to damage three B-29s, after losing in combat eleven Shokis to the powerful American defensive fire.

Some tests were also carried out with the Ho-301, using some Ki.44-II-Otsu of the 1st Field Reserve Squadron without suffering any structural damages. Afterwards, some Ki.44s of the 47th *Sentai* were transformed to test these 40-mm cannons in combat. The 47th was an elite squadron whose pilots had some success fighting against the Liberators at a medium altitude.

However, the flight altitude of the B-29 made the Ki.44 difficult to manoeuvre with the extra weight. Above 8,000 m, the small wings generated little lift, and the plane uncontrollably fell several hundred meters when trying any combat manoeuvring. Its only effective tactic was diving at 45 degrees, frontally attacking the 'bomber box' (to avoid the dangerous effect of the 20-mm cannon at the B-29 tail), firing against the vulnerable bomber cockpit, and then increasing the dive angle to avoid a collision.

These manoeuvres were already difficult with the Shoki standard, but with the extra weight of the guns, the flight controls barely responded due to the low air density at high altitude. It is, therefore, possible that some registered rammings were actually accidental collisions. After shooting, the two aircraft crossed just a few meters away, with a combined speed of 1,000 kph. Considering the limited range of the Ho-301, the Japanese pilot could either shoot four rounds and escape or shoot six rounds and die.

The *Ta-Dan* bombs used by the IJA for air-to-air bombing were also not effective. Some pilots—such as Capt. Yasuro Masazaki of the 47th *Sentai*—developed a special skill using these weapons and achieving some hits. However, their experience was not transferable, and *Ta-Dan* proved useful in combat at lower altitudes only.

On 4 February 1945, the Ki.44 fighters of the 70th *Sentai* destroyed B-29 42-24608 over Kobe and, six days later, the 42-24867 over Ota, using air-to-air bombing tactics. Some Ki.43 and Ki.44 aircraft of the 1st Field Reserve Squadron based in Singapore were used in experiments with the new *Ro-San Dan* spin-stabilised rockets that proved to have too erratic flight paths for use in air-to-air combat. Three types of spin-stabilised rockets were built for the IJA during the Second World War:

Ro-San Dan (Ro-3) of 10 cm and 10 kg
Ro-San Dan (Ro-5) of 20.2 cm and 76 kg
Ro-Sichi Dan (Ro-7) of 30.3 cm and 280 kg

All of them were stabilised in flight, rotating at 3,600 rpm thanks to the spin effect produced by six 25-degree-angled nozzles; they had incendiary and shrapnel warheads, time fuses, and percussion primers and could also be fired from simple iron tubes. Some tests were also performed with an unknown type of fin-stabilised rocket—possibly a modified Ro-3 using a Ki.43 with underwing rails—but there is no record that it was used in combat as with the efficient German R4M air-to-air rocket.

After all these failures, only the *tai-atari* (head-on ramming) tactics remained, using the plane as a weapon to destroy the B-29 in a deliberate collision course.

There are no records indicating the assignment of the Ki-44 to any *tokko* (suicide) unit as these aircraft were considered indispensable for air defence of the Japanese mainland. The structure of the Ki.44-II-Ko only supported the installation of a 150-kg bomb fixed for close-range attacks, instead of a centreline 200-l fuel tank. The Ki.44 of the following series could transport two fuel tanks under the central section of the wing in a rather rear position, not to interfere with the deployment of the landing gear. It could carry two 52-kg cluster-bomb containers for 30 Type 2 *Ta-Dan* bombs under the outer wings.

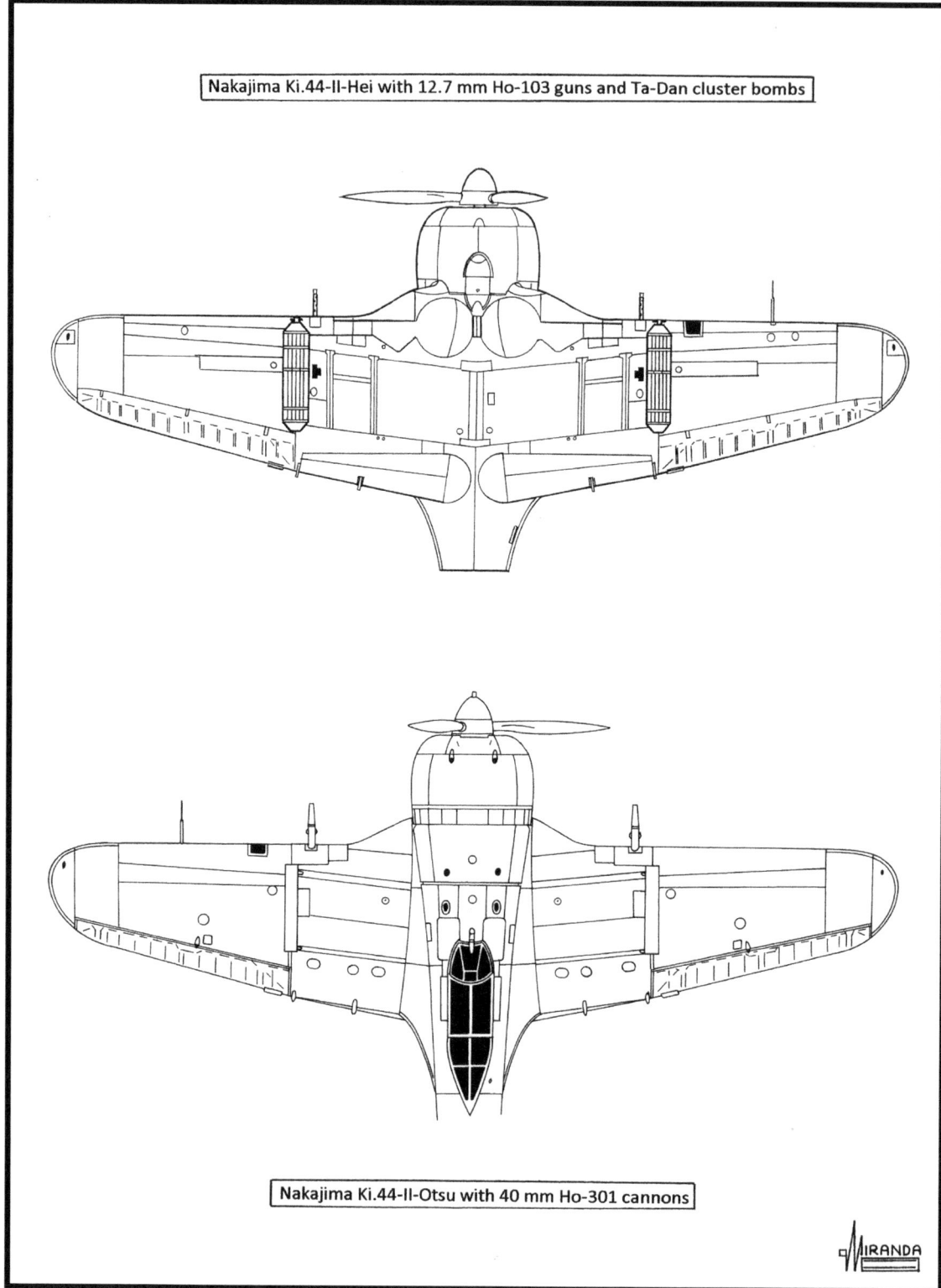

Nakajima Ki.44-II-Hei with 12.7 mm Ho-103 guns and Ta-Dan cluster bombs

Nakajima Ki.44-II-Otsu with 40 mm Ho-301 cannons

MIRANDA

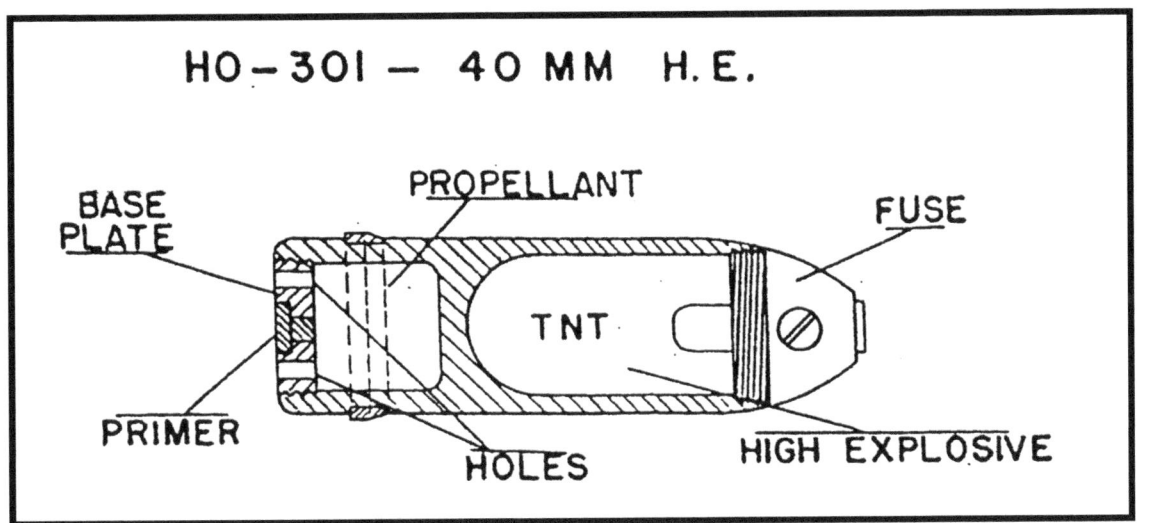

HO-301 — 40 MM H.E.

BASE PLATE

PROPELLANT

FUSE

TNT

PRIMER

HOLES

HIGH EXPLOSIVE

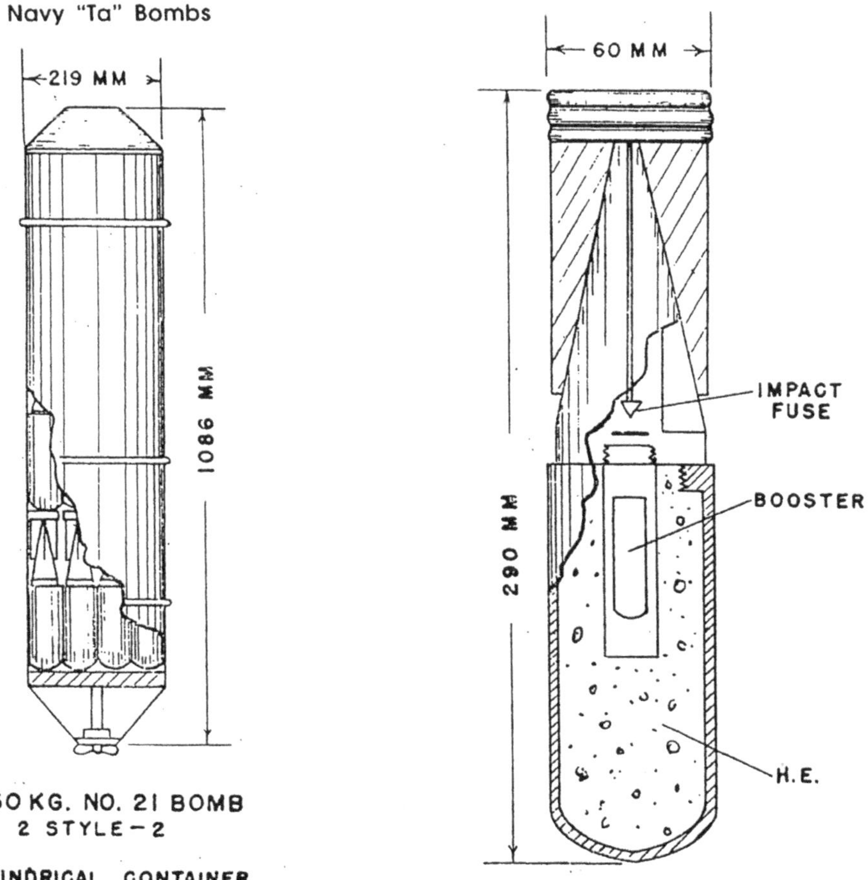

Navy "Ta" Bombs

←219 MM→

1086 MM

60 KG. NO. 21 BOMB
2 STYLE-2

(CYLINDRICAL CONTAINER
HOUSES 36 BABY BOMBS)

←60 MM→

290 MM

IMPACT FUSE

BOOSTER

H.E.

BABY BOMB

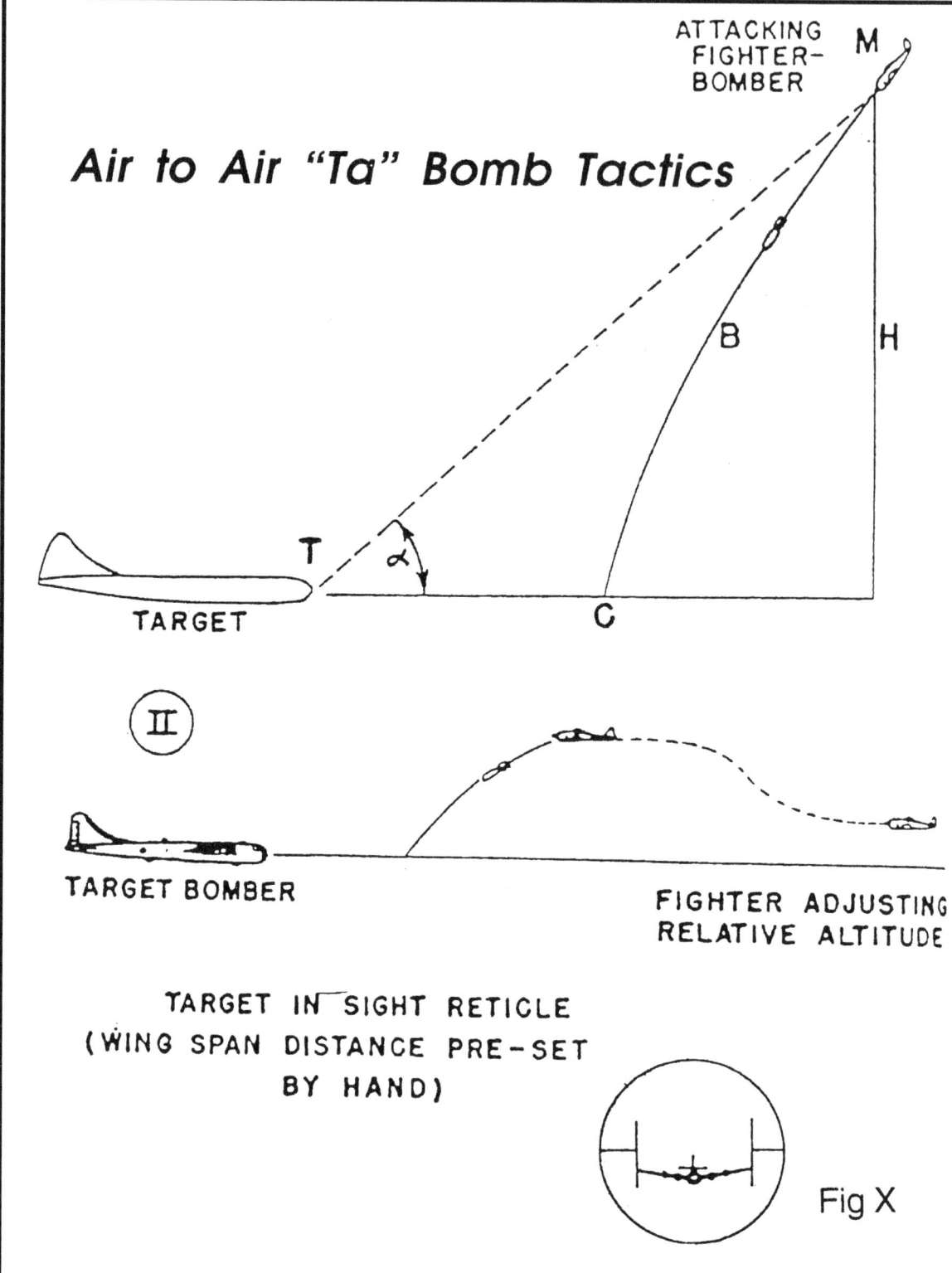

Air to Air "Ta" Bomb Tactics

ATTACKING
FIGHTER-
BOMBER

M

H

B

α

T

TARGET

C

Ⅱ

TARGET BOMBER

FIGHTER ADJUSTING
RELATIVE ALTITUDE

TARGET IN SIGHT RETICLE
(WING SPAN DISTANCE PRE-SET
BY HAND)

Fig X

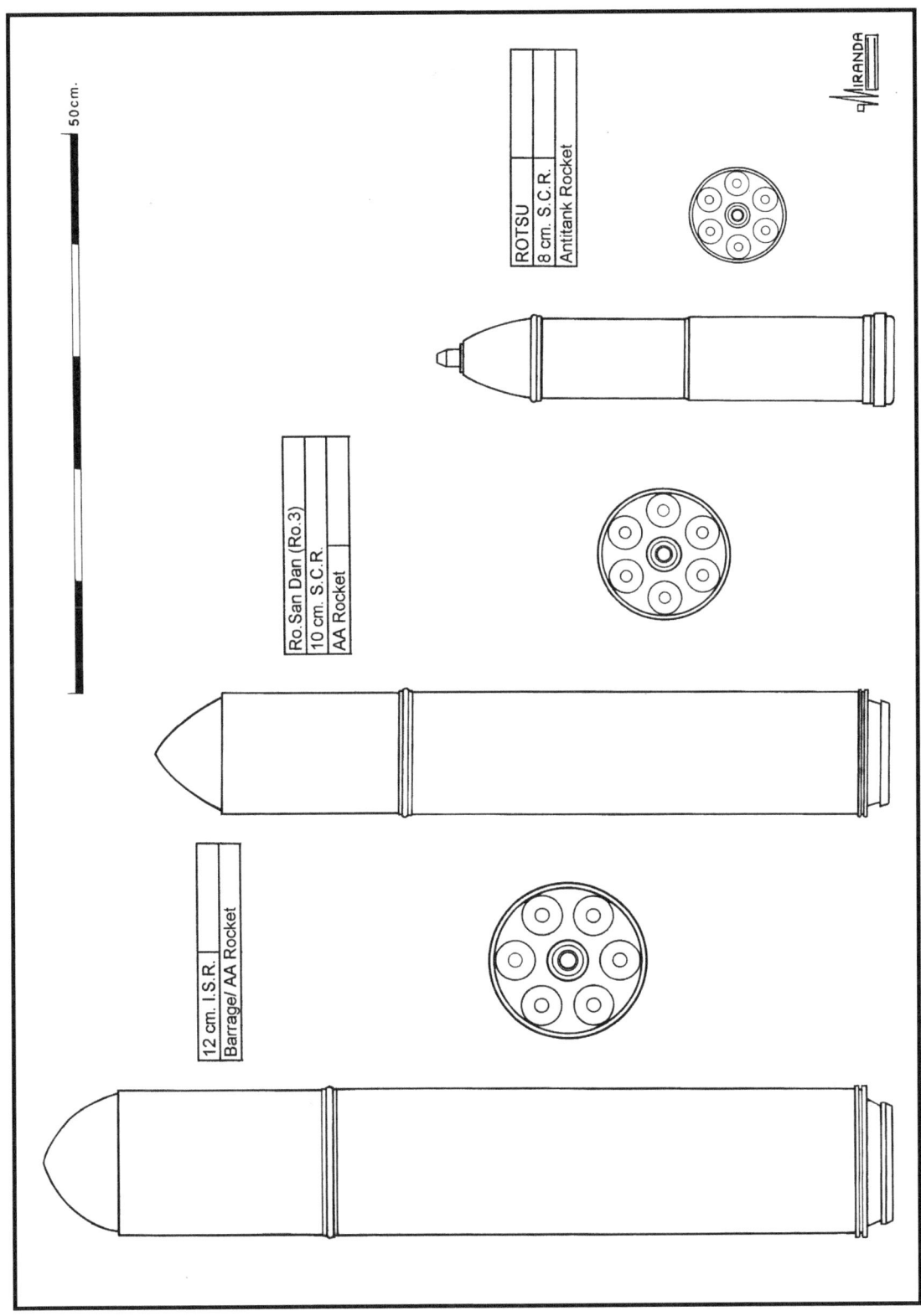

ROTSU
8 cm. S.C.R.
Antitank Rocket

Ro.San Dan (Ro.3)
10 cm. S.C.R.
AA Rocket

12 cm. I.S.R.
Barrage/ AA Rocket

50 cm.

Kawasaki Ki.45 Toryu

The writings of Giulio Douhet had convinced many influential persons in the mid-1930s that future wars would be won from the air by large fleets of bombers. Yet the combat experience gained in Spain and China clearly indicated that the bombers had to be escorted by fighters to be effective.

The limited range of the fighters of the time restricted the territorial ambitions of the countries a little over 300 km beyond its borders, but Germany dreamt of the Urals, Italy dreamt of Egypt, and Japan dreamt of China.

Trying to overcome that limit was how the *Zerstörer* concept was conceived—a heavy fighter with powerful weapons and a high range in which the Axis powers invested large resources with a more ideological than scientific basis. When the realities of war and the laws of physics were imposed over London in the summer of 1940, Göring was shocked to hear that his heavy Messerschmitt Bf 110 could not hunt the Hurricanes because they could make tighter turns. The Italians had similar luck with the Romeo 58 and Savoia 91, which never reached the production stage. Göring persevered in this error, favouring the construction of 300 units of the Messerschmitt Me 210, whose design flaws cost 3 million *Reichsmarks* and a major national scandal.

In Japan, the IJA ordered the design of the Kawasaki Ki.45, inspired by the operational philosophy of the Bf 110. After many tests using prototypes, the Ki.45-KAI-Ko entered service armed with two machine guns in the nose and one 20-mm cannon in a ventral tunnel. Over the course of its first combat over Kweilin, China, on 12 June 1942, five Toryus of the 84th *Chutai* faced five Tomahawks of the AVG, losing three to zero. According to reports coming from the fighting in Burma—where the Ki.45 of the 21st *Sentai* faced the British Hurricane Mk IIA and Mohawks Mk IV—the IJA realised that the *Toryu* was not able to fight against single-engined fighters.

The Ki.45 could face the British Beaufighters in New Guinea with dignity but it was almost impossible for this aircraft to bring them down, because of the low rate of fire of its antique cannon. The production of the Ki.45 was then reoriented towards ground attack specialised versions like the Ki.45-KAI-Otsu. This aircraft had a new 20-mm cannon Ho-3 with a 50-round magazine in the nose and a 37-mm Type 94 cannon, manually loaded, with a low rate of fire, in the ventral tunnel. It could carry two Type 98, number 25 land bombs of 242.2 kg under the wings.

Both the Ko and the Otsu versions were widely used in New Guinea, China, and Malaya against trains, patrol torpedo boats, and landing ships. In 1943, the surviving aircraft were sent to flight schools and replaced in combat units by the Ki.45-KAI-Hei. In this version, the 37-mm cannon was the Ho-203 automatic model with a 25-round magazine and was in the nose. The ventral tunnel carried a 20-mm Ho-3. The Hei retained the ability to carry two 250-kg bombs.

All the aeroplanes of this model manufactured by the Tachikawa Arsenal had the barrel visible, protruding from the rounded extreme nose, while those manufactured by Akashi were covered by a conical fairing. The Hei proved very useful in the fight against the Liberators, achieving some successes during the first months of 1943. When American bombers began to be escorted by Lightning fighters, the Ki.45 again performed ground attack missions. During the summer, the Ki.45 of the 5th, 13th, and 45th *Sentais* suffered heavy losses against the second generation fighters of the Corsair and Thunderbolt type, newcomers to New Guinea.

After receiving reports on the construction of airfields for the B-29 in China, the IJA began preparations for the defence of the Japanese mainland. The evaluation of the Hei showed that the aircraft possessed good flight performances at high altitude; it could also fight using all of its weapons between 8,200 and 9,750 m without losing any manoeuvrability, and up to 10,200 m with some weight loss, although it took it too long to reach that altitude.

On 15 June 1944, during a night raid on Yawata by the B-29 of the 468th BG, 42-6230 *Limber Dragon* was shot down by a Ki.45 of the 4th *Sentai*, piloted by Lt Sadamitsu Kimura. On 29 July, B-29 BS 42-6275 of the 794th BS was shot down over Chengshen, China, by a Ki.45 of the 25th *Sentai*. On 7 December, 42-6262 *Round Trip Ticket* of the 678th BS, was shot down over Manshū by another Ki.45 of the 25th *Sentai*. On 22 January 1945, during an attack on the Nakajima factory of Tokyo, 42-24769 *Rover Boy Express* was downed near Konoike by a Hei of the 4th *Sentai* piloted by Isamu Kashiide. On 4 February, a Ki.45 of the 4th *Sentai* downed 42-24629 *Devil's Darling* over Kobe. On 5 June, 42-69665 was downed by a Ki.45 of the 53rd *Sentai* also over Kobe.

Some of these victories were achieved via frontal attacks by firing against the cockpit of the bomber from a distance of 100 m or by 45-degree diving against the engines. When the IJA ordered every *Sentai* of air defence to create an air superiority company specialising in ramming, some Hei were expressly modified by removing the armaments to make them lighter.

The Ki.45 proved to be very suitable as a rammer because it had fast diving features that were superior to those of any other Japanese fighter. It was also very resistant to battle damage, especially when armoured plates were installed to protect the pilot. In this version, the radio operator was removed, and the rear opening of the cockpit was coated with metal plates. Even with its weight reduction, the Ki.45 weighed more than twice a Ki.44, which allowed it to cause much greater structural damage during a collision.

In early March 1945, the B-29s began a series of devastating low-altitude night raids against the sixty-seven major cities in Japan. Despite what happened in Germany, the IJA had not foreseen the need to build specialised night fighters. Taken by surprise by the change in strategy of the Americans, the Ki.45 pilots improvised some nocturnal technical interception techniques, coordinating their attacks with the ground searchlights regiments. They also used a B-17 caught in Bandung for nocturnal visual localisation practices. Some Hei aircraft suffered field transformations for night fighting, fitting them with two 20-mm Ho-5 guns angled at 35 degrees in *Schräge Musik* configuration.

The fires lit the undersides of the B-29s making them visible to the pilots of Toryus, Gekkos, and Zeros that awaited the opportunity of destroying them at a low altitude, firing at their belly from close range. When, at the end of May 1945, the Superfortress came to the imperial capital city escorted by numerous Mustangs based on Iwo Jima, the Ki.45 survivors were sent on *tokko* missions.

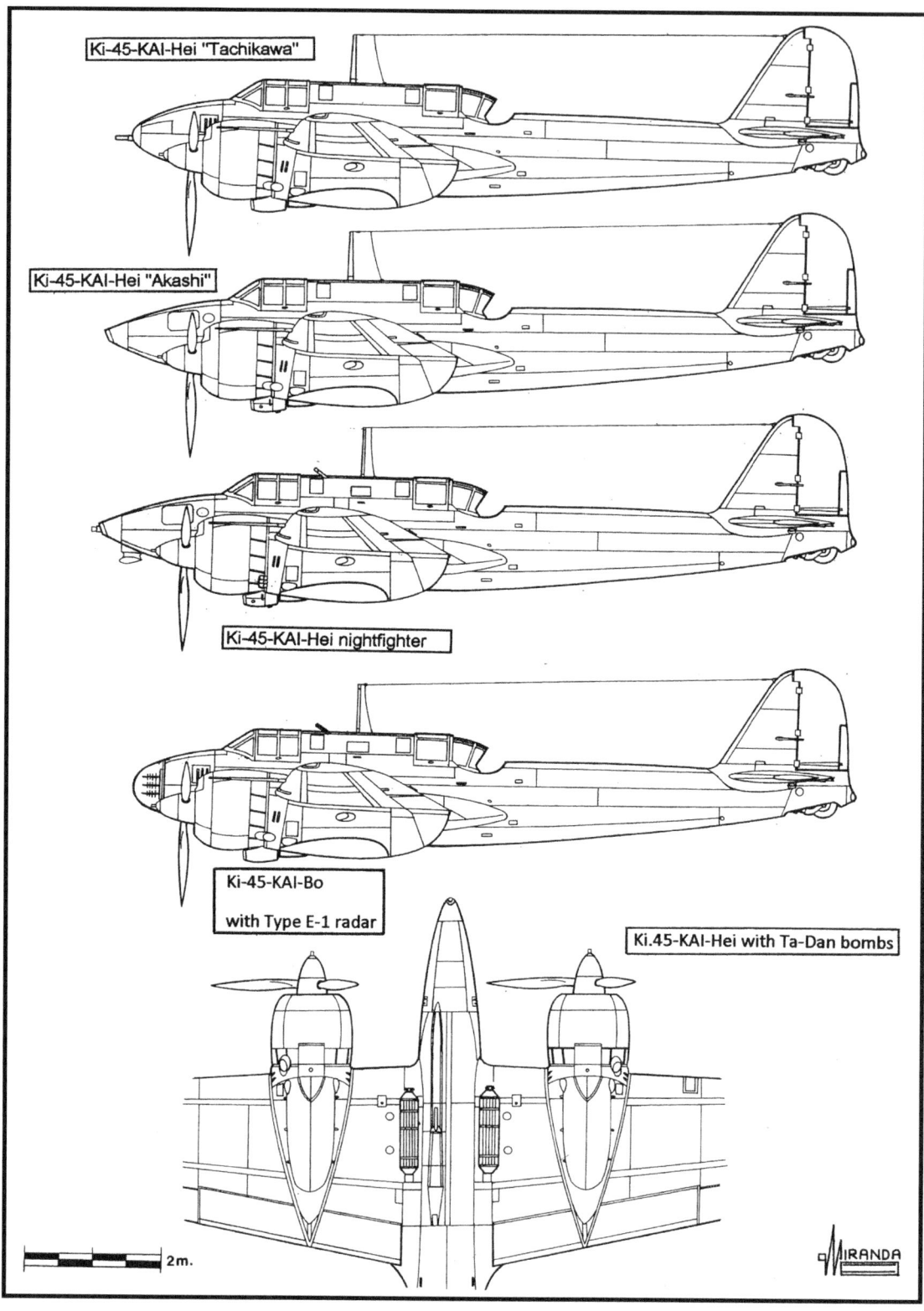

Ki-45-KAI-Hei "Tachikawa"

Ki-45-KAI-Hei "Akashi"

Ki-45-KAI-Hei nightfighter

Ki-45-KAI-Bo

with Type E-1 radar

Ki.45-KAI-Hei with Ta-Dan bombs

2m.

Mitsubishi Ki.46 Shin Shitei

The Mitsubishi Ki.46 was designed in 1938 as a high-altitude photographic reconnaissance aeroplane to monitor the movements of the Red Army and evade the Polikarpov I-16 fighters. The Mitsubishi design team emphasised its aerodynamic shape and lightweight minimal fuselage cross-section.

Manufacturing of thirty-four pre-production Ki.46-I units began in 1940, assigning them for training pilots at the Shimonoshizu Army Flying School and to some operational tests with the 81st *Sentai*, based in Indochina. Some of the 1,085 units of the Ki.46-II production version were manufactured, entering service in July 1941, just in time for reconnaissance missions over the future expansion areas of the IJA during the Second World War.

In October, some *Shin Shitei* recce aeroplanes of the 51st Independent *Chutai*, based in Kampong Trach, Cambodia, photographed the British defence installations in Malaya. The aircraft of the 76th Independent *Chutai*, operating from Taiwan, conducted reconnaissance missions over the airfields and naval US bases in the Philippines. After the conquest of Burma by Japanese troops, the Ki.46 based there began to spy on the movements of the Royal Navy in Trincomalee, Ceylon. They could also carry out reconnaissance missions over the harbour of Darwin, in northern Australia, taking off from airfields located in Timor, after the occupation of the Dutch East Indies.

With a top speed of 604 kph and a ceiling of 10,700 m, the *Shin Shitei* was immune to interception until the arrival of the new P-38-F Lightning and Spitfire Mk V fighters in the Far East. Flying at a cruising speed of 425 kph, they could remain aloft for nearly six hours. Impressed by their performance, the IJA made several attempts to obtain variants of the Ki.46 suitable for air-to-air combat.

By early 1943, seventeen Ki.46-II were modified by fitting one Type 94 37-mm cannon to their nose—a very heavy weapon taken from a medium tank. The Type 94 was to be loaded manually by the pilot and had a rate of fire lower than three rounds per minute. In February 1943, six modified Ki.46 were sent to Rabaul to fight against the B-17 and B-24. Operating with the 13th *Sentai*, they proved that the excessive weight made the aircraft noseheavy and difficult to manoeuvre.

On 24 November, six additional Ki.46s were modified as *Hyakushiki Shitei* III (Air Defense Fighter) with the installation of a Type 94 in a 57-degree *Schräge Musik* configuration activated by the radio operator. Integrated into the 17th Independent *Chutai*, they were used to defend the Nakajima factories against the B-29 of the 73rd BW. Fifteen *Shin Shitei* aircraft of the Ki.46-Hei version were manufactured in July 1944. They had two Ho-5 cannons in the nose and one Ho-204 37-mm automatic cannon in a *Schräge Musik* configuration.

In the autumn, some tests were conducted at the Hitachi Training Center using a Hei that was experimentally armed with a Type 94 cannon in a dorsal position. The plane achieved an altitude of 12,300 m using 95 octane fuel, but its flight was too unstable to properly aim the cannon. It was also too heavy and took over twenty minutes to reach the level of flight of the B-29.

Some of these aircraft were experimentally used as night fighters by the 16th *Dokuritsu Hikotai* and the 17th Independent *Chutai*. It turned out that they lacked stability for sustained shooting using the Ho-204 cannon because the fuselage structure was too light and could not absorb the recoil. The Ki.46-III-Ko version entered service in August 1944. It was faster (650 kph), with new Ha-112-II engines, direct fuel injection, rear armour plating, and an improved oxygen supply system. It could also transport a 600-l fuel tank under the fuselage, which provided an extended range of 4,000 km.

During the autumn, tests were performed at the Hitachi Training Centre using a Ko experimentally armed with a Type 94 in a dorsal position. The plane could attain an altitude of 12,300 m, using 95 octane fuel, but again, its flight at that altitude was too unstable to properly aim the cannon.

The IJA then ordered the manufacturer to transform ninety units of the Ki.46-III-Ko into fighters. The first seventy-five machines became the Otsu model, with a flat windscreen, two staggered Ho-5 20-mm cannons, and attachments under the wing roots to carry two Type 2, Number 6, Mk 21 *Ta-Dan* 60-kg air-to-air bombs. Fifteen further units were transformed into the Ki.46-III-Hei version, with two Ho-5s in the nose and one 37-mm Ho-204 in a 57-degree *Schräge Musik* configuration.

The 'Otsu' version was used against the B-29 by two *Sentais*, six *Chutais*, and one *Hikotai*, proving that its armament was too light to destroy the giants. Some success was only achieved by using *tai-atari* tactics and *Ta-Dan* bombs. On 20 August 1944, B-29 42-24474 of the 462nd BG was shot down over Yawata by a Ki.46 of the 28th *Sentai* using air-to-air bombs. On 6 November 1944, the Ki.46 made an attack with *Ta-Dan* bombs against the B-29 bases in Tinian.

On 21 November, the Otsu of the 19th Independent *Chutai* attempted interception of some B-29 of the 58th BW, over Cheju Island-Korea, but could not reach them due to its low rate of climb. Three days later, the 73rd BW bombed the Nakajima-Musashino factory. During the attack, a B-29 of the 500th BG (possibly the 42-24662) was rammed by a *Shin Shitei* of the 17th Independent *Chutai* from Chofu-Tokyo airbase, piloted by Lt Motokuni Ise, over Hachijo Island. On 3 December, another B-29 was damaged by *Ta-Dan* bombs launched by the Ki-46 of Sgt Kobayashi.

On the 18th of the same month, the B-29s of the 870th BS attacked Mitsubishi's Nagoya factory, and during this raid, 'Special Delivery' 42-24628 was rammed by a Ki.46 of the 16th Independent *Chutai* from Taisho airbase in Osaka, piloted by Sgt Nakamura. Three days later, the Ki.46 of the 81 Independent *Chutai* shot down B-29 *Wild Air* 42-24505 of the 769th BS, over Manshū. On the 22nd, the B-29 returned to Nagoya, being intercepted.

During combat, a bomber was damaged by *Ta-Dan* bombs and another named *Dragon Lady* 42-63425 made it back to their base in Saipan after being rammed first by a Ki.44 and then by a Ki.46 of the 16th Independent *Chutai*. Five days later, a B-29 of the 498th BS was shot down over Tokyo by a Ki.46 of the 28th *Sentai*, piloted by Sgt Etsuo Kitagawa, using air-to-air bombs.

On 7 April 1945, 42-24674 of the 878th BS was destroyed by a *Shin Shitei* of the 28th *Sentai* by the same method over the Nakajima factory. During the combat, five Ki.46s (with only a thin layer of armour plating and without self-sealing fuel tanks) were shot down by escorting Mustangs. The Japanese pilots from the reconnaissance units lacked dogfight training and so they were annihilated. During the spring of 1945, the Otsu series was retired from interception missions, assigning them to reconnaissance and swift courier duties.

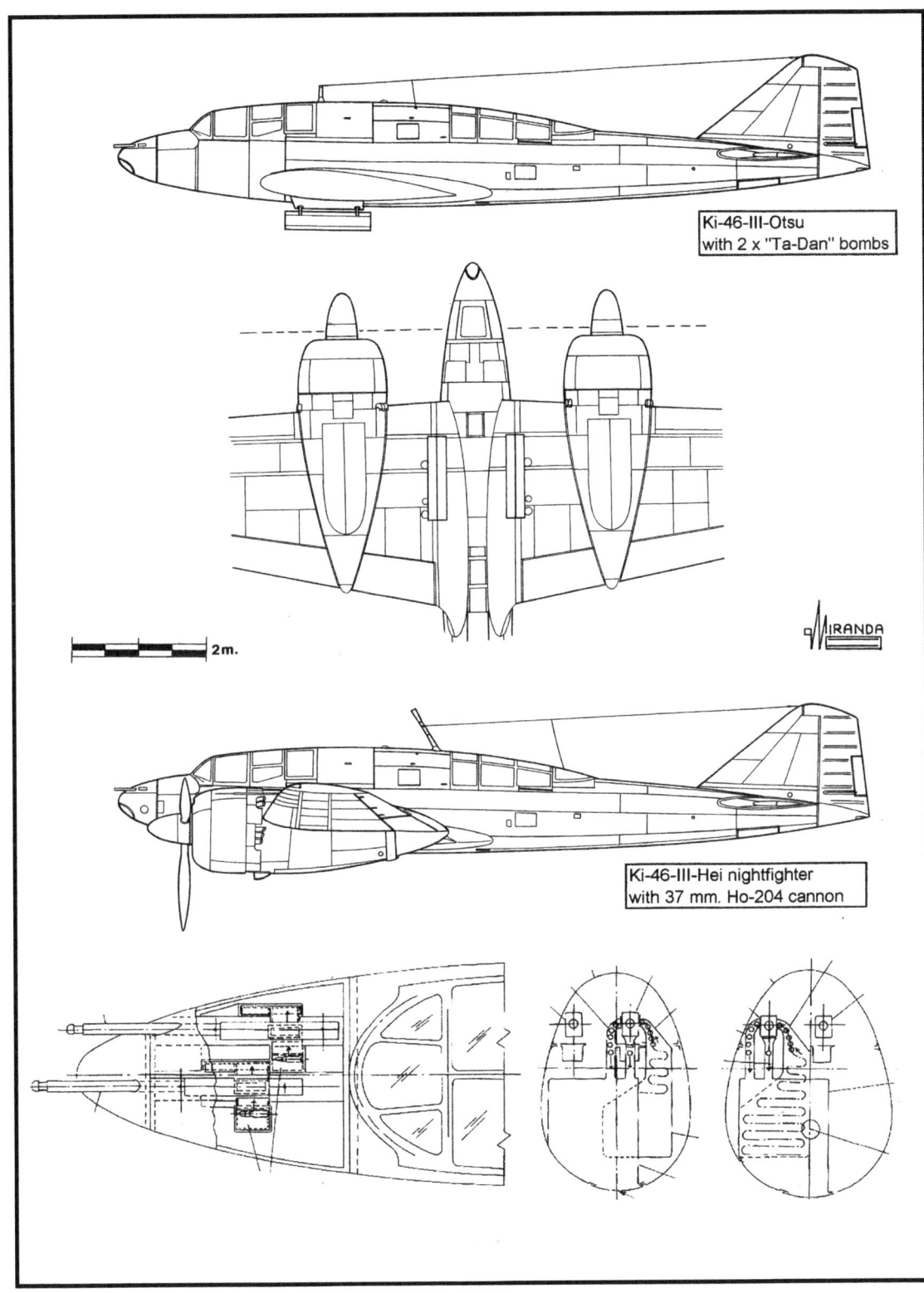

Ki-46-III-Otsu
with 2 x "Ta-Dan" bombs

2m.

Ki-46-III-Hei nightfighter
with 37 mm. Ho-204 cannon

Kawasaki Ki.60/Ki.61/Ki.100 Hien

Japan acquired the manufacturing license of the German Daimler-Benz DB 601 engine in 1938. In 1940, the IJA assigned their production to the Akashi plant of the Kawasaki firm, under the name Ha-40. The engine was to be used to propel the Ki.60 and Ki.61 fighters as well as a fast bomber commissioned by the IJN to Yokosuka.

The Ki.60 was built by the standards of the fighters used in Europe, but it was not satisfactory to the Japanese pilots due to its low manoeuvrability, excessive wing load, and high landing speed. These features were removed from the Ki.61, including many aerodynamic solutions already tested in the Heinkel He 100, as well as a larger wing surface and a lighter armament of four machine guns.

The Ki.61 began operations with the 68th and 78th *Sentais* in May 1944 in New Guinea. The tropical climate and poor maintenance conditions affected the delicate engines and the general availability of the aircraft. Many were immobilised on the ground and destroyed by the strafing attacks of the American P-38s. The Hien proved to be superior to the P-39s and P-40s in air combat, although these aircraft were quite difficult to shoot down using machine guns only due to its robust airframe, armoured cockpit, and self-sealing fuel tanks.

Even more difficult was fighting the strongly armed B-17s and B-24 heavy bombers, leading to the IJA ordering the construction of the Ki.61-I-Otsu version, equipped with 20-mm cannons and two droppable 200-l fuel tanks or two 250-kg bombs hanging under the wings. The IJA had no access to the Oerlikon cannons used by the IJN *Zeros* and was forced to buy 800 Mauser MG 151 20-mm cannons from Germany that were carried by submarine to Japan in August 1943. The special ammunition for the MG 151 was also imported and could not be renewed.

At the end of the year, the Ho-5 cannon built in Japan was already available. Its installation on the wings of the new Ki.61-I-KAI-Hei fighters started immediately, but the weapons proved insufficient against the B-29 bombers. Some aircraft of this series were experimentally provided with Ho-155 35-mm cannons that proved too heavy to quickly reach the altitude of the enemy planes.

Despite the encountered difficulties, the Ki.61 achieved some successes. On 3 December 1944, B-29 42-24656 was shot down over Tokyo by a Hien of the 244th *Sentai* piloted by Capt. Teruhiko Kobayashi. On 3 January 1945, a B-29 of the 73rd BW was shot down over Nagoya by an aircraft of the 55th *Sentai* piloted by 2Lt Takeo Adachi. On the 23rd of the same month, 42-24785 of the 882nd BS was destroyed over the Hamamatsu factory by a Ki.61. On the 27th, during a raid on the Nakajima factory, 42-24616 *Haley's Comet* and 42-24619 *Shady Lady* were shot down by two Hiens of the 244th *Sentai* piloted by Capt. Teruhiko Kobayashi and Sgt Chuichi Ichikawa.

The numerous problems experienced with the Ha-40 engine were due mainly to the weak construction of the cylinder block, improperly designed to make it lighter than the heavy Daimler-Benz. Failures also occurred in the operation due to dust and sand from the landing strips and the poor maintenance conditions in tropical climates. The engineers redesigned the engine as a Ha-140 that was somewhat more reliable, being used to propel the Ki.61-II-KAI from April 1944 onwards. Despite its excellent performance in tests, only 374 airframes were made, and when the Akashi factory was destroyed in a bombing raid on 19 January, only ninety-nine Ha-140s were completed, just enough to equip four *Sentais*.

The situation forced the Kawasaki engineers to consider installing a new Mitsubishi Type 4 Ha-112-II 1,500-hp radial engine. To achieve its integration into the Ki.61 airframe, they conducted a study of the only Focke-Wulf Fw 190 fighter existing in Japan to analyse how the Germans had solved the problem. Surprisingly, as happened with the Mustang, changing the engine produced an excellent fighter with greater manoeuvrability and climb rate that was also easier to maintain. Named Ki.100-I Type 5, it was used by six *Sentais* of elite, fighting on equal terms against Hellcats and Corsairs in Okinawa and against Mustangs over Japan.

The best combat altitude for Type 5 was 6,000 m, but it was almost useless against the Superfortress at 9,000 m. Some aircraft of the 111th *Sentai*, assigned to the defence of Osaka, removed the machine guns to save weight, but the head-on attacks carried with two 20-mm cannons only were not destructive enough to achieve results against a B-29 and some aircraft of the *Sentai* were experimentally fitted with air-to-air *Ro.San Dan* 10-cm rockets.

During the night from 14 to 15 April 1945, the B-29s of the 313rd and 314th BW conducted a medium-altitude attack against the Kawasaki factory losing eleven aircraft (42-24821, 42-63545, 42-93893, 42-93962, 42-94034, 44-69673, 44-69834, 44-69871, 44-69882, 44-69907, and 42-24664), one of them rammed by a Ki.100 of the 244th *Sentai* piloted by Capt. Chuichi Ichikawa.

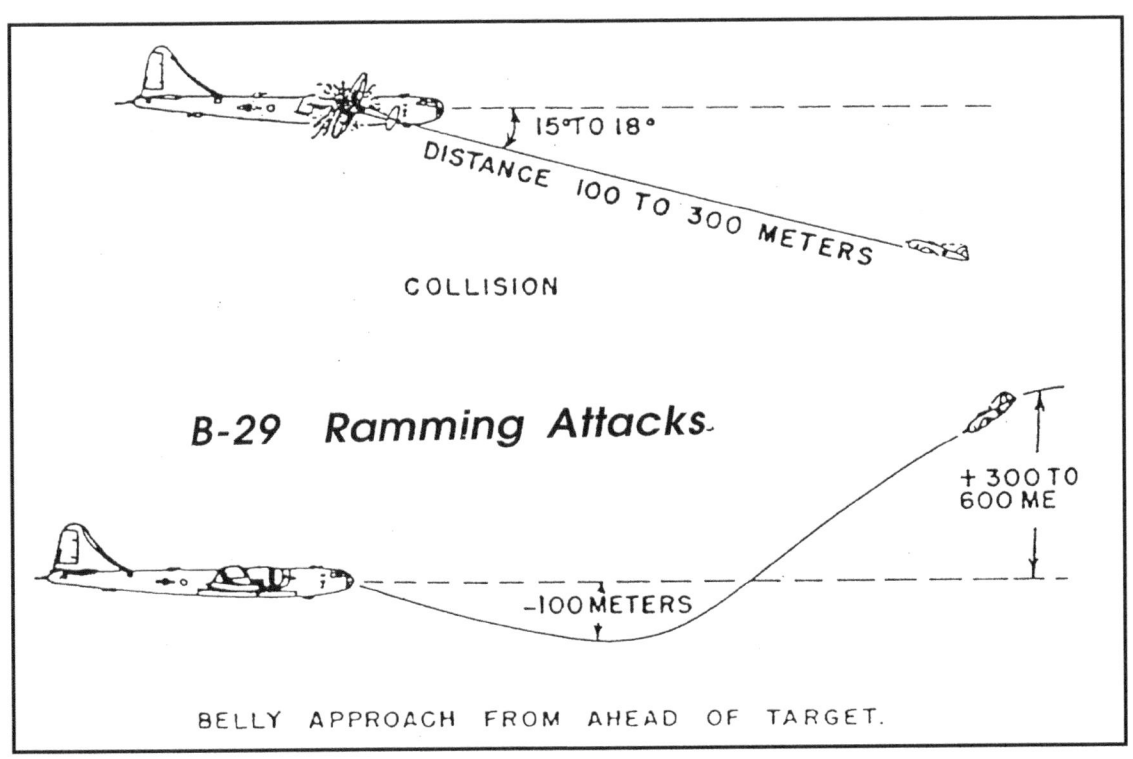

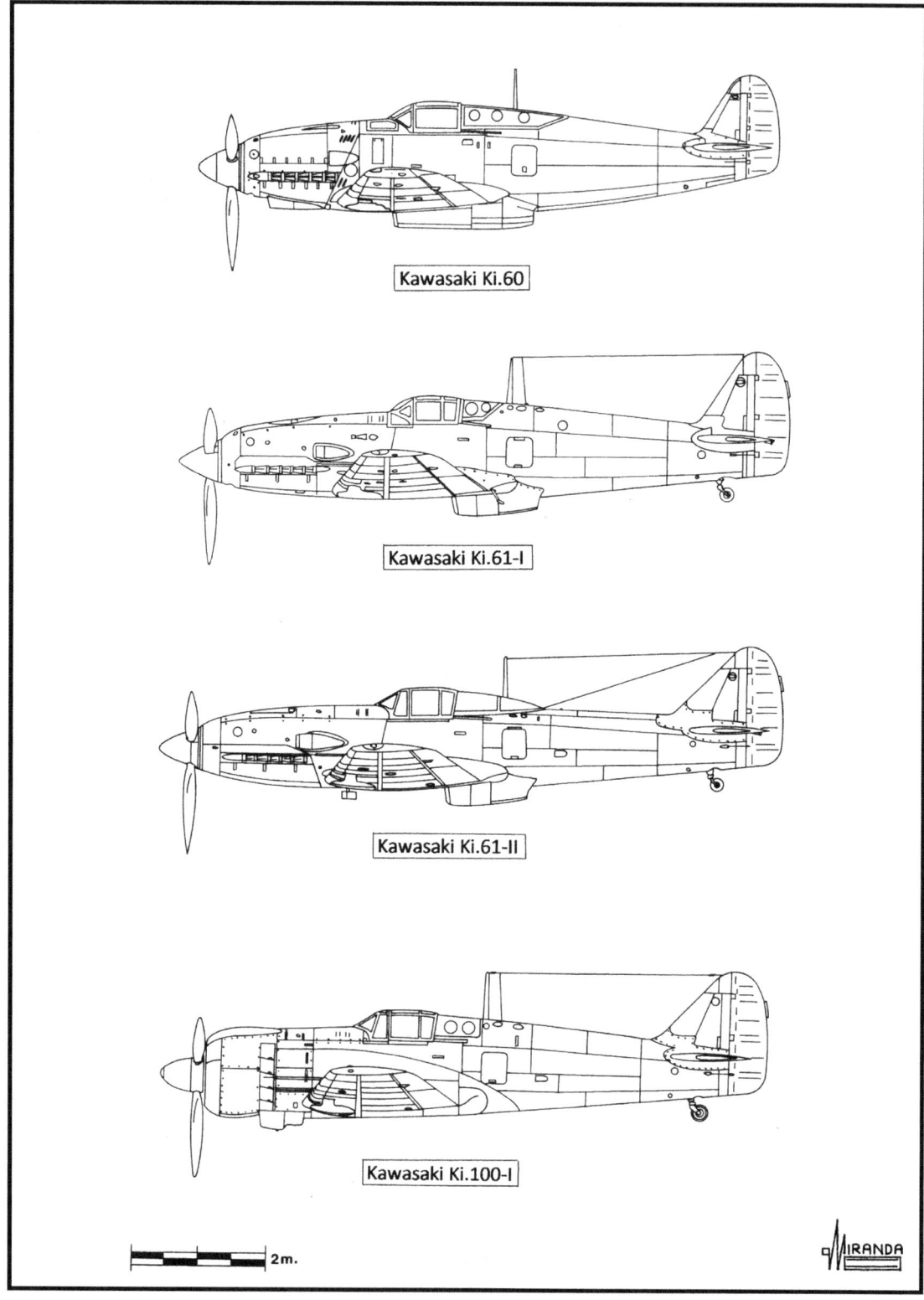

Kawasaki Ki.60

Kawasaki Ki.61-I

Kawasaki Ki.61-II

Kawasaki Ki.100-I

2 m.

Nakajima Ki.62, Ki.63, Ki.84, Ki.106, Ki.113, Ki.116, and Ki.117 Hayate

When Italian and Japanese designers could make use of the Daimler-Benz in-line engines made in Germany, instead of the radial engines of local manufacturing, the creation of high-performance interceptors followed two different concepts—Italians modified already existing fighters to install the new engine, whereas the Japanese started a special design programme that aimed to obtain the best possible fighter within its type, which was divided into two different parts.

The first one was to obtain a 'heavy fighter'. To the Japanese of the time, that meant a European designed fighter with a small wingspan, high wing loading, armoured plates, self-sealing tanks, and heavy armament. The result was the Kawasaki Ki.60 that never achieved mass production. The second part sought a multipurpose fighter—a lighter, more acrobatic plane that was, basically, easier to be manufactured by the local industry. Out of the two companies that presented similar projects, the Kawasaki option (manufactured as Ki.61) was chosen because this company was also in charge of manufacturing under licence the engine DB 601.

The Nakajima Ki.62, which never reached a prototype stage, was designed in 1941 by a team led by T. Koyama as a back-up project in case the Kawasaki fighter was a failure. The numerous problems experienced with the Ha-40 and Ha-140 engines forced the Kawasaki engineers to install the Ha-112-II radial engine in the Ki.100 series. In 1942, the Nakajima team also redesigned the Ki.62 as Ki.63, propelled by one 1,050-hp Mitsubishi Ha-102; one 1,870-hp Nakajima Ha-103; one 2,200-hp Nakajima Ha-107 air-cooled radial engine; one 1,900-hp Nakajima Ha-39; or one 2,600-hp Mitsubishi Ha-203 liquid-cooled in-line engine. This new fighter served as a transitional design between the Ki.43 Hayabusa and the Ki.84 Hayate. The latest was, in fact, an over-dimensioned Ki.63 with a wider wing chord, deeper fuselage, and scaled-up tail surfaces.

Surprisingly, both the Italian and Japanese systems produced formidable interceptors.

Ki.62 Technical Data

Wingspan: 12 m
Length: 8.75 m
Height: 2.30 m
Max. speed: 582 kph
Engine: one 1,100-hp liquid-cooled Kawasaki Ha-40 (DB 601A) with twelve cylinders in inverted Vee
Armament: 2 × 12.7-mm Ho-103 machine guns over the engine and 2 × wing-mounted 20-mm Ho-5 cannons

Ki.63 Technical Data

Wingspan: 12 m
Max. speed: 700 kph
Combat radius: 600 km
Engine: one 1,050-hp Mitsubishi Ha-102 air-cooled, radial engine
Armament: 2 × 12.7-mm Ho-103 machine guns over the engine and 2 × wing-mounted
20-mm Ho-5 cannons

Designed in 1942 to address the shortcomings experienced in combat by the Ki.43 and
Ki.44 fighters of the same firm, the Ki.84 was used with great success as an interceptor,
fighter bomber, and air superiority fighter, fitted with 13-mm bulletproof steel plating
and self-sealing fuel tanks.

Powered by one 1,990-hp Ha-45-21 radial engine and armed with two 12.7-mm Ho-103
machine guns and two 20-mm Ho-5 cannons, the Ki.84 had almost the same range as the
P-38L and was better at low-altitude manoeuvring than any Allied fighter, also besting
them at climb rate below 20,000 feet. The Ki.84 units were plagued by poor workmanship
and experienced numerous maintenance problems, with engine and undercarriage
failures that diminished its effectivity in the final years of the war. Most late-production
Hayates could not achieve even 400 kph when the standard level speed of the Ki.84 was
rated at 620 kph.

On 4 November 1944, out of the eighty Ki-84 units sent to Lingayen, only fourteen
arrived. The rest suffered problems with their engine, landing gear, and hydraulic or fuel
systems. The Ha-45 direct-injection Homare 21 engine entered into service prematurely
without being fully tested. Their injectors were not designed for the low-quality *Koku 87
Kihatsuyo* of 87 octane fuel and frequently got stuck. The oil temperature suffered serious
variations during flight, and the pressure at inverted flight was zero.

Like its predecessors Ki.43 and Ki.44, the Hayate was equipped with 'butterfly flaps'
that could be deflected for combat by an angle of 15 degrees. The maximum lift coefficient
of 1.70 allowed it to perform 360-degree turns in 17.05 seconds. Under good maintenance
conditions, the Ki-84-I-Ko reached a maximum speed of 686 kph with a service ceiling
of 11,830 m.

During the Battle of the Philippines, between 17 December 1944 and 8 January 1945,
twelve *Sentais* equipped with Ki.84-I-Ko aircraft conducted escort missions in *kamikaze*
groups, suffering heavy losses. The 12th, 52nd, and 102nd *Sentais* used them as fighter
bombers with a Type 99, No. 25, Model I 248.7-kg bomb suspended under the starboard
wing and a 200-l droppable fuel tank under the port wing. By mid-November 1944,
the pilots of some of these aircraft started to perform individual *tokko* attacks. On 16
November, a group of sixteen Ki.84s and seven Ki.43s participated in a raid against
Burauen airfield, destroying five B-29 bombers by using a combination of strafing and
Ta-Dan bombs.

On 17 December, twelve Ki.84 of the 21st *Hikodan* escorted a group of suicide planes
formed by three Ki.43-III of the *Hakko Tai* no. 7 and a Ki.84-I-Ko of the *Seika Tai*
off Mindoro. On 15 April, eleven Hayates of the 100th *Sentai* attacked US airfields in

Okinawa, destroying some planes on the ground. On 25 May, eleven Ki.84 of the 103rd *Sentai* attacked the Yontan airfield with strafing and *Ta-Dan* bombs.

Against the B-29, the Ki.84 did not have better luck than the Ki.44, achieving just a few successes with frontal attacks using Ho-155 cannons and *Ta-Dan* bombs. On 16 March 1945, during a raid against Kobe, the B-29s 42-65242 and 42-63546 were shot down by aircraft of the 246th *Sentai* piloted by Kenji Fujimoto and Yokio Ikute. On 13 and 14 April, another two bombers were shot down by Yoshio Yoshida of the 70th *Sentai*. During these battles, it was made patent that the best time to attack with *Ta-Dan* bombs was when the B-29s were launching their own bombs because they could not perform evasive actions during this operation. Finally, some pilots were forced to make *tai-atari* frontal attacks after exhausting their ammunition firing against the giant aircraft, with no apparent result.

To improve the firepower of the Hayate, Nakajima incorporated two new variants in the production lines. The Ki.84-I-Otsu appeared in November 1944, with four 20-mm Ho-5 cannons and, early in 1945, the Ki.84-I-Hei with two Ho-5 and two 30-mm Ho-155 cannons. Yet as with the Shoki, the flying tests showed that the excessive weight of the armament degraded the rate of climb, to the point of not being able to reach the flight altitude of the B-29s in time to intercept them. The IJA had not yet received the high-altitude interceptor requested from the industry three years before.

The situation worsened on 1 November when a B-29 flew over Tokyo without being intercepted by the Ki.44. The next day the IJA ordered all air defence *Sentais* formed a *Shinten Seiku Tai* unit that specialised in ramming attacks using Ki.43, Ki.44, and Ki.45 fighters, devoid of armament, to confront the American heavy bombers. After evaluating the first match between a Ki.48-I and a B-29 that occurred on 16 March 1945, Nakajima started an accelerated program to obtain a high-altitude version of the Hayate, and the design team began working simultaneously on five projects: Ki.84 Sa Go, Ki.84-III, Ki.84N, Ki.84P, and Ki.84R.

The Ki.84 Sa Go was a Ki.84-I-Ko airframe with a modified Ha-45 engine in which the methanol-water injection system had been replaced by oxygen injection to improve high-altitude performance. The Ki.84-III would have the same airframe powered by one Ha-44-13 engine with a Ru-302 mechanically driven supercharger. The Ha-44-13 generated 2,450 hp at take-off and was able to maintain 2,040 hp at 11,000 m but was heavier than the Ha-45 and never become operational. The Ki.84.III was still on the drawing board in August 1945.

The building of the Ki.84R (Ki.84-IV) was started with new wings of 12,138 m span and 22.5 sq. m. surface, but after a new calculation, it was decided to expand them to 12,238 m and 23.5 sq. m. The tail surfaces were also enlarged by 10 per cent. The proposed engine was a Ha-45-44 (with Ru-303 exhaust-driven turbo-supercharger) driving a four-bladed propeller that was 3.5 m in diameter, which made it necessary to lengthen the undercarriage legs. With the Ru-303, it was expected to obtain an engine power of 1,870 hp at 3,400 m, 1,640 hp at 6,000 m, and 1,550 hp at 9,000 m. The prototype was 80 per cent complete in August 1945.

The Ki.84P was a project only version of the Ki.48R with 24.5 sq. m. wing area and one Ha-44-13 engine.

The Ki.84N would have used a 2,450-hp Ha-44-13 or a 2,530-hp Ha-44-14 engines with a Ru-303 turbo-supercharger driving a four-bladed propeller that was 3.6 m in diameter. The proposed armament was four 20-mm cannons. It would have had a wingspan of 12.3 m, be 10.177 m in length and 3.85 m in height, have a wing surface of 22.3 sq. m., a max. speed of 610 kph, a maximum weight of 5,296 kg, and a range of 1.577 km. On 4 June 1945, the *Kaigun Koku Hombu* decided its mass production with the *kitai* number of Ki.117 (project only).

By mid-1943, the effective blockade by the US Navy Submarine Force began to strangle the Japanese economy, and the aeronautical industry was particularly affected by increasing shortages of aviation fuel and light alloys. Prior to the US embargo, the IJA normally used 91 octane fuel, then the worse 87 octane fuel was introduced, to the great detriment of aircraft performances and numerous engine maintenance issues.

Once the Allied Forces were established in the Philippines and in Okinawa, Japan was cut off from the oilfields of the Dutch East Indies. The last tanker reached Japan in March 1945. At the end of the war, the quality of fuel went down to 85 octane because the gas was mixed with oil extracted from pine tree roots. The scarce 95 octane fuel captured by the Allies was reserved for the use of some elite units, such as the IJA 21st Hikodan, whose Ki.84 fighters performed *kamikaze* escort missions, or the Shiden-Kai fighters of the IJN 343 *Kōkūtai* that protected strategic targets. In contrast, the Allies consumed between 40,000 and 70,000 tons of 100/150 Grade Aviation 44-1 fuel each month.

On 8 September, Nakajima, Tachikawa, and Mansyu were instructed by the *Koku Hombu* to use wood and steel as aluminium substitutes in the manufacture of Hayate.

Nakajima began building a version called Ki.84-II-Kai with wooden rear fuselage control rods and wingtips. The Hayate KAI (for Kaizen-improvement) entered in service in autumn 1944, powered by one Ha 45-21, Ha-45-23, or Ha-45-25 engine.

After studying the wreckage of a de Havilland Mosquito downed in Burma, Tachikawa Hikoki engineers designed the Ki.106, an all-wood version of the Ki.84 powered by one 2,000-hp Nakajima Ha-45-21 engine that was 9.95 m in length, 3.59 m in height, had a max. speed of 620 kph, and a range of 800 km. The Ki.106 weighed 430 kg more than the Ki.84-I-Ko, which had an adverse effect on manoeuvrability and climb rate. Late in 1944, three airframes were built for Tachikawa by Ohji Koku KK with two 20-mm cannons, vertical surfaces with increased area, and plywood skin with a lacquer coating.

In the Ki.113 version, designed in the fall of 1944, Nakajima used steel in as many sub-assemblies as possible, but the project was left aside after the completion of the prototype in early 1945 due to the excessive weight of the new airframe. Engine and dimensions are the same as with the standard Hayate.

The version proposed by Manshu Hikoki, called Ki.116, had enlarged tail surfaces and was powered by one 1,500-hp Ha-112-II Kinsei engine from a Ki.46-III, driving one three-bladed airscrew. Only one prototype was built.

In July 1942, the IJA issued a requirement for a night fighter to defend Rabaul base against B-17 attacks. In August 1944, Nakajima modified a Ki.84-I-Ko by installing a single 20-mm Ho-5 cannon, with 300 rounds, at 45 degrees in *Schräge Musik* configuration behind the cockpit. The bulletproof steel plate of 13 mm was removed, an aerodynamic cover tube was installed to protect the rear canopy from the blast, and a cut-out was made on the movable side so that it could slide backwards about 60 per cent of opening the before remodelling. In October, the second prototype was built by modifying a Ki.84-I-Otsu, and both aircraft performed test flights at Fusa airfield. It is believed that at least twelve aircraft were converted to this configuration.

In some documents written by Major Iwamiya, technical director of IJA General Affairs Division, and Lieutenant Commander Noboru Kimura of the Technical Department of the IJA Headquarters, it was considered the possibility of installing a Taki-2 radar in the version of Ki.84-I-Tei production. According to other authors, the Tei variant would be armed with two Ho-5 cannons firing at 45 degrees, and in the USAF Report 1946, this number was extended to three.

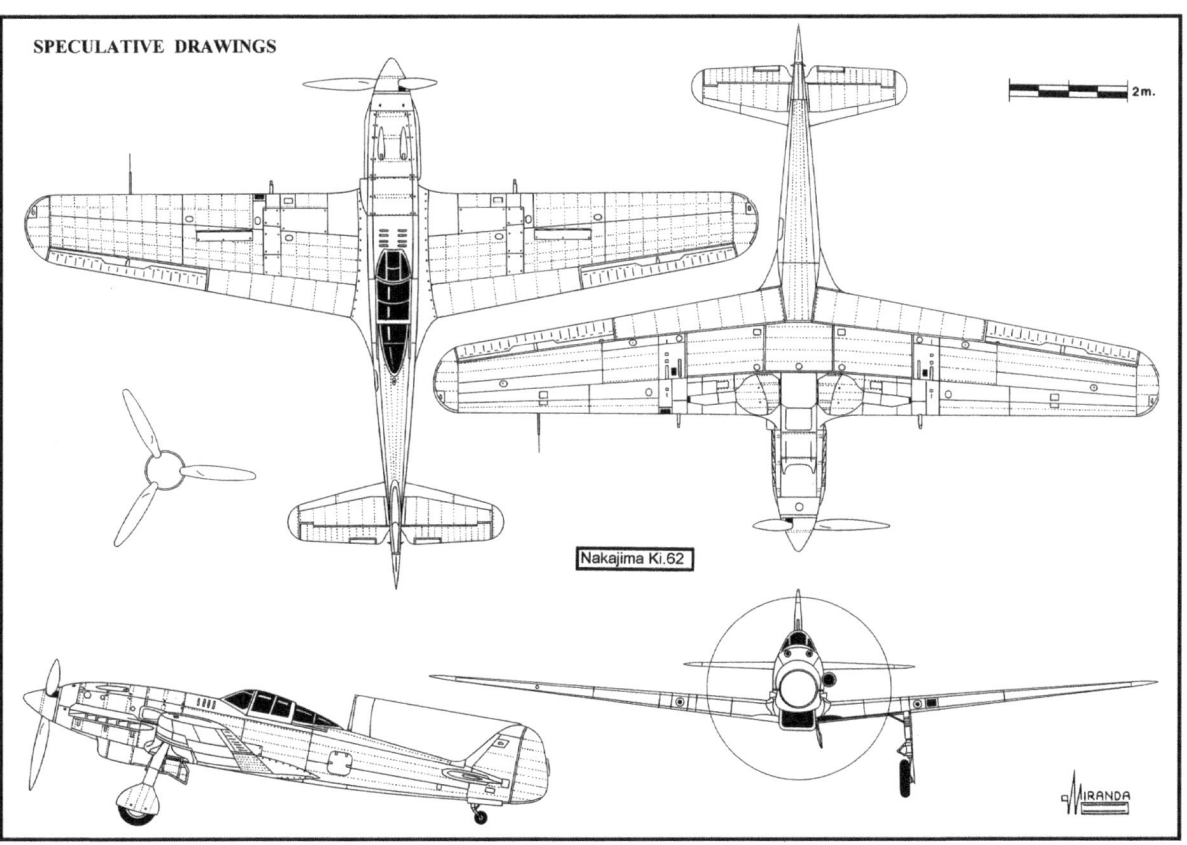

SPECULATIVE DRAWINGS

Nakajima Ki.62

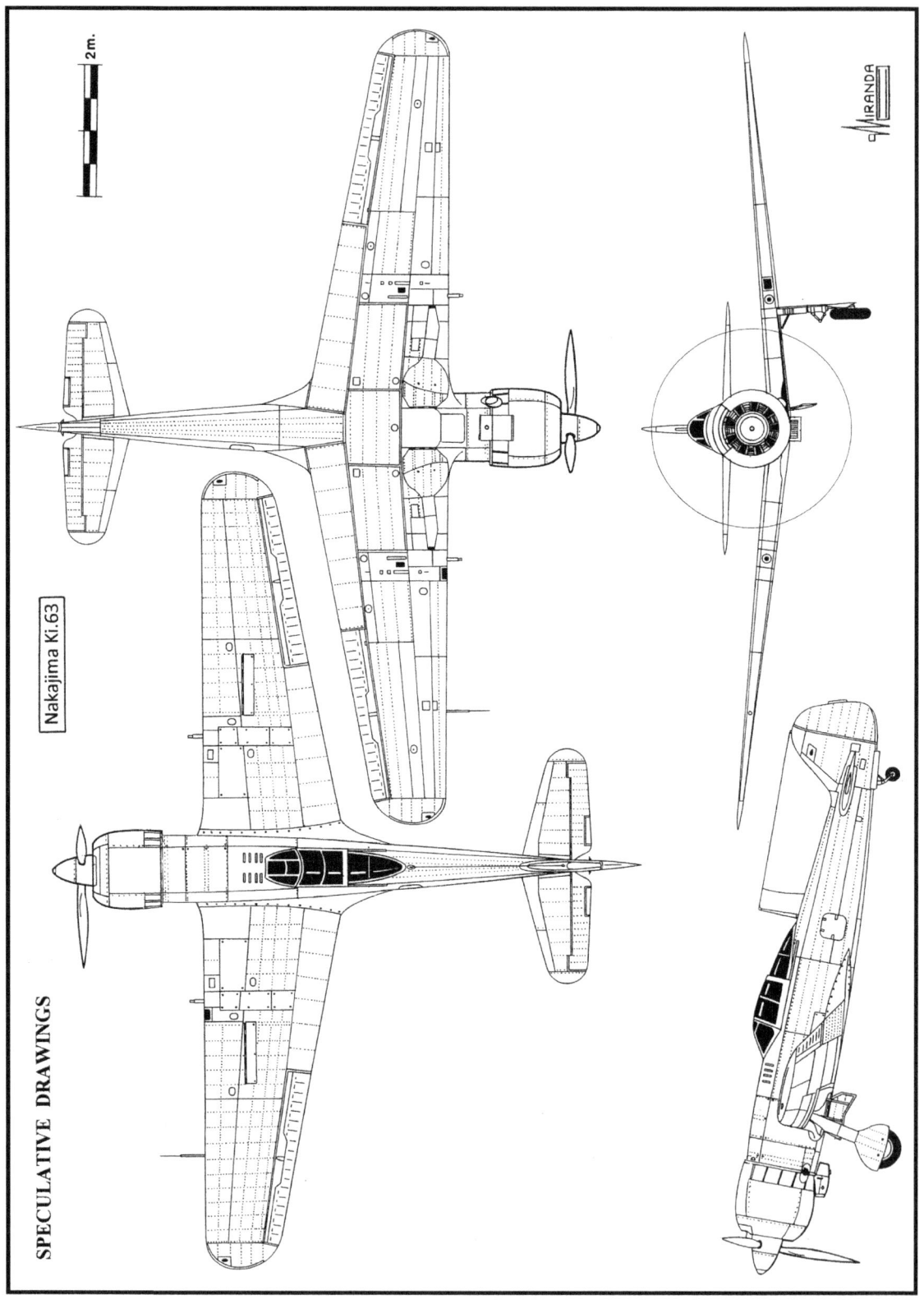

2 m.

Nakajima Ki.63

SPECULATIVE DRAWINGS

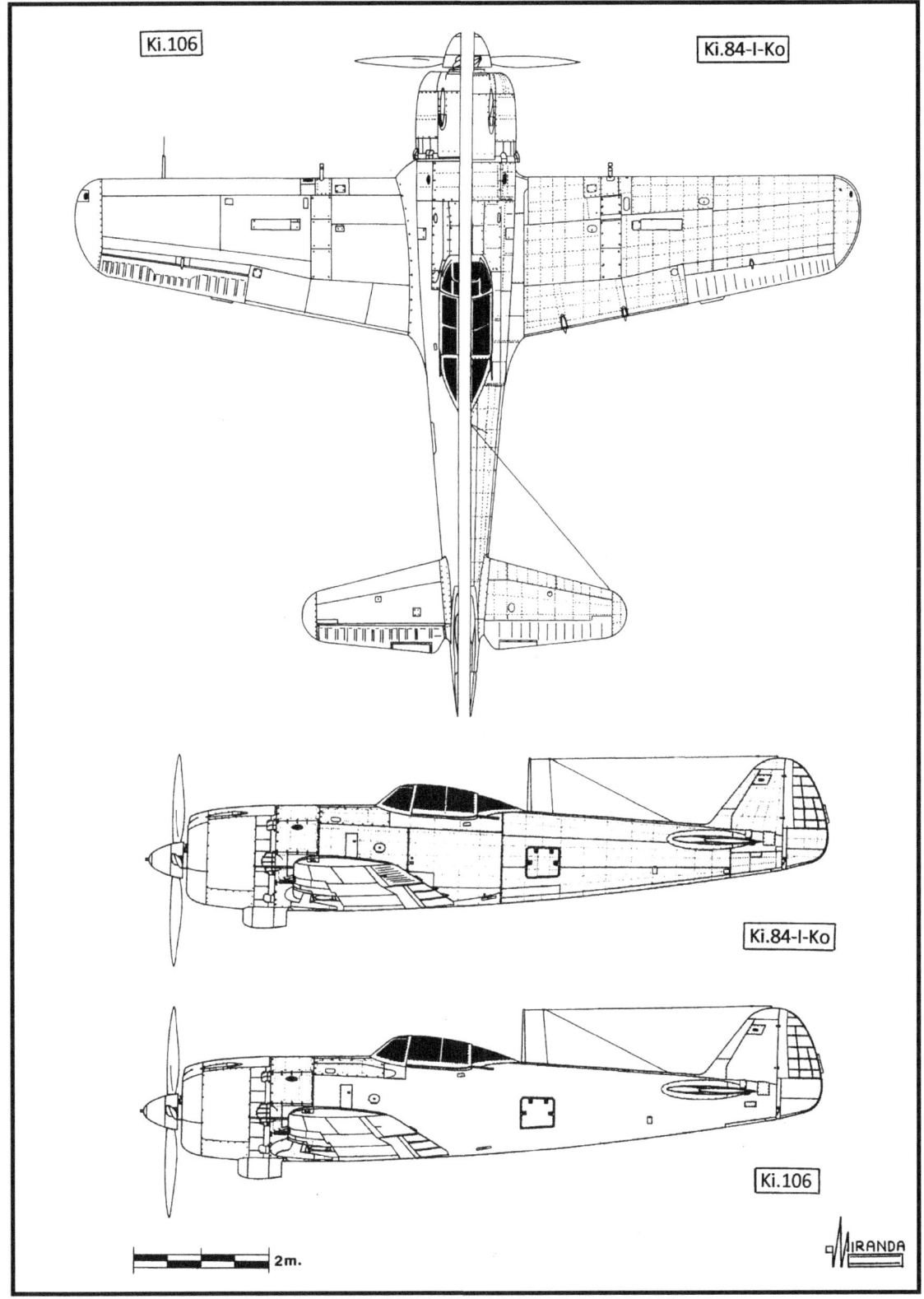

Ki.106

Ki.84-I-Ko

Ki.84-I-Ko

Ki.106

2m.

MIRANDA

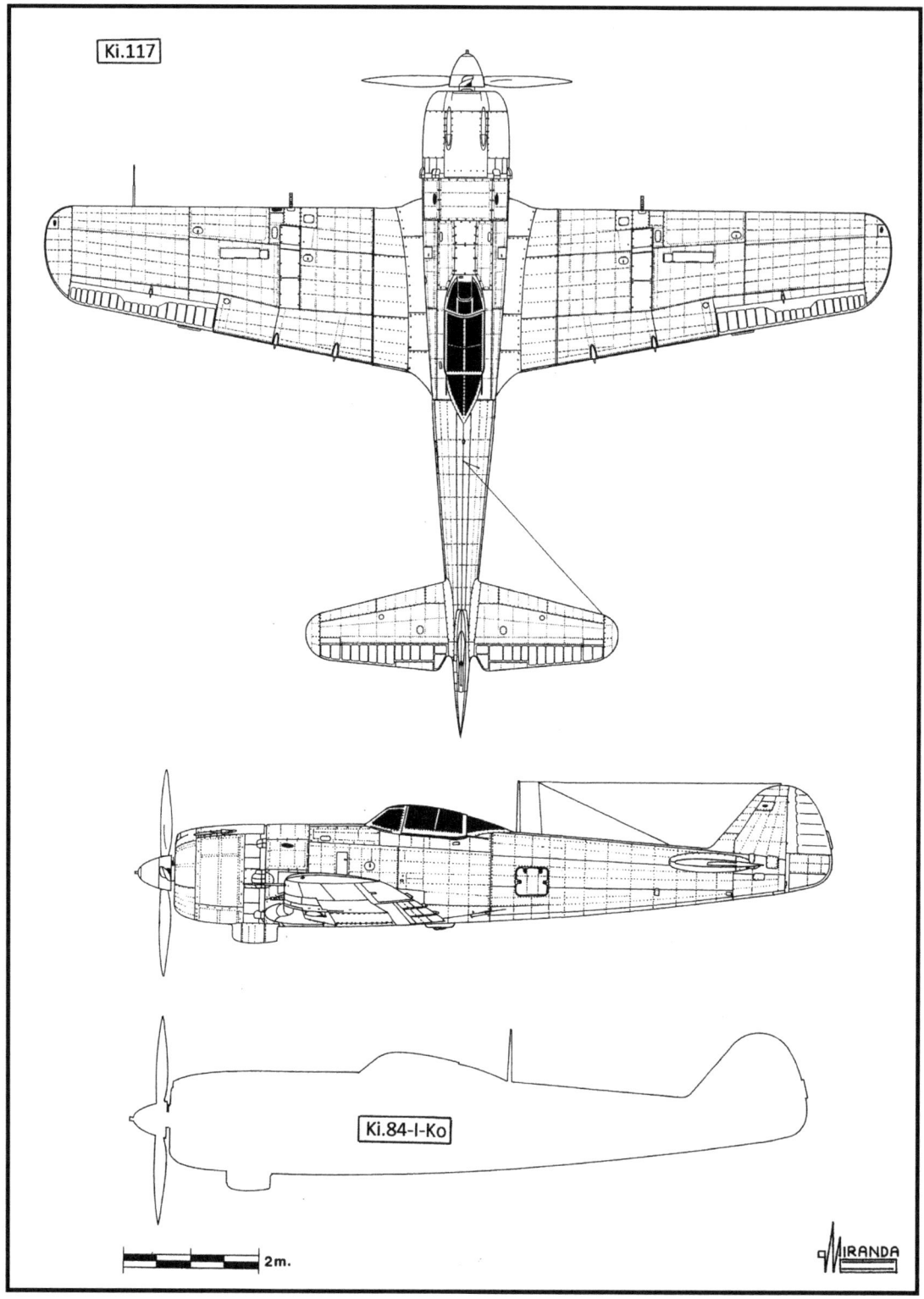

Ki.117

Ki.84-I-Ko

2 m.

MIRANDA

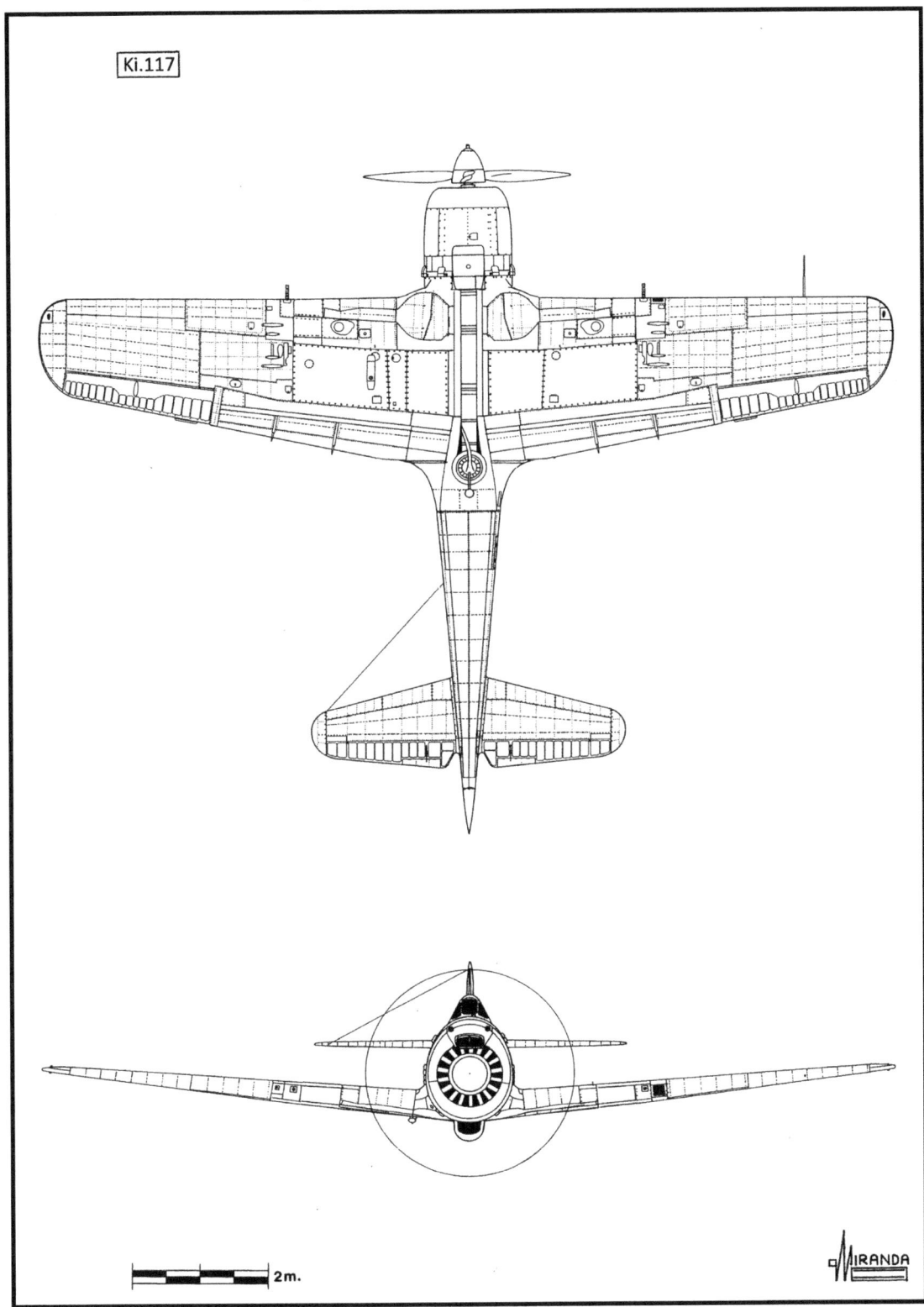

Ki.117

2m.

Kawasaki Ki.64, Ki.78 (*Ken-3*), and Ki.88

In the 1935 contest for the future fighter of the *Jagdwaffe*, the Heinkel He 112 lost against the Messerschmitt Bf 109 because of its elliptic wing, which was more difficult to manufacture.

In 1937, in an effort to remain in the contest, Dr Heinkel promised General *Luftzeugmeister* Udet that he would be able to manufacture a fighter that, propelled by a Daimler Benz DB 601, would be capable of reaching 700 km/h. Although Udet considered it impossible, the project—named Heinkel P1035—started on 25 May 1937. The design team, led by Siegfried Günter, followed the streamlining and drag reduction in the main guidelines. They adopted a well-fared cockpit, a fully retractable tail wheel, and a stressed skin wing covering, reducing the number of 'Butter' rivets.

The DB 601 engine had exhaust ejectors for a small amount of thrust, and the supercharger inlet was moved from the side of the cowling to a location under the propeller hub. The frontal radiator was replaced by a surface cooling system, inspired by the Macchi seaplane racers, which was already being tested on the He 119 V1.

The steam generated at high temperatures was separated from the cooling fluid from the engine using a centrifugal compressor and an expansion chamber. The heat exchangers, located in the wings, had a capacity of 345 l and transferred the heat outside through the stressed covering's light alloy. The steam was then condensed into liquid by cooling and returned to the engine circuit by means of twenty-two electric-driven centrifugal pumps.

A similar system was designed to refrigerate the oil by passing it through a heat exchanger where methyl alcohol was added. The resulting vapour was then being ducted to the tail surfaces, where it was to be condensed back to liquid before returning to the heat exchanger. By the end of October, the project was presented to the *Luftwaffe Technisches Amt*, receiving the He 100 number type.

During the flight tests of the first prototype, it turned out that the wing suffered a structural distortion, caused by the high temperatures. It was also confirmed that the oil-cooling system did not work at all. The second prototype had a reinforced wing cladding and was equipped with a retractable auxiliary cooler for the ground running and another, on the port wing root, for the oil.

On 30 March 1939, the prototype Heinkel He 100 V8, powered by one 1,800-hp Daimler Benz DB 601 ReV engine, set a world speed record flying at 746.6 kph. In order to minimise drag, the conventional radiator was replaced by one experimental surface-evaporation cooling system that used pressurised water at 110 degrees C.

More prototypes and a short preproduction series were built, and the He 100 achieved several speed records. Yet its unreliable cooling system, which made it very vulnerable in combat, together with its maintenance problems and the lack of DB 601 engines advised against its mass production, which had been foreseen for 1939.

However, Ernst Heinkel tried it again, following the RLM specifications for a piston-engined fighter that was to combine speed and high-altitude performance. By the end of 1944, Günter's team started to work on the P1076, possibly the fastest aircraft of its class ever designed. Based on the He 100, it adopted a more sophisticated version of the surface-cooling technology, where the steam circulated within the double layer of stressed skin covering that integrated the wings, the engine cowling, the rear fuselage, and the tailfin. The centrifugal compressor and the expansion chamber were located at the rear of the fuselage.

The design of the wings was very advanced for its time, with a perfectly smooth surface and slightly swept forward at 8 degrees, constructed as a two-piece, two spar all metal structure. The section between the spars housed the condensation deposits of the heat exchangers, the electric-driven centrifugal pumps, the main undercarriage, and two Mk 108/30 cannons and ammo tanks. Flaps and ailerons spanned the entire trailing edge, with the outermost as ailerons and the inside ones as landing flaps.

The armoured cockpit was pressurised for high-altitude flying and covered with a clear vision bubble canopy that was hinged to the port side. The 700-l fuel tank was located behind the pilot's seat. The tailwheel was fully retractable. To facilitate its cooling on both sides, the tailfin was designed with a 0-degree angle to the fuselage axis. Consequently, all the installed engines should be fitted with counter-rotating, three-bladed VDM propellers.

The P.1076 was projected in four different versions, to adjust to the new 2,000-hp class engines that were expected to be available in 1945. The P.1076/I was designed as a competitor of the Bf 109 K-14. Equipped with a DB 603M, it would have been faster and climbed to higher altitude, carrying heavier armament.

The P.1076/II, fitted with a Jumo 213 engine, should have reached similar performances. Its production was to compete against the Fw 190 D-9, to which could have equally exceeded in armament, maximum speed, and ceiling. The P.1076/III was designed as a competitor of the Fw Ta 152 H. Equipped with a DB 603N and a wingspan expanded to 12.4 m, it would have been a formidable high-altitude interceptor, as fast and well-armed as the Me 262, but with a superior ceiling.

The design of a V16 variant of the DB 603, known as DB 609, was started in September 1942. It was a sixteen-cylinder, 2,500-hp engine, yet the prototype showed serious vibration problems when tested in the Focke-Wulf 190 V19, due to the excessive length of the crankshaft.

The expectation was that the DB 609, with two-stage twin supercharger, integrated heat exchanger cooler, and contra-rotating three-bladed VDM propellers, would reach 3,400 hp at a ceiling of 12,000 m, but the vibration issue could not be solved and the program was cancelled in 1943. From some drawings of the time, one can infer that the purpose was to install it on the P.1076. The version III, with increased span, would possibly serve to compensate the lengthier engine. The new aeroplane would have had a length of 9.86 m and a central armament of 55-mm Mk 112B, Mk 214, or Mk 412 cannons.

He P.1076/I Technical Data

Wingspan: 11 m
Length: 9.6 m
Height: 2.9 m
Wing area: 18 sq. m
Max. weight: 3,260 kg
Max. speed: 860 kph
Ceiling: 14,500 m

Range: 1,340 km
Engine: one 2,100-hp Daimler Benz DB 603M, supercharged, with MW50 power boost.
Armament: one 30-mm MK 103 engine-mounted and two 30-mm MK 108 wing-mounted cannons.

He P.1076/II Technical Data

Wingspan: 11 m
Length: 9.64 m
Height: 2.9 m
Wing area: 18 sq. m
Max. weight: 4,480 kg
Max. speed: 880 kph
Ceiling: 14,000 m
Engine: one 2,100-hp Junkers Jumo 213E with two-stage, three-speed supercharger and MW50 power boost.
Armament: one 30-mm MK 103 engine-mounted and two 30-mm MK 108 wing-mounted cannons.

In 1934, the Italian Macchi 72 set a world speed record flying at 709.2 kph powered by two Fiat AS.5 engines coupled in tandem.

The same configuration could be used in the design of a twin-engined 2,000-hp super-fighter, removing a considerable amount of drag over two separate nacelles. Yet it also required the resolution of several problems suffered by the engines: ignition, coolant flow, exhaust valves, connecting rods, and dangerous backfires at high power and high speed.

The French were very interested in the military use of this new technology and concluded that the operational ensemble would work better by separating the engines so that they would work independently connected by an effective power transmission system. In 1935, they patented the electrically controlled Cotal gearbox to connect two air-cooled radial engines in tandem, which was used in the design of the Payen Pa 112 C.1 fighter in 1937.

In March of the same year, the engineer Michel Vernisse patented a gearbox that allowed him to connect two Hispano-Suiza 12V engines in tandem. These engines were built with a 20-mm cannon mounted between the two ranks of cylinders, firing through the propeller.

In June, the *Ministère de l'Air* placed an order for twenty-five Arsenal VG 20 fighters powered by two 910-hp Hispano-Suiza 12Y engines mounted in tandem and connected by one Vernisse gearbox. The construction program was delayed because of the priority given to the Arsenal VG 30 light fighter, and no VG 20 was ever built.

During the German occupation, Vernisse continued to refine the transmission system. On October 1942, two 860-hp HS 12Y-31 engines were installed, connected by one Vernisse gearbox, in the Latécoère 299-01 prototype to flight test the whole power system.

The Germans were not interested in the project. At that time, they had already dropped their own DB 615 system, with two DB 603 engines connected in tandem, to develop the side-by-side DB 606/610 that would be used by the He 177 bombers.

The Soviets acquired the manufacturing license of the HS 12Ybrs as Klimov M-103 A. In 1939, they began the construction of the Bolkhovitinov S-2, a fast bomber powered by two M-103 engines connected in tandem by a transmission system like the Vernisse. On 20 March 1940, the prototype was flown, reaching a top speed of 570 kph. After the German attack, the development of the S-2 was interrupted because of the priority given to the manufacture of the Petlyakov Pe-2 bomber.

In October 1940, after analysing the new combat tactics used in Europe, the Kawasaki firm started a high-speed aircraft research programme, working on closing the technological gap with the western world. They used two 1,175-hp Ha-40 (DB 601) engines connected in tandem by a 2-m-long DB 615 power shaft and an evaporation cooling system based on the He 100 V8. All necessary information was acquired in Germany by engineer Jun Kitano in 1940.

On 23 January 1941, Kawasaki was authorised by the *Kaigun Koku Hombu* to start the construction of one experimental prototype that combined both technologies. Engineer Takeo Doi designed the laminar flow wings that would house the cooling system, with 200 litres of pressurised water at 1.1 atmospheres and 103 degrees C. Some 86 per cent of the wing area would be evaporation surfaces, including flaps. The propulsion system, named Ha-201, drove two contra-rotating airscrews, the front propeller being of fixed-pitch type and the rear propeller being of variable-pitch with Hamilton-Standard hydraulic system.

In October 1942, one Ki.61-I fighter was modified to test the effectiveness of the cooling system. The prototype performed thirty-five flying tests, surpassing the top speed of the Ki.61 standard by 40 kph. The prototype was completed in November 1943, receiving the *kitai* number Ki.64. The flying tests started by the beginning of the month, experiencing vibration problems in the power shaft, the malfunctioning of the contra-rotating airscrews, and the overheating of the rear engine. The engine burnt during the fifth flight, and the pilot was forced to make an emergency landing, damaging the prototype that never flew again.

The production version, named Ki.64-Kai, would have been powered by two 1,350-hp Ha-140 turbocharged engines, with a methanol-water injection, driving a VDM/Sumitomo electrically controlled, constant-speed, contra-rotating propellers.

The cooling system was redesigned to operate a 4.8-atmosphere internal pressure and at 110 degrees C, hoping to achieve a max. speed of 800 kph. The proposed armament was two nose-mounted and two wing-mounted Ho-5 cannons.

In the run of a satisfactory cooling of the rear engine, in February 1943, engineer Takeo Tsuchii started working on the design of the Ki.88, a Ki.61 modified with a Ha-140 engine, mounted behind the cockpit, driving a three-bladed propeller via an extension shaft. The Ki.88 would be fitted with a conventional radiator mounted on the bottom of the fuselage, with the objective to perfect an alternative cooling system for the rear engine of the Ki.64.

The prototype was expected to be completed by October 1943, but the smooth functioning of the evaporation cooling system installed on the Ki-61-I in 1942 made the IJA doubt the usefulness of the project. The Kawasaki firm decided to modify the Ki.88 by updating it as a fighter armed with a 37-mm Ho-203 cannon firing through the propeller hub and two 20-mm Ho-5 (synchronised) cannons mounted in the nose.

In October 1943, the Ki.88 was dropped by the *Koku Hombu* due to poor combat results from the P-39 Airacobra, based on the same formula.

The Aeronautical Research Institute of the University of Tokyo (*Koken*) had been working since 1938 on the design of an experimental aircraft capable of flying at 850 kph powered by a DB 601 German engine. The project was known as Ken-3, for *Kensan* (Research). The airframe had been carefully designed with laminar flow wings and one streamlined fuselage made as narrow as possible. One 60-hp auxiliary engine, driving a cooling fan, would be installed behind the cockpit to improve the performance of the two 'P-38 style' radiators located inside the fuselage.

Following the presentation of the wooden mock-up to the IJA in May 1941, the Ken-3 received the *kitai* number Ki.78, and the construction of the prototype began four months later. The Ki.78 was flown in December 1942, powered by one DB 601A-Kai methanol-water boosted to 1,550-hp, for short periods.

On April 1943, at the same time as the Ki.61-I entered combat over New Guinea, the Ken-3 experimented tailplane flutter at the relatively low speed of 635 kph. The problem was cured by fitting a horn balance to the elevator. In early 1944, the prototype reached a top speed of 704 kph, but the IJA considered that the foreseen 850 kph in the initial design could only be reached with more powerful engines. The construction of the second prototype was cancelled on 11 January 1944.

The high-speed research programme was dropped on 1 February 1945 when Kawasaki stopped the manufacturing of the Ha-140 V-12 engine.

Ki.64 Technical Data

Wingspan: 13.5 m
Length: 11.03 m
Height: 4.25 m
Wing area: 28 sq. m
Max. speed: 700 kph
Max. weight: 5,100 kg
Ceiling: 12,000 m

Ki.78 Technical Data

Wingspan: 8 m
Length: 8.1 m
Height: 3.07 m
Wing area: 11 sq. m
Max. speed: 704 kph
Max. weight: 2,300 kg
Ceiling: 8,000 m

Ki.88 Technical Data

Wingspan: 12.4 m
Length: 10.2 m
Height: 4.15 m
Wing area: 25 sq. m
Max. speed: 600 kph
Max. weight: 3,900 kg
Ceiling: 11,000 m

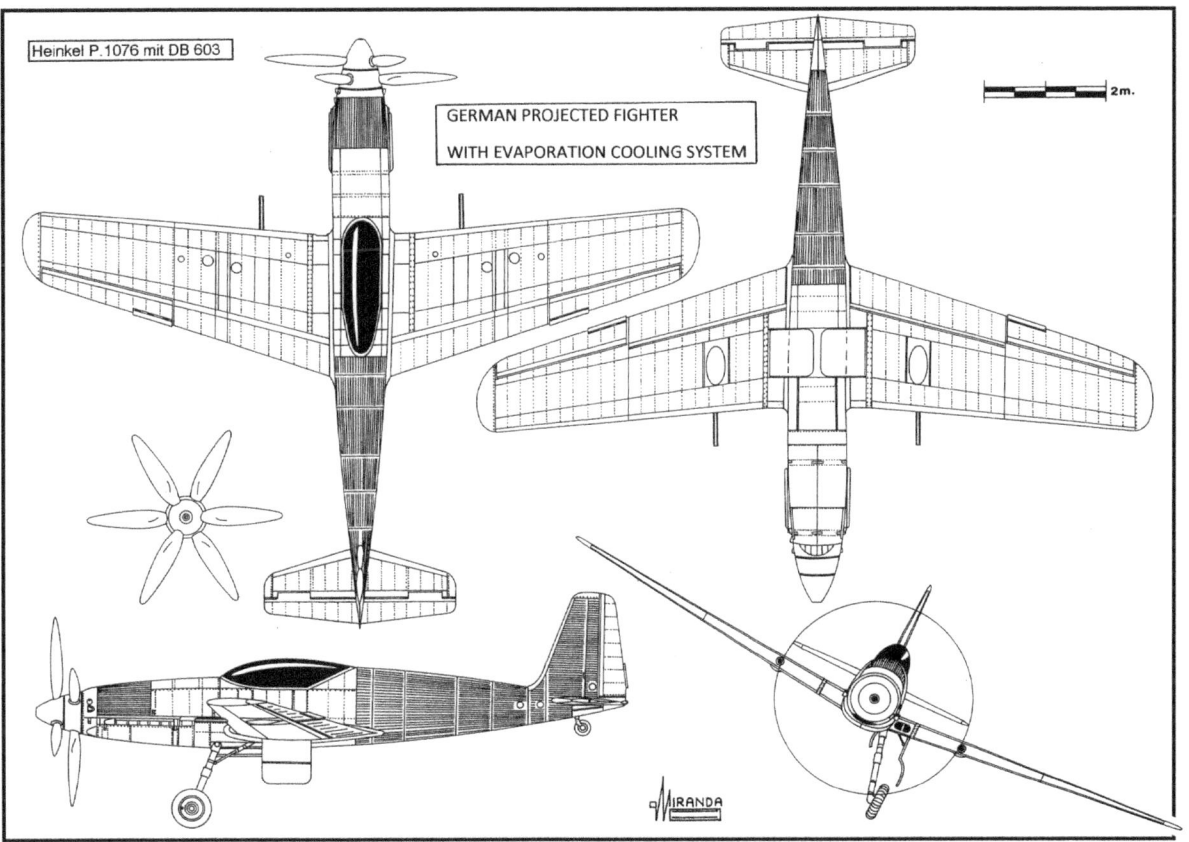

Heinkel P.1076 mit DB 603

GERMAN PROJECTED FIGHTER

WITH EVAPORATION COOLING SYSTEM

2m.

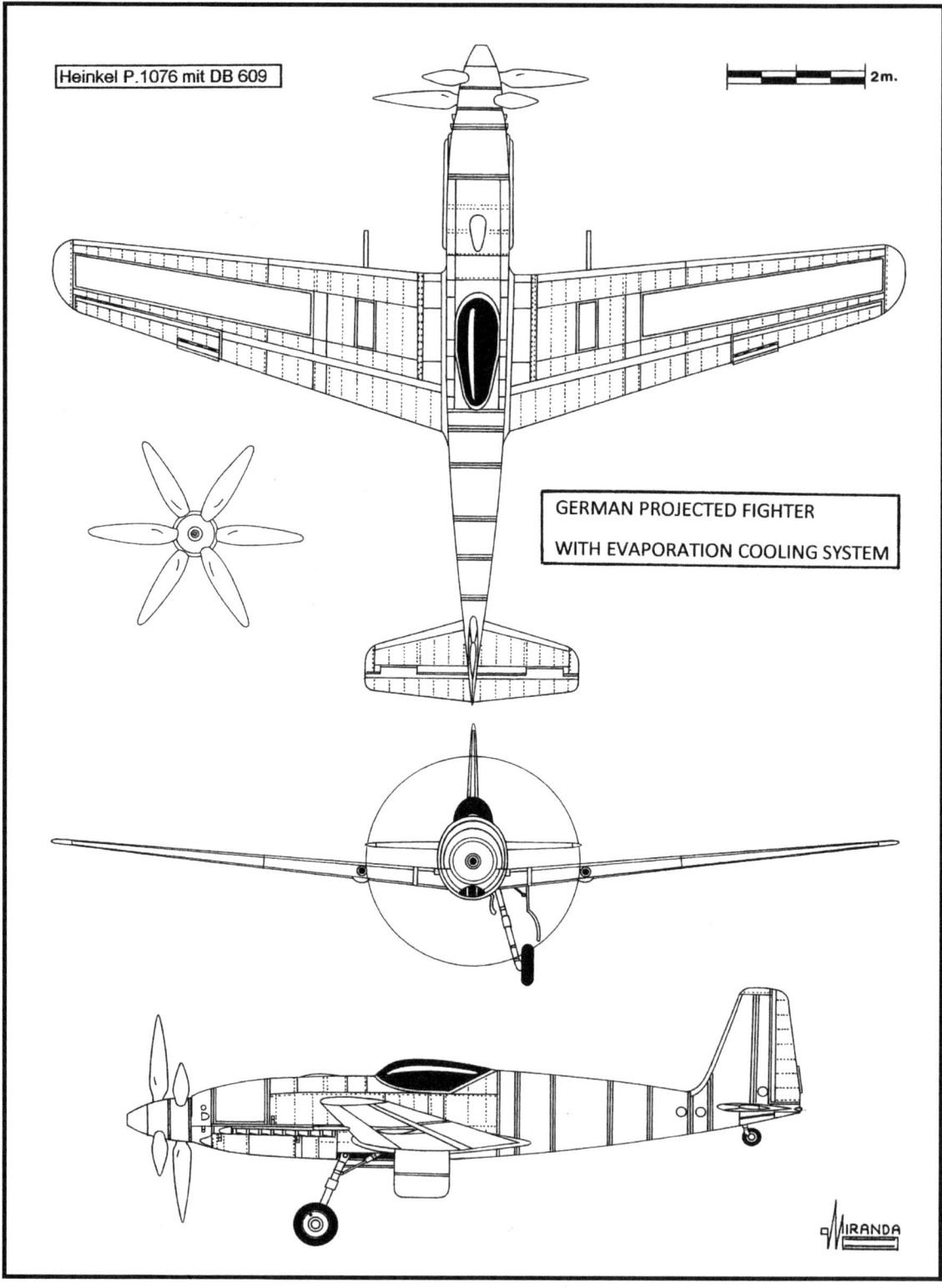

Heinkel P.1076 mit DB 609

2m.

GERMAN PROJECTED FIGHTER
WITH EVAPORATION COOLING SYSTEM

MIRANDA

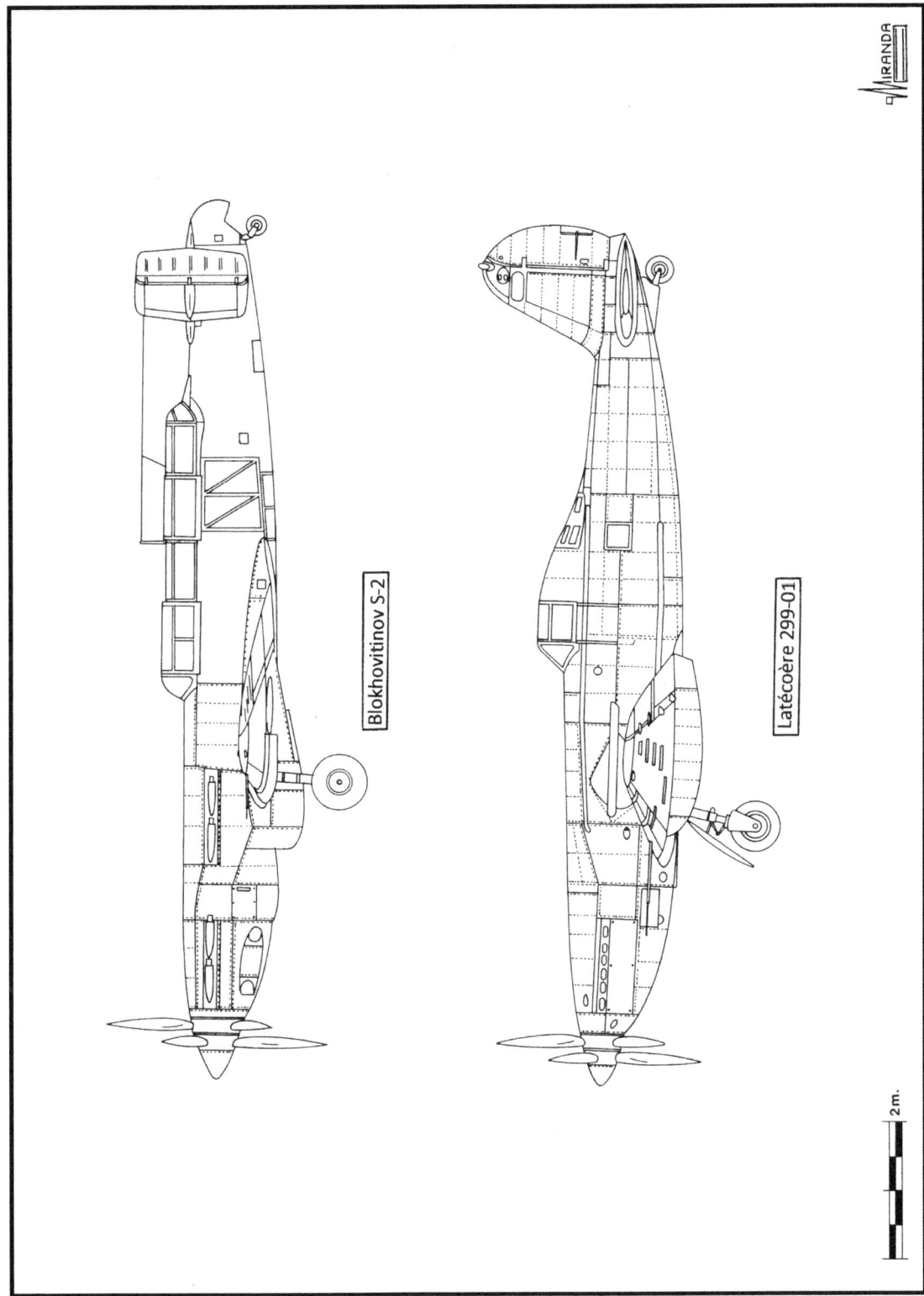

Blokhovitinov S-2

Latécoère 299-01

2 m.

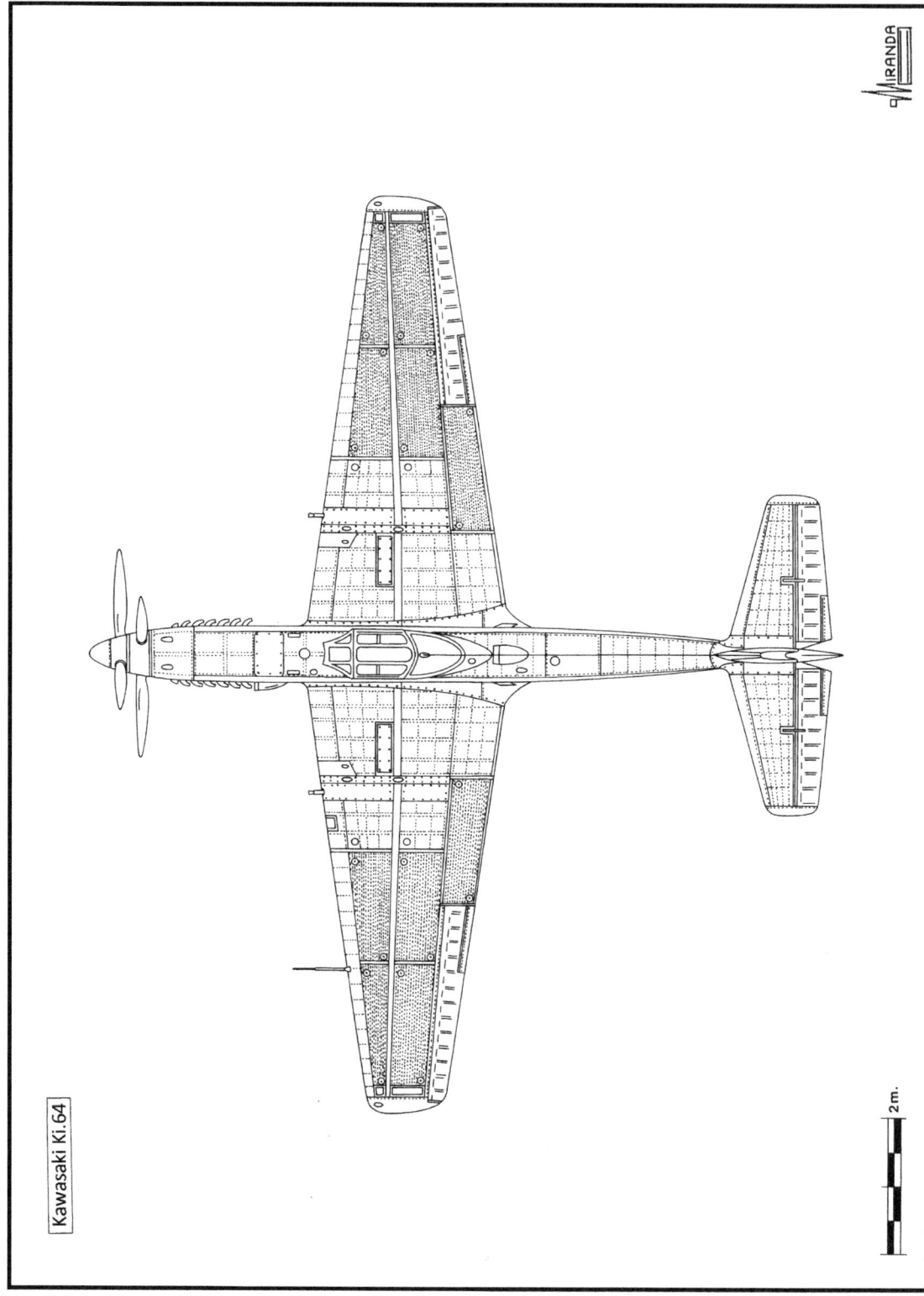

Kawasaki Ki.64

2 m.

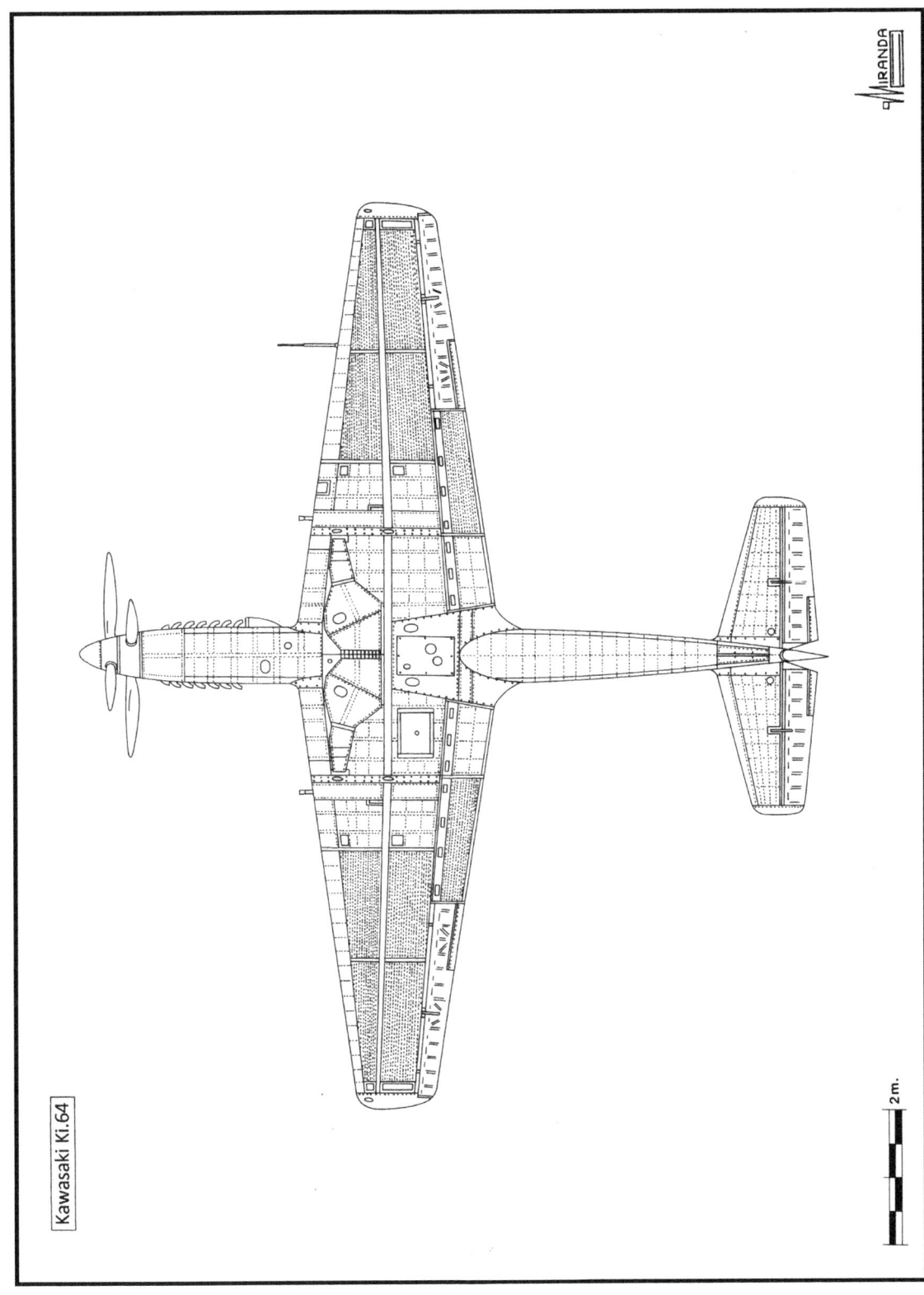

Kawasaki Ki.64

2 m.

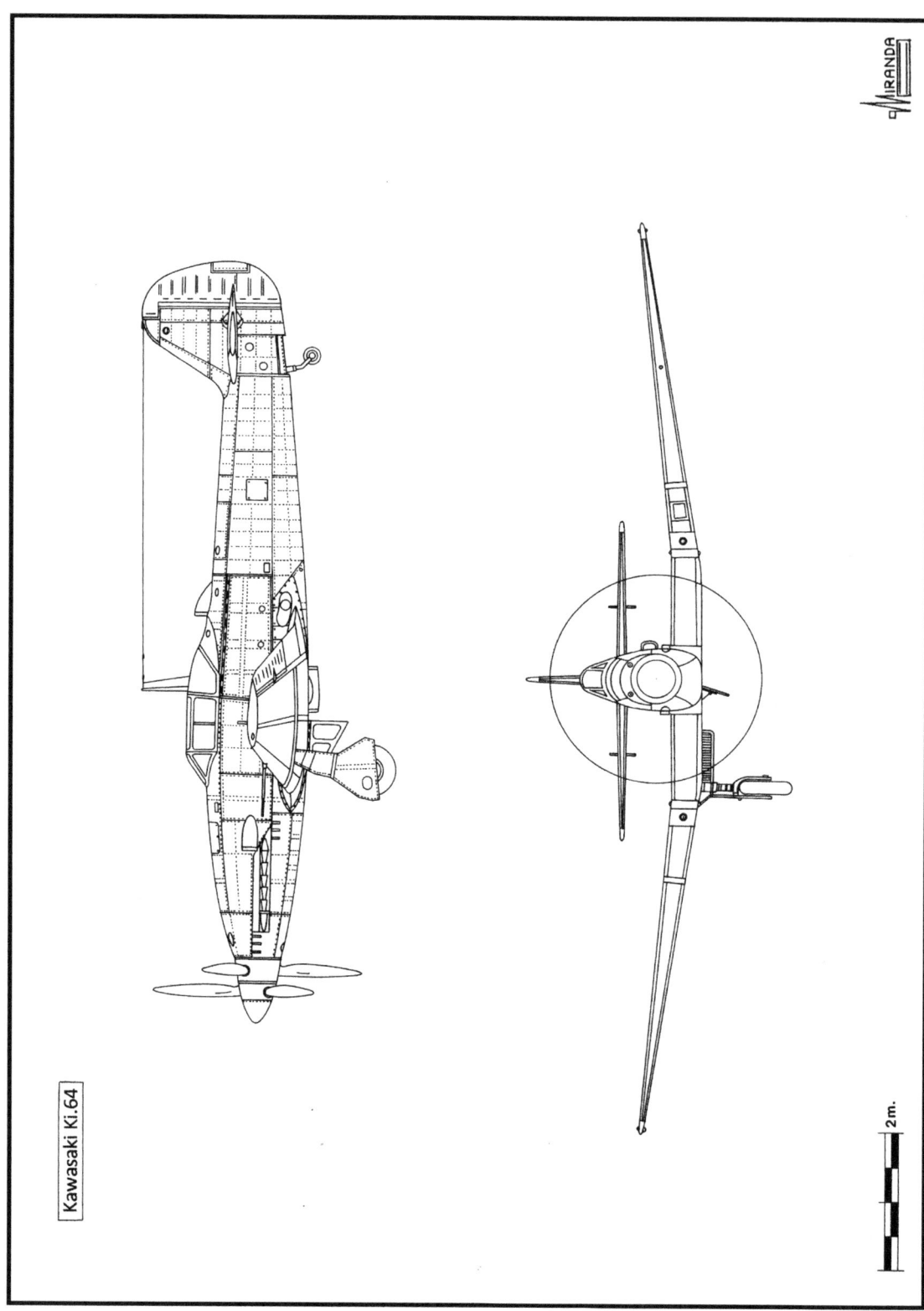

Kawasaki Ki.64

2 m.

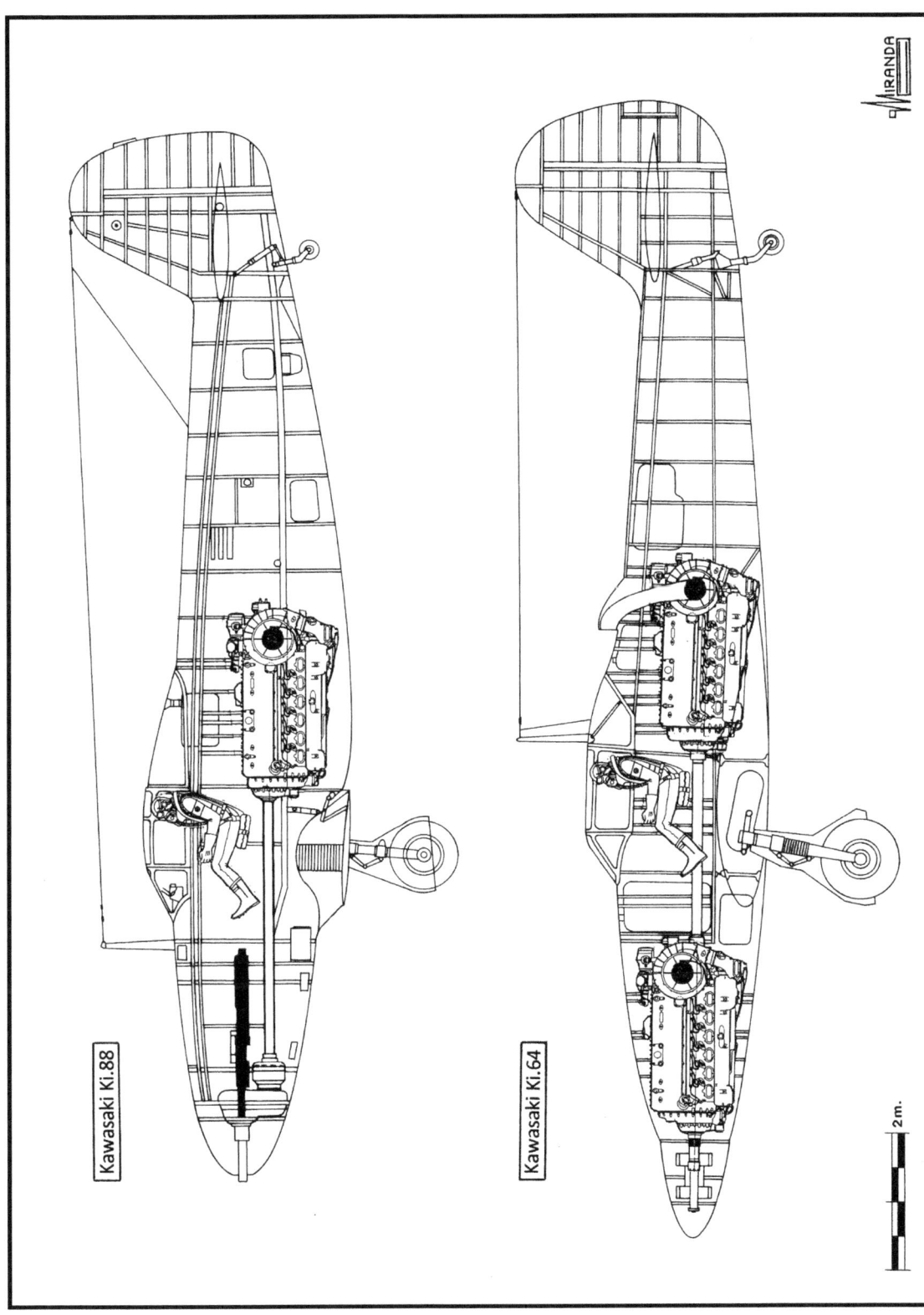

Kawasaki Ki.88

Kawasaki Ki.64

2 m.

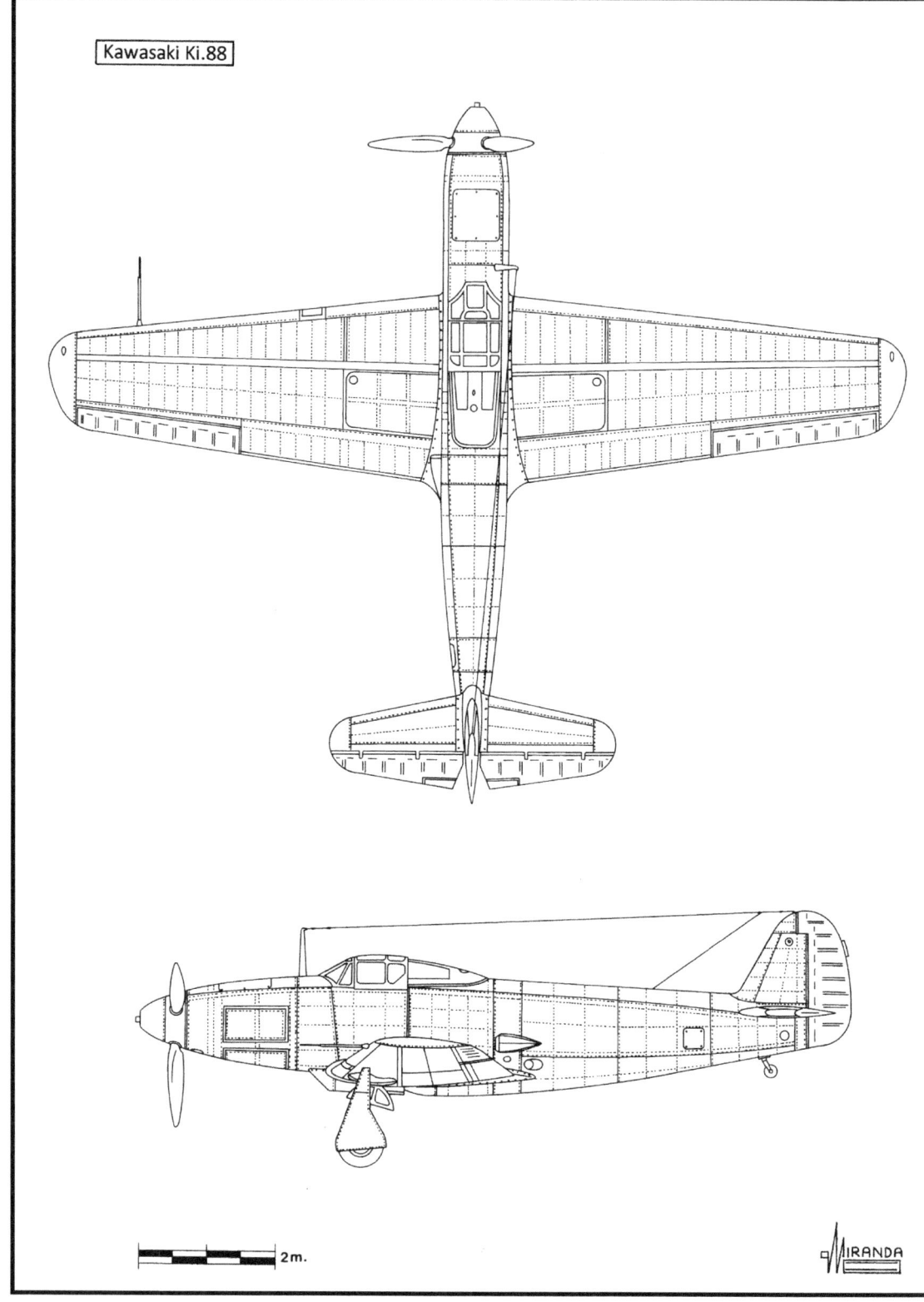

Kawasaki Ki.88

2m.

MIRANDA

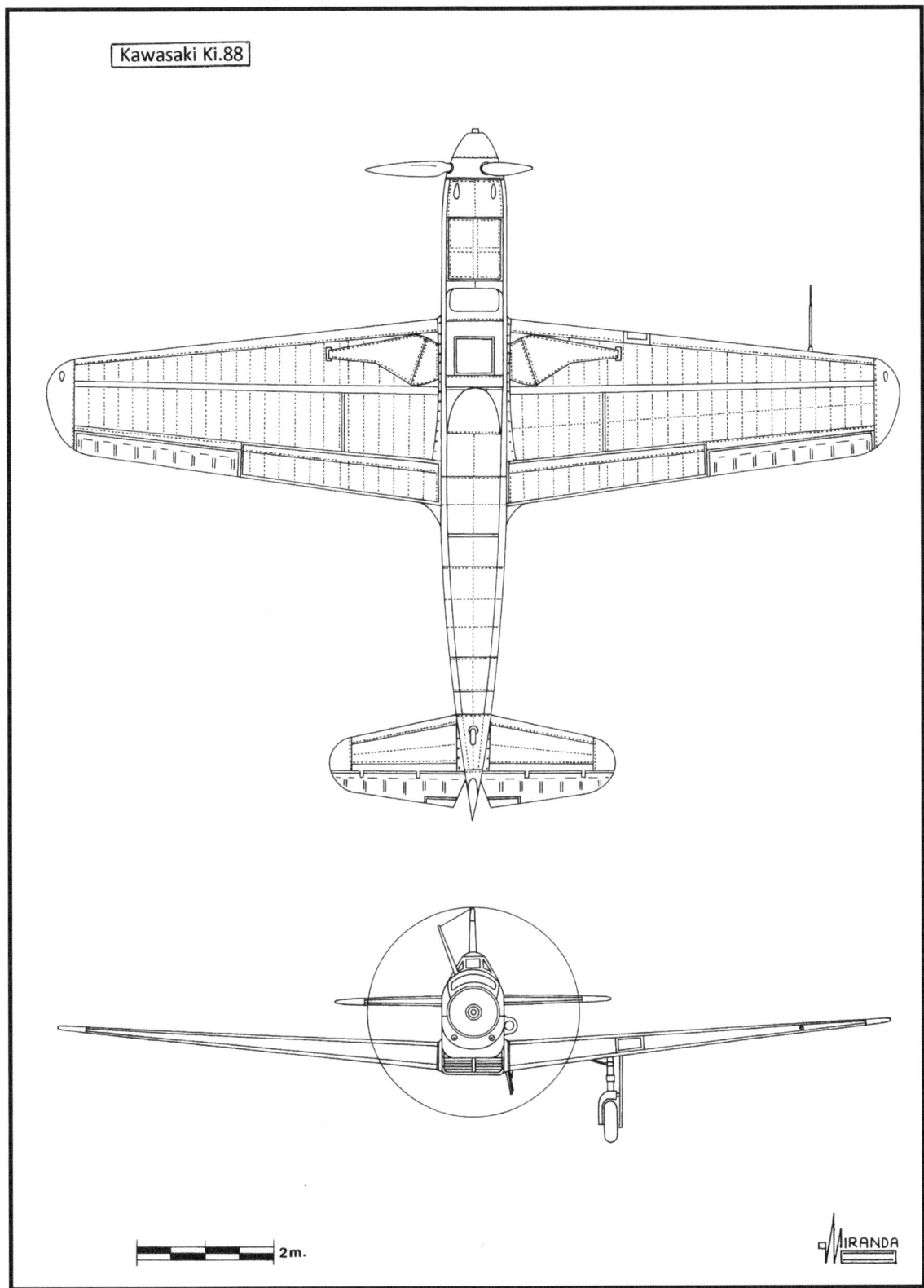

Kawasaki Ki.88

2m.

MIRANDA

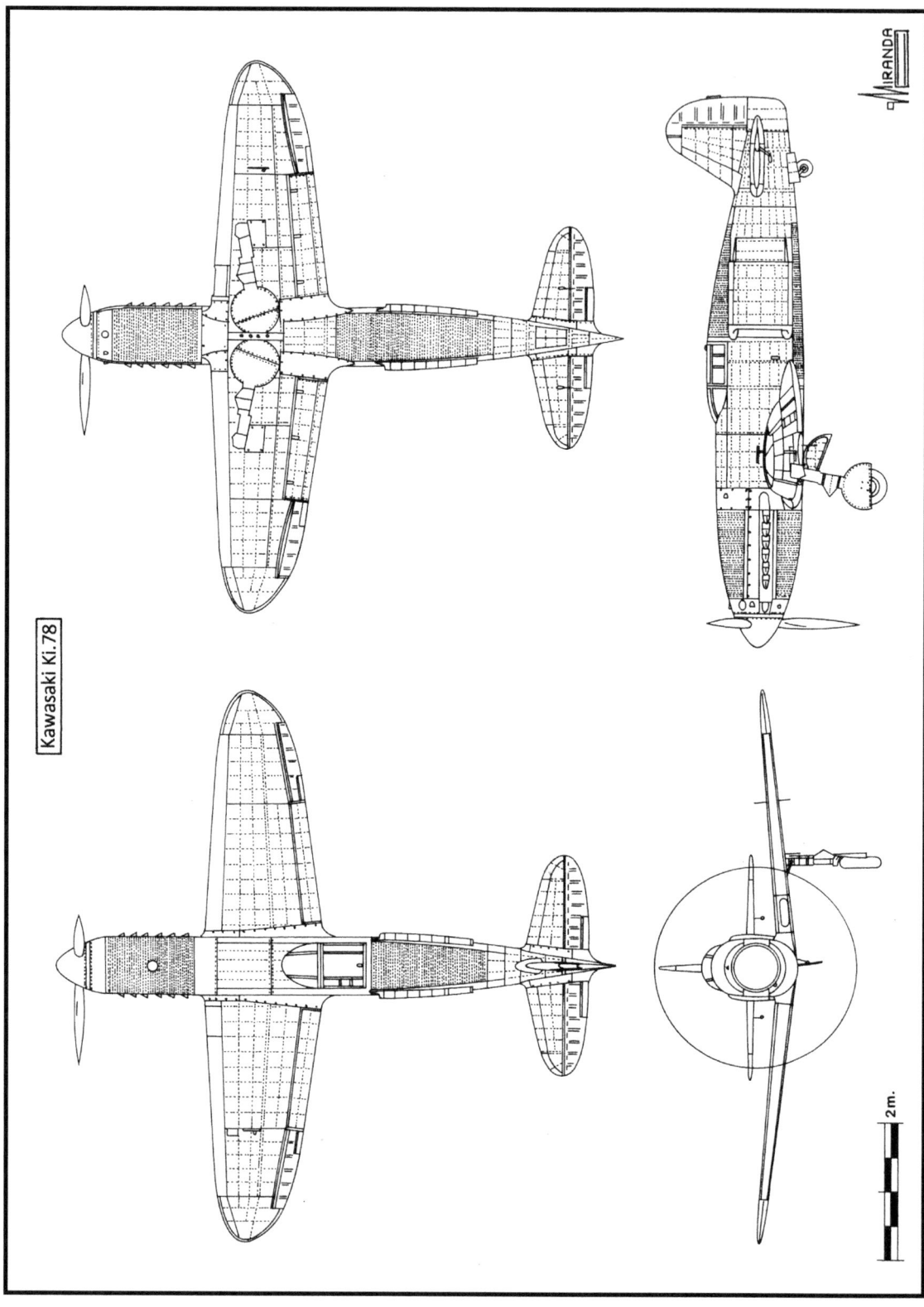

Kawasaki Ki.78

2 m.

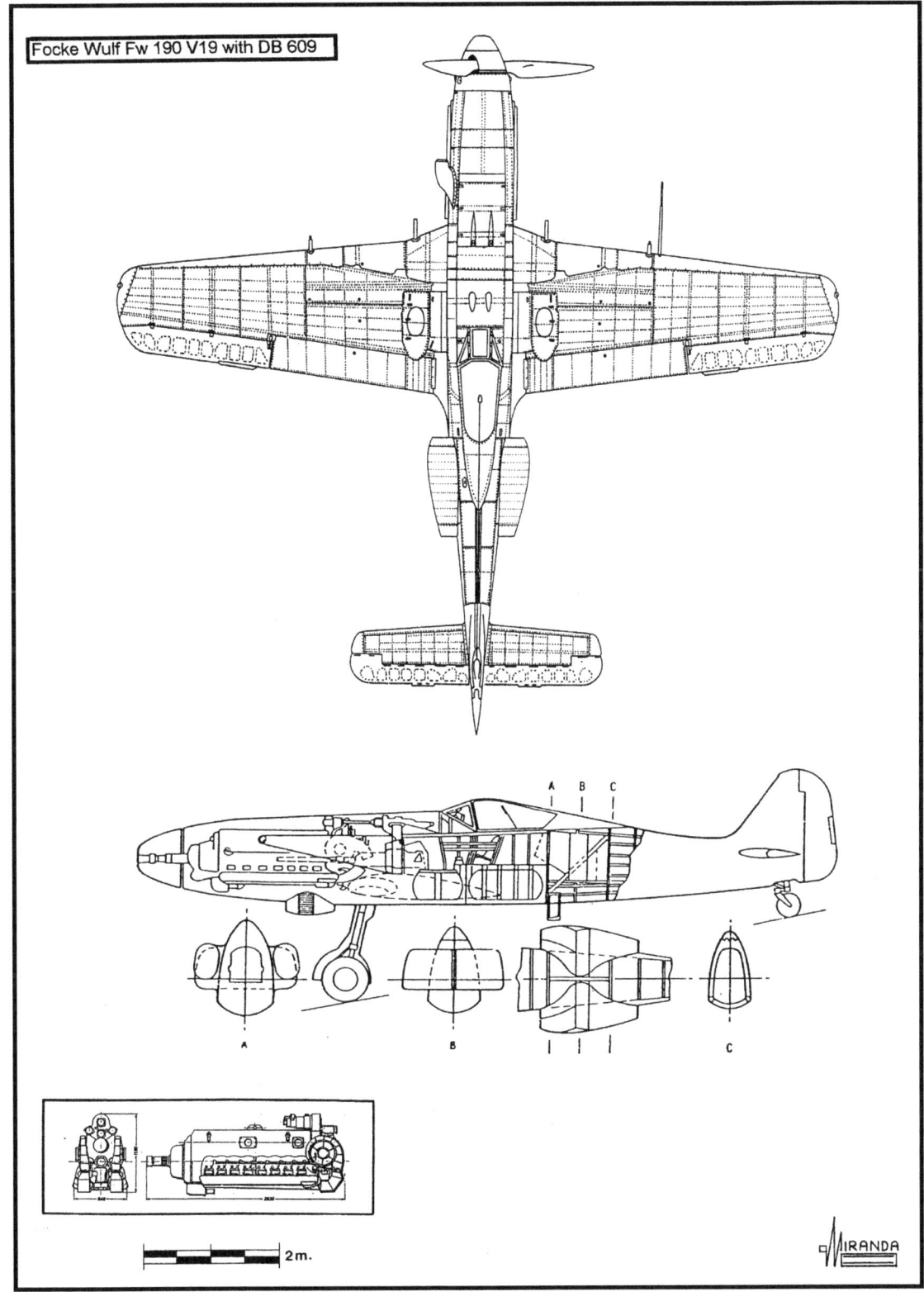

Focke Wulf Fw 190 V19 with DB 609

2 m.

High-Altitude Interceptors Nakajima Ki.87 and Tachikawa Ki.94

On March 1938, the Mitsubishi A5M2 fighters fighting in China started to use mechanically driven superchargers and oxygen equipment to face the new Gloster Gladiator of the Chinese Air Force that could fly at an altitude of 6,000 m.

These primitive forced induction devices, based on a Rateau French patent of 1926, consisted of a rapidly spinning impeller powered by the engine via a short drive shaft that sucked in ambient air then injected it into the carburettor.

By acquiring the manufacturing license of the German engine Daimler Benz DB 601, the Japanese gained access to the Vulkan coupling technology, a supercharger fitted with a continuously variable transmission device that automatically regulated the rotation speed of the impeller by means of a barometric control.

The study of a Merlin XX British engine, from a Hawker Hurricane Mk II captured in Singapore, allowed Kawasaki engineers to build their first two-stage supercharger for the Ha-140 engine. The British system used two impellers that rotated at different speeds, selected by the pilot by means of a gearbox. The use of two impellers in engines of more than 1,500 hp requires the installation of an intercooler, to avoid the premature detonation problems that occur when air is injected into the carburettor at an excessive temperature.

Based on the Swiss model acquired in 1937, the Hitachi, Nakajima, and Mitsubishi engineers received the assignment to develop their own turbocharger. By the end of 1942, Mitsubishi produced the mechanically driven Ru-302 supercharger with two stages and two speeds for the Ki.46-IV high-altitude reconnaissance aircraft. The Ru-302 did not perform well during the tests, which were conducted in May 1944 with a J2M4 Raiden-33 fighter. The Hitachi turbo was manufactured with the best available alloys of chrome-molybdenum steel, but its development was too slow and was still being tested, installed in a C6N *Saiun*, by the end of the Second World War.

The Nakajima team tried to modify one A6M2 standard fighter by installing one Sakae turbo-charged engine without intercooler. The prototype was named A6M4 and started its flight test at Yokosuka Arsenal in 1943, experiencing fires and multiple ruptures in the compressor and ducting. The origin of these failures was that the imported Swiss turbo was actually a design for 500-hp diesel engines with an operating temperature that was 200 degrees C lower than that of the Japanese petrol engines. Despite all these problems, the Mitsubishi engineers managed to build the A6M3 series in 1942, powered by a *Sakae* 21 and able to climb up to 11,000 m thanks to a modest two-speed supercharger.

The Japanese tried to increase the power of their engines with methanol-water and oxygen-injection devices, but the system only worked below 10,000 m. Mitsubishi engineers tried to develop an exhaust-driven turbo-supercharger based on the study of North American P-43 and B-17 aircraft captured in China and the Philippines. By mid-1944, turbo-superchargers were indispensable to fight the B-29 bombers at altitudes over 10,000 m, but the Japanese industry was unable to duplicate the captured aircraft.

The General Electric turbo-supercharger was a product that required enormous technical and manufacturing resources that were not available in Japan. The high temperatures reached by exhaust gas and the high rotation speeds of turbines (26,000 rpm) required the use of austenitic stainless-steel chrome-molybdenum alloys and the development of work-hardening techniques that enabled the turbocharger to withstand stresses caused by centrifugal forces. The precision machining of turbines and impellers could only be made possible by sophisticated machine tools and a surplus of raw materials.

The availability of high-octane fuel let the American engines run hotter without detonation problems, but the Japanese had 87-octane only and had to use forced air-cooling fans to avoid the overheating of their supercharged engines.

In August 1944, the Mitsubishi J2M4 Raiden 34 flew with one Ru-303 exhaust-driven turbo-supercharger mounted in the starboard side of the fuselage, just behind the Kasei 23c engine. The new supercharger did not work properly either, provoking fires during the tests, and never became operational.

The exhaust-driven turbo-superchargers were larger, involved extra piping, and increased an aircraft's size, weight, complexity, and cost. It is not possible to install them in a conventional single-engined fighter, and its use requires specially designed aircraft, with enough room for the installation of the turbo, the intercooler, and the heavy tubing system.

In February 1942, the US Government placed an order for 1,600 Boeing B-29 superbombers, able to fly at 595 kph and 9,700 m altitude. In April, the *Koku Hombu* Technical Branch issued a specification calling for a high-altitude interceptor with a 800-kph max. speed, 13,000-m service ceiling, and 3,000-km range, armed with four 30-mm cannons. The specification was so demanding that most Japanese aircraft manufacturers decided not to submit projects.

In the summer of 1942, the Tachikawa firm began the design of the Ki.94-I, a twin booms heavy fighter powered by two 2,000-hp Ha-211 Ru air-cooled radial engines (mounted in push-pull configuration) driving two VDM constant-speed propellers with a diameter of 3.32 m. With the use of the new Ru-302 mechanically-driven superchargers, a service ceiling of 14,000 m was expected. In October 1943, the mock-up was presented to *Koku Hombu*, but IA experts decided that the plane was too heavy and with an overly complex propulsion system. The project was dropped.

Ki.94-I Technical Data

Wingspan: 15 m
Length: 13.05 m
Height: 3.85 m
Wing area: 37 sq. m
Max. speed: 780 kph
Max. weight: 9,400 kg
Ceiling: 14,000 m
Range: 4,520 km
Proposed armament: 2 × 37-mm Ho-203 and 2 × 30-mm Ho-105 cannons

The IJA intelligence services awaited the first B-29 attack in April 1944, but this was delayed by a lack of supplies at the Chinese airfields of Kweiling and Liuchow. The first contact with the B-29 occurred in 26 April, when six Ki.43 fighters of the IJA 204th

Sentai had a worrying combat with a B-29 of the 444th BG, which was flying supplies from India to China. The giant plane, heavily loaded and with the tail gun out of service, was shot twelve times without apparent results; it just ascended until the Hayabusas were forced to abandon the pursuit due to a lack of oxygen.

It was known that the B-29 could fly at high altitudes thanks to its turbo-charged engines, but when it first appeared 10,000 m above Tokyo on a reconnaissance mission, it was flying so fast that the Ki.44 of the 47th *Sentai* could not reach it. By contrast, the J2M4, J2M5, and N1K5-J fighters that had been designed to face it had not even begun to be manufactured.

In March 1944, the IJA decided to lower the requirements for the high-altitude specification of 1942, asking the Nakajima firm to build the Ki.87-I, a high-altitude interceptor with a less heavy pressurisation system than the Tachikawa pressure cabin.

Three versions of the Nakajima fighter are known: the Ki.87-I; the Ki.87-II, powered by one 3,000-hp Ha-46 engine (with Ru-303) driving a six-bladed propeller; and the Nakajima 20-Shi-Ko, with Ha-44-21 engine developed for the IJN. The Ki.87-I prototype was flown in April 1945, powered by one 2,450-hp Ha-44-12 air-cooled radial engine, with one Ru-303 turbo-supercharger mounted at the starboard side of the forward fuselage.

This configuration seemed safer than the ventral position installation. Mitsubishi engineers feared that the fuel contact with the turbo would cause fires. In 1942, the Chinese lost 139 P-43 fighters for this cause due to a defect in the Fairplane cement used to seal the fuel tanks. The IJA disagreed and preferred a ventral installation, such as in the P-47 Thunderbolt, which delayed serial production of the Ki.87 until the end of the war. Nakajima preferred to devote its efforts to obtaining a high-altitude interceptor based on the Hayate airframe and yielded its pressurisation technology to Tachikawa so they could use it in the design of the Ki.94-II.

Ki.87-I Technical Data

Wingspan: 13.423 m
Length: 11.82 m
Height: 4.5 m
Wing area: 26 sq. m
Max. speed: 697 kph
Max. weight: 5,633 kg
Ceiling: 12,855 m
Proposed armament: 2 × 30-mm (synchronised) Ho-155 and 2 × 20-mm Ho-5 cannons

The Ki.94-II design was approved by the *Koku Hombu* in April 1944. An order was placed for three prototypes and eighteen pre-production aircraft. The aircraft was equipped with laminar flow wings, designed by Tatsuo Hasegawa, and one Nakajima pressurised cabin with an armoured windshield. The engine used was a 2,450-hp Ha-44-13 (with Ru-303, cooling fan and two intercoolers) driving a four-bladed propeller. The prototype was completed in July 1945, but it was not flight tested because the war ended.

A second prototype, in construction phase, was powered by one 3,000-hp Ha-46 engine, driving a six-bladed VDM/Sumitomo airscrew with a diameter of 3.8 m. Development of the Ki.94 was too slow, and when the B-29s attacked Yawata on 14 June 1944, Japan had no fighters capable of confronting them successfully.

Ki.94-II Technical Data

Wingspan: 13.4 m
Length: 12 m
Height: 4.61 m
Wing area: 28 sq. m
Max. speed: 720 kph
Max. weight: 6,427 kg
Ceiling: 14,250 m
Range: 2,200 km
Proposed armament: 2 × 30-mm Ho-155 and 2 × 20-mm Ho-5 cannons

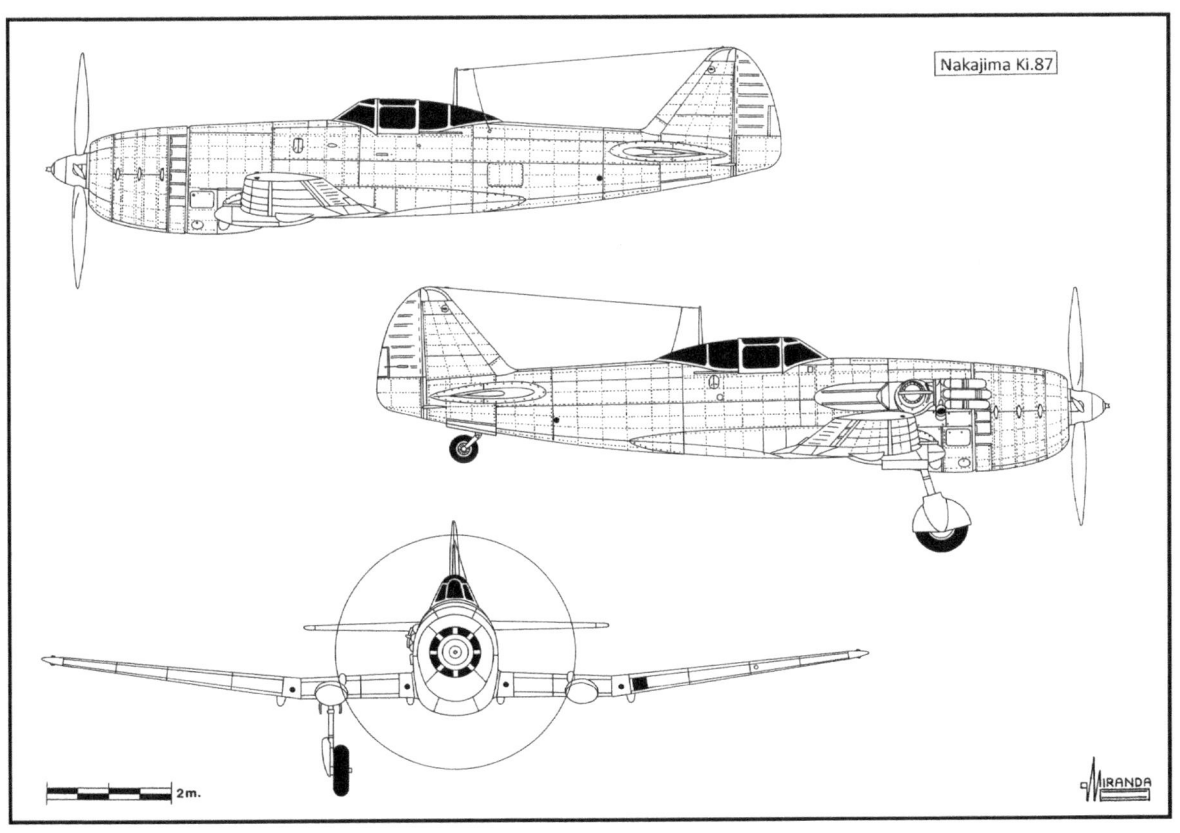

Nakajima Ki.87

Nakajima Ki.87

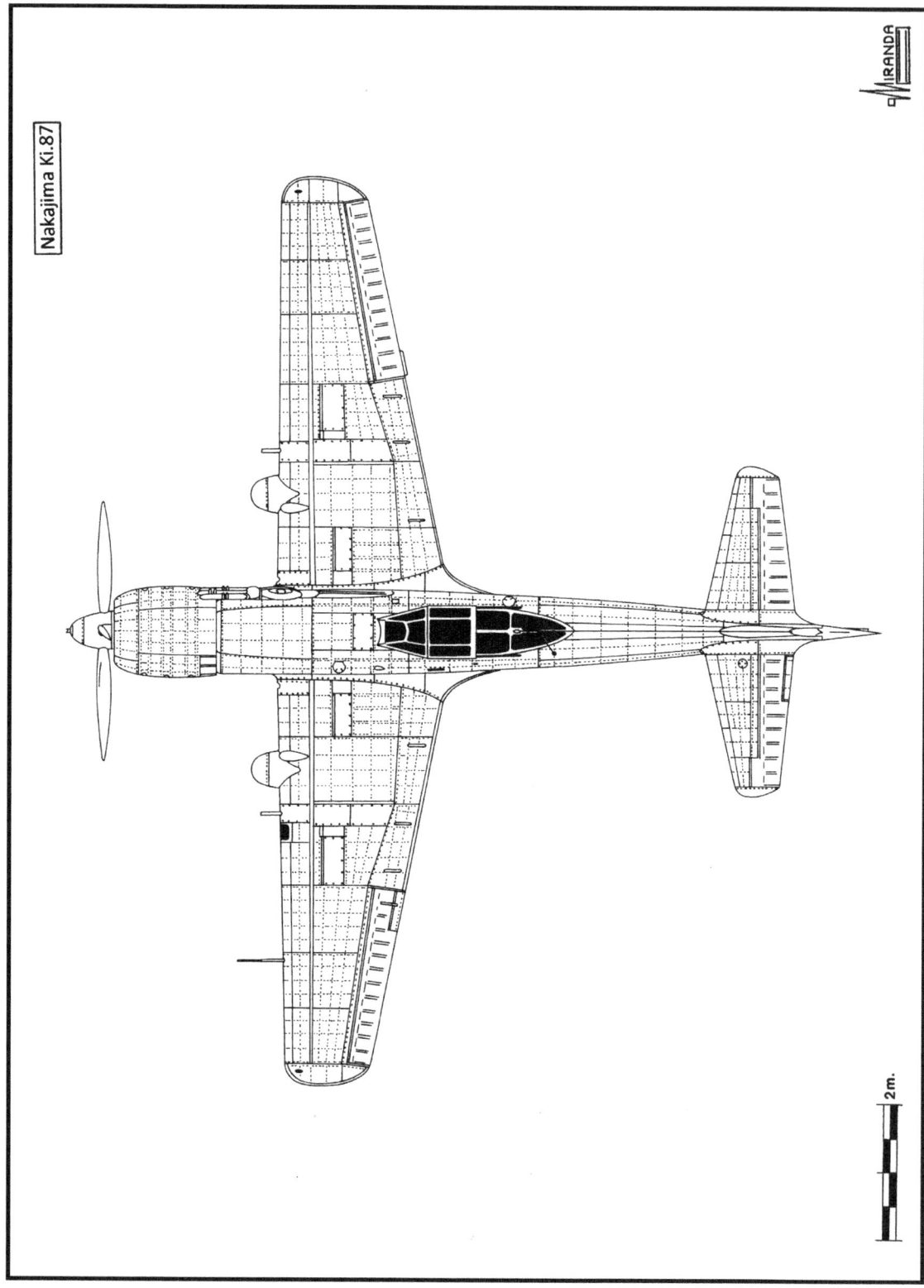

2m.

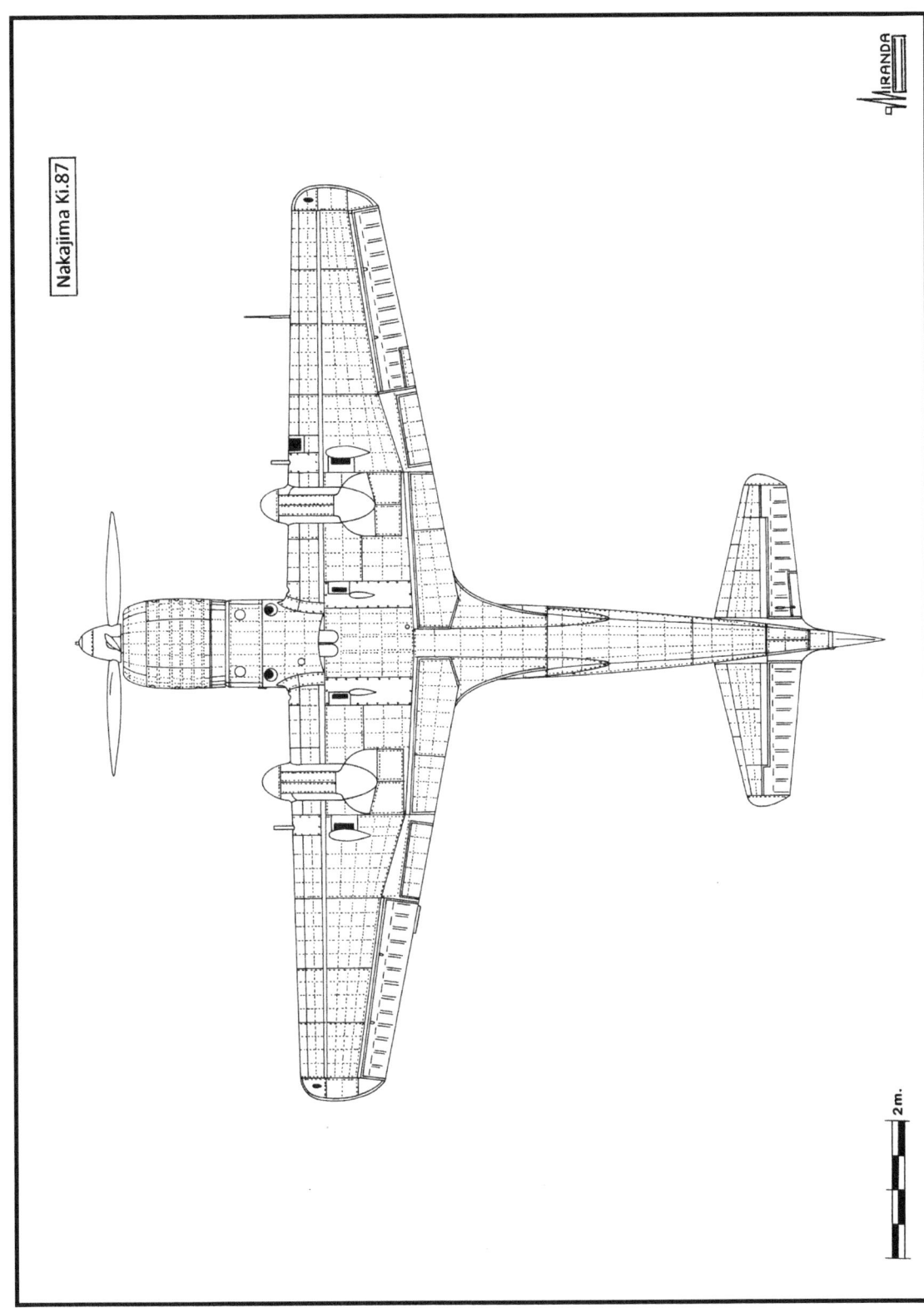

Nakajima Ki.87

2 m.

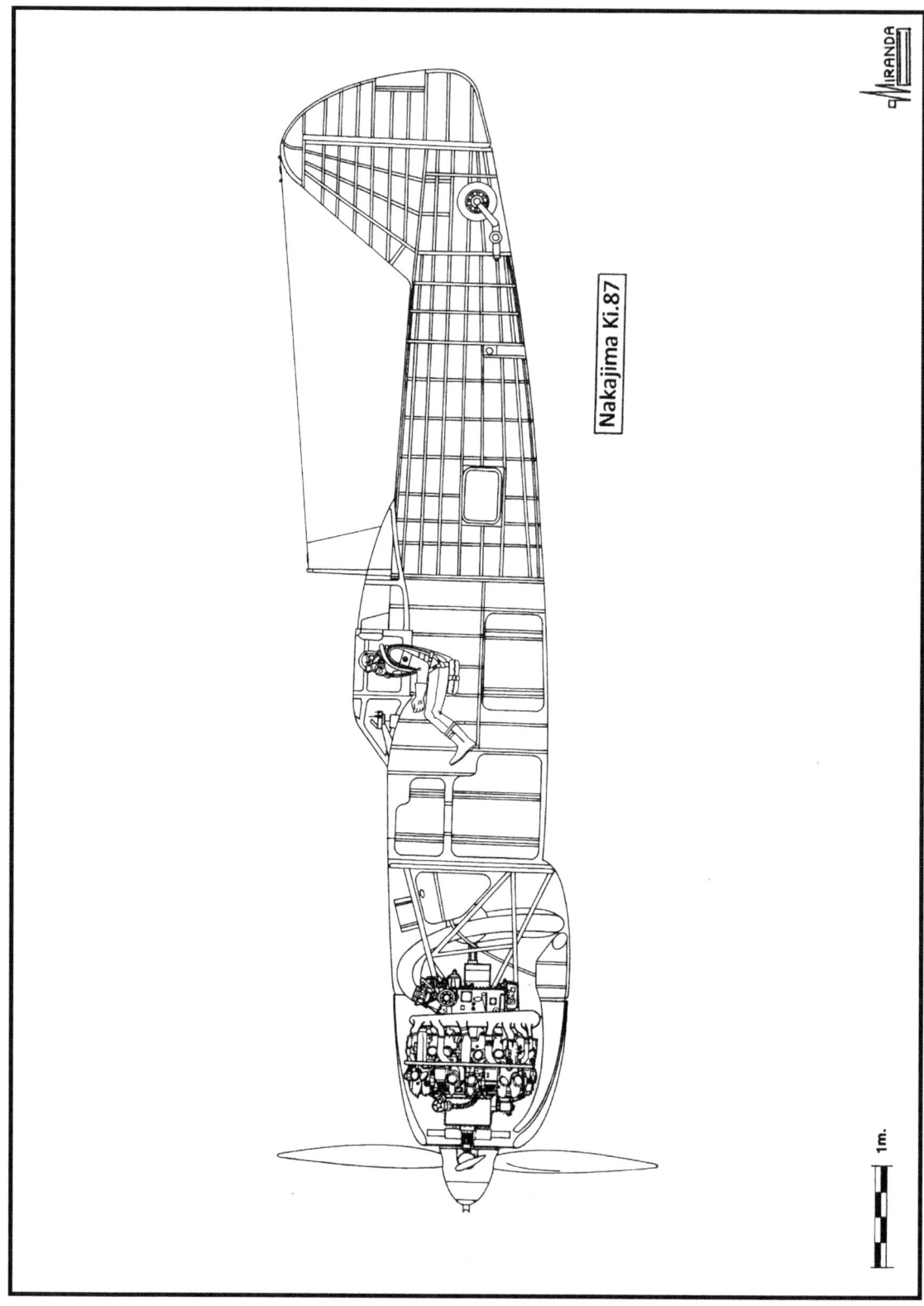

Nakajima Ki.87

1 m.

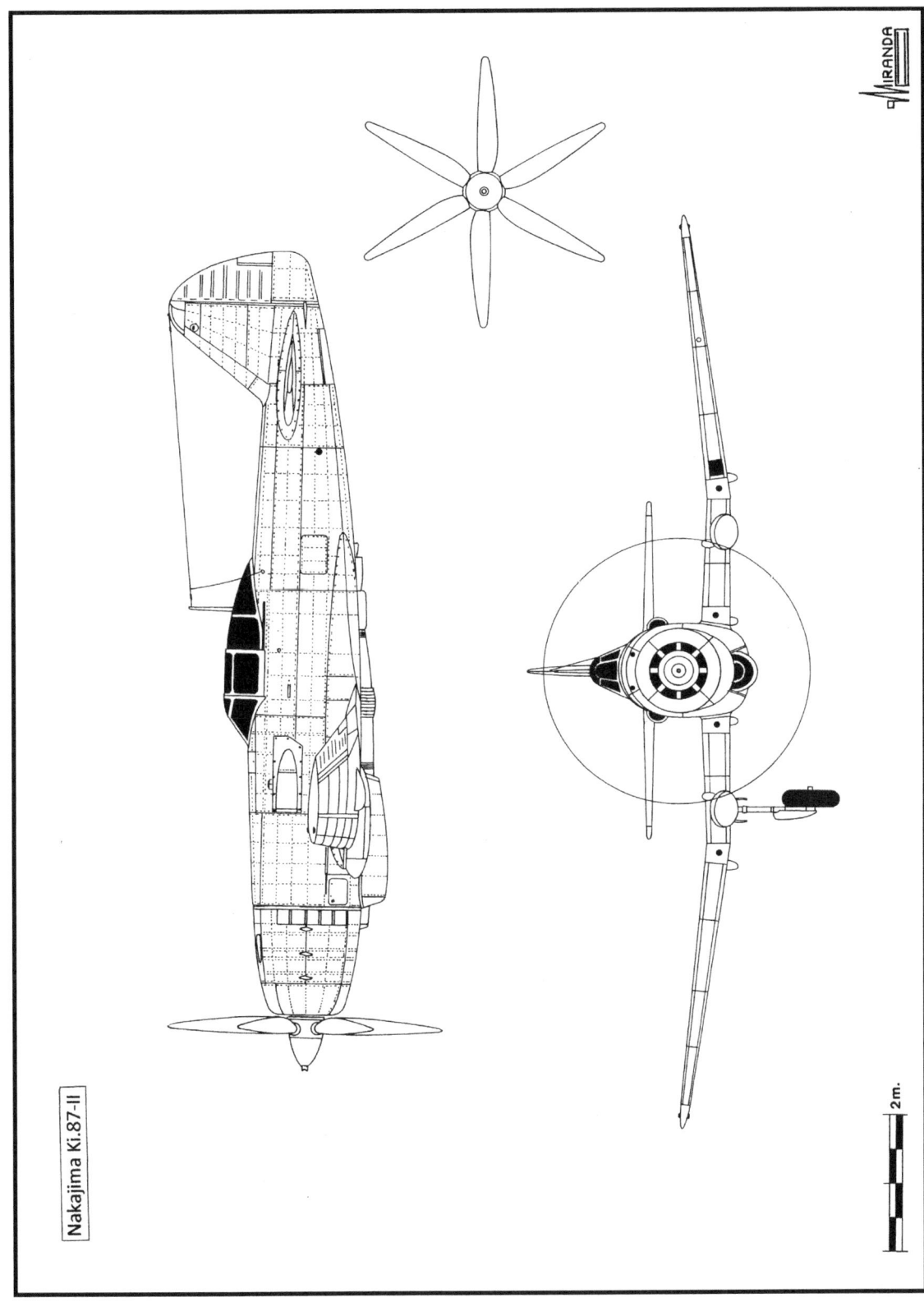

Nakajima Ki.87-II

2 m.

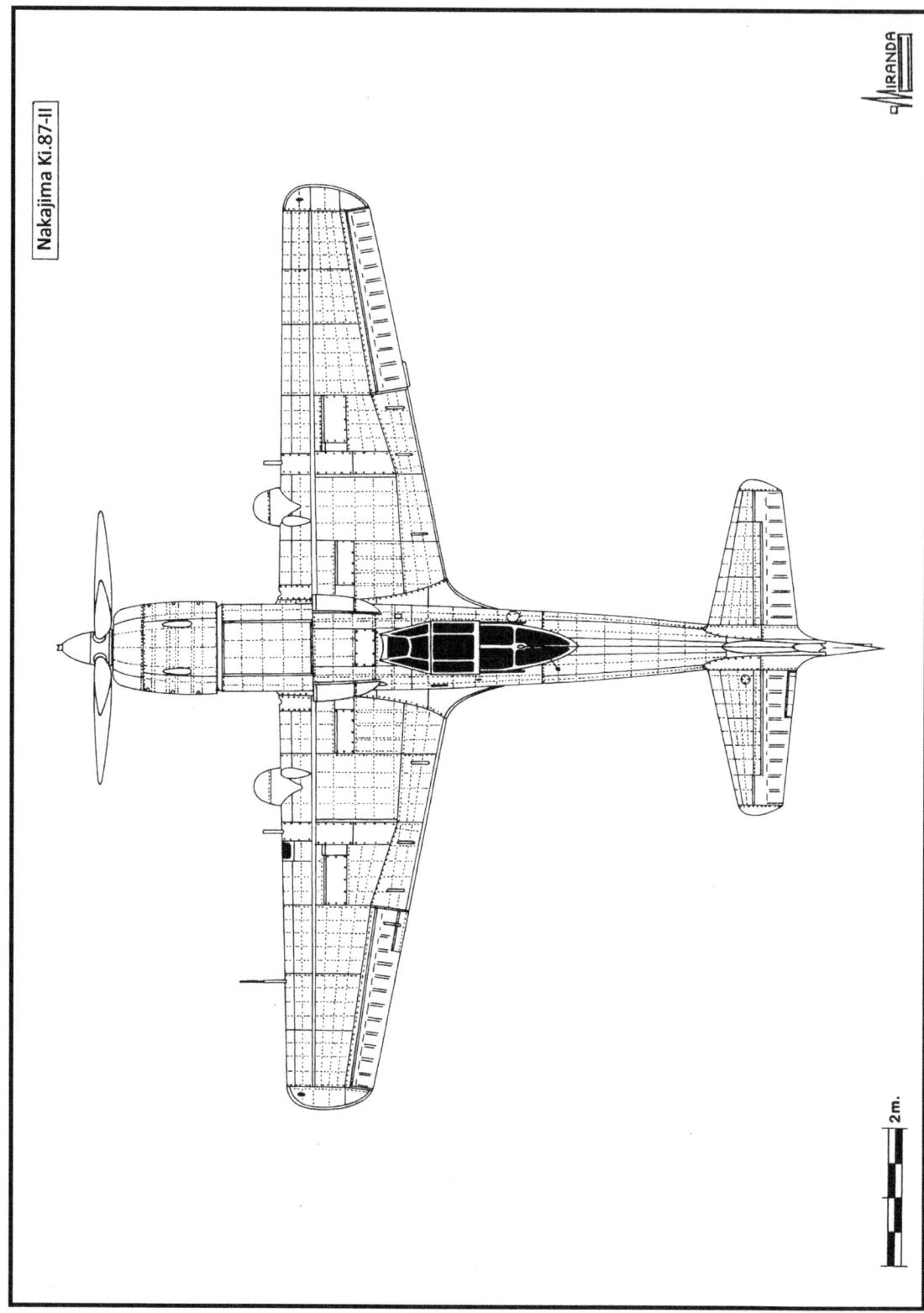

Nakajima Ki.87-II

2m.

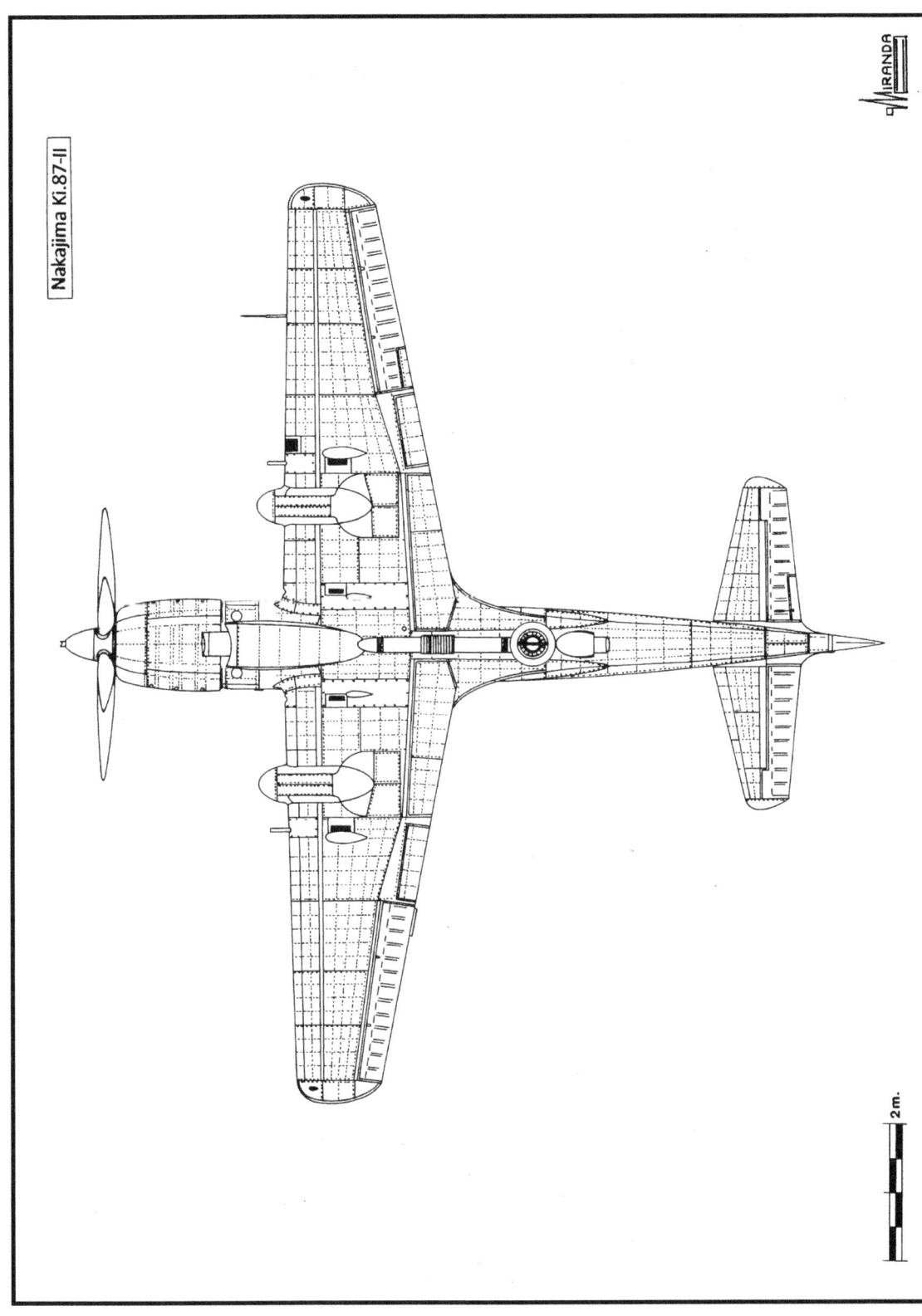

Nakajima Ki.87-II

2 m.

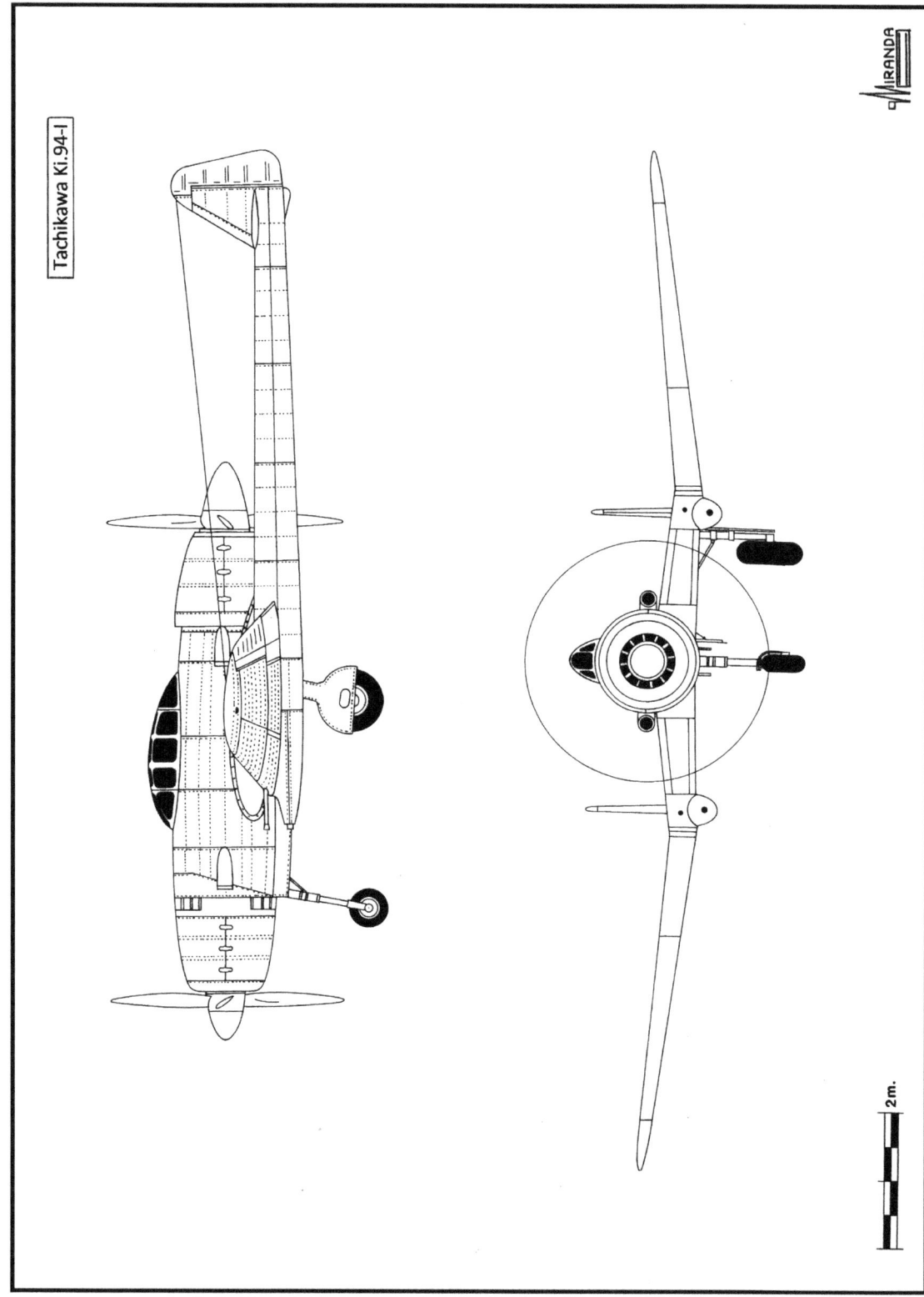

Tachikawa Ki.94-I

2 m.

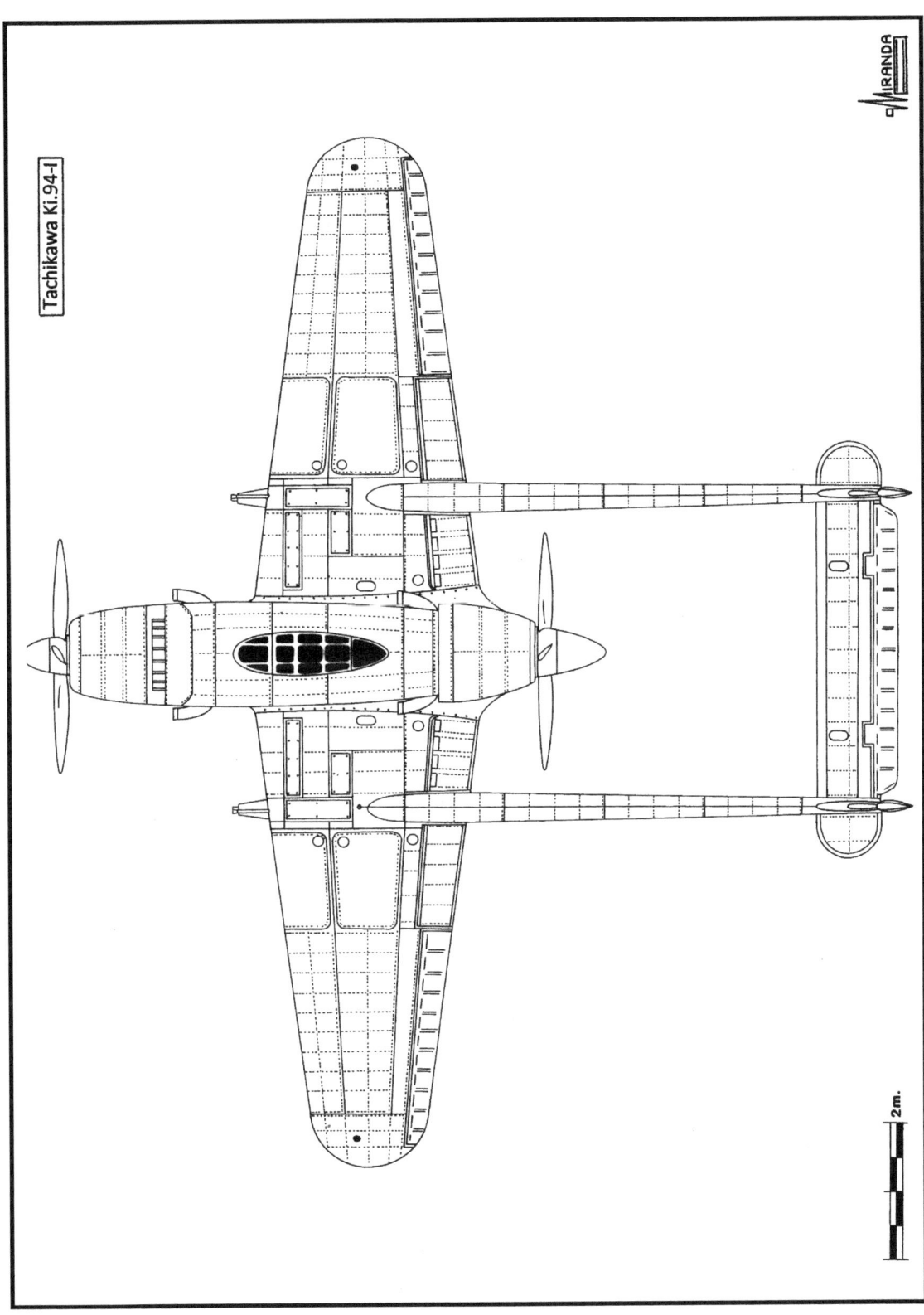

Tachikawa Ki.94-I

2 m.

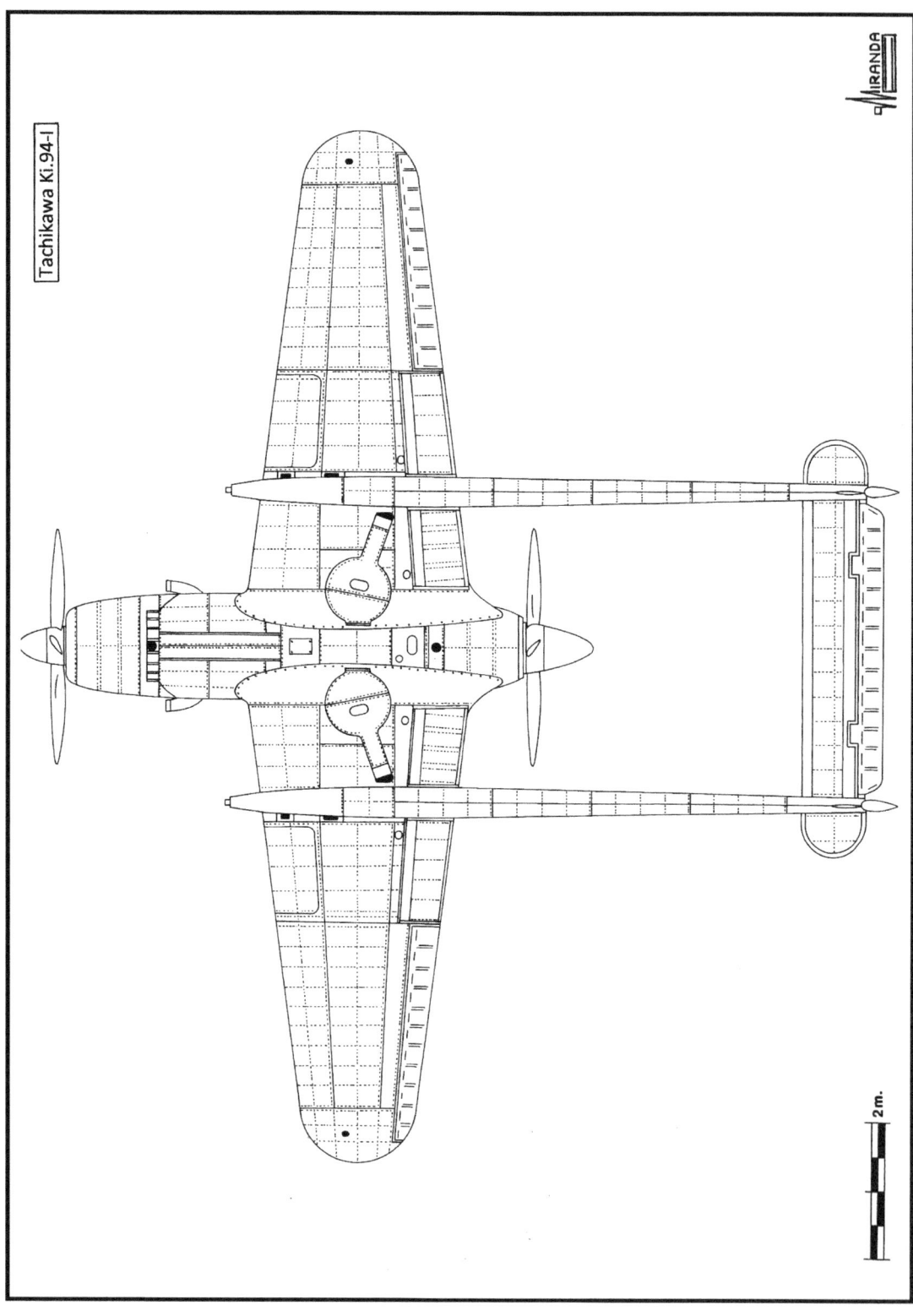

Tachikawa Ki.94-I

2 m.

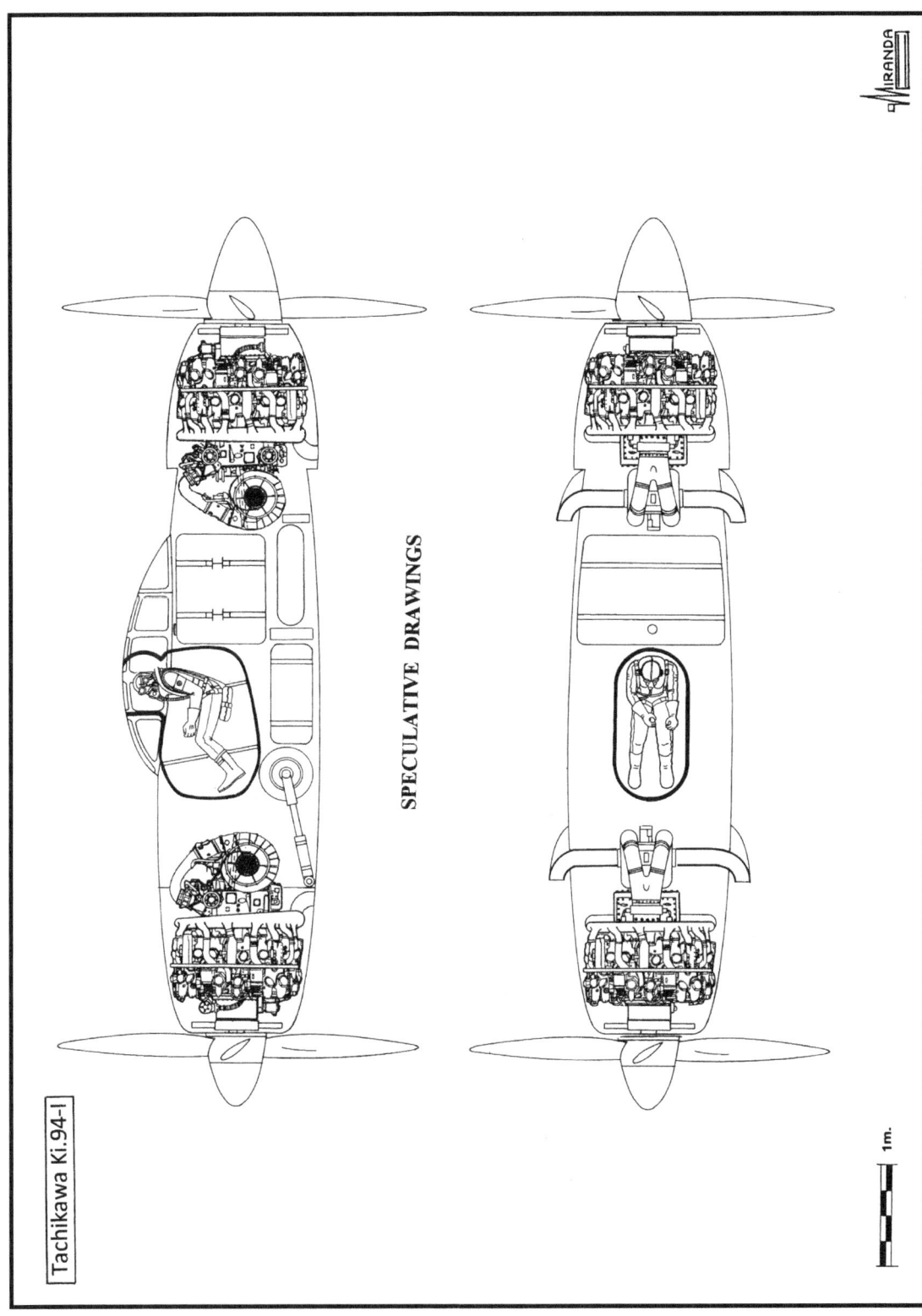

SPECULATIVE DRAWINGS

Tachikawa Ki.94-I

1 m.

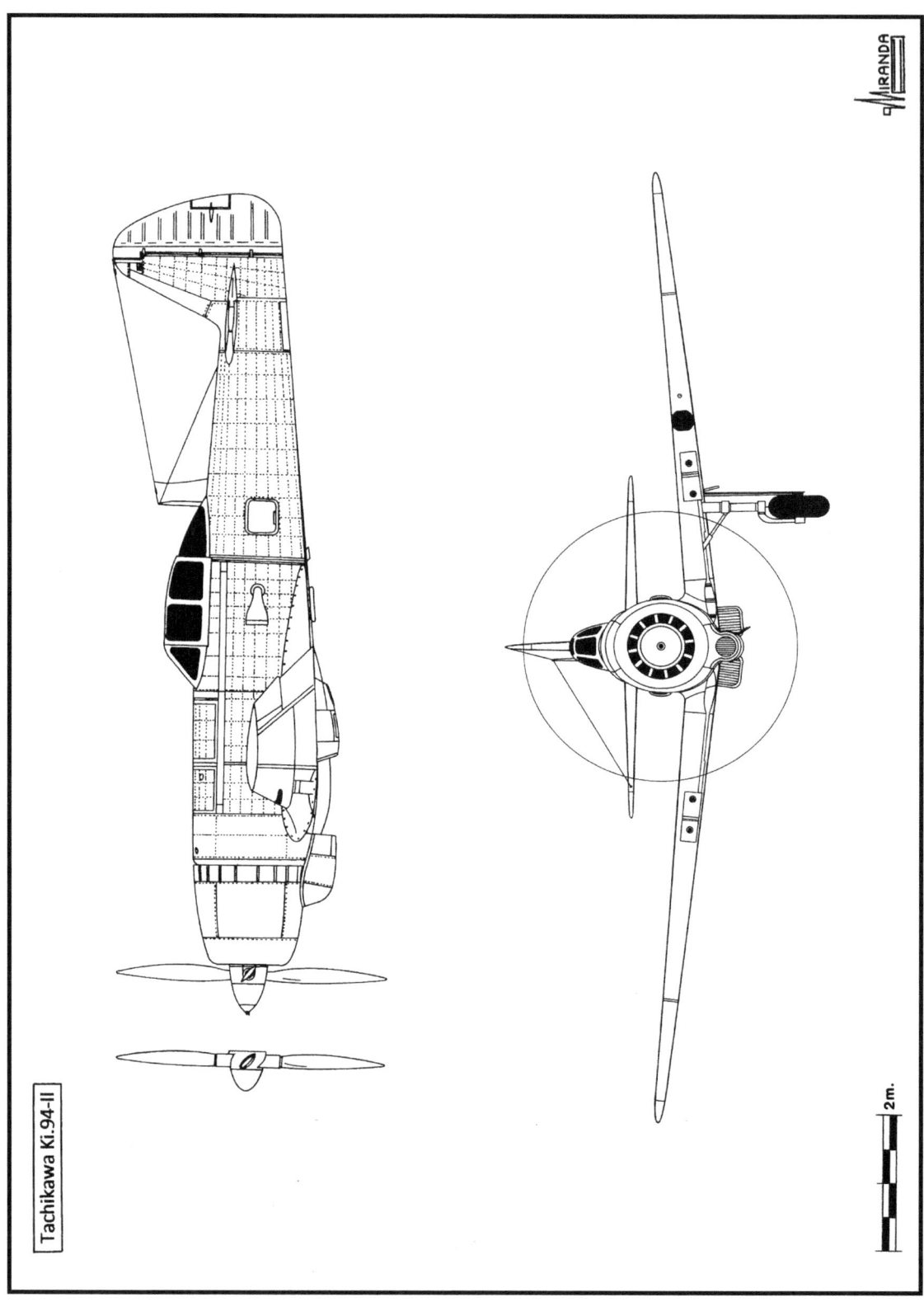

Tachikawa Ki.94-II

2m.

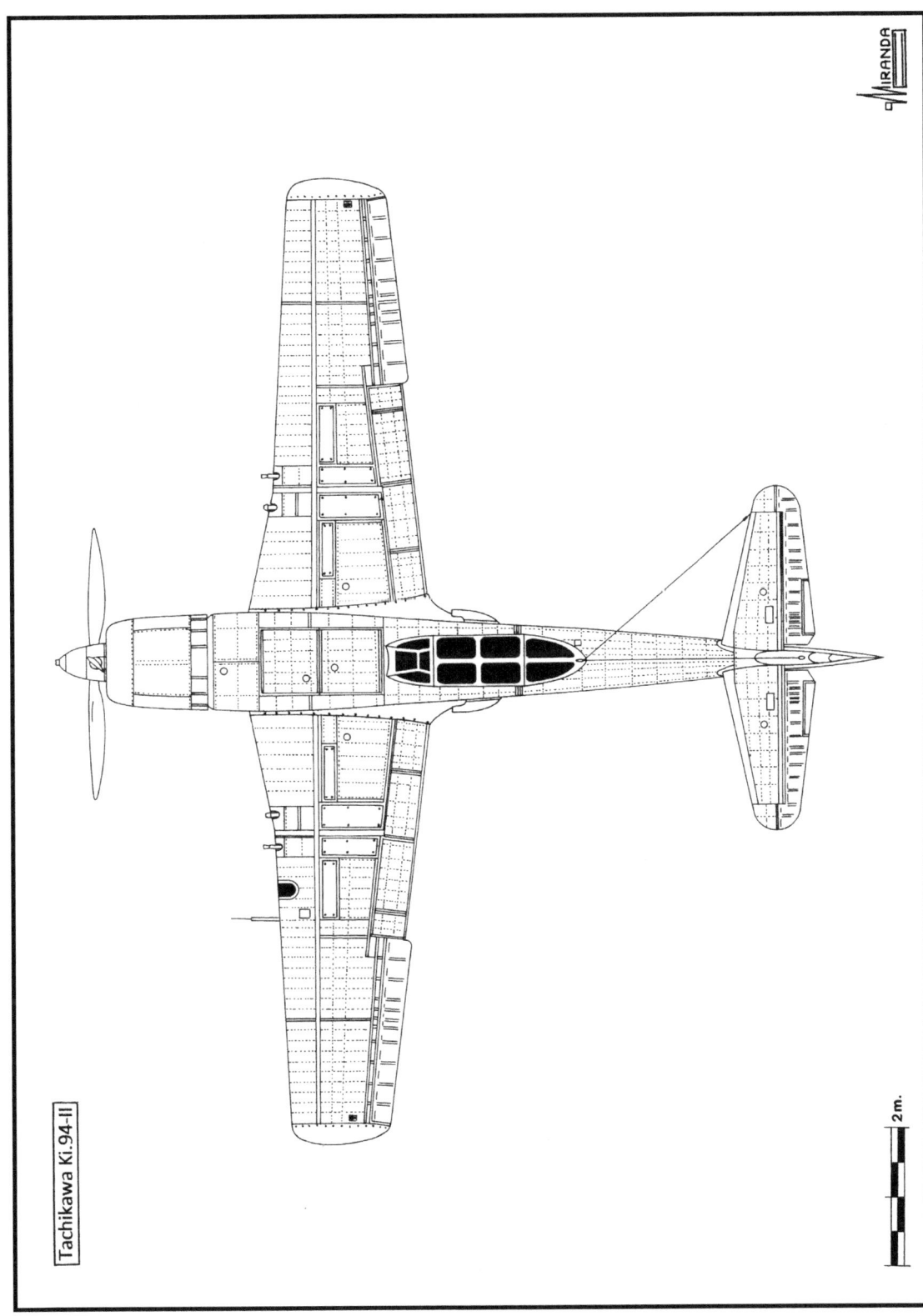

Tachikawa Ki.94-II

2m.

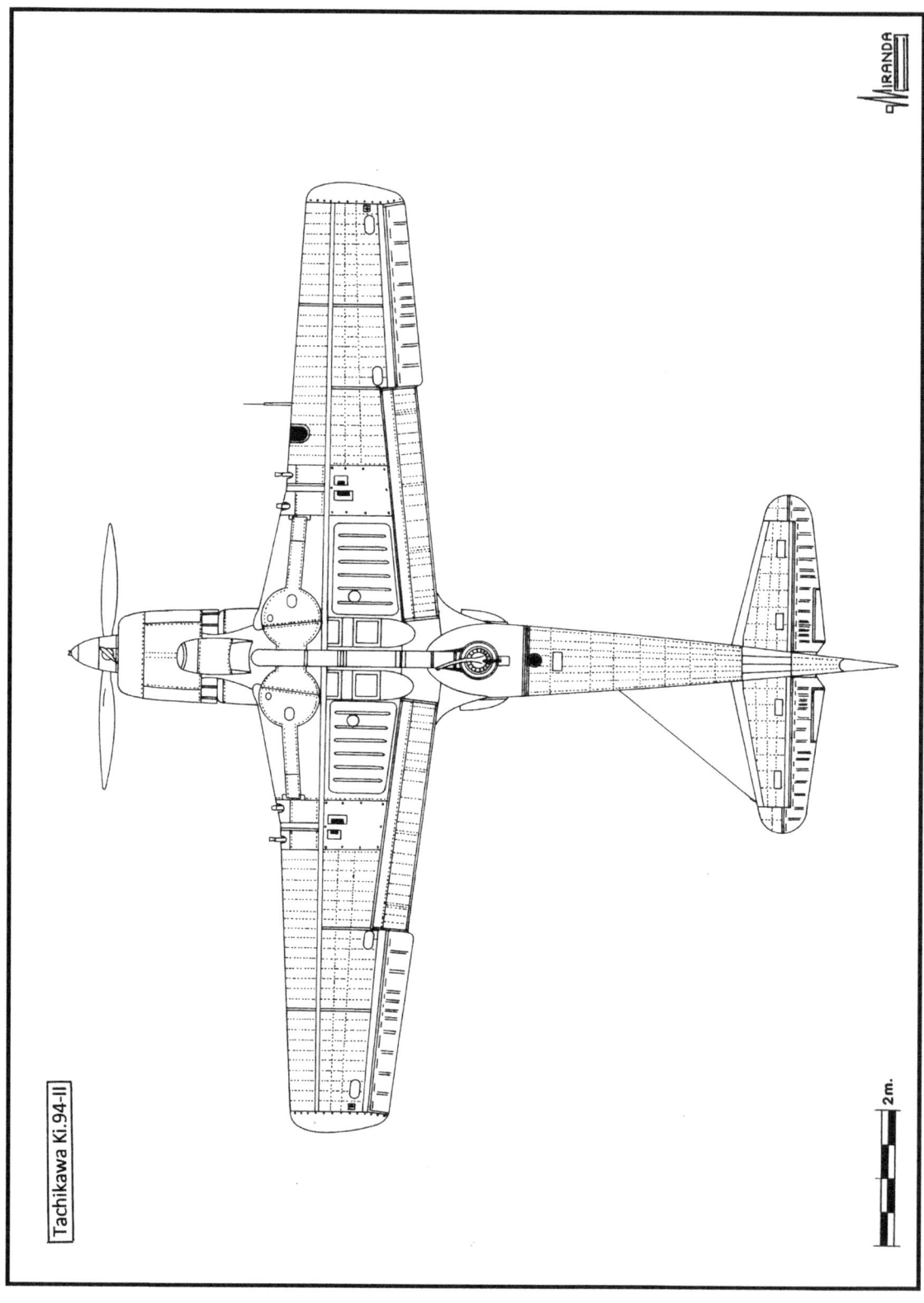

Tachikawa Ki.94-II

2m.

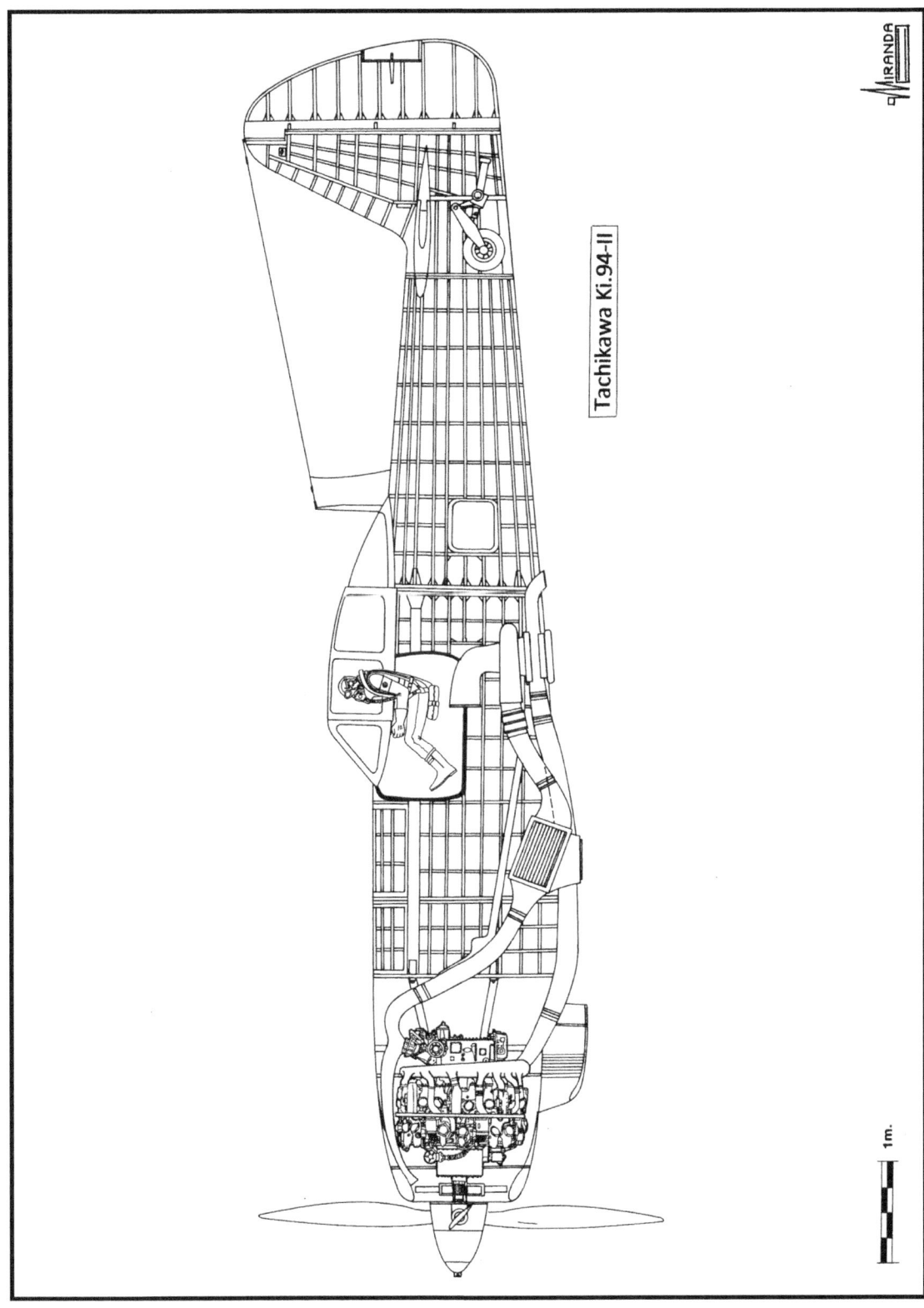

Tachikawa Ki.94-II

1 m.

Manshu Ki.65 and Ki.98

In February 1940, the IJA Aero-Technical Research Institute (*Rikugun*) requested several Japanese aircraft manufacturers develop a high-performance interceptor that would replace the Ki.44.

Kawasaki received orders to develop the Ki.60 and the Ki.61 fighters, powered by one 1,100-hp Ha-40 in-line, liquid-cooled engine. Nakajima developed the Ki.62, powered by one Ha-40, and the Ki.64m powered by one 1,050-hp Ha-102 radial, air-cooled engine. Mitsubishi proposed to modify the J2M Raiden to suit the needs of the IJA.

The new aircraft, named Ki.65, should be powered by a 1,080-hp Ha-102 Zuisei or a 1,850-hp Ha-101 Kasei radial engines. Mitsubishi hoped to have its first prototype completed in March 1942, but the firm was so overworked getting ready for the war that the IA decided to transfer the project to Manshu Hikoki Seizo KK. in the spring of 1941.

The *Koku Hombu* suggested using a 1,850-hp Ha-111 engine for the prototype and a 2,200-hp Ha-43/Ha-211 eighteen-cylinder double-star radial engine for the production version. The diameter of the Ha-211 was 11 cm shorter than that of the Ha-101 used by the Raiden, allowing Manshu designers to use a reduced front section fuselage, shortening the shaft extension. Increased engine power allowed a new wing with increased span and surface to improve high-altitude manoeuvrability.

Late in 1942, the *Koku Hombu* issued a heavy fighter specification, calling for one high-altitude interceptor that could be modified for use in ground close-support and anti-landing ships duties. The armour required for this type of attacks and the weight of the armament required the use of very powerful engines, so most of the projects presented (Kawasaki Ki.102, Mitsubishi Ki.83, and Rikugun Ki.93) were twin-engined aircraft.

The firm Manshu Hikoki Seizo KK decided to adopt the aerodynamic solutions of the Focke-Wulf with BMW 803A for its single-engined project Ki.98, which could meet the specification with half the power of the Ki.83. By 1941, the German firm BMW had developed a 4,500-hp, twenty-eight-cylinder, four-row radial, liquid-cooled monster engine called BMW 803.

Following the cancellation of the Focke-Wulf 238 bomber project, Kurt Tank's team designed a 9,000-kg high-altitude interceptor powered by one BMW 803A with two-stage, four-speed supercharger. The twin boom configuration allowed the installation of a heavy engine in the centre of gravity of the aircraft, which improved manoeuvrability and allowed them to build smaller airframes with material and weight savings. The forward section of the fuselage allowed for the installation of dual use, anti-tank, and anti-bomber heavy non-synchronised cannon.

The main drawback of this configuration was the cooling of the engine; therefore, it was necessary to design a new tricycle landing gear and a bail-out system for the pilot. In July 1943, the IJA authorised the construction of a prototype, powered by one 2,200-hp Ha-211-III air-cooled radial engine and armed with one 37-mm Ho-204 and two 20-mm Ho-5 cannons. In the spring of 1944, the *Koku Hombu* was informed of the operational characteristics of the new Ru-303 turbo-supercharger, which Mitsubishi would begin producing in 1945.

The IJA decided to prioritise the construction of the high-altitude version of the 1942 specification and instructed Manshu that the Ki.98 should be for modified B-29s interception duties, powered by one Ha-211 Ru turbocharged engine. Manshu expected to have the prototype finished by mid-1945, but when the Red Army began the invasion of Manchuria in August, the plane was destroyed, along with all project documentation to avoid capture by the Soviets.

Mitsubishi Ki.65 Technical Data

Wingspan: 10.8 m
Length: 9.5 m
Height: 3.81 m
Wing area: 20 sq. m
Max. speed: 620 kph
Max. weight: 2,720 kg
Ceiling: 10,000 m
Endurance: 7.5 hours with drop tank
Engine: one 1,530-hp Mitsubishi Ha-101 Kasei radial
Armament: 2 × 20-mm Ho-5 cannons in the wings and 2 × 7.7-mm Type 97 light machine guns in the nose

Manshu Ki.65 Technical Data

Wingspan: 12.5 m
Length: 9.7 m
Height: 2.97 m
Wing area: 24 sq. m
Max. speed: 680 kph
Max. weight: 4,160 kg
Engine: one 2,200-hp Mitsubishi Ha-211 radial
Armament: 2 × 20 mm Ho-5 cannons in the wings and 2 × 12.7-mm Ho-103 heavy machine guns in the nose

Manshu Ki.98 Technical Data

Wingspan: 11.26 m
Length: 11.4 m
Height: 4.3 m
Wing area: 24 sq. m
Max. speed: 731 kph
Max. weight: 4,500 kg
Ceiling: 10,000 m
Range: 1,250 km

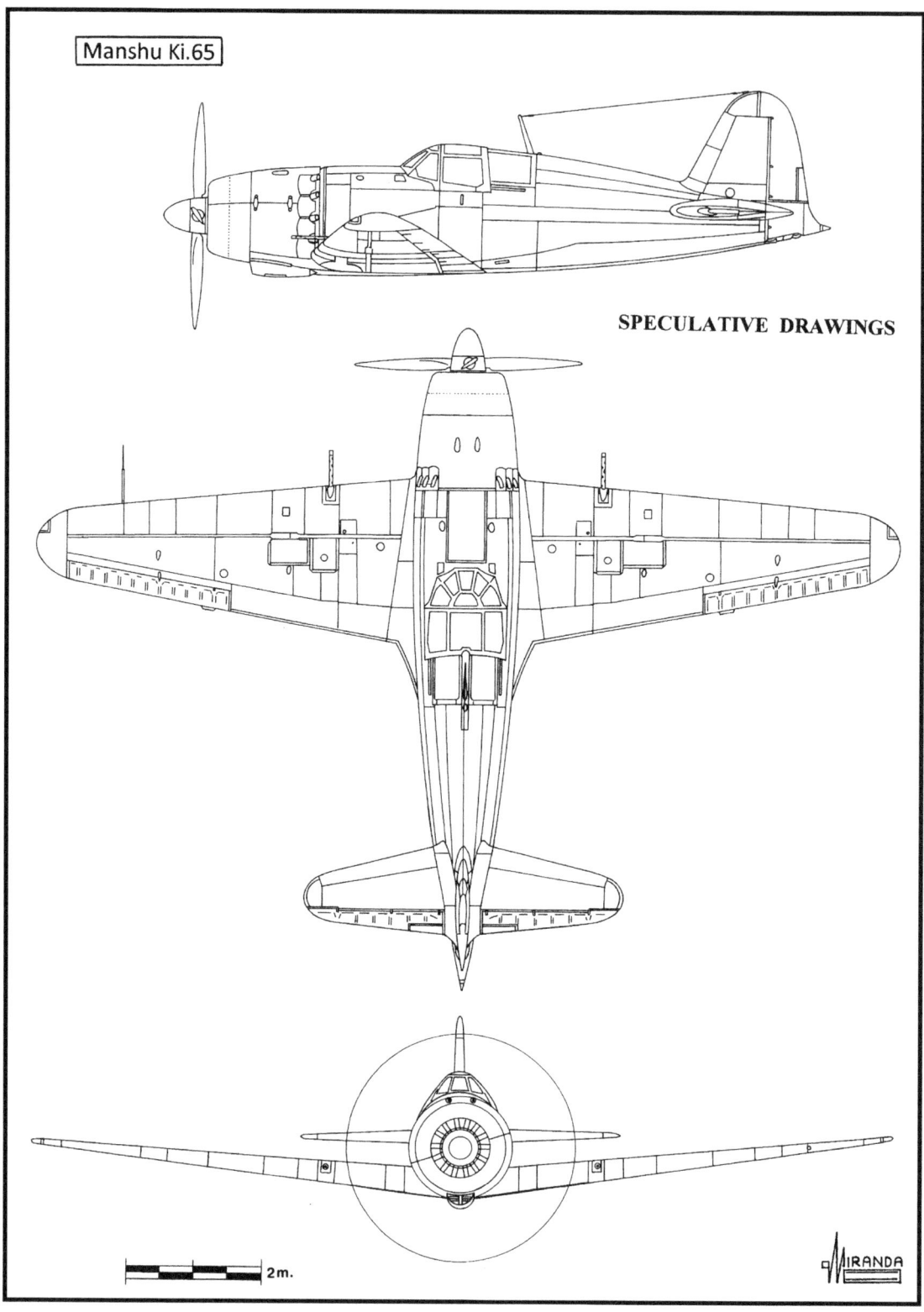

Manshu Ki.65

SPECULATIVE DRAWINGS

2m.

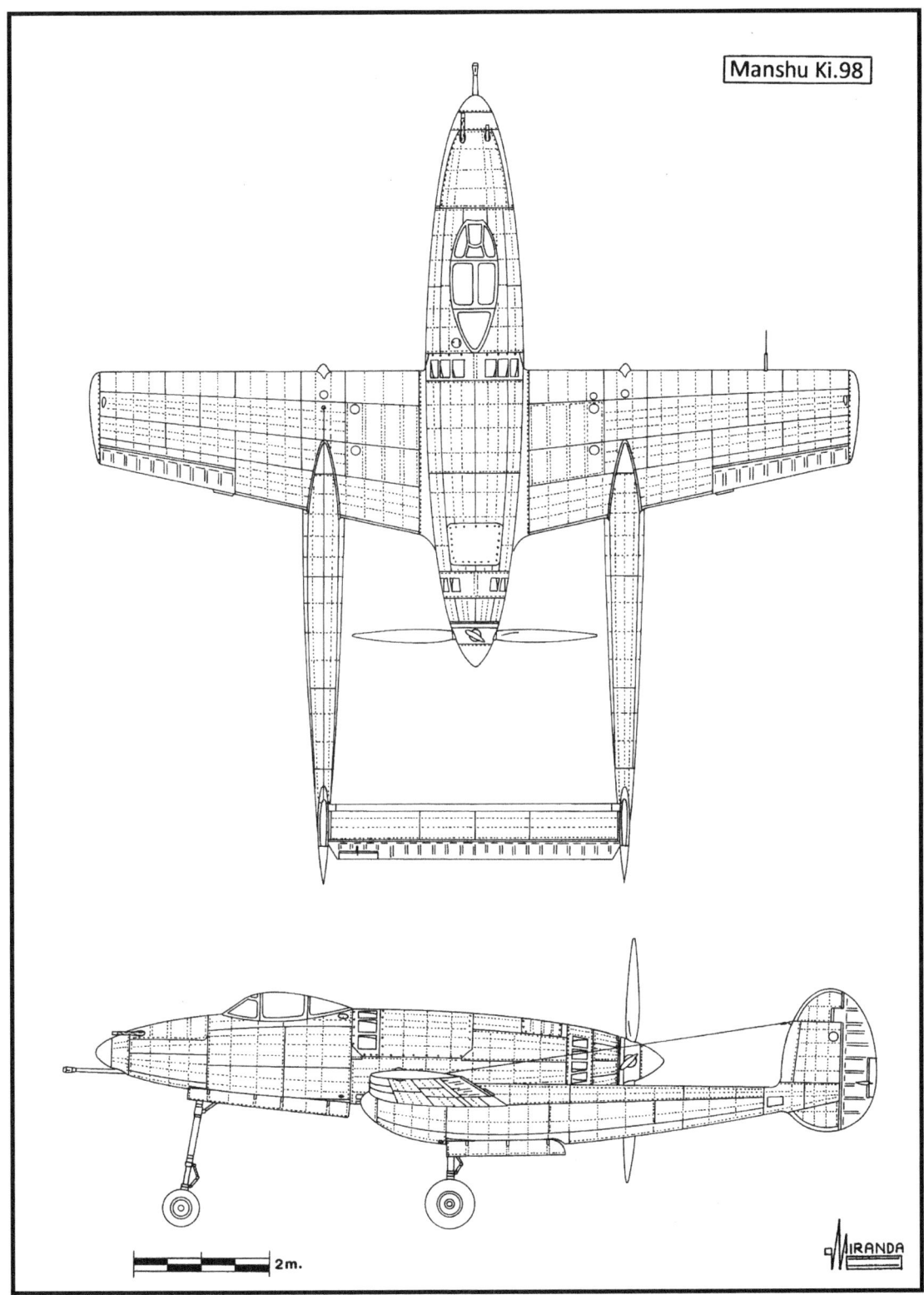

Manshu Ki.98

2m.

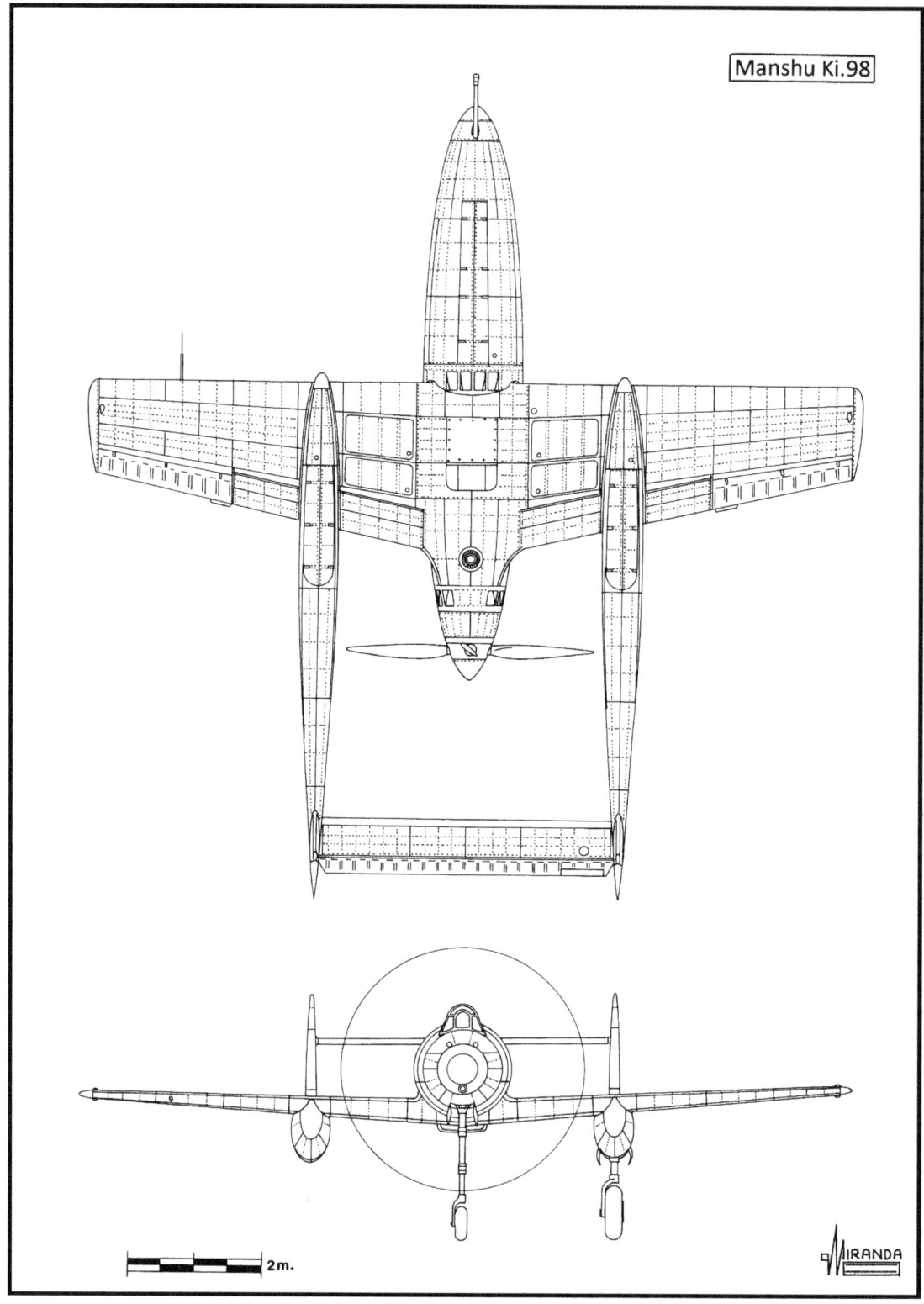

Manshu Ki.98

2m.

MIRANDA

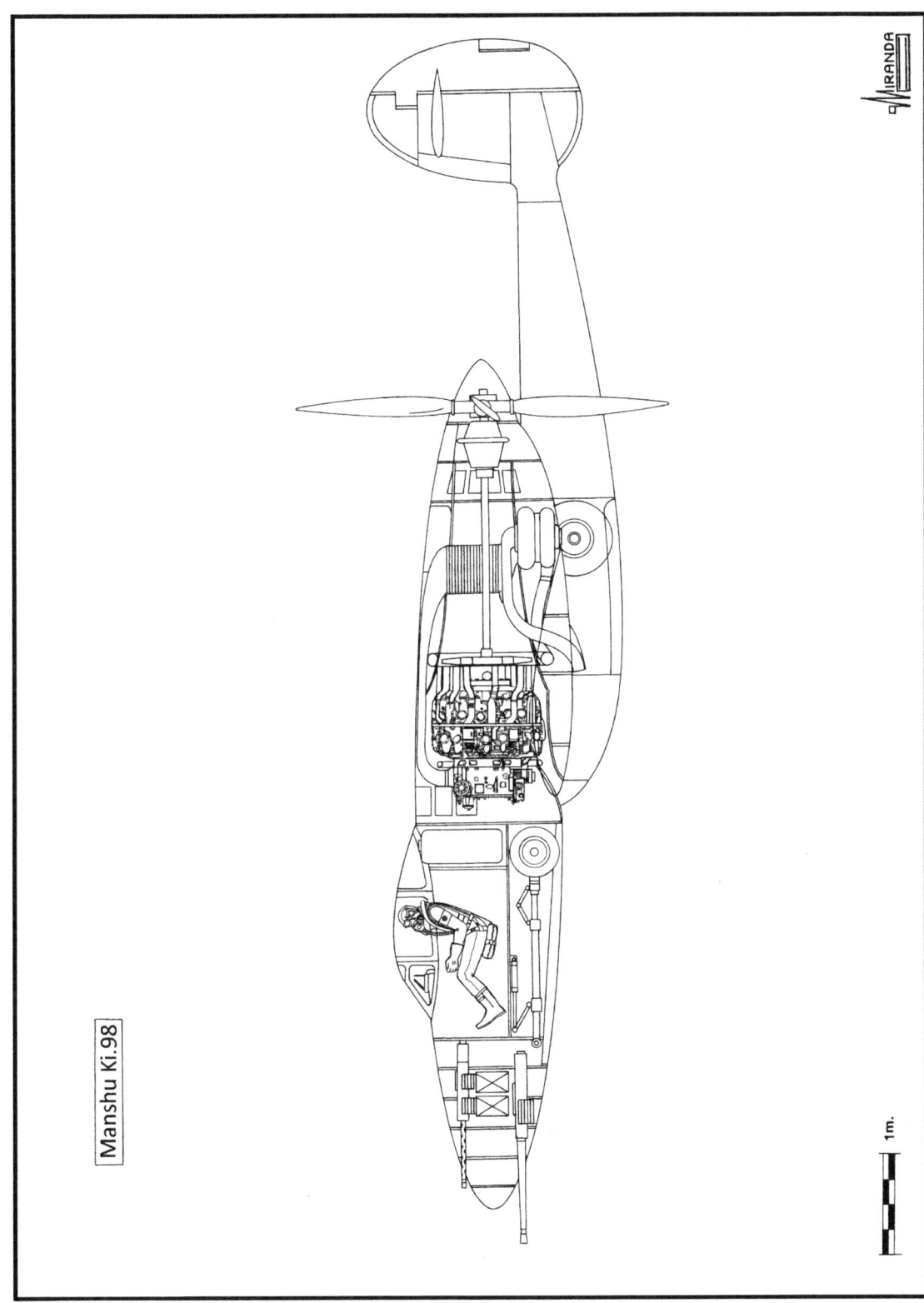

Manshu Ki.98

1 m.

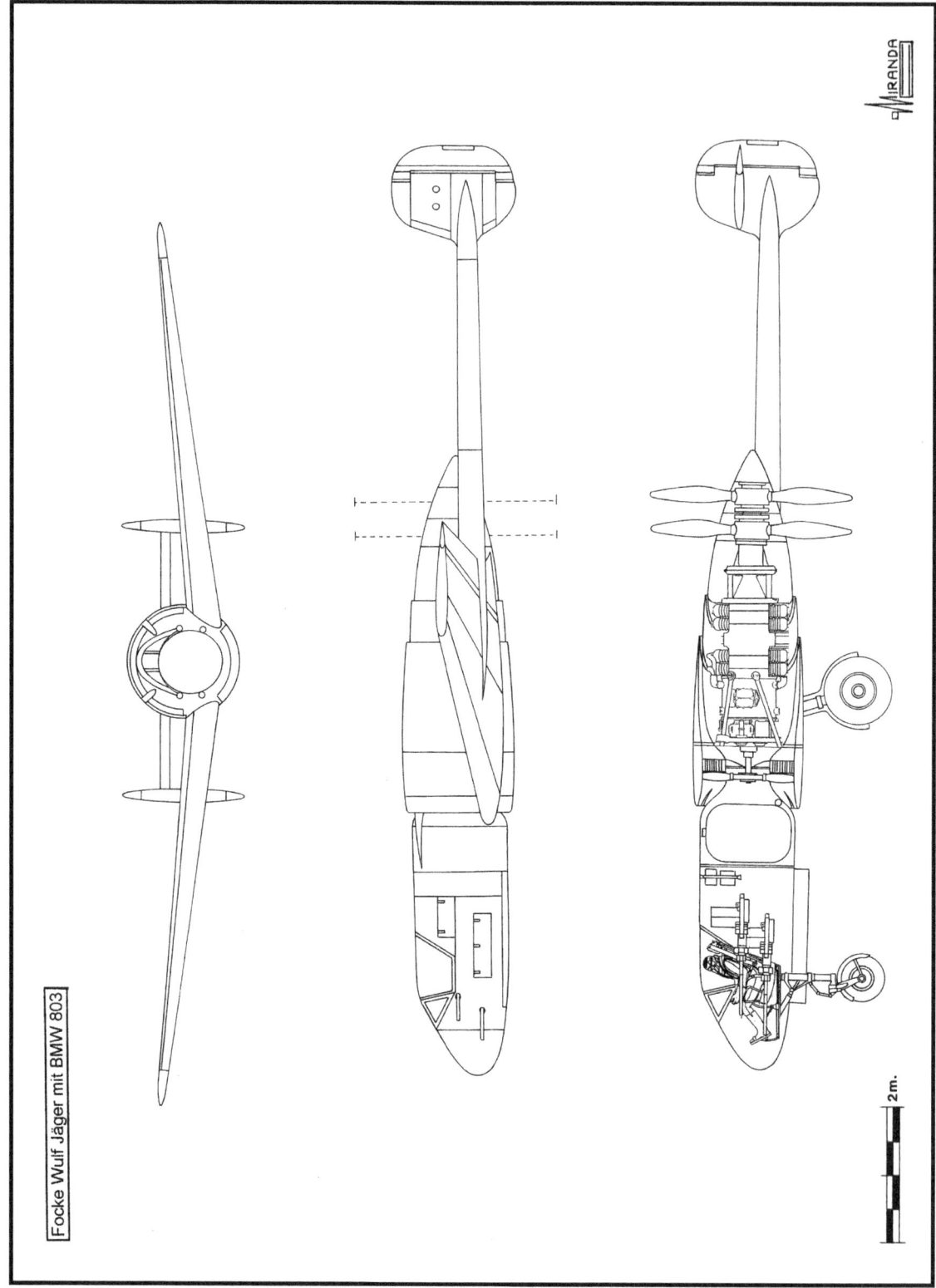

Focke Wulf Jäger mit BMW 803

2 m.

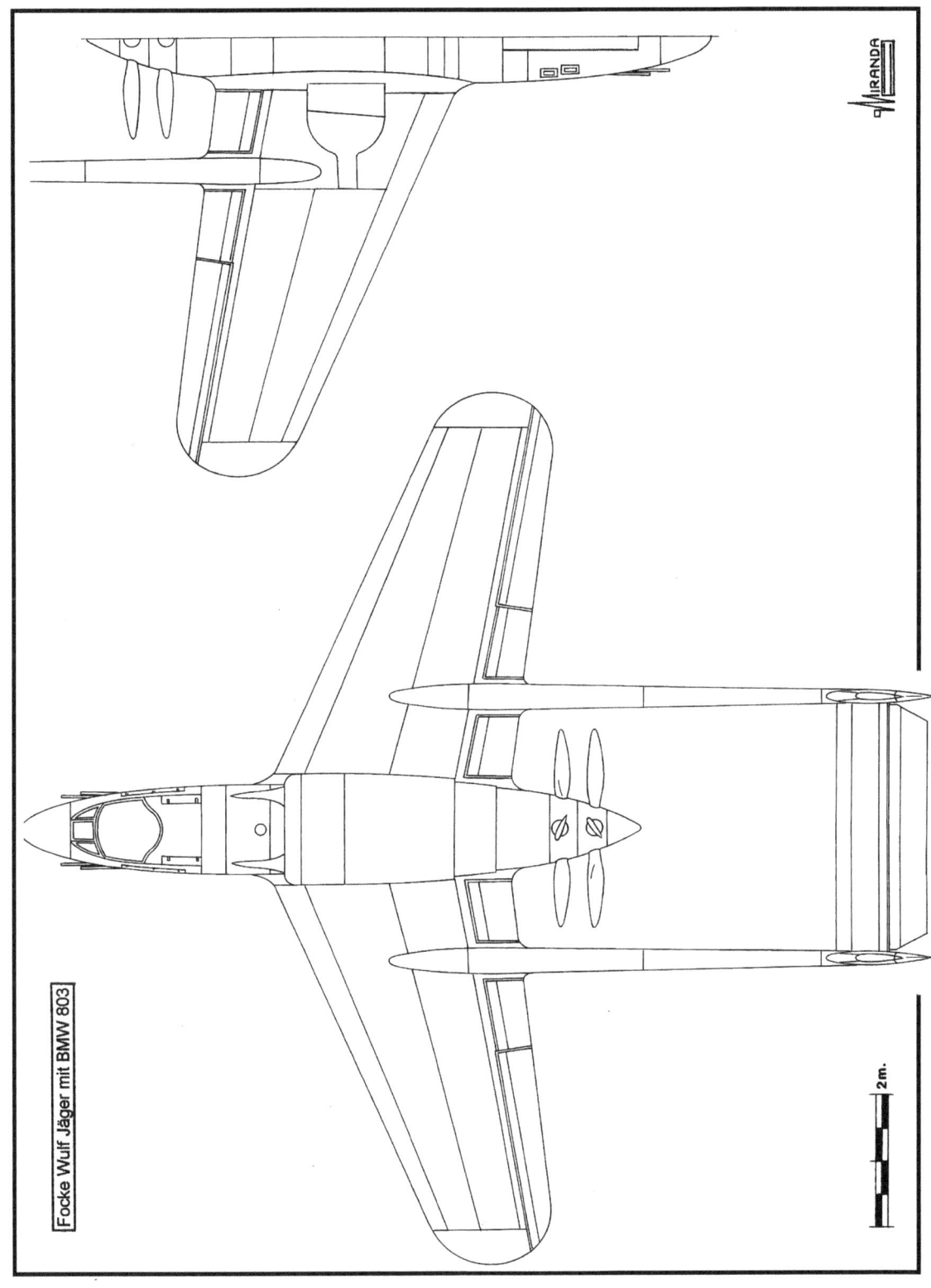

Focke Wulf Jäger mit BMW 803

2 m.

Rikugun Kogiken Heavy Fighter

In the summer of 1941, the Kogiken design team, from the Army Aero-Technical Research Institute (*Rikugun*), under the leadership of Ando Sheigo, proposed to the IJA the construction of a heavy fighter powered by one 1,460-hp Nakajima Ha-45 air-cooled radial engine, driving a four-bladed airscrew by means of an extension shaft.

The engine was buried into the fuselage and mounted over the wing, a configuration that had been used by the Italian fighter Piaggio P.119 in 1940. Such an installation offer improved manoeuvrability and visibility from the cockpit and the possibility of mounting several heavy guns grouped in the nose. Many problems had to be solved before a suitable cooling system was obtained. For the first project, named Plan I Type A, Kogiken proposed using two air scoops positioned on both sides of the cockpit, but the system was found to be inefficient.

Type A would be armed with 20-mm Ho-5 cannons, firing trough the propeller hub, two 12.7-mm Ho-103 heavy machine guns mounted in the nose, and two wing-mounted Ho-103. In the second configuration, Plan I Type B, the cockpit was placed behind the engine for easy cooling. In order to reduce drag, the nose was prolonged to allow a finely tapered cowling, with a narrow annular intake and cooling fan.

The Type B would be armed with a 20-mm Ho-5 cannon, firing trough the propeller hub, two 12.7-mm Ho-103 heavy machine guns mounted in the nose, two wing-mounted Ho-103, and two 7.7-mm Type 97 light guns in front of the windscreen. The third Plan I Type B-1 configuration had the air scoop located under the nose and one 37-mm Ho-203 cannon, firing through the propeller hub. The engine proposed for this version was a 1,990-hp Mitsubishi NK9H Homare 21 or a 2,000-hp Nakajima Ha-145.

Type A Technical Data

Wingspan: 9.35 m
Length: 8.74 m
Height: 3.3 m
Wing area: 14.6 sq. m
Max. speed: 700 kph
Max. weight: 2,291 kg
Range: 600 km

Type B Technical Data

Wingspan: 9.35 m
Length: 8.87 m
Height: 3.7 m
Wing area: 14.6 sq. m
Max. speed: 700 kph
Max. weight: 2,295 kg
Range: 600 km

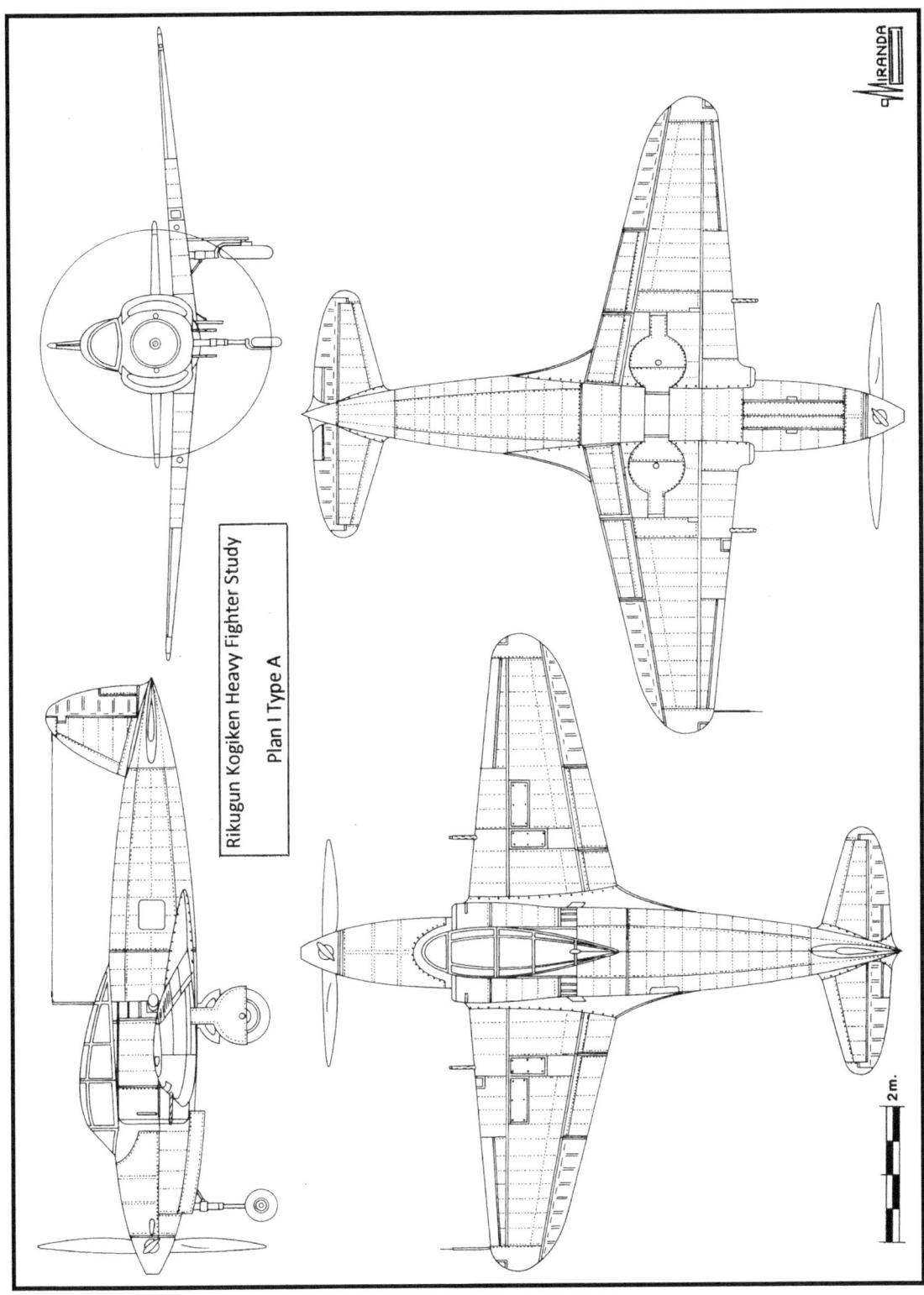

Rikugun Kogiken Heavy Fighter Study
Plan I Type A

2 m.

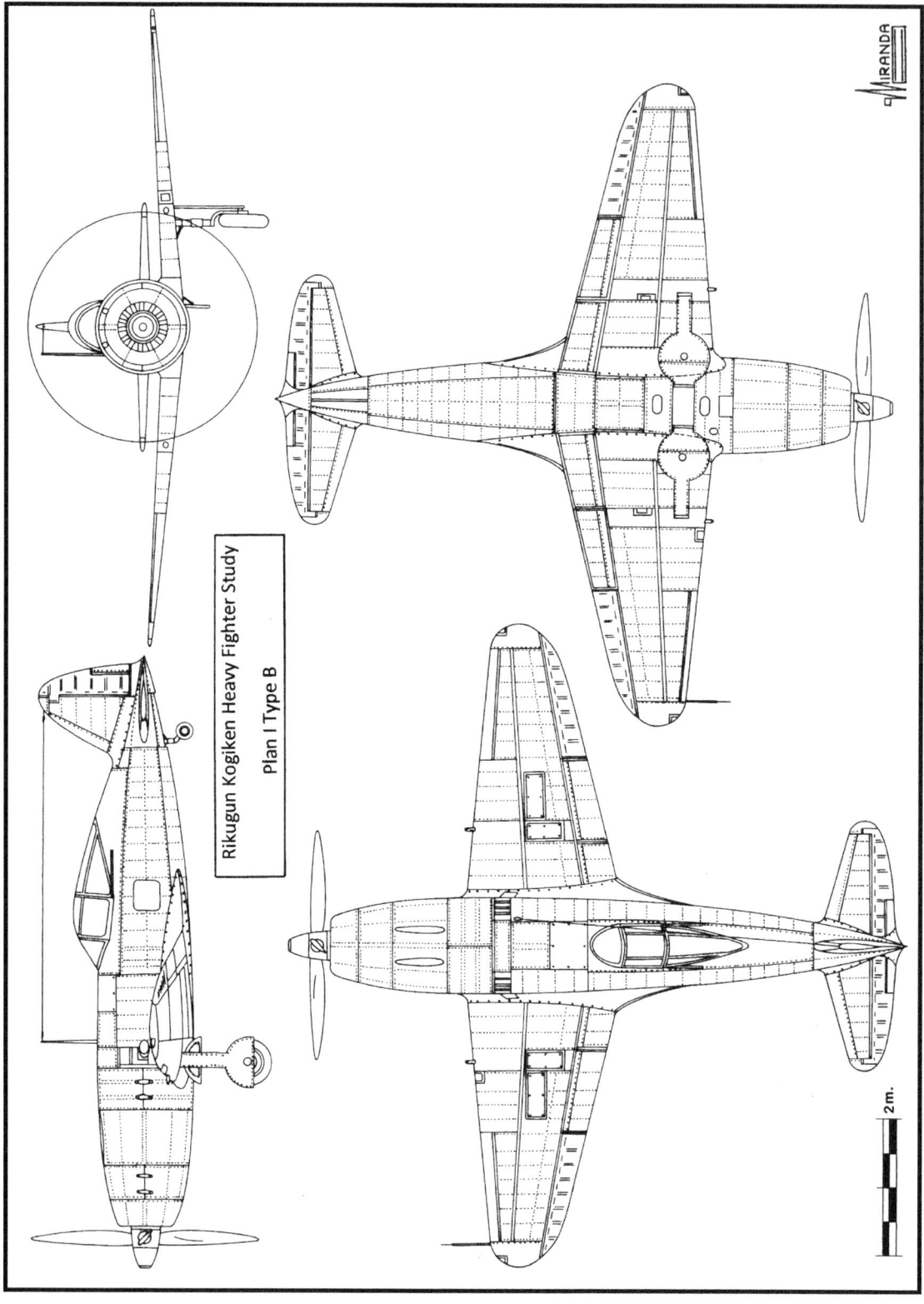

Rikugun Kogiken Heavy Fighter Study

Plan I Type B

2 m.

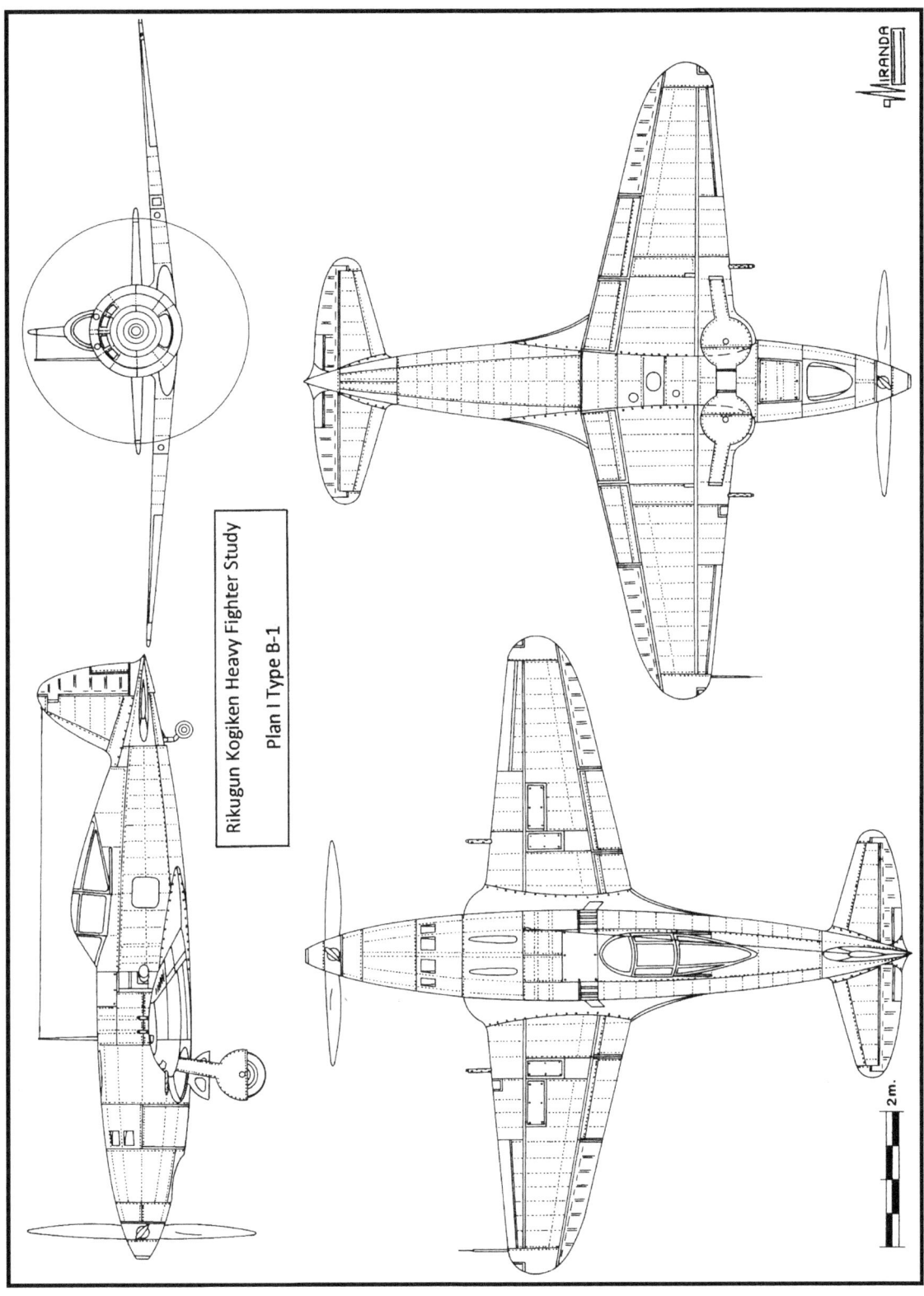

Rikugun Kogiken Heavy Fighter Study
Plan I Type B-1

2 m.

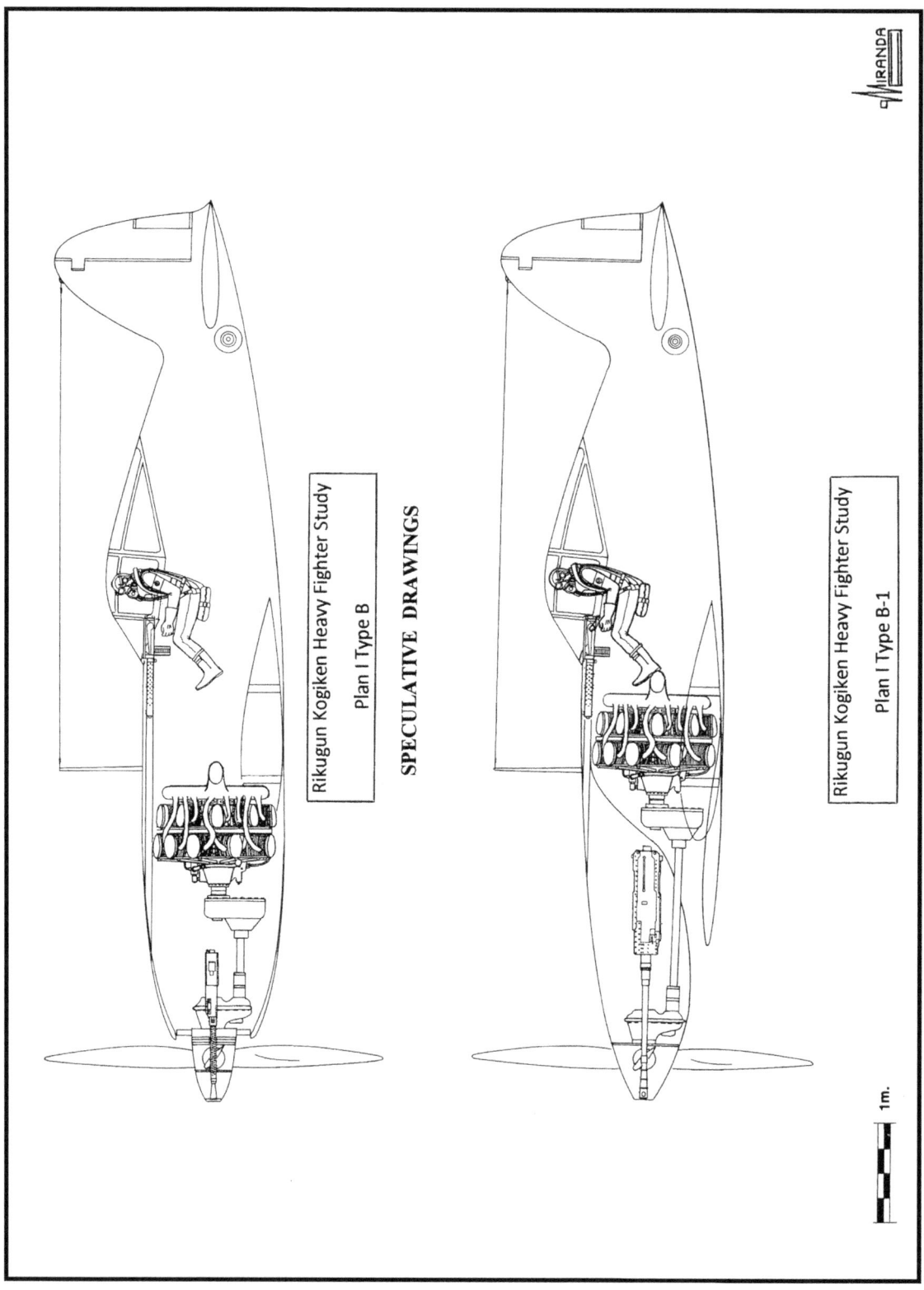

Rikugun Kogiken Heavy Fighter Study

Plan I Type B

SPECULATIVE DRAWINGS

Rikugun Kogiken Heavy Fighter Study

Plan I Type B-1

1 m.

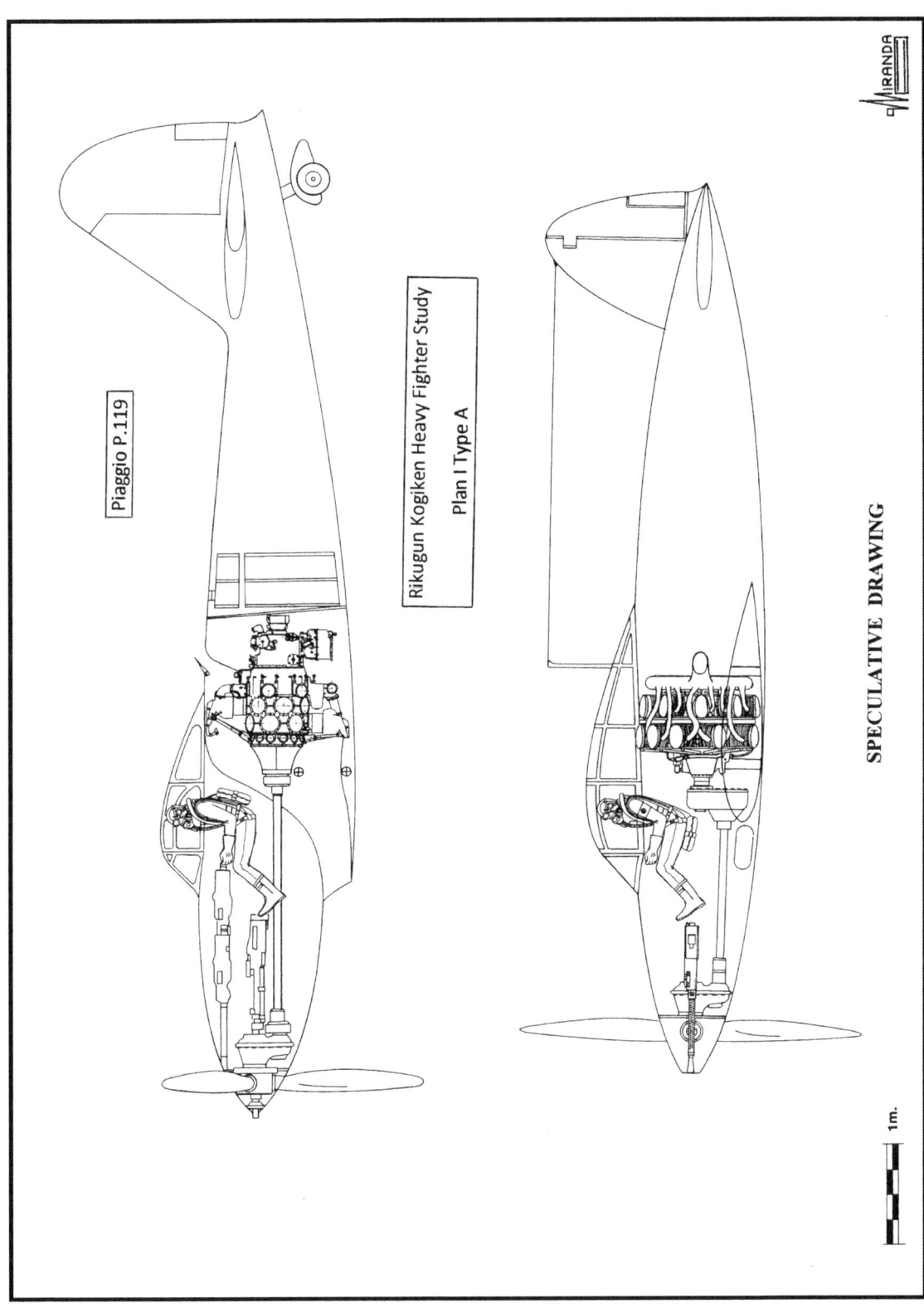

Piaggio P.119

Rikugun Kogiken Heavy Fighter Study
Plan I Type A

SPECULATIVE DRAWING

1 m.

Nakajima Ki.201 Karyu

Just one week before the outbreak of the Second World War, the German prototype Heinkel He 178 was flown, piloted by *Flugkapitän* Erich Warsitz. The He 178 was the first aeroplane in the world powered by a turbojet.

The new HeS 3B engine had been designed by Dr Hans-Joachim Pabst von Ohain and consisted of a large 120-cm diameter drum capable of producing 450-kgf static thrust at sea level. Its shape was due to the centrifugal compressor—essentially a centrifugal turbine gas—whose efficiency increased with diameter.

The Allies were also researching centrifugal engines. In May 1941, they built the Power Jets W.1 with a 107-cm diameter and 387-kgf, and by 1943, they already had the de Havilland Halford H-1 with a 127-cm diameter and 1,225-kgf static thrust. With this power, it was possible to build a single-engined jet fighter, with the centrifugal turbojet installed inside the fuselage. In 1943, the British chose the Halford to propel their new fighters Gloster E5/42 and de Havilland E6/41 Vampire. The Americans used the same turbojet to power the Lockheed XP-80 prototype, early in 1944.

In 1939, the Heinkel-Rostock team was working on the development of the HeS 8 centrifugal turbojet, which was expected to be used to propel the He 280 fighters. With a planned thrust of 700 kgf and a diameter 20 per cent shorter than the HeS 3B, the new turbojet required a great research effort and an extensive test program. Numerous technical problems had to be solved before starting its large-scale production, and the HeS 8 suffered numerous delays. By March 1941, it only produced 500 kgf of static thrust, increasing to 550 kgf by early 1942 and 600 kgf in early 1943.

The root cause was the reduction of the diameter, recommended by the aerodynamicists to minimise the drag produced by the engine nacelles when installed under the wings of the He 280. Trial experience revealed that the most effective way to increase thrust in this type of turbojets was to also increase their diameter and improve the performance of the centrifugal compressor. In 1939, the HeS 3B, with a diameter of 93 cm, produced 450 kgf. In the spring of 1943, the *Oberkommando der Luftwaffe* decided to cancel all research work with centrifugal turbojets to focus on the development of axial-flow type engines.

The first Japanese turbojets were centrifugal engines based on the German Heinkel HeS 3B. They burnt a great amount of fuel and could only increase its power by augmenting the diameter of its central section. Yet such a big size of the engines and their position in the underwing nacelles would have generated too much drag. In 1942, Vice Admiral Misao Wada, chief of Yokosuka Naval Aero-Technical Arsenal (Kugisho), directed the development of the TR-10 turbojet, the Japanese version of the HeS 3B, with a one-stage centrifugal compressor.

Redesignated Ne-10, the engine was first tested in the summer of 1943 with a thrust of 300 kgf, which was deemed insufficient by the IJN. To increase its efficiency, it was necessary to reduce the RPM, and an additional four-stage axial compressor was mounted in the air-intake. The new engine, Ne-12B, was just 7 per cent more powerful than the previous model, weighed 315 kg, and had a high rate of fuel consumption of 510 kg per hour. Only forty units were built to power the Nakajima Maru-Ten, the suicide version of the Kikka.

In December 1944, Kugisho was working on the Ne-30, a scaled-up variant of the Ne-12B with 850 kgf static thrust, to power the Keiun recce aircraft and the Tenga fast bomber. At any rate, only one prototype of the Ne-30 was built for evaluation purposes. Its manufacturing was cancelled in favour of the new axial-flow type turbojets that were more efficient and could be positioned under the wing without generating too much drag.

In 1945, the Japanese abandoned the development of centrifugal turbojets, just as the Germans did, to focus on the development of the new turbojets, with multi-stage compressors and low RPM, inspired by the BMW 003A. Kugisho manufactured twenty-one Ne-20 engines, with 475 kgf static thrust and 11,000 rpm. Two Ne-20 were flight tested successfully with the Kikka prototype in August 1945. Kugisho continued to work until the end of the war on the Ne-20-KAI, with special steel Mn-Cr-V alloy, 570 kgf, and a 650-degree C temperature limit, to power the Kikka pre-production series.

Ishikawajima-Shibaura built a prototype of the Ne-130 turbojet, 900 kgf, and 9,000 rpm to power the production series of the Tenga fast bomber and the Karyu fighter. Nakajima-Hitachi built the prototype of the Ne-230, with 885 kgf and 8,100 rpm, to power the Karyu fighter. Mitsubishi could not complete the prototype of the Ne-330, which was damaged by an air raid.

The Ne-330 had 1,300 kgf (estimated) static thrust and 7,600 rpm; it had been designed to power the *Keiun* heavy fighter. The Japanese turbojets started with gasoline and, during the acceleration, were run on pine root oil with 20 per cent gasoline or with a mixture of wood turpentine and charcoal.

In January 1945, the *Koku Hombu* instructed Nakajima to design a version of the Messerschmitt Me 262 A-1 adapted to suit Japanese production capabilities. The new aircraft, named Karyu, was a common project of the IJA/IJN; the design phase ended in June 1945. The IJA version, with the *kitai* number Ki.201, would be powered by two Ne-230 turbojets and armed with two 30-mm Ho-155 II and two 20-mm Ho-5 cannons.

The IJN version, powered by two Ne-130 turbojets, would be armed with two 30-mm Type 5 and two 20-mm Type 99 cannons. The Karyu was designed by Iwao Shibuya as a high-altitude interceptor and anti-landing ships strike fighter able to carry a 500–800-kg bomb. It was hoped the Karyu could act as an all-weather interceptor guided by the *TaChi-3* ground radar with a Taki-15 airborne IFF transponder with a range of 150 km. By the end of war, the prototype was only 50 per cent completed at Nakajima-Mitaka plant.

Ki.201 Technical Data (with Ne-230)

Wingspan: 13.7 m
Length: 11.5 m
Height: 4.05 m
Wing area: 25 sq. m
Max. speed: 812 kph
Max. weight: 6,962 kg
Ceiling: 12,000 m
Range: 980 km

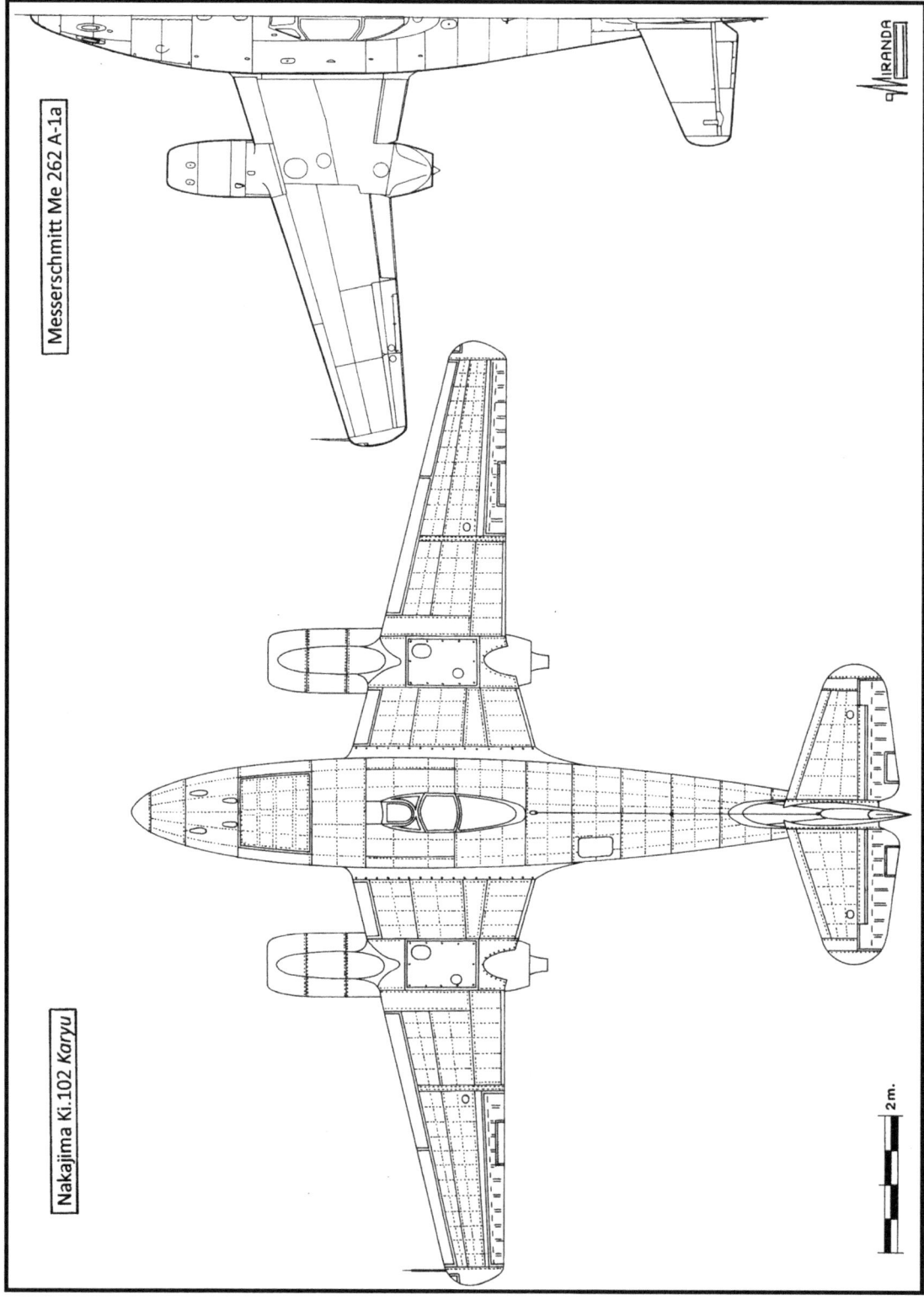

Messerschmitt Me 262 A-1a

Nakajima Ki.102 *Karyu*

2 m.

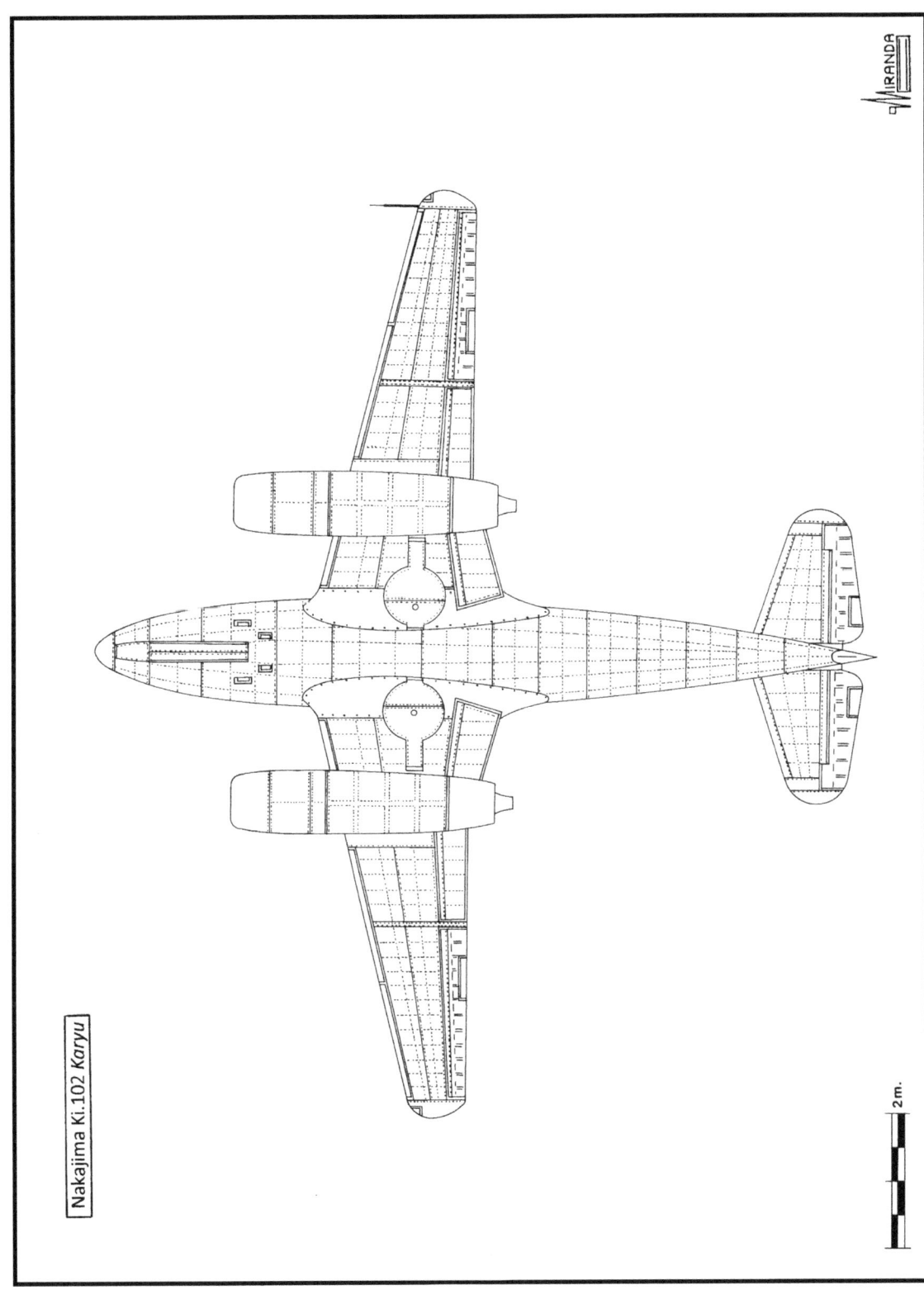

Nakajima Ki.102 *Karyu*

2 m.

Fighters of the Dying Sun

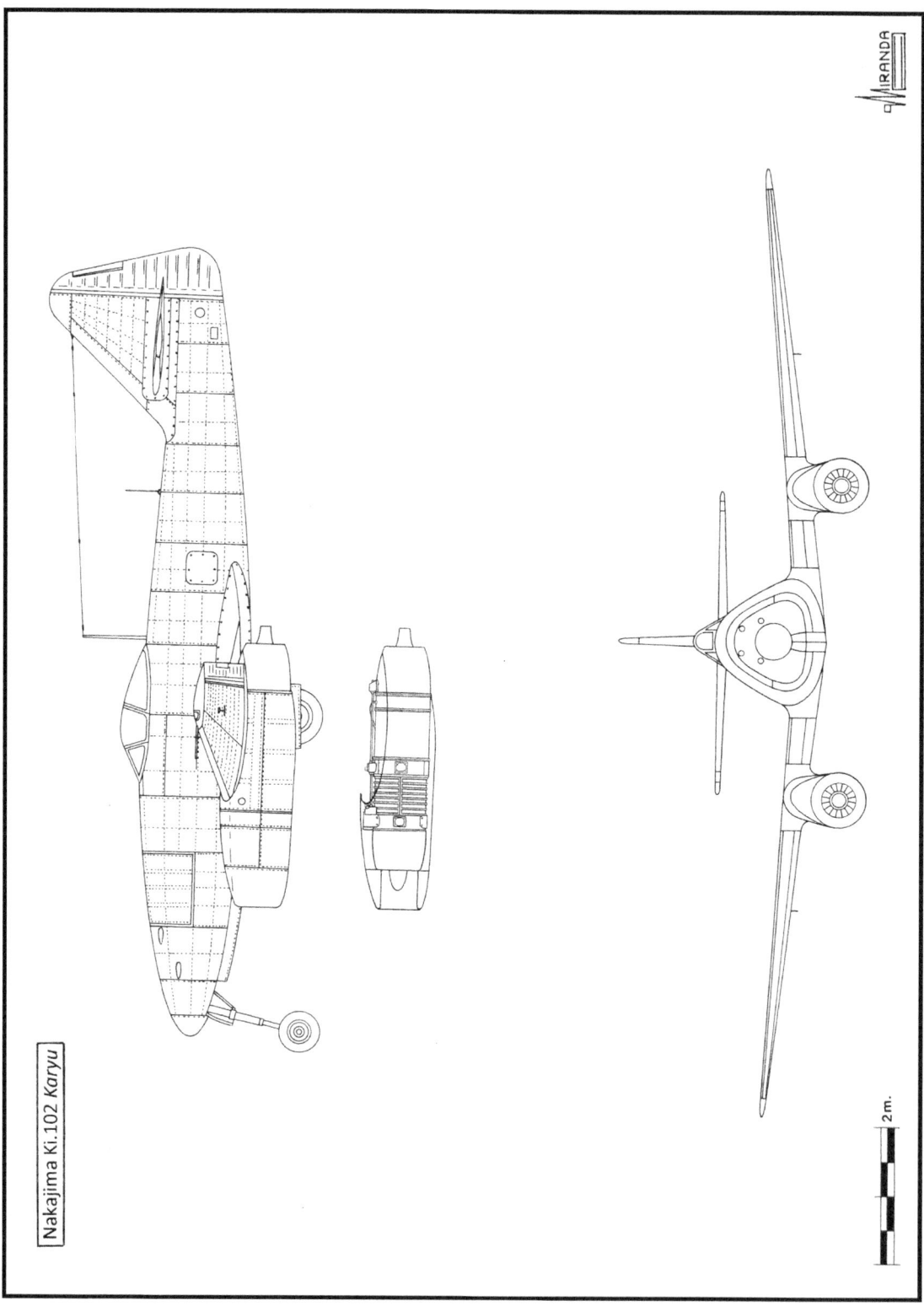

Nakajima Ki.102 *Karyu*

2 m.

3

Imperial Japanese
Navy Aircraft and Projects

Mitsubishi A6M Zero

Designed in 1938 to defend the Imperial Fleet against the low-level attacks of the torpedo-bombers and the dive bombers at medium altitude, the Zero did not need to perform well above 8,000 m.

The IJN did not consider the American B-17, conceived as strategic bomber at high altitude, to be a threat to the warships in open sea, although the great range of the Fortress would allow it to attack Japanese naval bases on the periphery of the empire. The answer seemed to be the Raiden, a high-altitude point defence interceptor with a high rate of climb, but it was too complex and difficult to maintain; it finally went into service too late and in small numbers.

When the B-17 and B-24 began to operate against areas of Japanese influence, there were only three types of available fighters to intercept them—the Hayabusa, the Shoki, and the Zero. However, neither of them had enough fire power to effectively fight against the American aircraft, a task considered difficult even for the *Sturm* German fighters equipped with heavy armour and weapons.

After many experiments and losses, the Japanese learned to fight these giants using air-to-air bombing tactics. The IJA used the Type 2, No. 6, Mk 21 52.5-kg bomb—a hexagonal breakaway canister containing 1 kg of 36 HE submunition Model II with an impact fuse or forty 0.4-kg hollow charge baby bombs designed to attack airfields. The naval model was very similar but made in a circular shape. They were known as *Ta-Dan* bombs, first used in 1944 together with the 3-Go aerial burst bombs of 33.7, 56.6, and 251.8 kg. The 3-Go tailfins had offset tailfins that rotated at 1,000 rpm after release as well as a clockwork tail fuse. When the bomb detonated, explosive charges blew white phosphorus filled with steel pellets outwards, causing fires in the engines and upper surfaces of the bombers.

In 1945, they began using the Type 3, Mk 27 rocket-propelled burst bombs that could be launched from the altitude of the bomber formation without flying over it. The air-to-air bombing used to be complemented by a *tai-atari* ramming attack against the bombers that had been hit.

Another suicide method used by the Zero pilots was to position at the centre of the 'box' and manually detonate a 250-kg bomb carried under the belly of the plane. On 8 May 1942, one A6M2 of the *Shokaku* aircraft carrier, piloted by the PO Takeo Miyazawa, rammed one TBD torpedo-plane of the USS *Yorktown*. On 4 July, a B-26 of the 22nd BG was rammed over Lae by the Zero of the Flyer First Class Mitsuo Suizu. On 1 August, a Rufe of the *Yokohama Kōkutai*, piloted by Shigeto Kobayashi, shot down a B-17 by ramming over Gavutu Island.

On 26 October, one A6M2 of the IJN *Shokaku* carrier, piloted by Shigetaka Omori, rammed an SBD dive bomber during the Battle of Santa Cruz. On 1 December, B-17F 41-24534 was rammed by an A6M2 over Vella Lavella. On 3 March 1943, one A6M2 piloted by Masano Maki of the Zuiho Fighter Group rammed a B-17, 41-24356, while over Kavieng.

On July 1944, one Zero of the 201st *Kōkutai*, piloted by Naoshi Kanno, rammed a B-17 over Yap Island. On 10 October, B-24 44-40774 was destroyed by ramming over Balikpapan by one A6M2 of the 331st *Kōkutai*. On 26 April, six Ki.43 fighters of the IJA 204th *Sentai* had a worrying first contact with a B-29, which was shot twelve times without apparent results. The giant plane, heavily loaded with supplies and the tail gun out of service, just ascended until the Japanese fighters were forced to abandon the pursuit due to lack of oxygen.

It was known that the B-29 could fly at high altitudes thanks to its turbo-charged engines. When it first appeared 10,000 m above Tokyo on a reconnaissance mission, it was flying so fast that the Ki.44 of the 47th *Sentai* could not reach it. By contrast, the J2M4, J2M5, and N1K5-J Japanese fighters that had been designed to face it, had not even begun to be manufactured. The problem was the technology of the turbochargers, whose manufacturing methods were kept so secret that the Americans refused to share them even with their allies.

Hitachi, Nakajima, and Mitsubishi engineers received the assignment to develop their own turbocharger based on the Swiss Brown, Boveri & Cie. The three-stage Mitsubishi turbocharger was installed in Raiden prototypes J2M4 and J2M5, with such poor results that its series production was dismissed. The Hitachi turbo was manufactured with the best alloys of chrome-molybdenum steel, but its development was too slow and was still being tested, installed in a Saiun, by the end of the Second World War.

The Nakajima team tried to modify an A6M2 by installing a Sakae turbo-charged engine without an intercooler. The prototype was named A6M4 and started its flight test in Yokosuka Arsenal in 1943, experiencing fires and multiple ruptures in the compressor and ducting. The origin of these failures was that the imported turbo actually was a design for 500-hp diesel engines with an operating temperature that was 200 degrees C lower than that of the Japanese petrol engines. Despite all these problems, the Mitsubishi engineers managed to build the A6M3 series in 1942, powered by a *Sakae* 21 that was able to climb up to 11,000 m thanks to a modest two-speed supercharger.

In 1943, the A6M5 already had an absolute ceiling of 11,740 m, but it took nearly thirty minutes to reach that altitude. For lack of a better weapon, the IJN was forced to use the Zero fighters to defend its bases, its fleet, and the imperial capital. On 21 November 1944, B-29 42-93848 was rammed by an A6M5 of the 352nd *Kōkutai*, piloted by Lt Mikihiko

Sakamoto, over Omura. On 3 December, the night fighters A6M3 of the 302nd *Kōkūtai* managed to destroy two B-29s (42-63461 and 42-24656) over Tokyo using *Ta-Dan* bombs and 20-mm cannons installed in *Schräge Musik* configuration. On 23 January 1945, one A6M5-Ko of the 302nd *Kōkūtai* based in Atsugi shot down B-29 42-24785 over Nagoya. It was the first B-29 destroyed by the 60-kg Mk 27 rocket bombs.

With more than 11,000 Zeros manufactured, it was inevitable that the IJN ordered its use in *kamikaze* missions. However, the plane was not suitable for such attacks as it became very difficult to control during a terminal dive. Fortunately for the Allies, many inexperienced pilots lost control of their Zero at the last moment, missing its targets by just a few meters. There are numerous reports of this type of failed attacks that at the time were attributed to the effect of the anti-air fire on the plane or on the driver, but they always referred to single seat fighters of the Hayabusa and Zero type. Instead, the dive bombers Val and Judy, equipped with airbrakes, had the record of impacts as they could be controlled until the last moment.

An inexperienced suicide pilot could only direct his Zero to the sea by continually accelerating from 3,000 m to the impact. In some cases, a nearby AA explosion destabilised the plane and it was no longer possible to regain control. According to some reports, the plane passed over the ship in inverted flight before hitting the water. In other cases, the Zero threw the bomb at the last moment, something that only makes sense if the bomb was accidentally dropped due to vibration or g-forces as it used to be screwed under the wing centre section. The original release mechanism had already caused problems, especially to the A6M5 of the 201st *Kōkūtai* during testing with skipping bombs made in Davao in July 1944. It was finally replaced by a fastening system that did not allow the bomb to be dropped.

The A6M2 was the most used version in *tokko* attacks. It had a maximum (theoretical) diving speed of 657 kph, but at 460 kph, elevator stick manoeuvring forces became quite heavy. Following complaints from pilots, servo tabs were installed on the ailerons in 1941, but it turned out that their use at high speeds damaged the fragile cladding of the wings. The A6M2 Bakusen modified for *tokko* missions carried Type 99, No. 25, Model I 248.7-kg anti-ship bomb. The servo tabs were removed in the A6M3 Model 32, reducing instead the surface of the ailerons.

The structural strength of the wing was increased in the A6M5, thus achieving a maximum diving speed of 740 kph, from which it was almost impossible to recover. At that speed, the stick seemed welded to the floor of the cockpit, and it was impossible to alter the path of the plane, especially when carrying a Number 50, Model II, streamlined, airship bomb of 507 kg. The A6M5 suicidal variant was named Kembu.

Although most of the suicide Zeros belonged to the aforementioned versions, it is possible that some A6M7 fighter-bombers of the Omura, Yokosuka, and 302nd *Kōkūtais* would fight in Okinawa. Some two seat trainers of the A6M2-K type from the *Genzan* and *Yatabe Kōkūtais* also made *tokko* attacks. On 29 April 1945, seven aeroplanes of the Showa Unit No. 5 equipped with 248.7-kg bombs attacked an allied carrier task force 60 nautical miles from Okinawa. On 4 May, fourteen aircraft from the Shinken Unit No. 5 attacked and sank the US picket destroyer *DD-560*. The escort missions of the A6M5 that should face the Hellcats and Corsairs in numerical and technological inferiority could also be considered suicidal. It was not uncommon to have 100 per cent losses per mission, several of them by ramming.

Some escort Zeros also voluntarily joined the *kamikaze* attacks when they were not required to report the results of the mission. Between 21 October 1944 and 13 August 1945, no fewer than 700 suicide Zeros, escorted by another 146, made attacks against Allied ships in Amami Oshima, Badubg, Bohol Sea, Bacolod, Camotes Islands, Cape Naga , Cape Toi, Cape Encanto, Dumagueted, Iwo Jima, Iba, Kikai Island, Kyushu, Kerama, Leyte, Lamon Bay, Lubang Island, Lingayen Gulf, Manila, Magong, Miyato Jima, Murcielagos Bay, Mindoro, Nano, Naha , Negros Island, Ormoc, Okinawa, San Jose, Sulu Sea, Siquijor, Surigao, Suluan, Tanegashima, Tacoblan, Taitung, Taiwan, Tokunoshima, Yoronjima, and Yonaguni. They belonged to the following *tokko* units: *Asahi, Baika, Byakko, Chihaya, Hatsuzakura, Hazakura, Jinrai, Kasagi, Kasuga, Kasumigaura, Kenmu, Kikusui, Kongo, Kotoku, Mitate, Niitaka, Oka, Reisen, Sakon, Sakurai, Seiko, Shikishima, Shomu, Showa, Suisei, Shichisei, Shinken, Taigi, Tokimune, Tsukuba, Ukon, Yamazakura, Yamato, Yamamoto*, and *Wakazakura*.

They made impacts on the following ships: USS *Enterprise* CV-6, USS *Bunker Hill* CV-17, USS *Belleau Wood* CVL-24, USS *Sangamon* CVE-26, USS *Suwanee* CV-27, USS *Santee* CV-29, USS *Natoma Bay* CVE-62, USS *St. Lo* CVE-63, USS *White Plains* CVE-66, USS *Kitkun Bay* CVE-71, USS *West Virginia* BB-48, USS *Missouri* BB-63, USS *Columbia* CL-56, USS *Brooks* DD-232, USS *Oberrender* DE-344, USS *Reid* DD-369, USS *Hazelwood* DD-531, USS *Evans* DD-552, USS *Morrison* DD-560, USS *Bryant* DD-665, USS *Allen M.Summer* DD-692, USS *Hank* DD-702, USS *Walke* DD-723, USS *Hugh W. Hadley* DD-774, USS *Mannert L. Abele* DD-733, SS *Marcus Daly*, LCT 1075, HMS *Indomitable*, HMS *Indefatigable*, HMS *Victorious*, and HMS *Ulster*.

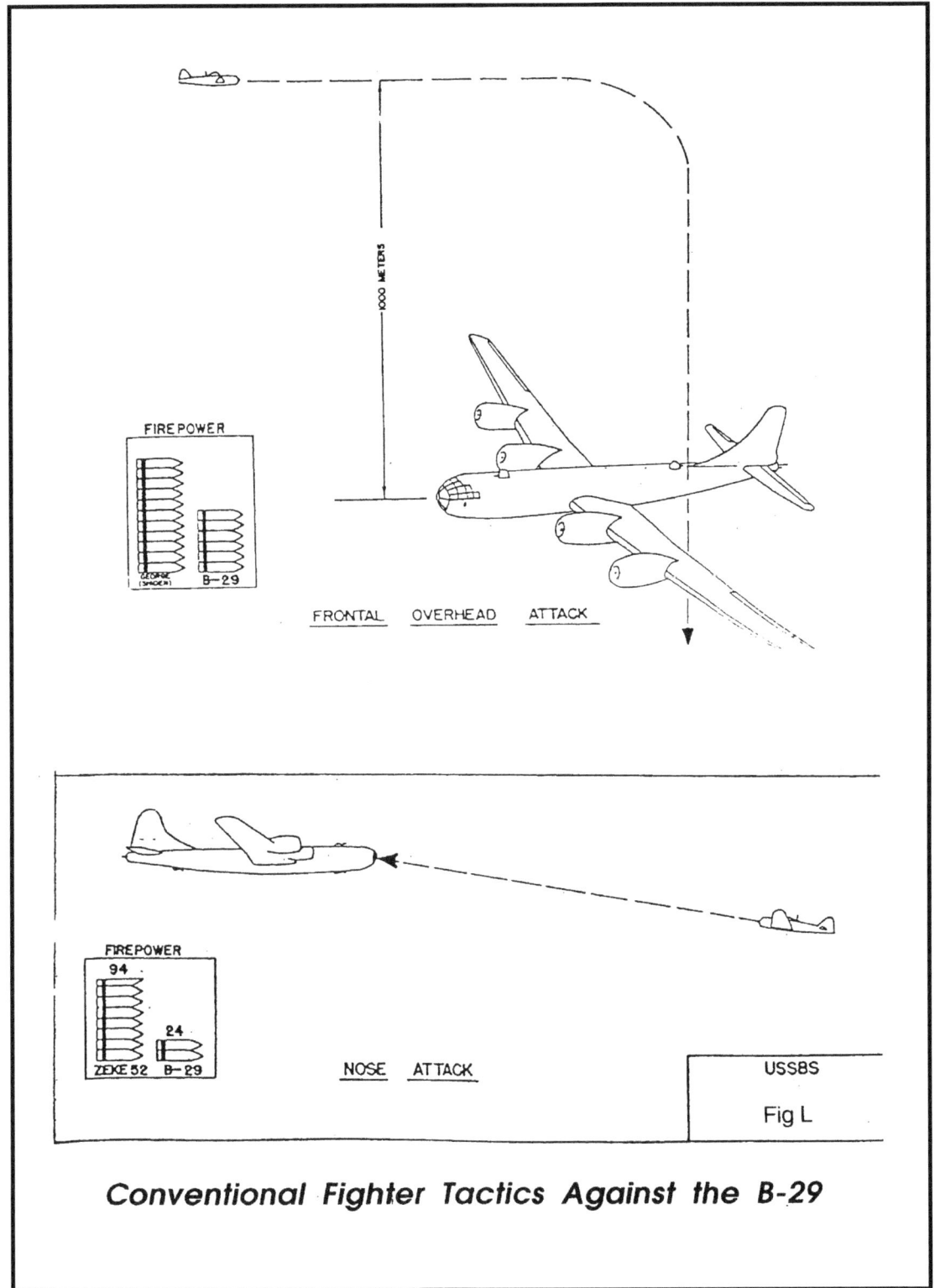

FIRE POWER

GEORGE (SHODEN) B-29

FRONTAL   OVERHEAD   ATTACK

1000 METERS

FIREPOWER

94

24

ZEKE 52   B-29

NOSE   ATTACK

USSBS

Fig L

Conventional Fighter Tactics Against the B-29

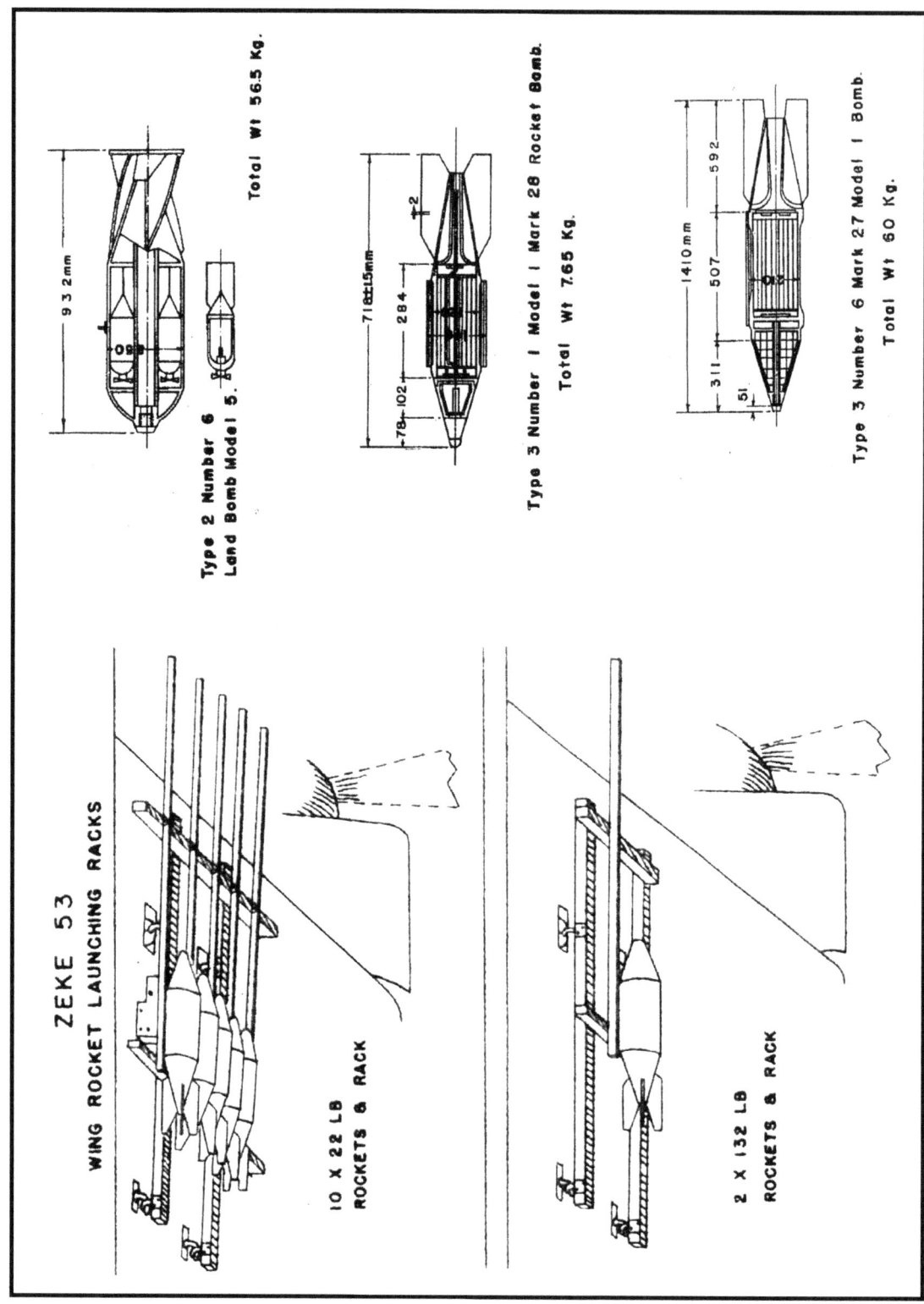

Type 2 Number 6
Land Bomb Model 5.

Total Wt 56.5 Kg.

Type 3 Number 1 Model 1 Mark 28 Rocket Bomb.

Total Wt 7.65 Kg.

Type 3 Number 6 Mark 27 Model 1 Bomb.

Total Wt 60 Kg.

ZEKE 53

WING ROCKET LAUNCHING RACKS

10 X 22 LB
ROCKETS & RACK

2 X 132 LB
ROCKETS & RACK

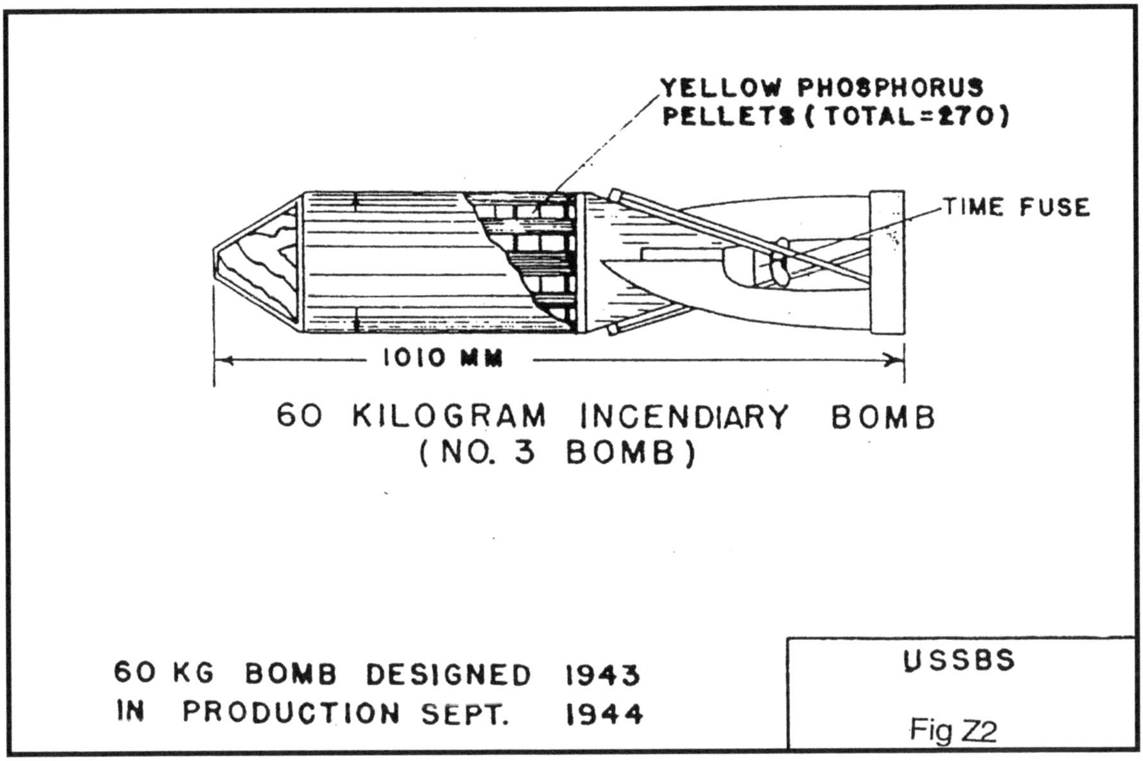

YELLOW PHOSPHORUS
PELLETS (TOTAL = 270)

TIME FUSE

1010 MM

60 KILOGRAM INCENDIARY BOMB
(NO. 3 BOMB)

60 KG BOMB DESIGNED 1943
IN PRODUCTION SEPT. 1944

USSBS

Fig Z2

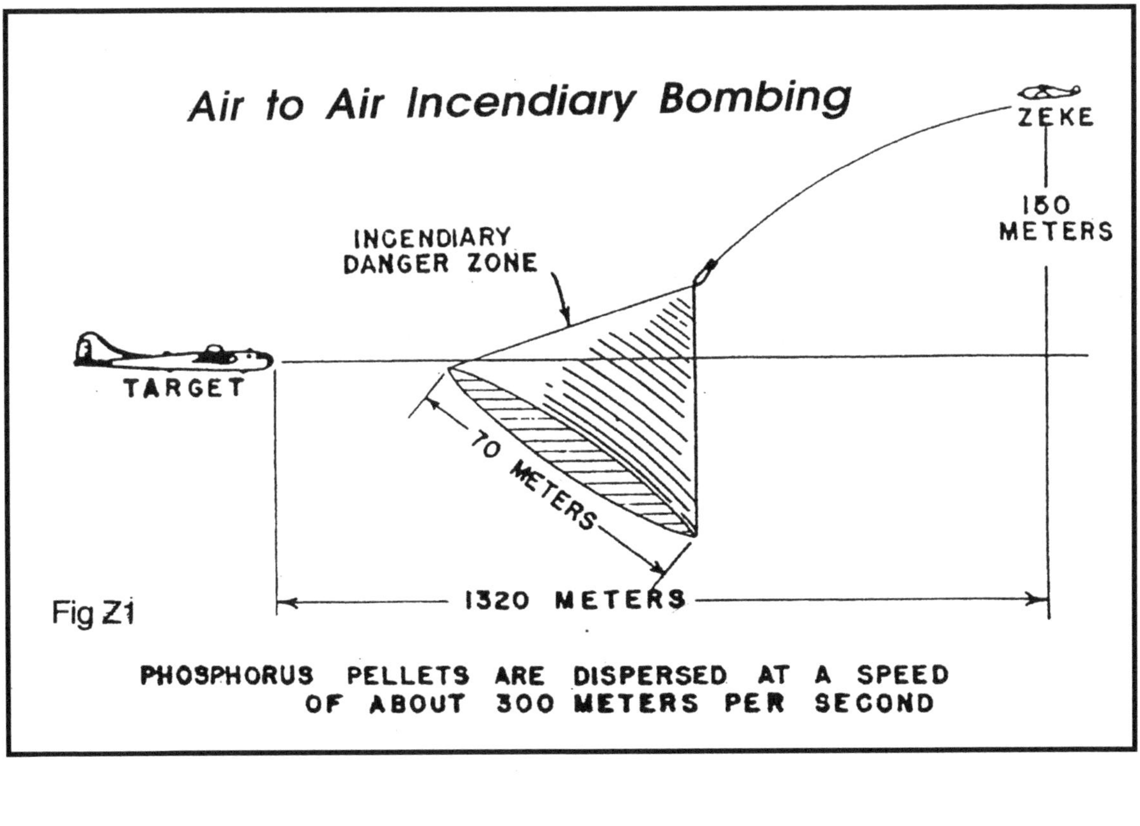

Air to Air Incendiary Bombing

ZEKE

150
METERS

INCENDIARY
DANGER ZONE

TARGET

70 METERS

1320 METERS

Fig Z1

PHOSPHORUS PELLETS ARE DISPERSED AT A SPEED
OF ABOUT 300 METERS PER SECOND

Mitsubishi J2M Raiden

Aircraft manufacturers competed for the few in-line engines available in 1939. With the potentially deteriorating situation that a long war could create, some aerodynamic essays were performed to reduce the radial engines drag in Germany, Belgium, and the USA. The Renard R-37 was introduced to the public in July 1939 as an emergency solution, in face of the prospect that France and the United Kingdom might cancel the exports of the Hispano-Suiza and Merlin in-line engines. The R-37 was propelled by a large 1,100-hp Gnome-Rhône engine with a large propeller spinner that completely covered the engine's front air intake.

In Germany, the Focke-Wulf company had the same problem after realising that the whole production of Daimler Benz in-line engines had been assigned to Messerschmitt. Kurt Tank's design team was forced to use the BMW radial engine for the new Fw 190 fighter, a prototype that flew in June 1939 with an extremely aerodynamic cowling and a large ducted spinner to reduce drag.

In USA, the NACA published a report at the beginning of 1939 about the methods to improve the volume of cooling air flowing over radial engines. In February 1939, Seversky performed the first flight tests with the NX2597 AP-4 Lancer prototype, equipped with ducted and non-ducted large propeller spinners. In March, the Curtiss Company decided to experiment with the new technology, transforming the P-36A s/n 38-004 into the XP-42 prototype by adding a large propeller spinner and extension shaft with air intake under the engine.

In May, the Japanese flight tested the third prototype of the Kawasaki Ki.45 with a spinner that was almost identical to that of the Fw 190 V1. The NX21755 s/n 142 Vultee 48 fighter flew for the first time in September with equipment that was similar to that of the Curtiss XP-42.

By mid-1939, the Northrop Company tested the A-17A s/n 36-184 bomber with ducted and non-ducted large propeller spinners and several nose and side-mounted blower configurations. In United Kingdom, the Hawker company performed several late experiments by the beginning of 1945, modifying the Tempest Mk V NV768 with several types of ducted spinners.

As a result of all this research, however, there was not any significant aerodynamic achievement. The R-37 was captured by the Germans before starting its flight tests, and the Fw 190 V1, the Curtiss XP-42, the Vultee 48, the Kawasaki Ki.45-03, and the Seversky Lancer all encountered insurmountable cooling problems and had to be refitted with conventional cowlings. The A-17 A was turned back to its original configuration and back to operations.

When the team of Jiro Horikoshi started the design of the Raiden, by the end of 1939, the result of experiments (that have been described above) that were understandably kept secret at the time was unknown at Mitsubishi. It was also ignored that the XP-42 extension shaft had suffered serious problems with vibrations. At this time, the main worry of the IJN was the possibility that the North American B-17, able to fly at 11,000 m, would be operational.

Every naval fighter of the 1930s was designed to protect the fleet against low-altitude attacks by torpedoes and dive bombers, but a four-engined heavy bomber could attack the Japanese naval bases from a high altitude without any opposition. The whole Zero manufacturing programme might have been modified or even cancelled if the B-17 was mass produced and operated from the airbases of Philippines and Central China.

So, the IJN published a specification for the design of a fighter able to intercept a B-17 flying at a speed of 600 km/h and an altitude of 6,000 m with a climbing time of five minutes. However, when the enemy bombers first appeared over Tokyo, they were of the B-29 type, flying at a speed of 575 km/h and an altitude of 7,600 m with an absolute ceiling of 9,700 m. They were so large, heavy, and powerful that the turbulence they created in the air could produce a total loss of control to the small Ki.44 fighters of the IJA that tried to intercept them. The key was in the superchargers of their huge engines. Their manufacturing techniques were considered top secret to the extent that not even the Australian or British had access to them.

Japan lacked the experience or the technology to duplicate the samples obtained from the aircraft that were shot down, and their attempts with the Ki.100 and the J2M4 did not achieve practical results. It was also impossible for the IJN to have access to the German Daimler Benz in-line engines, given their rivalry with IJA, who acquired the manufacturing licence of the DB 601A for the Ki.60 fighter. Like the Italians, they could only pursue the aerodynamic solution.

The Raiden was designed with a spindle-shaped fuselage with a propeller extended shaft, like that in the XP-42, to permit a finely tapered cowling, a narrow annular air intake like that in the Renard R-37, and the engine-driven fan like that in the Focke-Wulf Fw 190 V1. The cockpit was extremely shallow with a curved windscreen and the wings were shorter than those used by the Zero with a laminar flow aerofoil section.

The selected radial engine was the most powerful available with water-methanol injection system. The armament was the same than that of the Zero: two 7.7-mm Type 97 machine guns and two 20-mm Type 99 cannons. Real combat experience showed that all this was wrong; pilots complained of lack of visibility and the curved windscreen cockpit was replaced by a flat panel windscreen to avoid optical distortion. The extended shaft caused serious problems with vibrations, and as a consequence, the engine attachment points and the cowling fasteners had to be reinforced, the number of fan blades reduced, and the propeller replaced by a more rigid one with a hydraulically controlled system.

The water-methanol injection system behaved hazardously, and although capable of providing extra power during take-off, it was useless above 8,000 m. At higher altitude, they should have used the German GM-1 system that generated an extra power boost for the nitrous-oxide injection. However, this technology was apparently either not shared or not properly used. The short wings were not right for combat at high altitude; controls did not work well at high speed and manoeuvrability was poor at any altitude. The Raiden could not face the P-47 and P-51 escort aircraft. The machine guns (weighing 35 kg, excluding the synchronisation system) were practically useless against the well-armoured American fighters and bombers. The Type 99-I cannon were the lightest 20-mm weapon in the world; they had short barrel and low muzzle velocity and were fed by a sixty-round drum.

The J2M3 replaced the machine guns with a pair of Type 99-II cannons with major muzzle velocity and belt feed, but the simultaneous usage of both types of guns with different ballistic hindered the aiming. Some units of the J2M3-Ko with four Type 99-II cannons were manufactured to solve this issue, which led to increasing the structural resistance of the wing and reducing fuel capacity even further. The J2M2 was able to transport two 30-kg bombs under the wings, and two 60-kg bombs in the case of the J2M3.

Considering that the *Taki 18* warning radars of the time could not accurately estimate the flight altitude of hostile aircraft and that the alert was issued with an advance of thirty minutes at its best, the Raiden interceptors had just the time to scramble up to 10,000 m and wait for the arrival of the bombers. Reaching that altitude, however, took them around 19.5 minutes, and fuel did not last more than forty minutes under those conditions, given that they could not afford the additional weight of a detachable fuel tank. If the B-29s did not arrive on time or deviated towards another target, the Raiden had to abort the interception due to a lack of fuel. Otherwise, they could only make a 'hit and run' type frontal attack to avoid the threat posed by the 20-mm guns on the tail of the B-29 bombers.

The attack was performed at an altitude between 6,000 and 9,000 m and required that both aircraft crossed at a compound speed between 970 and 1,000 kph. The practical range of the Type 99-I was of 1,000 m and of 400 m in the case of the Type 97 machine guns. If the Raiden J2M2 started shooting within the lethal area of 1,000 yards (under the fire of all the heavy dorsal machine guns of the group that would not be less than sixty per box) and should start deviating at least 100 m before the impact, it could only shoot fifty-eight 20-mm rounds. In the case of the J2M3, it could shoot 108 20-mm rounds and around 100 rounds in the case of the J2M3-Ko.

The Luftwaffe statistics on the probability to shot down a B-29 with a 95 per cent of certainty, from a distance of 1,000 m, stated that at least 203 20-mm projectiles should be shot to make thirty-six impacts, equivalent to approximately 500 gr of HE or to the impact of a 55-mm gun. The J2M2 carried only 120 20-mm projectiles and the J2M3-Ko around 400 projectiles. The Raiden was difficult to control at 600 kph, with its heavy ailerons and lack of manoeuvrability, and therefore, the probability to shoot down a B-29 in a single attack was below 50 per cent.

A unique attack is all that the Japanese could afford with just forty minutes of fuel. On the way back to the base, the Raiden were pursued by the P-51 that were superior in manoeuvrability. Many were shot down, and those that could escape in a vertical dive suffered compressibility buffeting when reaching Mach 0.75. The bigger structural resistance of the J2M3 wing gave them some advantage under 5,000 m with at least one Mustang losing its tail when trying to reach them over Yokohama on 29 March 1945.

The Raiden were scarce and the IJN had forbidden their usage for ramming both to them and to the valuable Shiden KAI. In September 1944, they used small Type 99, Number 3, Mark 3 33.7-kg cluster bombs to shoot down seventeen B-24 bombers over Menado. This tactic was used by the J2M2 of the 381st *Kōkutai* that had been specially modified to carry small weight under the wings. Only the 303rd, 332nd, 343rd, and 352nd *Kōkutais* actually ever fought against the B-29s.

From April 1945 onwards, the J2M3 started to use the new Type 3, Number 6, Mark 27, Model I 60-kg rocket-bombs that were shot from the rails installed under the wings. They reached a speed of 270 m/s, exploding at a predefined distance by means of a clockwork fuse, disseminating 140 iron pellets and 4 kg of white phosphorus in a conical pattern of 60 degrees. The rocket-bombs were shot from 1,200 m and before the attack with guns started.

However, the B-29 was difficult to shoot down. Some bombers could even return to base after being rammed by two fighters. The 302nd *Kōkūtai* claimed several damaged B-29, as well as the 42-24735 downed over Tokyo on 3 December 1944 and during some fighting at high altitude against B-29 and P-51 over Yokohama on 29 May 1945. Several damaged bombers were reported, along with 42-24735 downed over Kyushu at the beginning of April, 44-69966 over Nagoya on 14 May, and 42-63567 over Omiya on 10 June. The 302nd *Kōkūtai* could also shoot down B-29 42-65295 over Kyushu using the burst bombs on 29 April.

The 352nd *Kōkūtai* claimed the downing of 42-93848 over Omura on 21 November 1944. The 332nd *Kōkūtai* reported another shot down while flying over Hansin on 22 December 1944. The Yokosuka *Kōkūtai* had some success against the naval aircraft of the Task Force 58 during their attack against Tokyo on 16 February 1945 when several F6F-5 fighters were destroyed.

Between the end of 1943 and the end of 1945, a small number of Raiden fighters were sent for operational testing to the Yokosuka, Yatabe, Genzan, Tainan, Konoike, and Chusi *Kōkūtais*, as well as to the 256th, 301st, 381st, 1001st, and 1081st *Kōkūtais*. They were used for the specific defence of the Chosen, Genzan, Ranan, Funei, Rashin, Konan, Guam, Saipan, and Philippine airfields. Although in the great battles over Okinawa and Kyushu, the pilots preferred to replace the Raiden by Zeros whenever possible.

By the end of 1942, Mitsubishi produced the mechanically driven Ru-302 supercharger, with two stages and two speeds, like the Ki.46-IV high-altitude reconnaissance aircraft. The Ru-302 did not perform well during the tests, conducted in May 1944 with a J2M4 Raiden fighter.

On August 1944, the Mitsubishi J2M5 was flown with one Ru-303 exhaust-driven turbo-supercharger mounted in the starboard side of the fuselage, just behind the Kasei 23c engine. The new supercharger also did not work properly, causing fires during testing, and never became operational.

In the face of such lacklustre results, the IJN decided to manufacture the Kawanishi N1K2-J Shiden KAI on a mass-scale and to assign the remaining Shiden and Raiden to the *Kokoku Heiki Go.1* programme of modifications that would transform them into suicide aircraft.

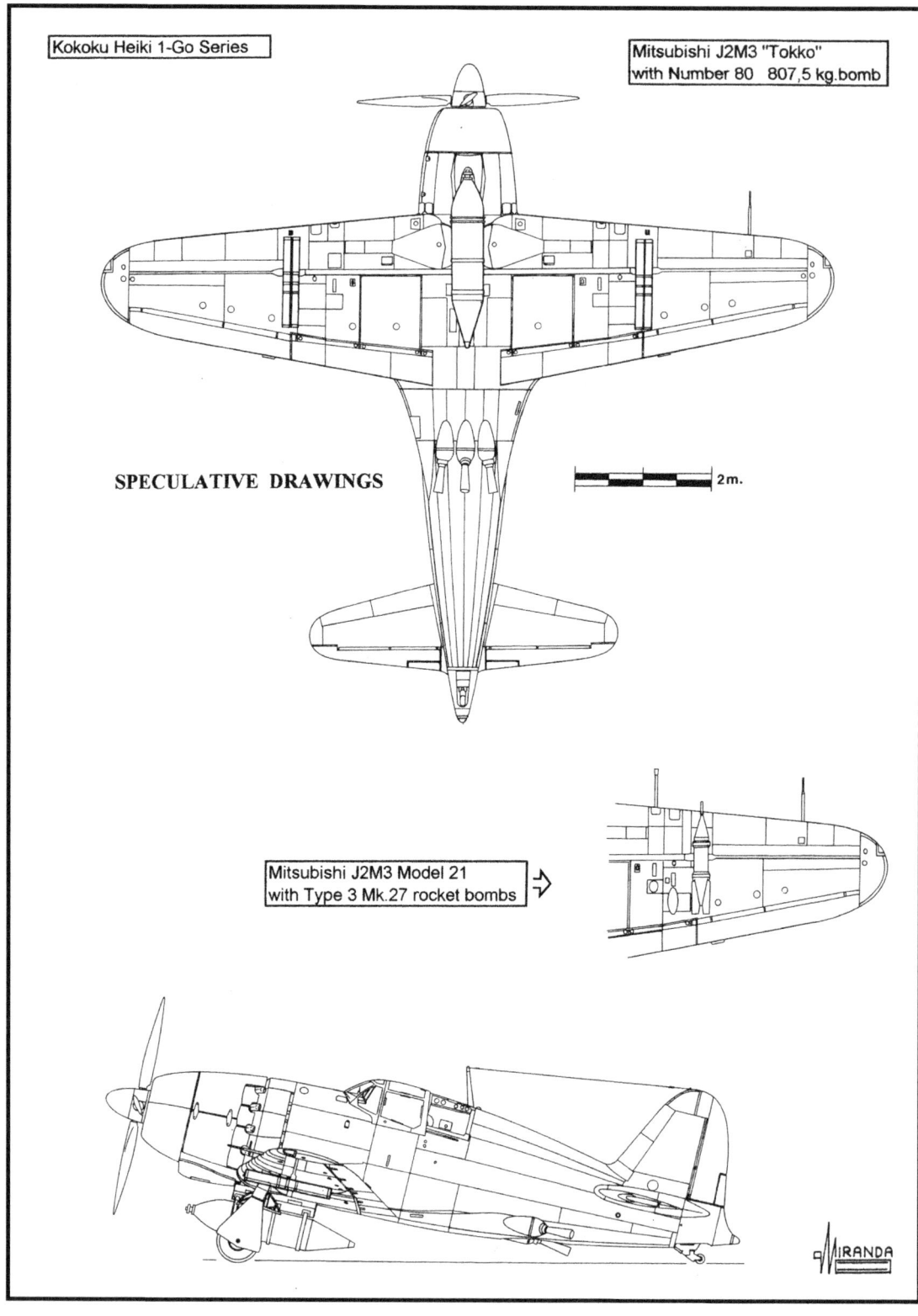

Kokoku Heiki 1-Go Series

Mitsubishi J2M3 "Tokko"
with Number 80   807,5 kg.bomb

SPECULATIVE DRAWINGS

2m.

Mitsubishi J2M3 Model 21
with Type 3 Mk.27 rocket bombs

MIRANDA

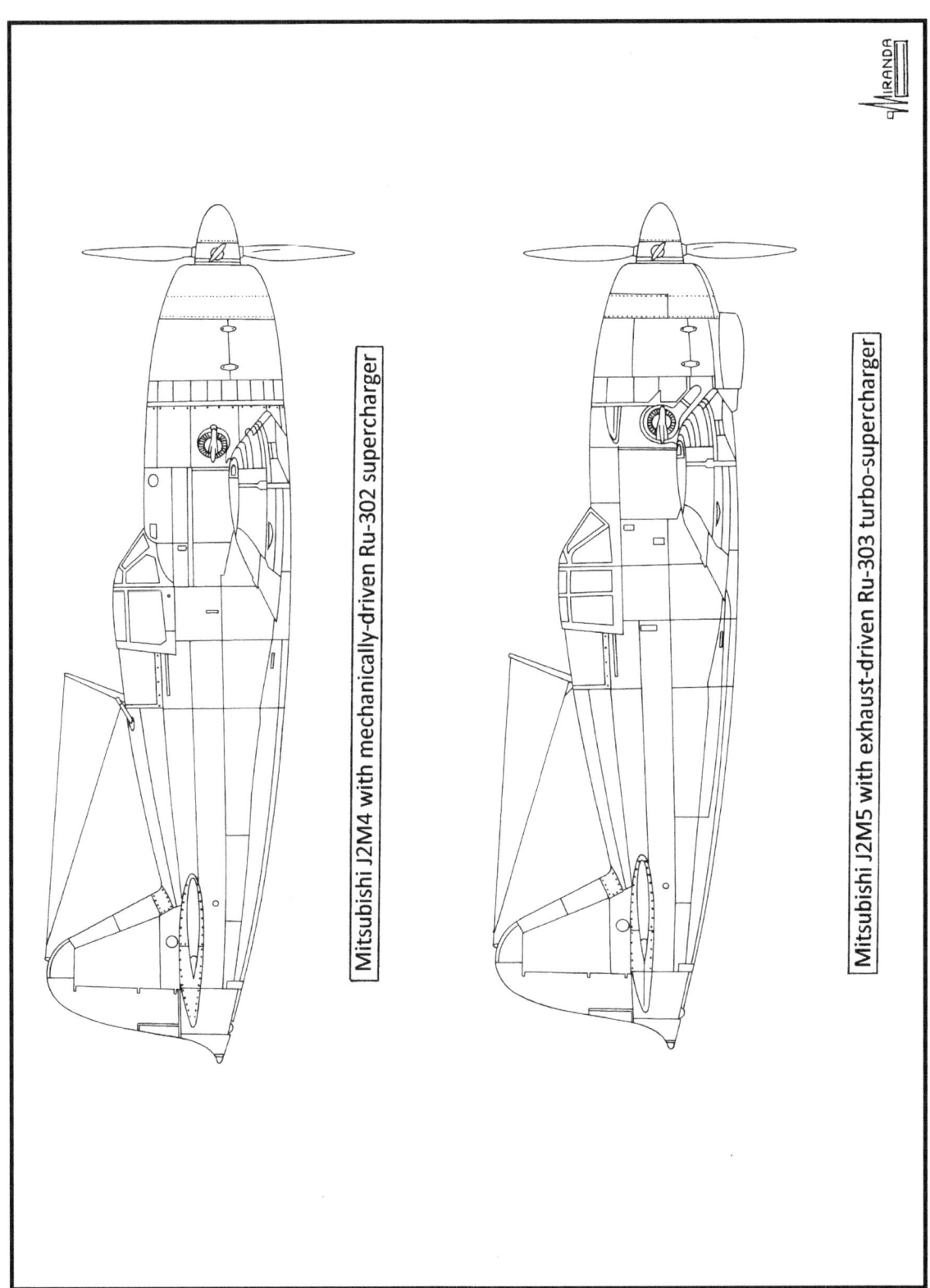

Mitsubishi J2M4 with mechanically-driven Ru-302 supercharger

Mitsubishi J2M5 with exhaust-driven Ru-303 turbo-supercharger

Kawanishi N1K1-J Shiden

With a mid-mounted wing and laminar flow aerofoil, the Shiden was designed at the end of 1941 to replace the Zero as standard carrier-based fighter of the IJN.

The choice was based on the mid-wing designs of the American naval fighters Wildcat and Buffalo that, at that time, looked better equipped to operate from aircraft carriers. The Shiden also considerably improved the roll rate compared to other low-wing designs.

However, while the American aircraft had a retractable belly undercarriage, the Shiden's main legs retracted within the wing, as with the Zero. This solution was to be problematic because the structure of the wing—originally designed for a floatplane—lacked the resistance to stand the impacts of deck landing.

To solve this issue, the joint of the main legs with the wings had to be positioned near the fuselage; therefore, the legs were not long enough, and the propeller hit the ground. The Kawanishi designers specialised in floatplanes and had no experience with retractable undercarriages; hence they tried to solve this problem with telescopic legs of great mechanical complexity, like those of the P-47 American fighter. When the Shiden was operational in February 1944, Japan had lost most of their aircraft carriers and almost all its naval pilots with experience on deck landing.

The aircraft of the IJN continued to operate from the ground bases, but the aerodrome's conditions were quite poor. A strip of pounded earth and a few hastily built sheds on a remote tropical island were incompatible with the sophisticated mechanics of the Shiden.

The first aeroplanes of the 401st *Kōkutai* arrived at the Takao (Formosa) airdrome on August 31, 1944. Their mission was to intercept the B-29 aircraft based in Chengdu (China) on their route to Japan. The operation was a failure. Despite themselves, the Japanese pilots discovered that their maximum speed at an altitude of 6,000 m was almost the same as the cruising speed of the B-29 at 9,000 m. They simply could not intercept them. When the alarm was sounded with enough notice, the Shiden tried to climb up to 9,500 m to perform just one frontal attack, facing the intense fire of dozens of the B-29 heavy machine guns. Besides, they could not afford the additional weight of an extra detachable fuel tank and had just fuel enough to return to base.

Another unpleasant surprise revealed the low performance of the brakes, something that should not be extremely important over aircraft carriers, although it was vital in a strip of earth when raining. To stop the aircraft, pilots acquired the habit of getting out of the landing strip, to brake over the loose earth on the sides, with disastrous consequences for the delicate telescopic mechanism of the legs. The efficiency of the next take-off was seriously hindered as the legs incompletely retracted within its housing under the wing, thus considerably reducing the aeroplane's speed and making landing a very dangerous exercise.

Engines also failed. Originally designed for the 91-octane fuel available in 1941, they had to work with 87-octane or even sometimes mixed with a volatile oil extracted from pine tree roots that lowered the fuel to 85-octane. It was so contaminated with impurities that American Jeeps that used this fuel during occupation suffered engine failures.

The Nakajima NK9H Homare 21 engine was not easy to start at tropical temperatures, and its cowling design was inadequate for efficient refrigeration. During climbing, the cowl air control flaps were fully opened to avoid excessive heating of the cylinder heads, generating considerable drag. The Homare also lost power above 7,000 m at a fast rate; although it was designed to generate 1,990 hp with 85-octane, it was only able to generate 1,800 hp.

The Shiden was at its most efficient in fighting at medium and low altitude, thanks to its automatic flaps and powerful weapons. Its performance equalled that of the Hellcat and Thunderbolt, being slightly below the Mustang and Corsair models.

The Shiden was very useful for defending the aerodromes of Formosa and Luzon against the strafing operations of the American naval fighters. However, it was incapable of defending its own bases to the south of Kyushu against the B-29 offensive during the spring of 1945.

During the last days of December 1944, the 402nd *Kōkūtai*, based in Marcott (Luzon), was converted into a suicide unit to perform attacks against US landings on Mindoro Island. By the beginning of January, the squadron received twelve Shiden of the N1K1-Jb model that could transport two 250-kg bombs under the wings and one 400-l detachable fuel tank under the fuselage. On 2 January, when they were ready for take-off, they suffered an attack by P-47s, destroying eight Shidens. The four remaining machines were used to perform raids against Allied ships in the Lingayen Gulf during the following days.

Meanwhile, the technicians of the Yokosuka naval test centre had concluded that neither the Kawanishi N1K1-J Shiden nor the Mitsubishi J2 M3 Raiden was right to fight against the B-29. They recommended the manufacturing of the N1K2-J Shiden KAI, an improved version of the Shiden, as a land-based standard fighter for the IJN. It was a painful decision, considering over 1,000 Shidens and 566 Raidens had already been manufactured.

By August 1944, both models, together with the Yokosuka D4Y Suisei, the Nakajima B6N Tenzan and the Aichi B7A Ryusei, were allocated to the *Kokoku Heiki Go.1* programme of reforms that had the objective to optimise the design of these aeroplanes for *kamikaze* missions. They installed supports for the new RATO rockets, developed by the IJN for take-off from their light aircraft carriers, and one 500–800-kg bomb.

The N1K1-J KAI-Ko was the first modified version of the Shiden. It had a Toku-Ro.1 Type 2 rocket, with 600 kg peak thrust and thirty seconds of life, under the rear (strengthened) fuselage. Its objective was to help the aircraft take off from short airstrips when heavily loaded. Another addition was the installation of a launch device for one 507-kg No. 50 Model 2 anti-ship bomb under the central section of the fuselage.

The concept was outdated in 1945, so the Shiden was provided with the new rocket booster package developed by Kugisho. Aerodynamically adapted to the Shiden belly, it contained four Toku-Ro.1 Type 1 rockets with 600 kg peak thrust and ten seconds of life, two Toku-Ro.1 Type 2 rockets, and a Number 80 Model 2 anti-ship bomb, fixed and without any tailfin.

The two Type 2 rockets were used in RATO configuration during take-off while the two central Type 1 rockets were used to gain speed when confronting the defence fighters of the US Fleet. The two forward Type 1 served to provide a 60-km speed increase during the terminal dive over the Allied ships, thus reducing the time of exposure to the 40-mm anti-aircraft artillery.

The 20-mm guns were removed from the 'KAI-Otsu' to reduce weight, leaving the two 7.7-mm Type 97 machine guns that were installed behind the engine as the only armament to defend from the Allied fighters. It had been ascertained that the *kamikaze* pilot could better estimate distances and angles for an optimal impact if the tracer bullets were shot during the terminal dive.

By the end of 1944, both the conventional and suicide version of the Suisei started to use 12-cm ISR-type rockets to distort the aiming of the AA Allied gunners during the terminal dive. These rockets had been originally developed for anti-aircraft artillery usage, with incendiary pellets and a shrapnel warhead, in imitation of the German *Föhn*. They could be mass shot from a square matrix or one by one from iron tubes similar to the German W.Gr 21. The Suisei carried two or four tubes under the wings, something that was generalised for all the aircraft of the *Kokoku Heiki Go.1*.

Four Shiden had been already modified by the end of the war, but they were preserved to counteract the invasion of Kyushu and never went into operation.

Kawanishi N1K2-J Shiden KAI

Designed in the spring of 1943 to succeed the Shiden, the Kawanishi N1K2-J Shiden KAI was its simplified version with a more reliable and similarly powerful engine that was 222 kg lighter. A total number of 23,000 parts were removed, and it had a lower wing and simpler undercarriage.

These changes improved the chances to compete against B-29s, although its armament of four 20-mm guns was somehow insufficient to destroy these gigantic machines. Thanks to the use of Type 3 Number 6 Mark 27 Model 1, with 60-kg rocket bombs (launched from rails installed under the wings) but also through ramming attacks, the Shiden KAI was able to shoot down some Superfortresses.

On 7 April, B-29 42-63512 was rammed over Tokyo by a KAI of the 301st *Kōkūtai*. Between 18 April and 11 May 1945, the Shiden KAIs of the 343rd *Kōkūtai* performed 120 interception operations against the B-29 that were striking the *kamikaze* bases of Oita, Tachiarai, Kanoya, and Chiran, to the south of Kyushu. On 22 April, two KAIs of the 407th *Kōkūtai* shot the belly of an unidentified B-29 at 8,000 m over Kanoya. The bomb bay exploded as a result, and the three aircraft were destroyed.

On 5 May, two B-29 bombers (nos 42-65305 and 44-69899) were shot down by Shiden KAIs of the 343rd *Kōkūtai* over Oita, one by the rocket bombs and the other by ramming. On 7 May, B-29s 42-63549 and 44-69887 were also destroyed over the same place and following the same pattern of attack.

During the combats of these days, three KAIs of the 343rd *Kōkūtai* were shot down by the machine guns of the B-29 bombers, seven by forced landing and fifteen by bombing. At medium-altitude fighting, the KAI was more efficient than the Shiden, a serious opponent to the Mustang under 4,000 m and to the Corsair at a low level. On 22 June 1945, one KAI of the 343rd *Kōkūtai* rammed Corsair FG-1D BuNo.88441 in a fight over Amami Oshima.

A total of just 428 Shiden KAIs were manufactured to be used by the elite units. The KAI was too valuable to be used in suicide missions, but during the Okinawa battle, the IJN lost twenty-nine aircraft against the US Navy fighters while escorting various *kamikaze* groups.

By mid-1943, the effective blockade by the US Navy Submarine Force began to strangle the Japanese economy, and the aeronautical industry was particularly affected by increasing shortages of high aviation fuel and light alloys. On 8 September, Nakajima,

Tachikawa, and Mansyu were instructed by the IJA to use wood and steel as aluminium substitutes in the manufacture of the Hayate fighter.

In the Ki.113, designed in autumn 1944, Nakajima used steel in as many sub-assemblies as possible, but the excessive weight of the new airframe caused the abandoning of the project after the completion of the prototype early in 1945. Kawanishi proposed the construction of the N1K5-J, a steel version of the Shiden-KAI with an extended wingspan of 13.92 m, powered by one Mk 9A engine, but the project was dismissed because of excessive weight.

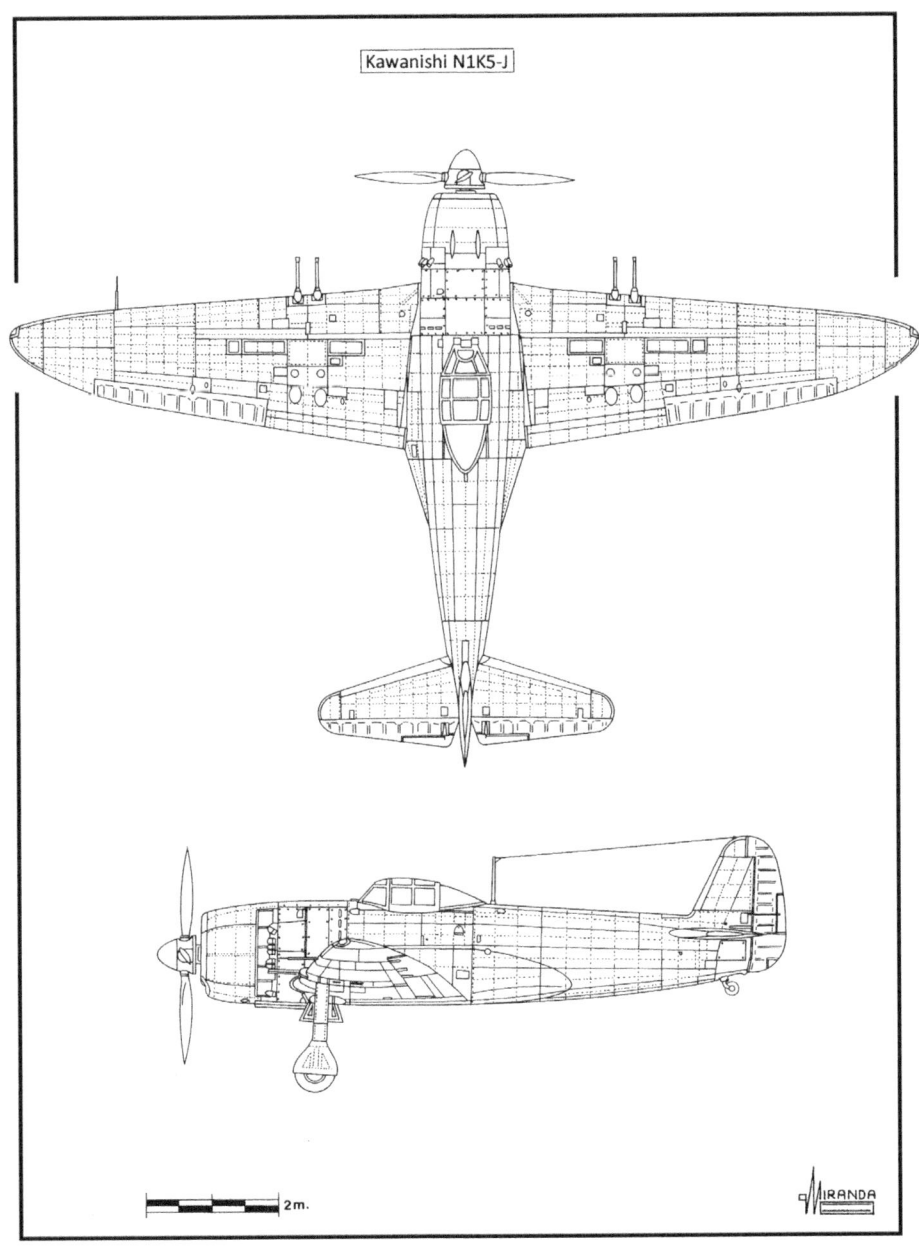

Kawanishi N1K5-J

2 m.

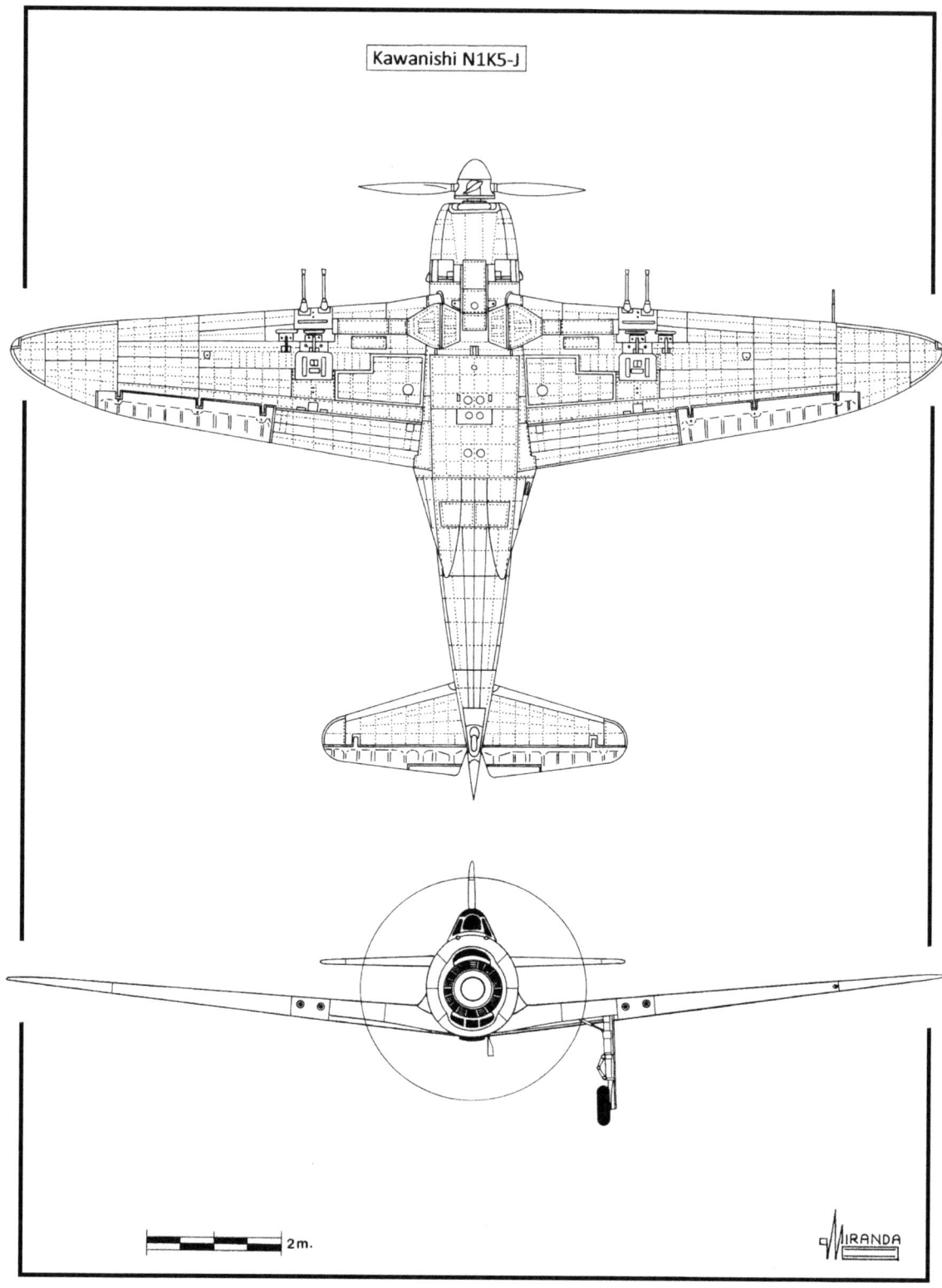

Kawanishi N1K5-J

2 m.

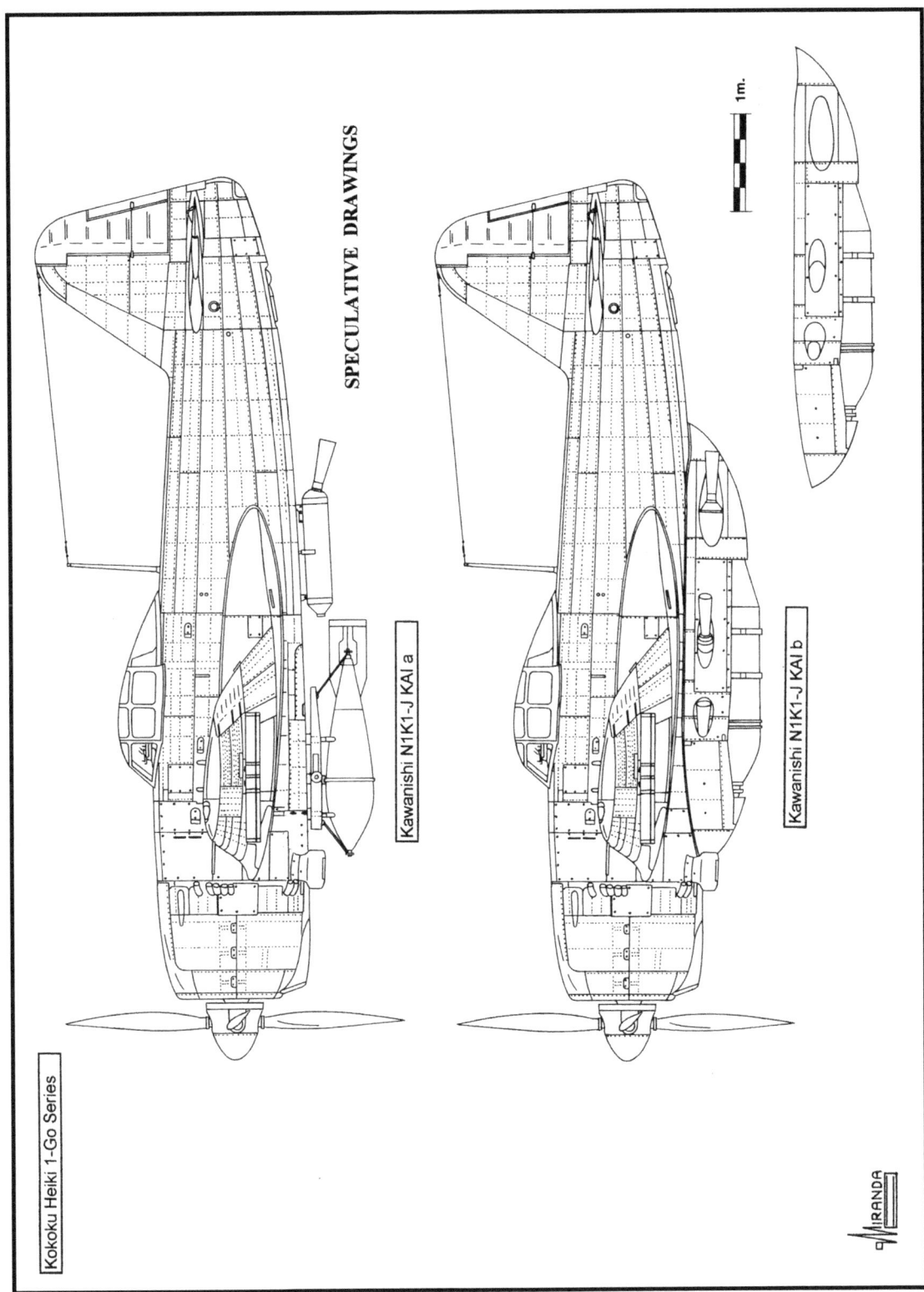

SPECULATIVE DRAWINGS

Kokoku Heiki 1-Go Series

Kawanishi N1K1-J KAI a

Kawanishi N1K1-J KAI b

1 m.

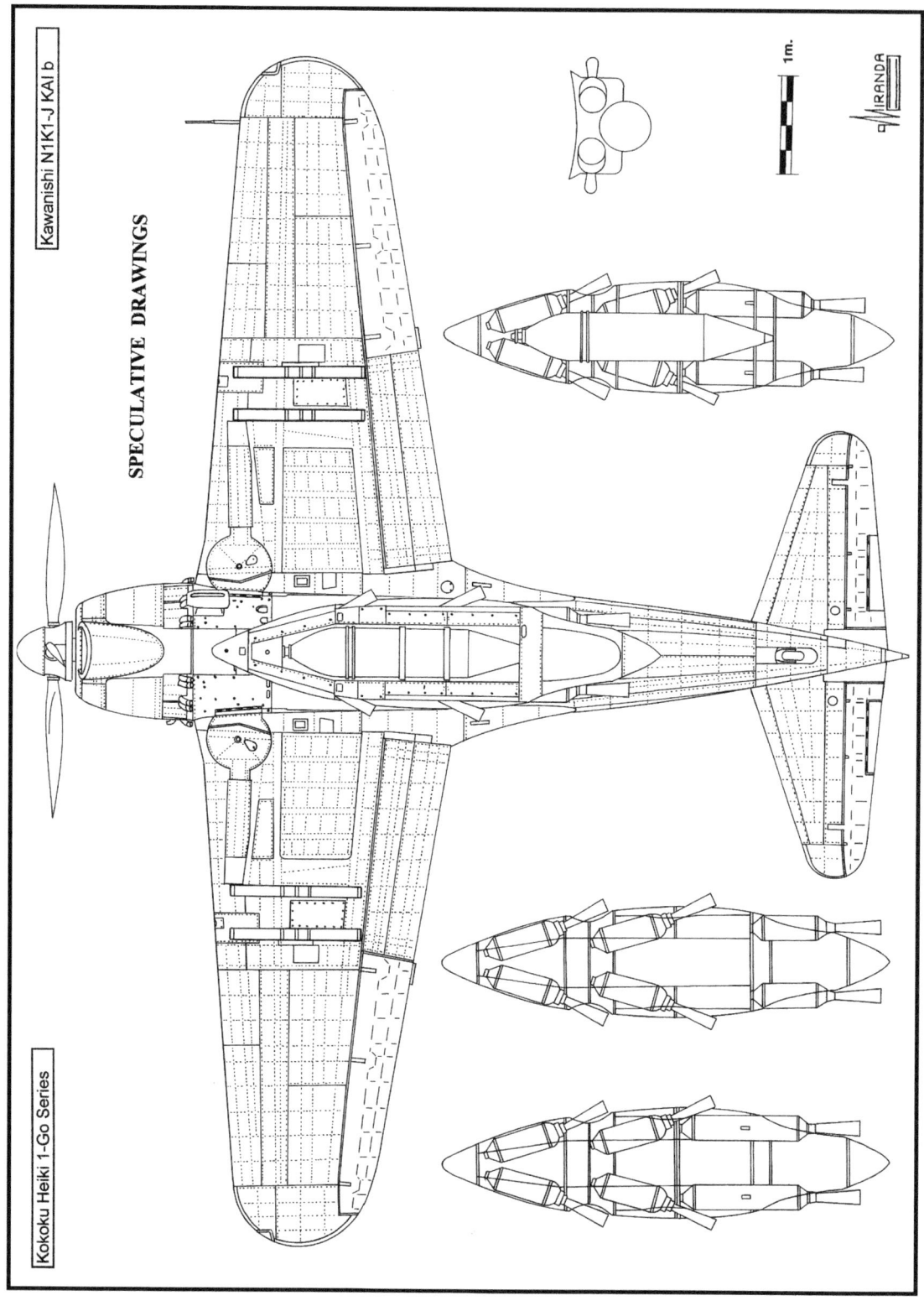

SPECULATIVE DRAWINGS

Kawanishi N1K1-J KAI b

Kokoku Heiki 1-Go Series

1 m.

The IJN '20-shi-Ko' Specification

The '20-shi-Ko' is just an expression used by some authors to refer to the 23 May 1945 IJN requirement for the future air-superiority fighter, which was supposed to have entered service in 1947. In fact, the IJN ended the use of the 'shi' naming system for experimental aircraft in 1943 (Showa 18).

After this decision, experimental aircraft names were such as 'Experimental Shiden-KAI' or 'Experimental Reppu-KAI'. The IJN used the 'shi' specification system for the last time in 1942, calling for a '17-shi-Ko' air-superiority carrier fighter (Mitsubishi M-50, A7M1 Reppu) and for the '17-shi-Otsu' interceptor fighter (Kawanishi K-90, J3K Shiden 31 and Mitsubishi M-70, and J4M Senden).

The '18-shi-Otsu' 1943 interceptor fighter specification (Nakajima J5N Tenrai, Kawanishi J6K Jinpu, and Kyushu J7W Shinden) and the '20-shi-Ko' 1945 air-superiority fighter specification (Mitsubishi A8M, Kawanishi A8K, and Nakajima A8N) exist only in specialised literature as 'historic license'. The official definition of the IHN for the 1945 air-superiority fighter was just 'Next air-superiority Ko fighter'.

The 23 May 1945 specification requirements were for a maximum speed of 704 kph at 10,000 m, a landing speed below 148 kph, fifteen minutes to reach 10,000 m altitude, a 13,500 m service ceiling, 2.5 hours endurance, four 20-mm cannons with 250 rounds per gun, self-sealing fuselage tanks, automatic extinguish device for the wings tanks, armour protection for the pilot, and automatic combat flaps. Mitsubishi, Kawanishi, and Nakajima submitted several projects based on the Reppu, the Jinpu, the Shiden-KAI, and the Ki.87-II.

Mitsubishi

In April 1942, the *Kaigun Koku Hombu* (IJN Aviation Bureau) issued the 17-shi-Ko specification for a 638-kph air-superiority carrier fighter to supersede the A6M Zero-Sen.

The Mitsubishi team envisaged the design study of a 125 per cent scaled-up version of the A6M3 Model 22, the best Zero of the time, powered by one 2,200-hp Mitsubishi MK9A (Ha-43-11) eighteen-cylinder, air-cooled radial engine with a water-methanol injection system that existed only in prototype form. The *Kaigun Koku Hombu*, fearing that the engine would not be ready for service in time, preferred to use a 2,000-hp Nakajima NK9K (Ha-45-22) Homare 22 engine with a Raiden-style small-diameter forced cooling fan.

During the flying trials made in May 1944, the A7M1 prototype revealed excellent flight characteristics, but the maximum speed of 574 kph reached was below specification. The Homare 22 produced only 1,300 hp at 6,000 m altitude.

A7M1 Technical Data

Wingspan: 14 m
Length: 10.995 m
Height: 4.28 m

Wing area: 30.86 sq. m
Max. weight: 4,410 kg
Max. speed: 574 kph

On 30 July 1944, the *Kaigun Koku Hombu* decided to cancel the A7M1 development in favour of the A7M2, powered by an MK9A (Ha-43) engine with a single-stage, two-speed mechanically driven supercharger. The four-bladed constant-speed VDM propeller had a diameter of 3.6 m. The new engine made it necessary to redesign the cowling, and the cooling fan was replaced by two Shiden-style air scoops. During flight tests performed in October, the A7M2 reached a top speed of 628 kph and with a twelve-second full circle turn time, which proved superior in manoeuvrability to the Zero 52, the F4U-1 Corsair, the F6F-3 Hellcat, and the P-51D Mustang, thanks to the installation of the two automatic combat flaps initially developed for the Kawasaki Shiden.

The A7M2 was chosen for large-scale production as Navy Carrier Fighter Reppu Model 22. Production models had hydraulically operated folding outer wing panels, 55-mm bulletproof glass for pilot protection, and a self-sealing body fuel tank with 22-mm rubber thickness. Tanks in the wings were equipped with only automatic extinguish devices. It was planned to mount two Type 99, model 2/4, 20-mm cannons and two Type 3, 13.2-mm heavy machine guns in the wings. The normal range of 917 km could be expanded with the installation of two external 350-l drop tanks. Only six prototypes and one production aircraft were completed in the last days of the Second World War.

A7M2 Technical Data

Wingspan: 14 m
Length: 10.984 m
Height: 4.28 m
Wing area: 30.86 sq. m
Max. weight: 4,720 kg
Max. speed: 628 kph
Ceiling: 10,900 m

The A7M2 airframe served as the base design of the A7M3, the proposed variant of the Reppu as Carrier Fighter Model 23. The new fighter was expected to operate from the IJN Shinano class's large aircraft carriers, making the wing-folding mechanism that was removed unnecessary. The weight they saved allowed them to expand the proposed armament to six Type 99, Model 2/5, 20-mm cannons, with 200 rounds per gun. The selected engine was a 2,150-hp Mitsubishi MK9C (Ha-43-51) with a mechanically driven single-stage, three-speed supercharger. The four-bladed constant-speed Sumitomo/VDM propeller had a diameter of 3.7 m. Development of the A7M3 began in March 1945; a wooden mock-up examination was scheduled for 16 August, and construction of the prototype was expected to end in December.

A7M3 Technical Data

Wingspan: 14 m
Length: 10.984 m
Height: 4.28 m
Wing area: 30.86 sq. m
Max. weight: 5,040 kg
Max. speed: 642 kph
Ceiling: 11,300 m

The 17-shi-Otsu A7M3-J was a high-altitude project of a land-based interceptor equivalent to the IJA Nakajima Ki.87-II. Development proceeded in parallel with the A7M3, which differed in armament, wing surface, and the 2,200-hp MK9A-Ru (Ha-43-11Ru) turbocharged engine, with two intercoolers, a forced cooling fan, and one Ru-303 exhaust-driven turbo-supercharger. The propeller was the same used in the A7M2.

The powerful armament, designed to combat the B-29 bombers, consisted of four wing-mounted Type 5, 30-mm cannons and two others (in 60-degree *Schräge Musik* configuration) mounted behind the cockpit. The design of the A7M3-J, officially named Reppu-KAI Model 34, was completed in November 1944. The mock-up examination was scheduled for February 1945, and the construction of the prototype should have been completed in October.

Mitsubishi engineers tried to develop an exhaust-driven turbo-supercharger based on the study of North American P-43 and B-17 aircraft captured in China and the Philippines. By mid-1944, turbo-superchargers were indispensable to fight the B-29 bombers over 10,000 m, but the Japanese industry was unable to duplicate the captured units. The General Electric turbo-supercharger was a product of enormous technical and manufacturing resources that were not available in Japan.

The high temperatures achieved by exhaust gas and the high rotation speeds of turbines (26,000 rpm) required the use of austenitic stainless-steel chrome-molybdenum alloys and the development of work-hardening techniques that enabled the turbocharger to withstand stresses from centrifugal forces. The precision machining of turbines and impellers was made possible by sophisticated machine tools and a surplus of raw materials.

In August 1944, the Mitsubishi J2M4 Raiden 34 was flown with one Ru-303 exhaust-driven turbo-supercharger mounted in the starboard side of the fuselage, just behind the Kasei 23c engine. The new supercharger did not work properly, causing fires during testing, and never became operational. The exhaust-driven turbo-superchargers were larger, involved extra piping, and increased an aircraft's size, weight, complexity, and cost. It is not possible to install them in a conventional single-engined fighter, and its use requires the design of special aeroplanes with enough room to install the turbo, the intercooler, and the heavy tubing system.

With the entry into service of the first Focke-Wulf Fw 190 fighters with the Luftwaffe in late 1941, it was necessary to upgrade the Merlin Mk 60, which used the Mk IX Spitfires, giving them with a two-stage, two-speed supercharger. Each stage had its own impeller, diffuser, and horn; the stages were placed in series, with the first stage feeding into the second. At the end of the war, the Merlin engines had two-stage superchargers, each with three-speeds, and the German BMW 801R radial engine, which powered the latest versions of the Fw 190, had a two-stage, four-speed supercharger.

The study of a Merlin XX British engine from a Hawker Hurricane Mk II captured in Singapore allowed Kawasaki engineers to build their first two-stage supercharger for the Ha-140 engine. The British system used two impellers that rotated at different speeds selected by the pilot by means of a gearbox. The use of two impellers in engines of more than 1,500 hp requires the installation of an intercooler (sits between the supercharger and the engine) to avoid the premature detonation problems that occur when air is injected into the carburettor at an excessive temperature.

Availability of 100- to 130-octane type 44-1 fuel let the American engines run hotter without detonation problems, while the Japanese only had 87-octane fuel and had to use forced air-cooling fans to avoid the overheating of their supercharged engines. By acquiring the manufacturing licence of the German engine Daimler Benz DB 601, the Japanese gained access to Vulkan coupling technology, a supercharger fitted with a continuously variable transmission device that automatically regulated the rotation speed of the impeller by means of a barometric control. With the use of the new mechanically driven Ru-302 superchargers, it was expected to reach a service ceiling of 14,000 m.

By the end of 1942, Mitsubishi produced the mechanically driven Ru-302 supercharger, with two stages and two speeds, for the Ki.46-IV high-altitude reconnaissance aeroplane. The Ru-302 did not perform well during the tests, conducted in May 1944 with a J2M4 Raiden 33 fighter. Mitsubishi began working on a new type of supercharger for the 2,130-hp Ha-43-42 engine, which combined the British two-stage, three-speed technology with the Vulkan coupling device. The first stage was mechanically driven by the engine, and the continuously variable speed of the second stage was driven using the Vulkan hydraulic transmission.

Nakajima preferred to continue the development of the British two-stage, three-speed mechanically driven supercharger for the 2,200-hp Ha-44-21 engine.

Numerous technical problems had still to be solved in the development of a suitable turbocharger. Fearing that the new turbo-supercharged engines would not be available in time, the *Kaigun Koku Hombu* decided to use the Ha-43-42 (with water-methanol injection and without intercooler) to power the short-range, large climb rate 18-shi-Otsu Shinden interceptor and the Ha-44-21 with the 20-shi-Ko high-altitude interceptor.

On 23 May 1945, Mitsubishi submitted three kinds of plans to meet the '20-shi-Ko' air-superiority fighter specification requirements:

The A7M3, with 2,000-hp Ha-43-51 engine (forced cooling fan, single-stage, three-speed mechanically driven supercharger) and automatic combat flaps.

The A7M3-J-KAI, modified with an extended wingspan of 15.58 m, a 2,200-hp Ha-44-21 engine (forced cooling fan, two-stage, three-speed mechanically driven supercharger), and automatic combat flaps.

A new design, equivalent to the Focke-Wulf Ta 152 H German fighter, denominated A8M1 *Rikufu* by some authors, with an extended wingspan of 16.6 m, a 2,200-hp Ha-44-21 engine (forced cooling fan, two-stage, three-speed mechanically driven supercharger), and automatic combat flaps.

A7M3-J-KAI Technical Data

Wingspan: 15.58 m
Length: 11.964 m
Height: 4.28 m
Max. weight: 5,753 kg
Max. speed: 658 kph
Ceiling: 14,000 m

A8M1 Technical Data

Wingspan: 16.6 m
Length: 11.964 m
Height: 4.28 m
Wing area: 36.6 sq. m
Max. weight: 6,379 kg
Max. speed: 645 kph
Ceiling: 14,200 m

The A7M3-J-KAI armed with four Type 99, Model 2/5, 20-mm cannons, was selected by the IJN as the 'Next Fighter' and decided to develop from Mitsubishi and Nakajima joint work because the Ha-44-21 engine was Nakajima design.

Kawanishi

To meet the requirements of the 17-shi-Otsu IJN specification, calling for a high-performance, land-based, Kyokusen interceptor, Kawanishi proposed its project K 90, with a Nakajima Homare engine, in 1942.

The IJN ordered the development of the K 90, as J3K1, powered by one Mitsubishi MK9B (Ha-43-21) engine with a two-stage mechanical supercharger and a first-stage Vulkan coupling drive. In August 1943, the project was modified as J6K1 Jinpu, to adapt it to the '18-shi-Ko' specification, calling for a high-altitude, air-superiority fighter powered by one Nakajima NK9A-O Homare 40, two-stage, three-speed mechanical supercharged engine, with an intercooler, forced cooling fan, and oxygen injection.

In July 1944, the J6K1 was superseded by the N1K2-J Shiden-KAI that was chosen by the *Kaigun Koku Hombu* for large-scale production. In April 1945, Kawanishi proposed the modification of the J6K1 to the IJN to adapt it to the requirements of the '20-shi-Ko' specification, to be powered by a Ha-44-21 engine with an intercooler and forced cooling fan, with an armament of six Type 99, Model 2/5, 20-mm cannons. According to some authors, the new design was named A8K1 Toppu.

A8K1 Technical Data

Wingspan: 12.5 m
Length: 10.118 m
Height: 3.94 m
Wing area: 26 sq. m
Max. weight: 4,373 kg
Max. speed: 685 kph
Ceiling: 13,000 m

Along with the A8K1, Kawanishi submitted the 'High-Performance Shiden-KAI' project that basically was a N1K5-J Shiden 25 powered by one 2,200-hp Nakajima Ha-45-44 engine, with a two-stage, three-speed mechanical supercharger, intercooler, and six Type 99, Model 2/5, 20-mm cannons.

'High-Performance Shiden-KAI' Technical Data

Wingspan: 11.99 m
Length: 9.346 m
Height: 3.96 m
Wing area: 23.5 sq. m
Max. weight: 4,768 kg
Max. speed: 663 kph
Ceiling: 12,000 m

Nakajima

On 23 April 1945, the Nakajima firm submitted its project '20-shi-Ko' based on the Ki.87-II high-altitude interceptor. Replacing the turbocharged Ha-46 engine with the required Ha-44-21 necessitated a new wing with a laminar profile, combat flaps, and an extended wingspan to improve high-altitude manoeuvrability. In this version, the pressurised cabin was removed, and the armament was reduced to just four 20-mm cannons to save weight.

Nakajima '20-shi-Ko' fighter Technical Data

Wingspan: 15.19 m
Length: 12 m
Height: 4.61 m
Wing area: 28 sq. m
Max. weight: 6,110 kg
Max. speed: 676 kph
Ceiling: 13,200 m

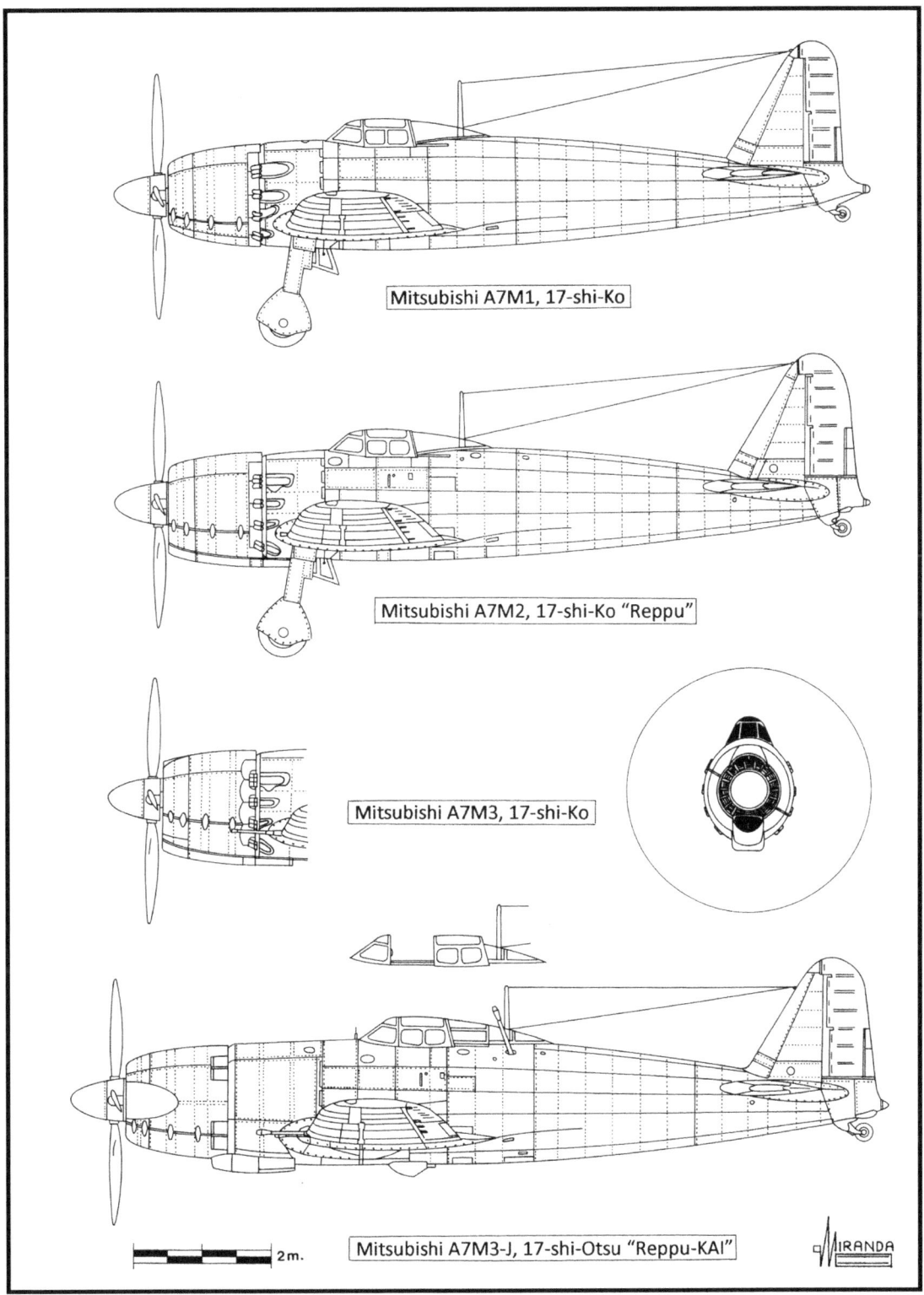

Mitsubishi A7M1, 17-shi-Ko

Mitsubishi A7M2, 17-shi-Ko "Reppu"

Mitsubishi A7M3, 17-shi-Ko

Mitsubishi A7M3-J, 17-shi-Otsu "Reppu-KAI"

2 m.

MIRANDA

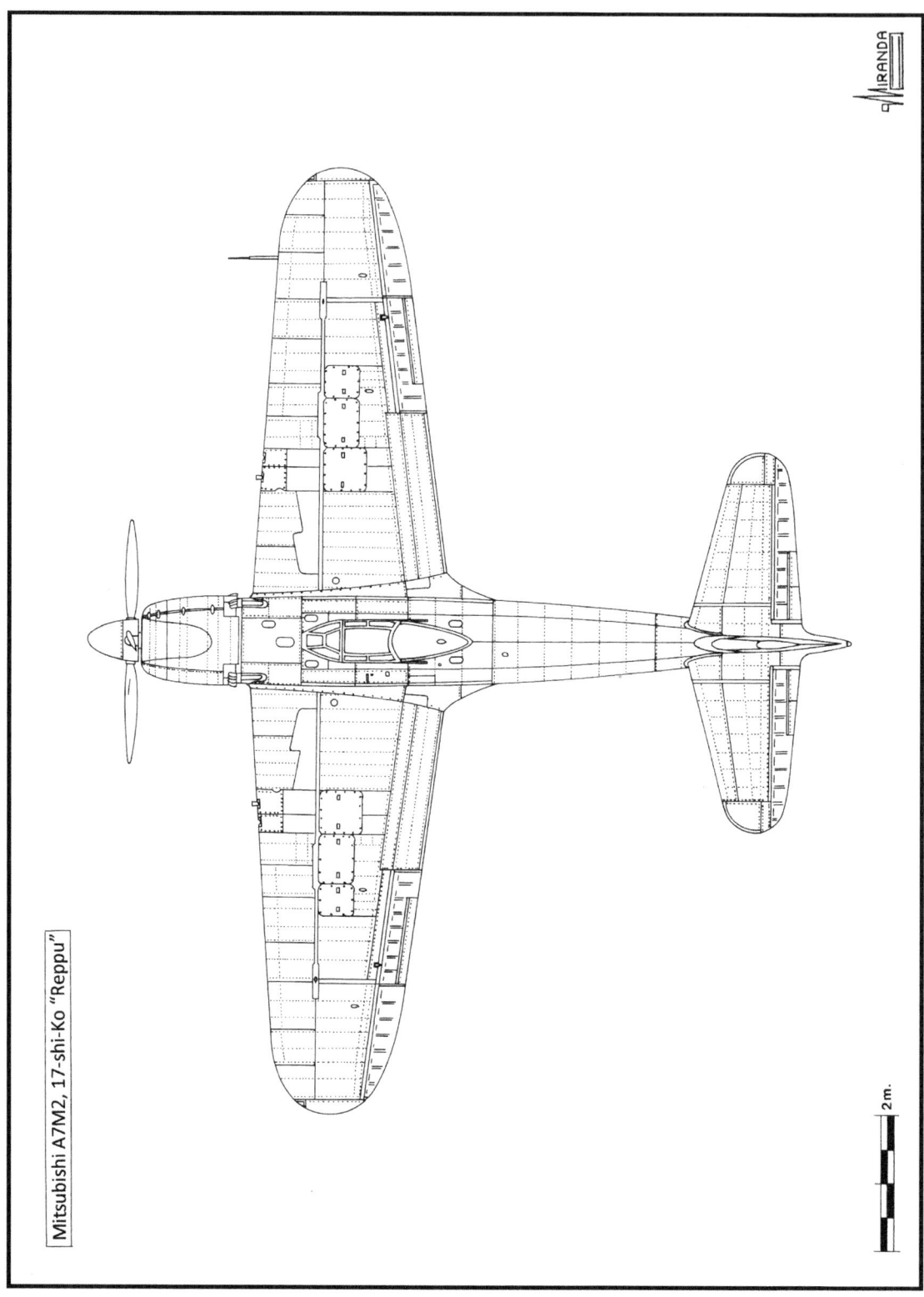

Mitsubishi A7M2, 17-shi-Ko "Reppu"

2 m.

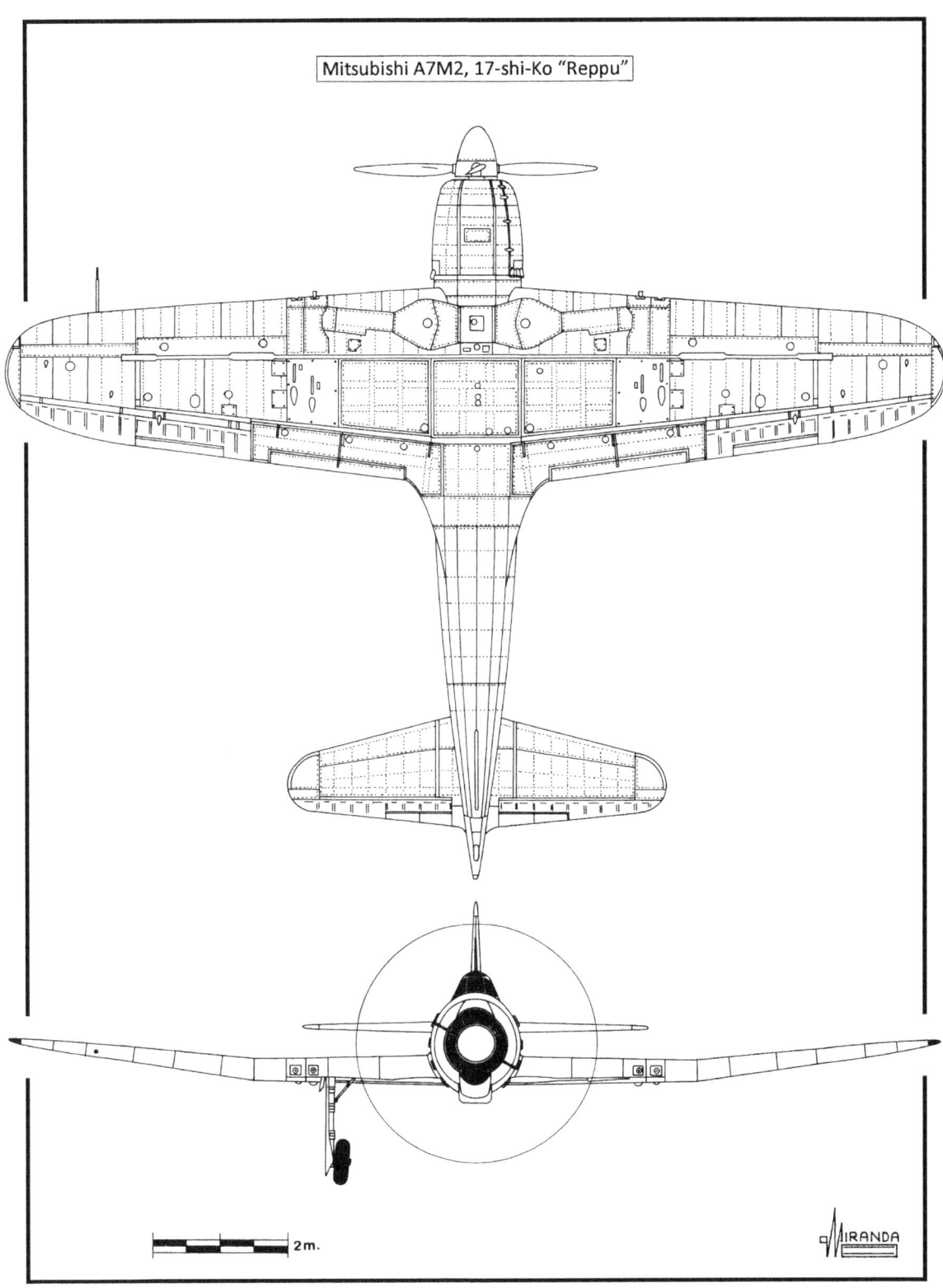

Mitsubishi A7M2, 17-shi-Ko "Reppu"

2m.

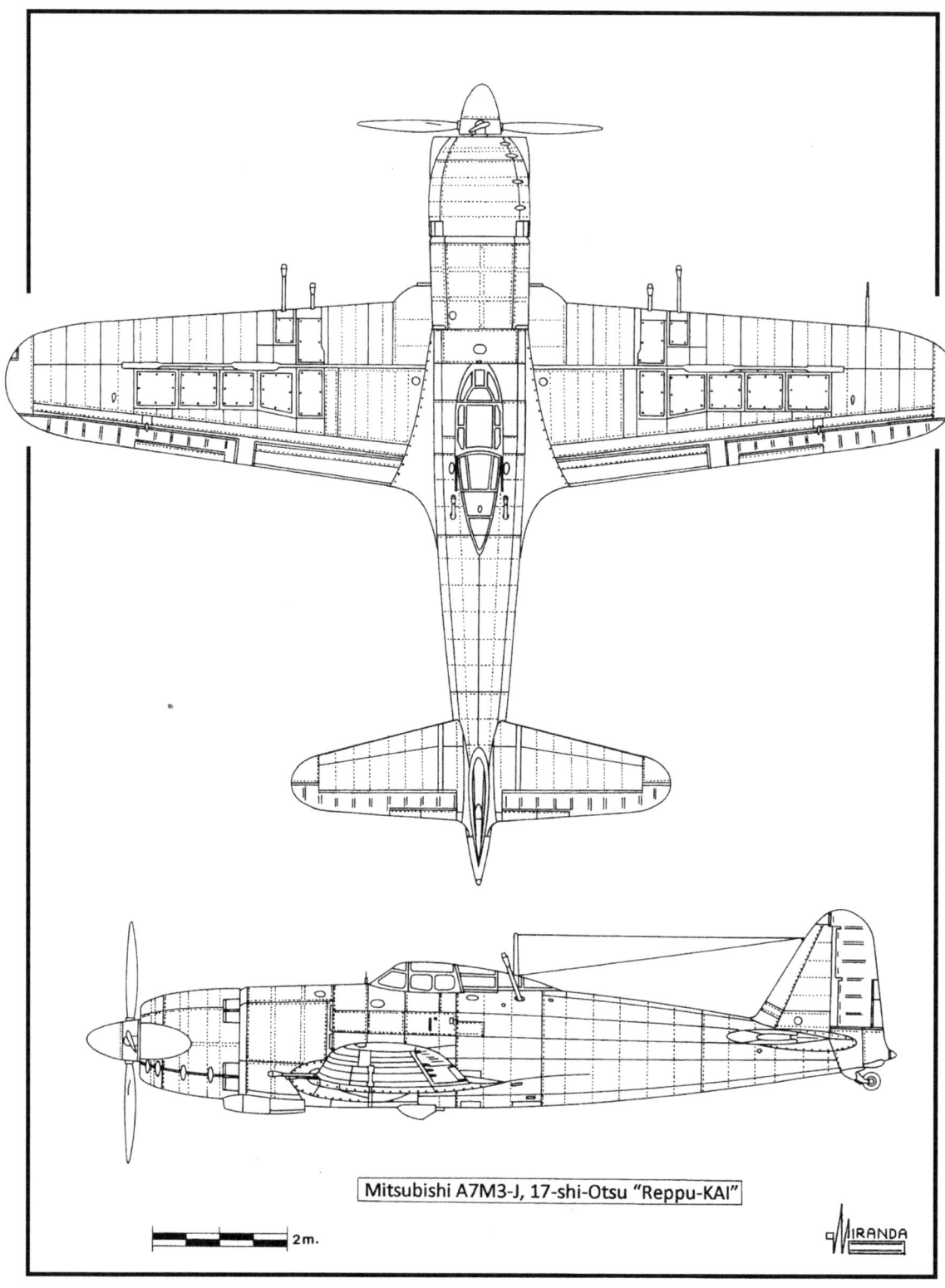

Mitsubishi A7M3-J, 17-shi-Otsu "Reppu-KAI"

2 m.

MIRANDA

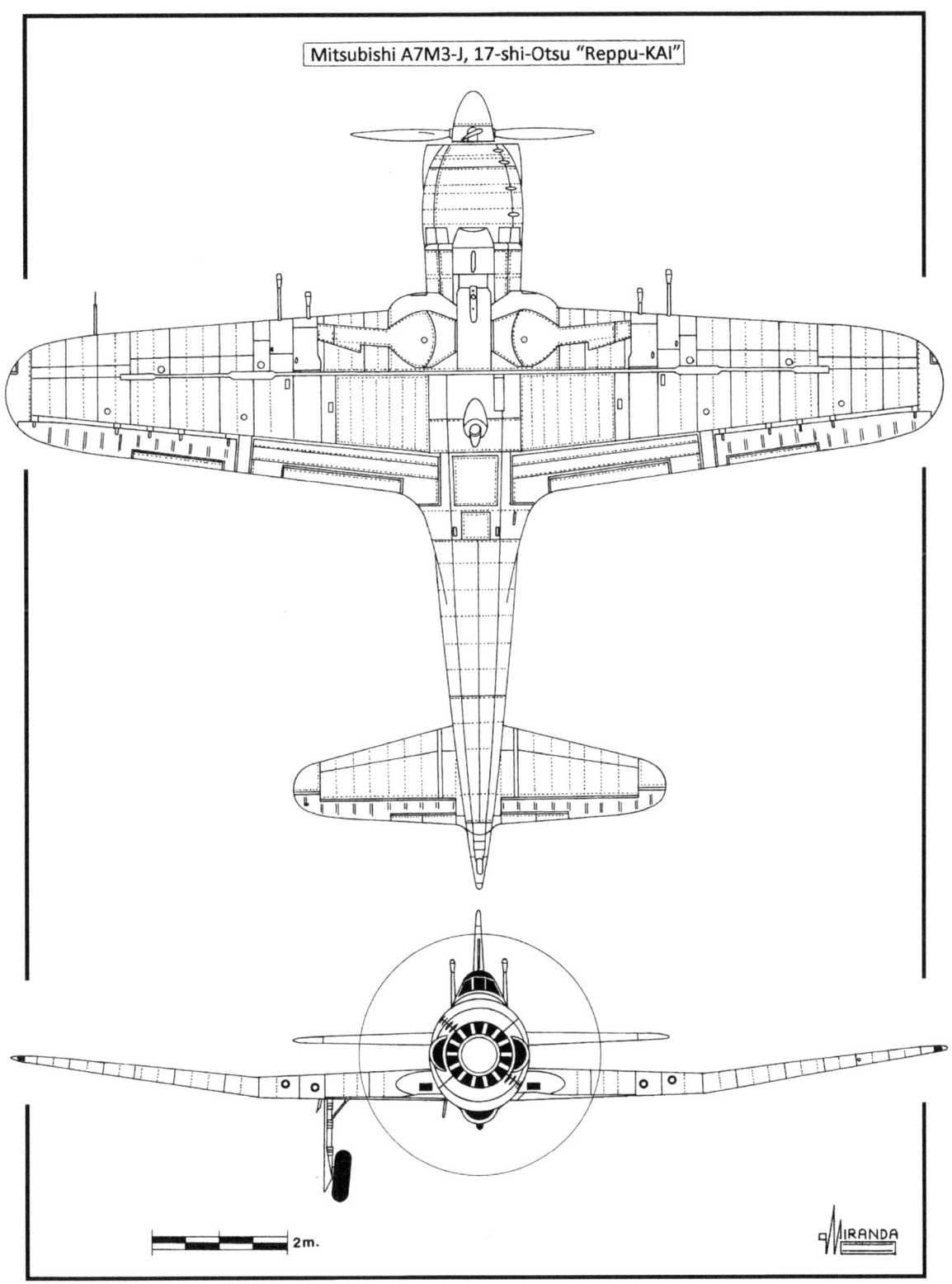

Mitsubishi A7M3-J, 17-shi-Otsu "Reppu-KAI"

2m.

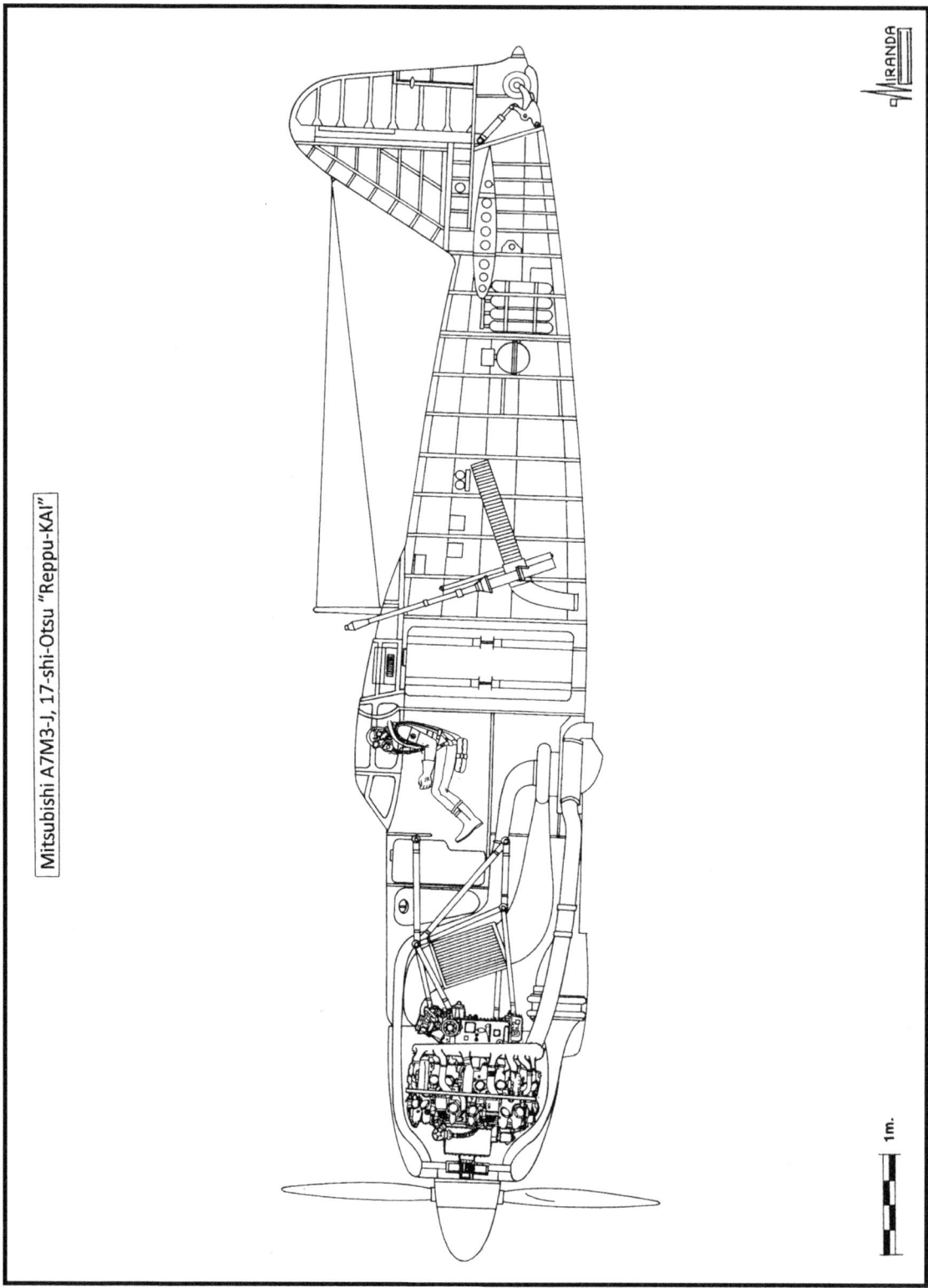

Mitsubishi A7M3-J, 17-shi-Otsu "Reppu-KAI"

1 m.

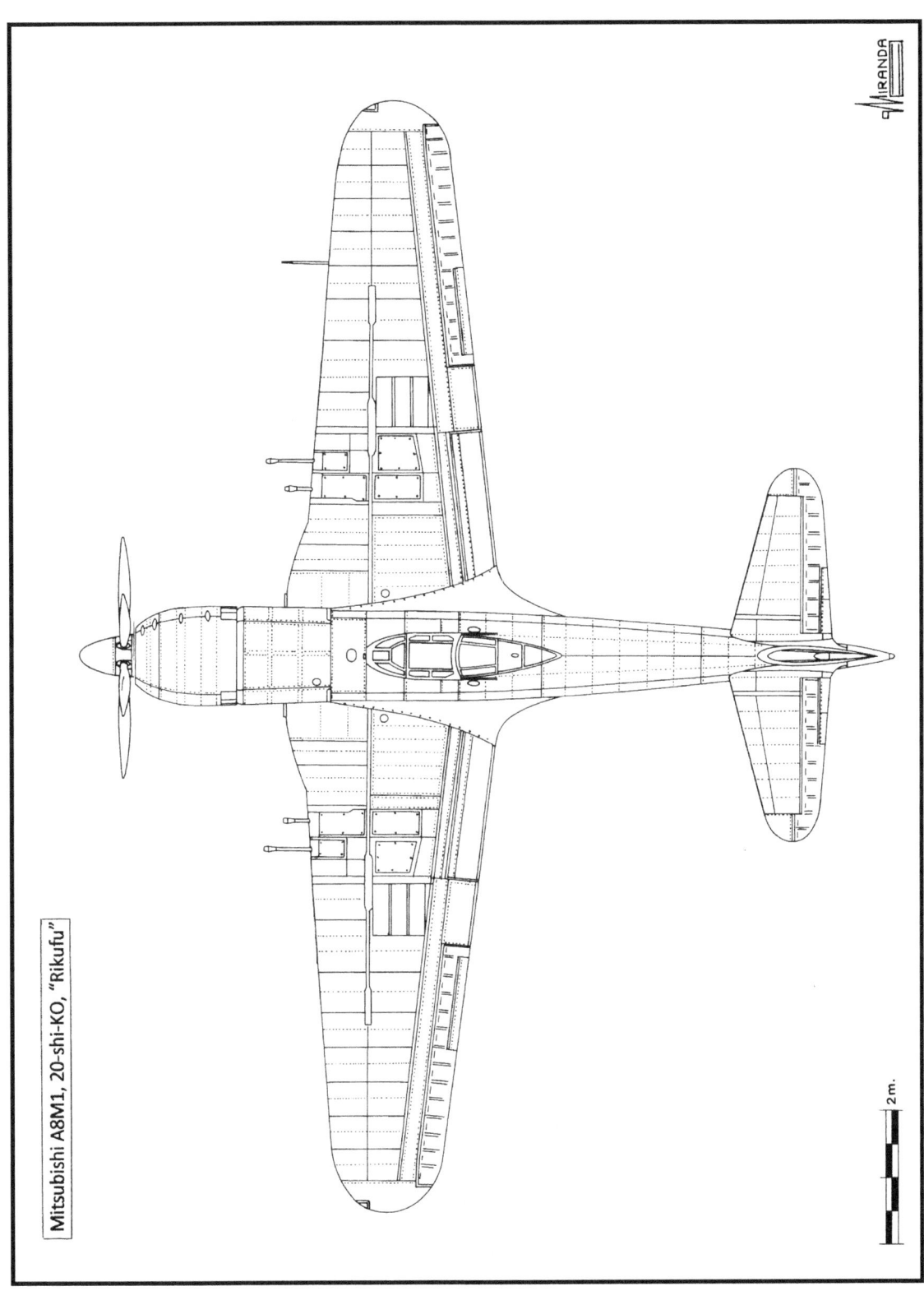

Mitsubishi A8M1, 20-shi-KO, "Rikufu"

2 m.

Mitsubishi A8M1, 20-shi-KO, "Rikufu"

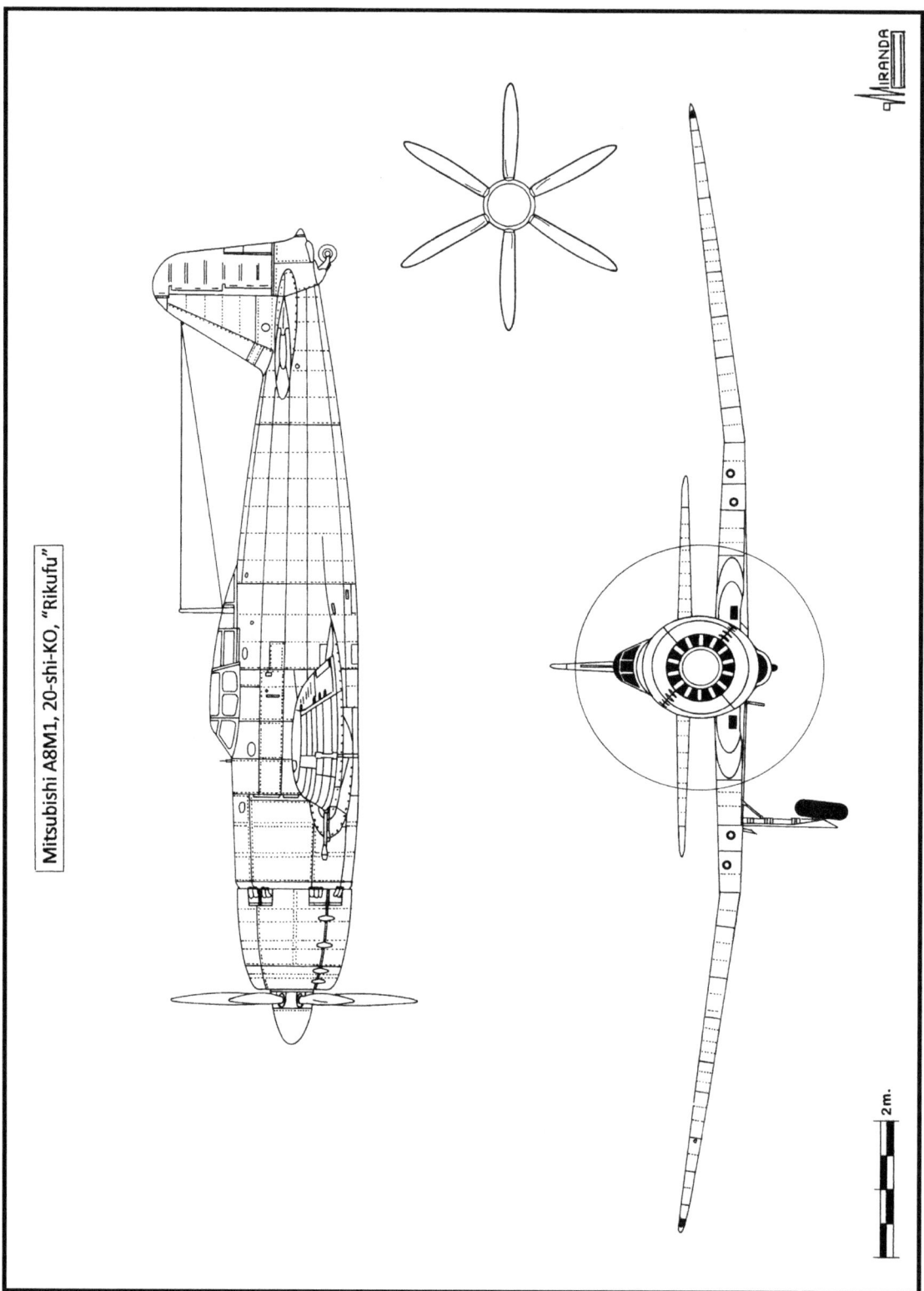

2 m.

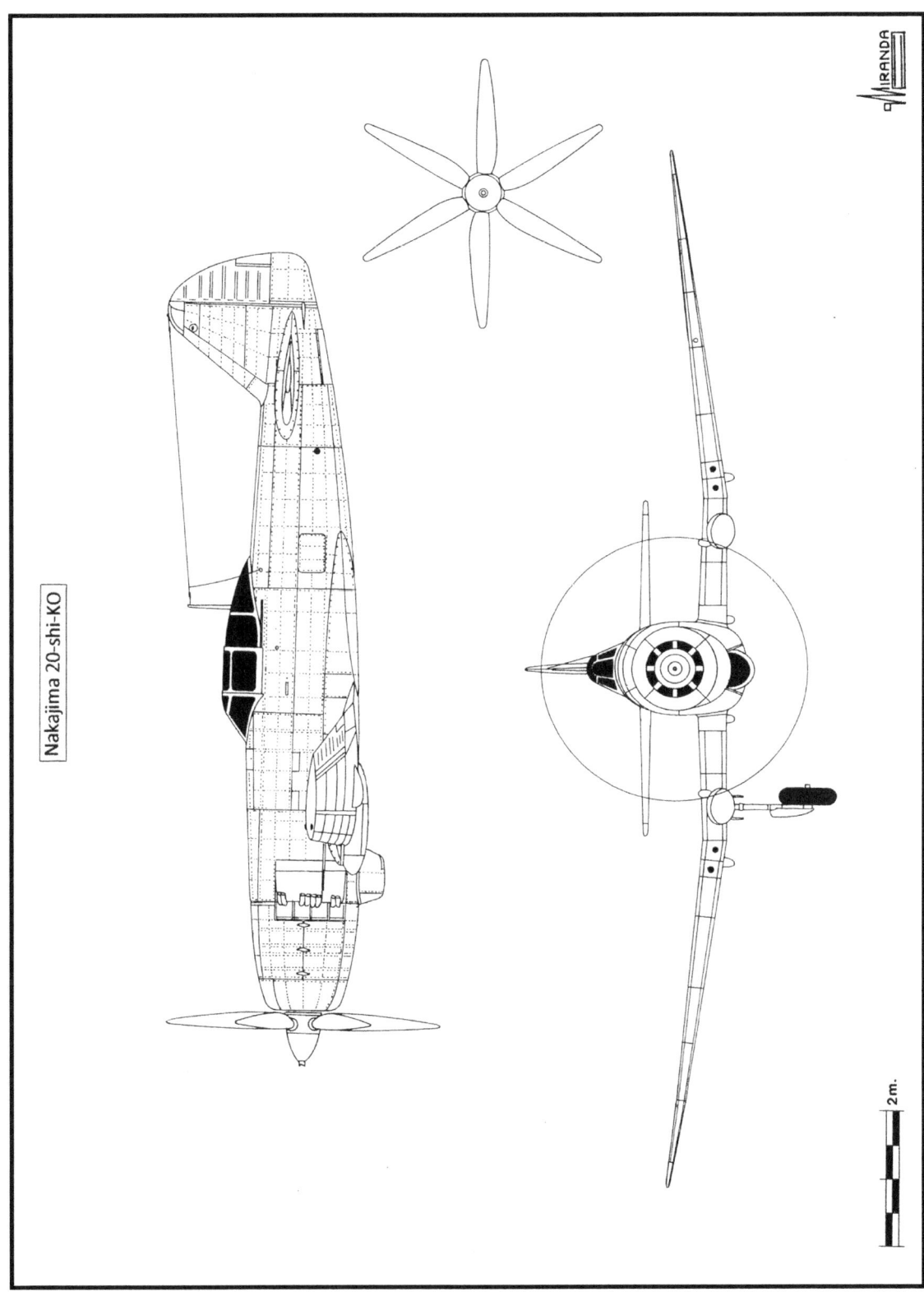

Nakajima 20-shi-KO

2 m.

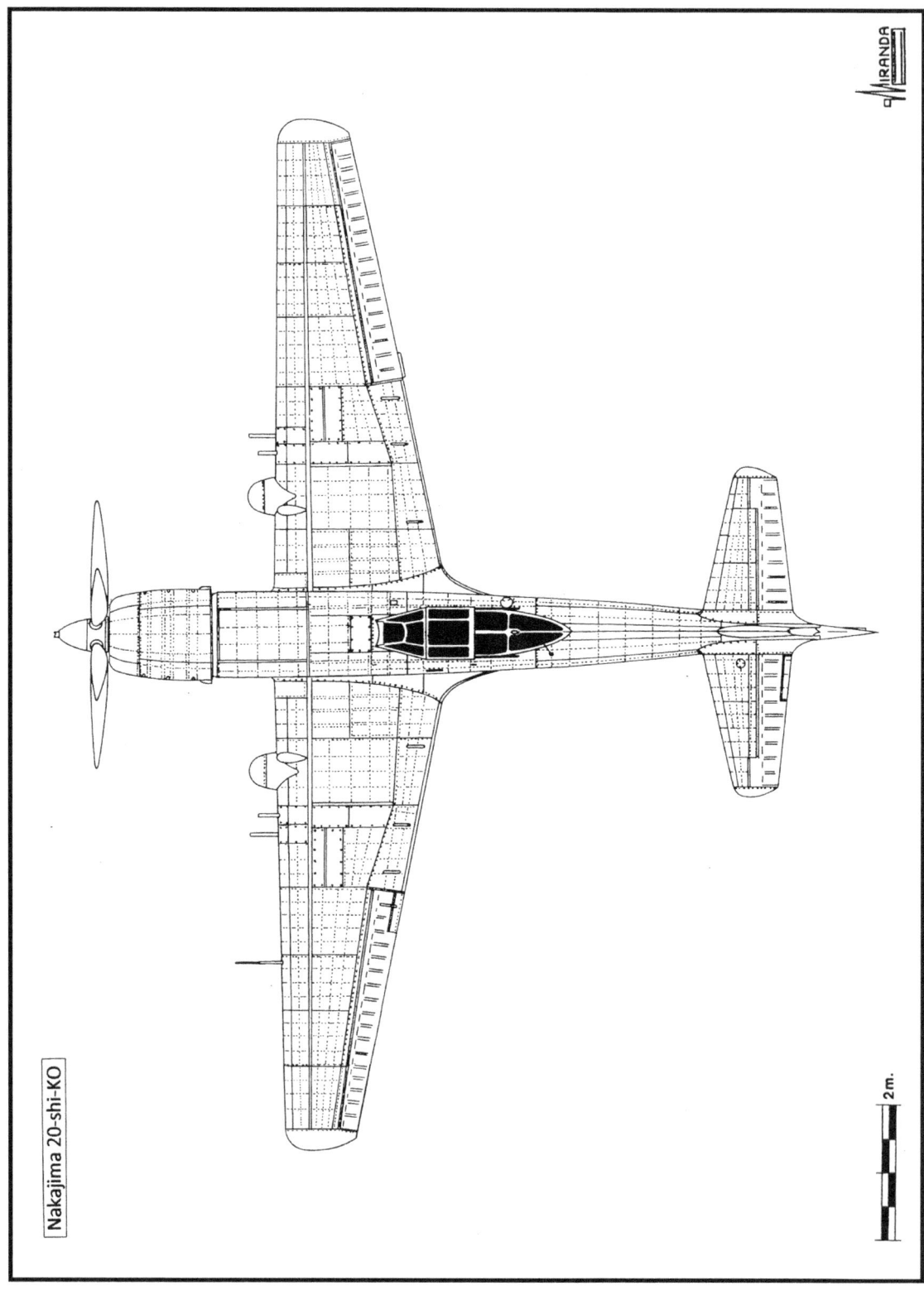

Nakajima 20-shi-KO

2m.

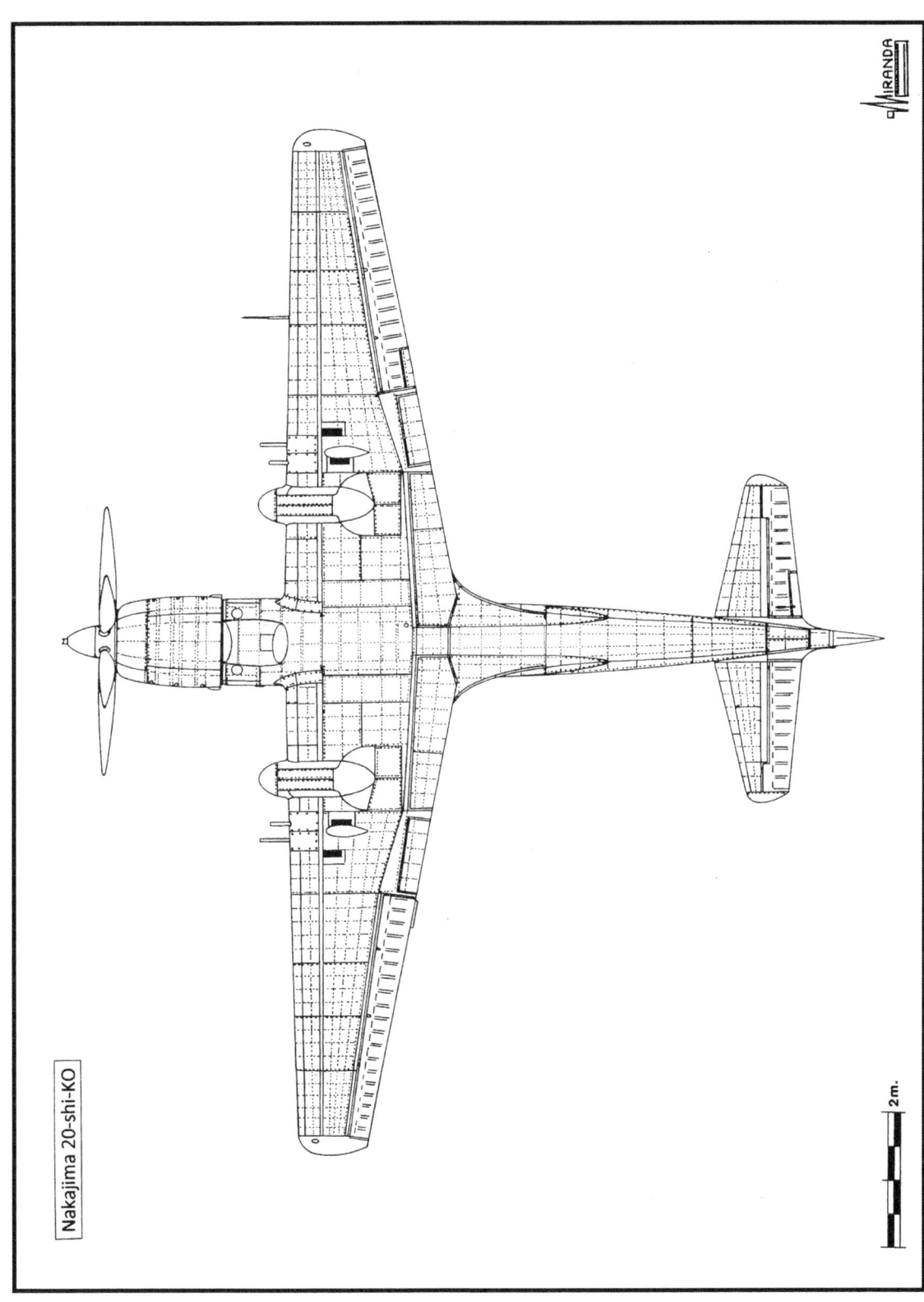

Nakajima 20-shi-KO

2 m.

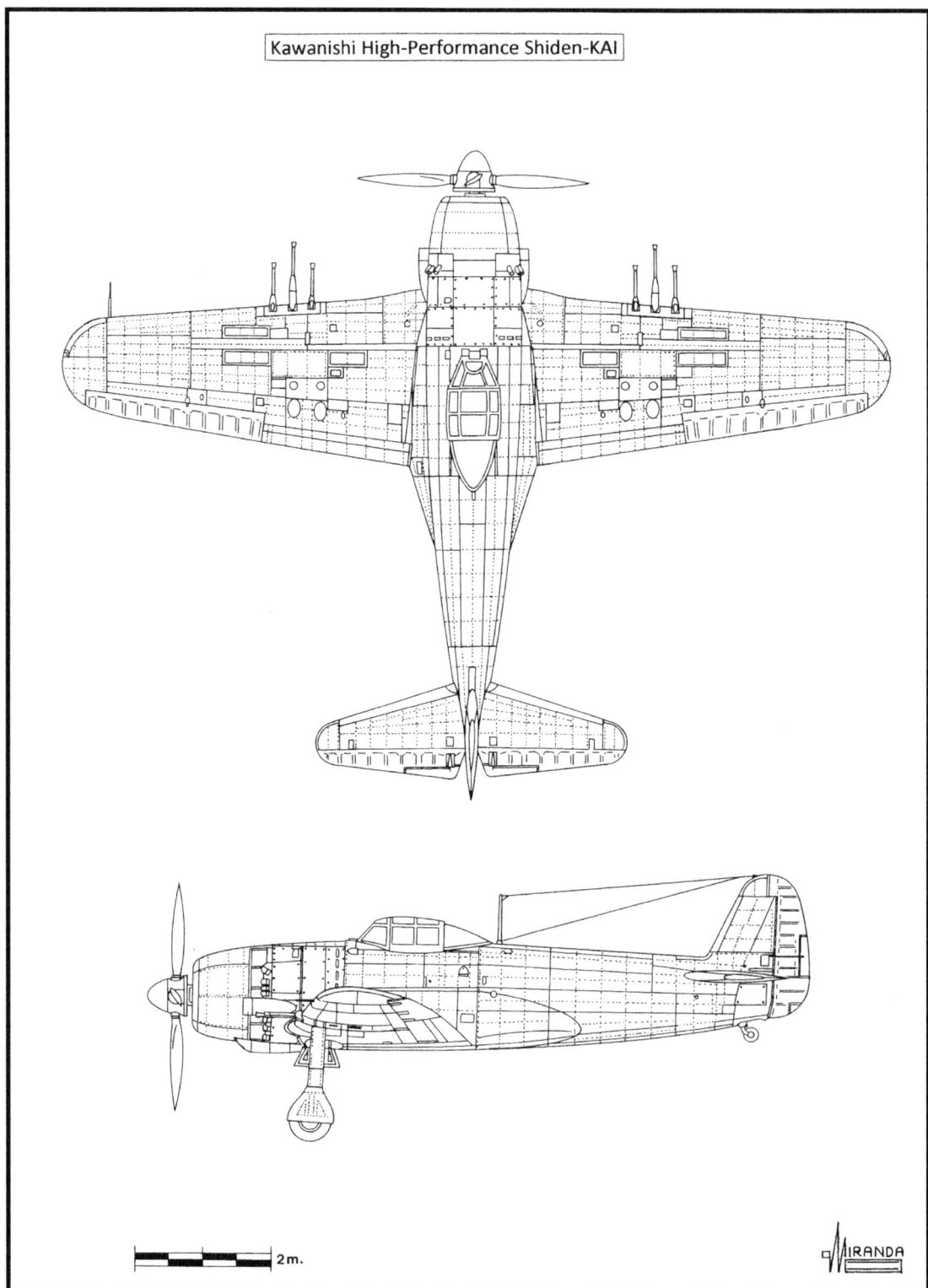

Kawanishi High-Performance Shiden-KAI

2m.

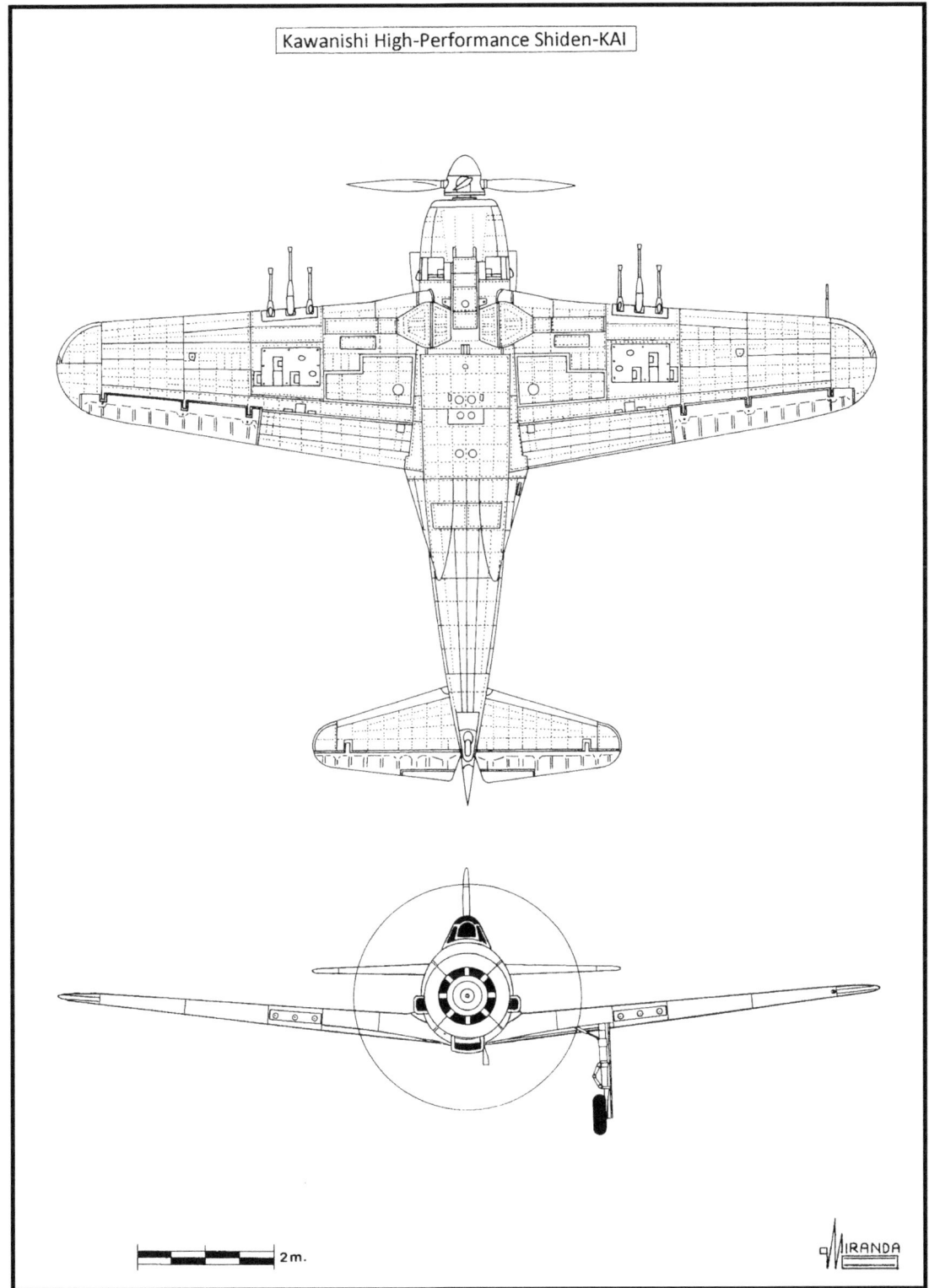

Kawanishi High-Performance Shiden-KAI

2 m.

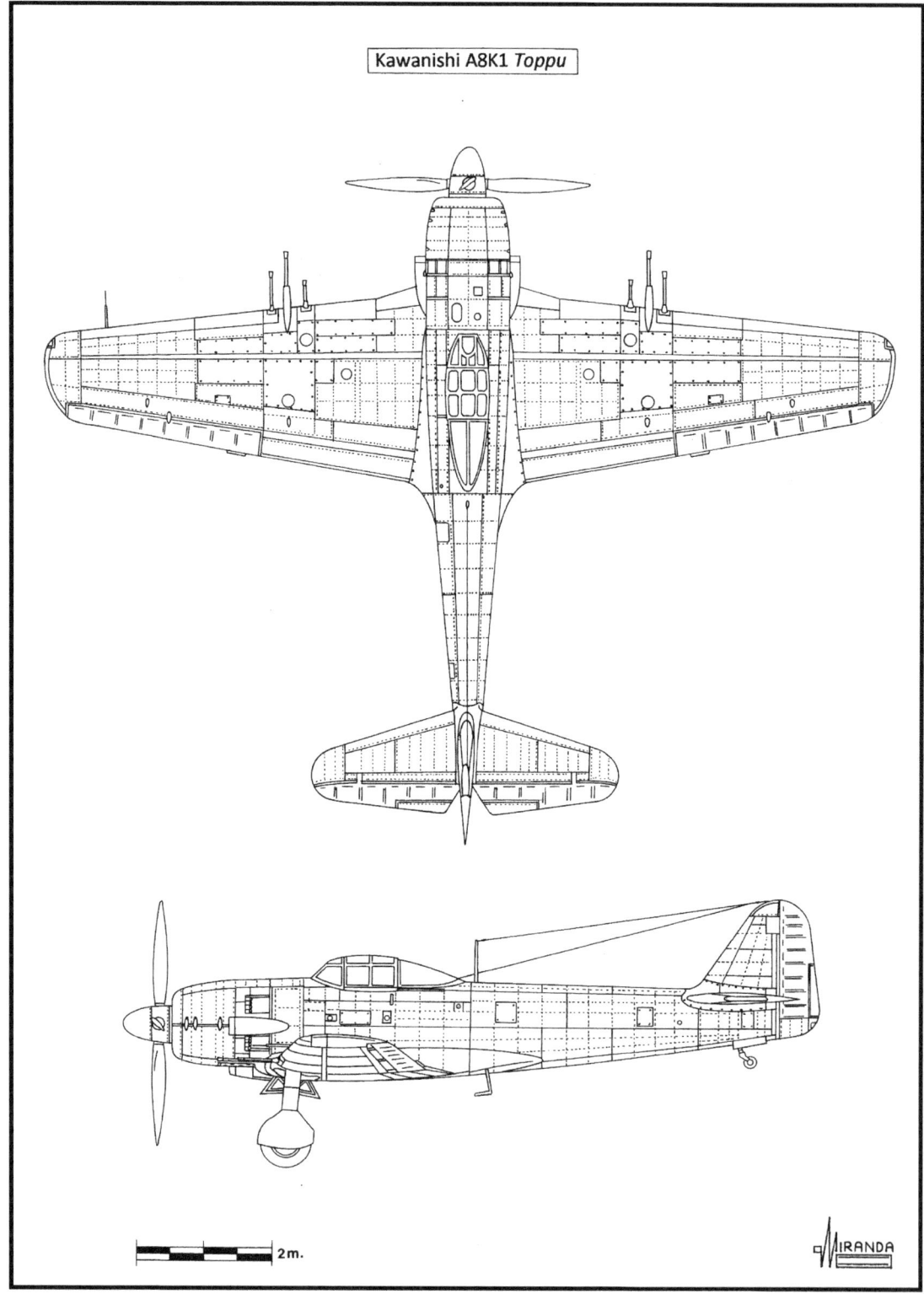

Kawanishi A8K1 *Toppu*

2 m.

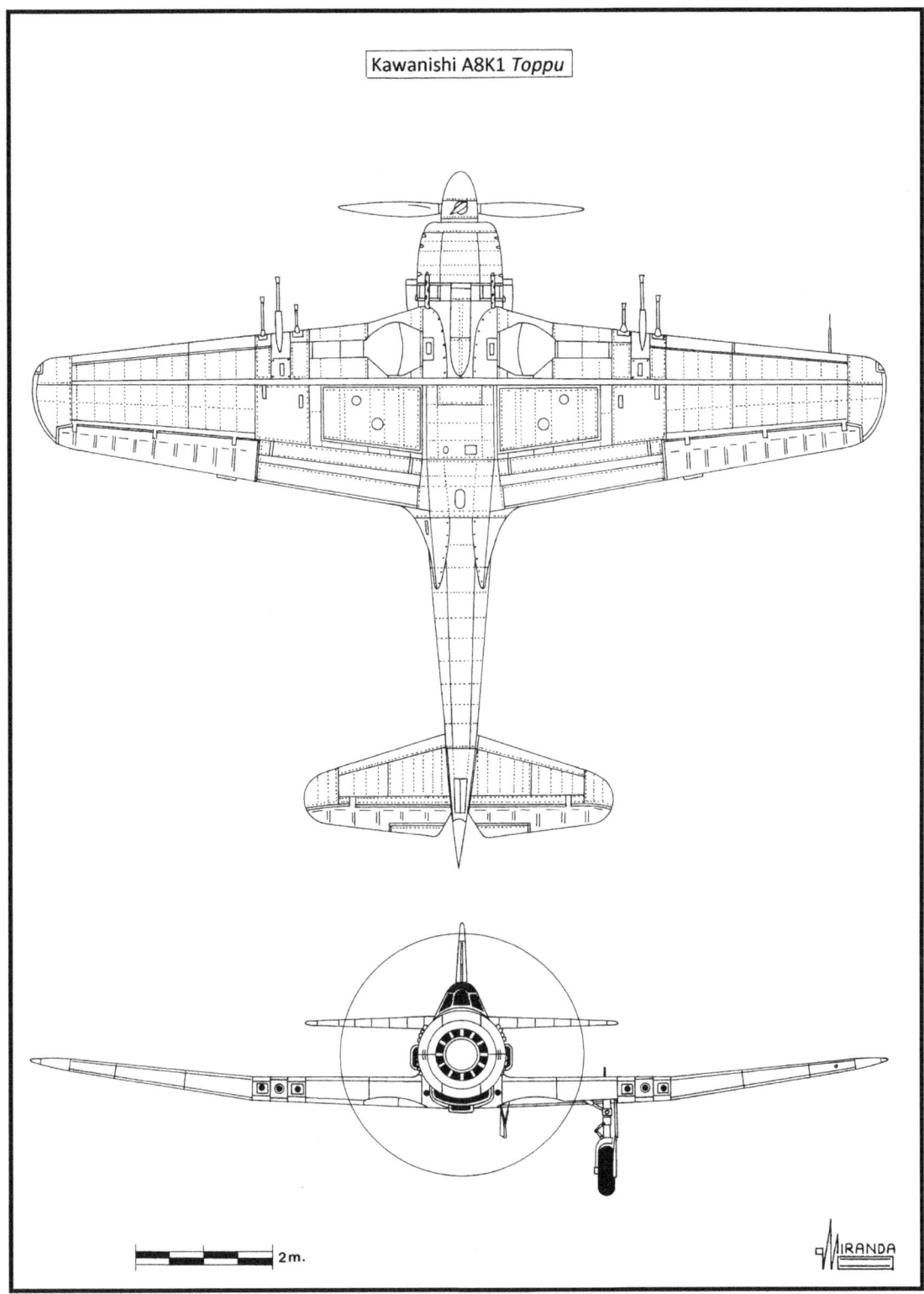

Kawanishi A8K1 *Toppu*

2m.

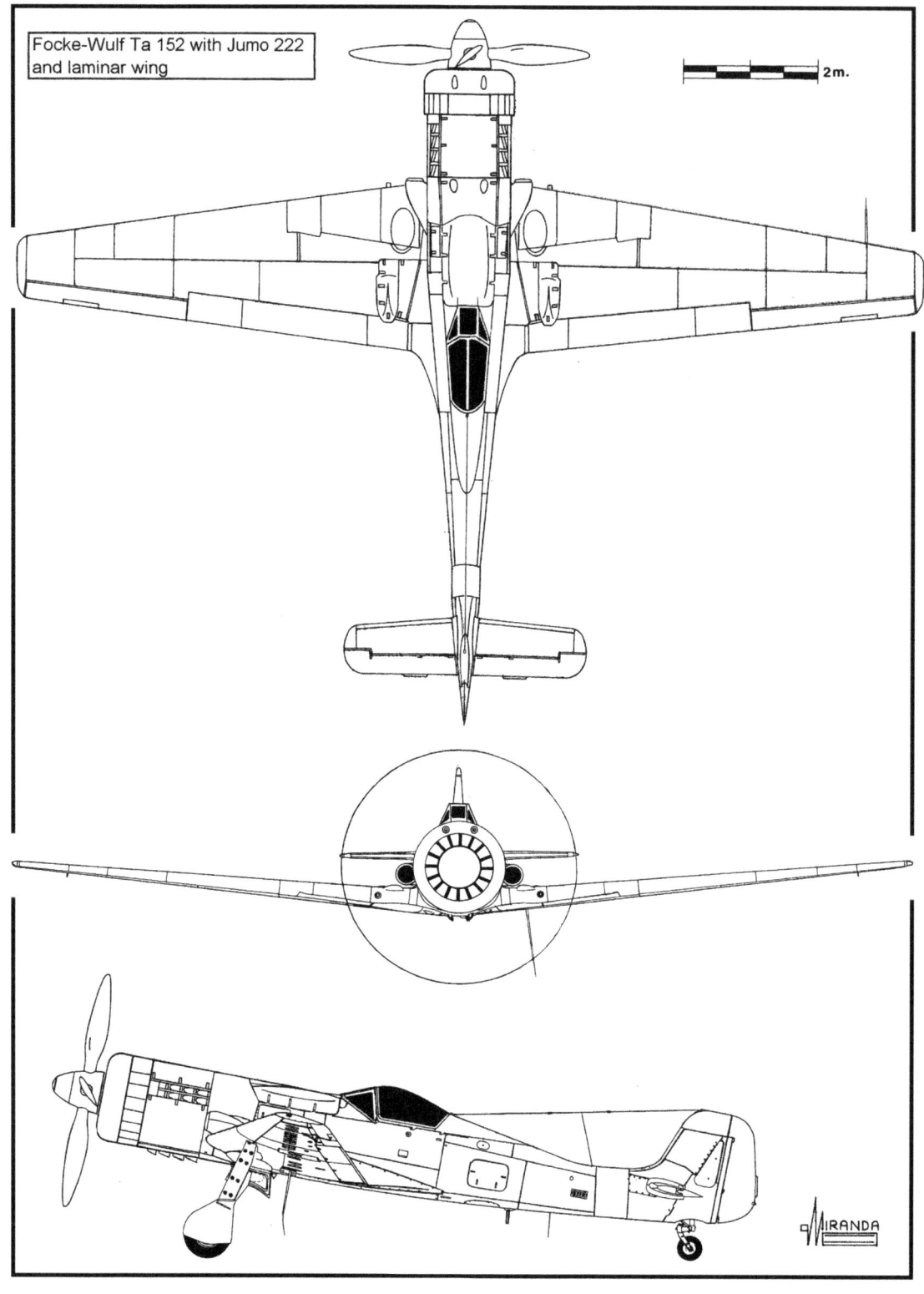

Focke-Wulf Ta 152 with Jumo 222
and laminar wing

2m.

Mitsubishi J4M Senden

Early in 1942 the *Kaigun Koku Hombu* issued the 17-shi-Otsu specification calling for a high-performance, land-based interceptor to supersede the Raiden.

The Kawanishi firm proposed the K-90/J3K project—a first version of the Jinpu with a Nakajima Homare engine. Mitsubishi submitted the M-70/J4M Senden, a twin-boom airframe powered by one 2,130-hp MK9D (Ha-43-42) supercharged engine, with Vulkan coupling and a forced cooling fan, driving a six-bladed pusher propeller. It was like the North American Vultee XP-54 and Swedish SAAB J-21, equipped with a tricycle landing gear.

In August 1942, Mitsubishi started the wind tunnel tests with a wooden model provided with three-bladed contra-rotating propellers. This first design, called J4M1, would be armed with a Type 5, 30-mm cannon mounted on the nose leg and two Type 99, 20-mm cannons located on both sides. The two tailfins were oval-shaped like those of the Lockheed P-38.

J4M1 Technical Data

Wingspan: 12.5 m
Length: 12.5 m
Wing area: 24.7 sq. m

The IJN considered that the engine cooling system was insufficient, and in the next version (J4M2 in March 1943), two dorsal air intakes and one ventral were installed. This version was called 'Plan-A' and had triangular tailfins and a modified windshield. The counter-rotating propellers were replaced by a four-bladed, constant-speed propeller with a diameter of 3.2 m and a breakaway mechanism to allow the pilot to bail-out.

J4M2 Technical Data

Wingspan: 12.5 m
Length: 12.5 m
Wing area: 22 sq. m
Max. weight: 4,886 kg

The J4M2 wind tunnel tests showed the hard vibration of the tail horizontal stabiliser, which was replaced by one with a smaller surface area located in an elevated position to avoid compressibility problems. In March 1943, the J4M3 mock-up was ready for *Kaigun Koku Hombu* inspection. The new design, called 'Plan-B', had evolved aerodynamically to compensate for the excessive drag generated by the high tailplane.

The windshield design was changed to a bubble canopy and the air scoops were replaced by eight suction inlets. The tailfins had more rounded shapes and the armament was increased to four cannons. It was proposed to replace the propeller with a Sumitomo six-bladed, constant-speed propeller with a diameter of 3.2 m.

J4M3 Technical Data

Wingspan: 12.5 m
Length: 13 m
Wing area: 22 sq. m
Max. weight: 4,400 kg

The J4M4 was the definitive version, with triangular tailfins and three cannons, proposed to *Kaigun Koku Hombu* in October 1944, but the Senden was cancelled shortly after, due to the failure of the Vulkan coupling development and excessive vibrations in the extended shaft.

J4M4 Technical Data

Wingspan: 12.5 m
Length: 13 m
Wing area: 22 sq. m
Max. weight: 5,260 kg
Max. speed: 703 kph
Service ceiling: 12,000 m

To circumvent the numerous problems caused by the engine, Mitsubishi considered using the Sakae IPR, a Campini thermojet with 600–740 kgf static thrust. This type of power plant consisted of a 920-hp Nakajima Sakae 11 radial engine driving a five-stage axial compressor at 5,280 rpm.

The compressed air was mixed with 74-octane sprayed fuel in a 2.43-m-long combustion chamber, burning at 1,000 degrees C before being ejected by an exhaust nozzle at 350 m/s. Unofficial drawings have been published depicting a J4M1 powered by a Yokosuka Ne 12 (TR 30) centrifugal turbojet, a J4M3m and a J4M4 with Kugisho Ne 330 axial turbojets.

The Swedes came to the same conclusion and in 1947 replaced the Daimler-Benz 605 piston engine of the SAAB J-21 with a DH Goblin centrifugal turbojet.

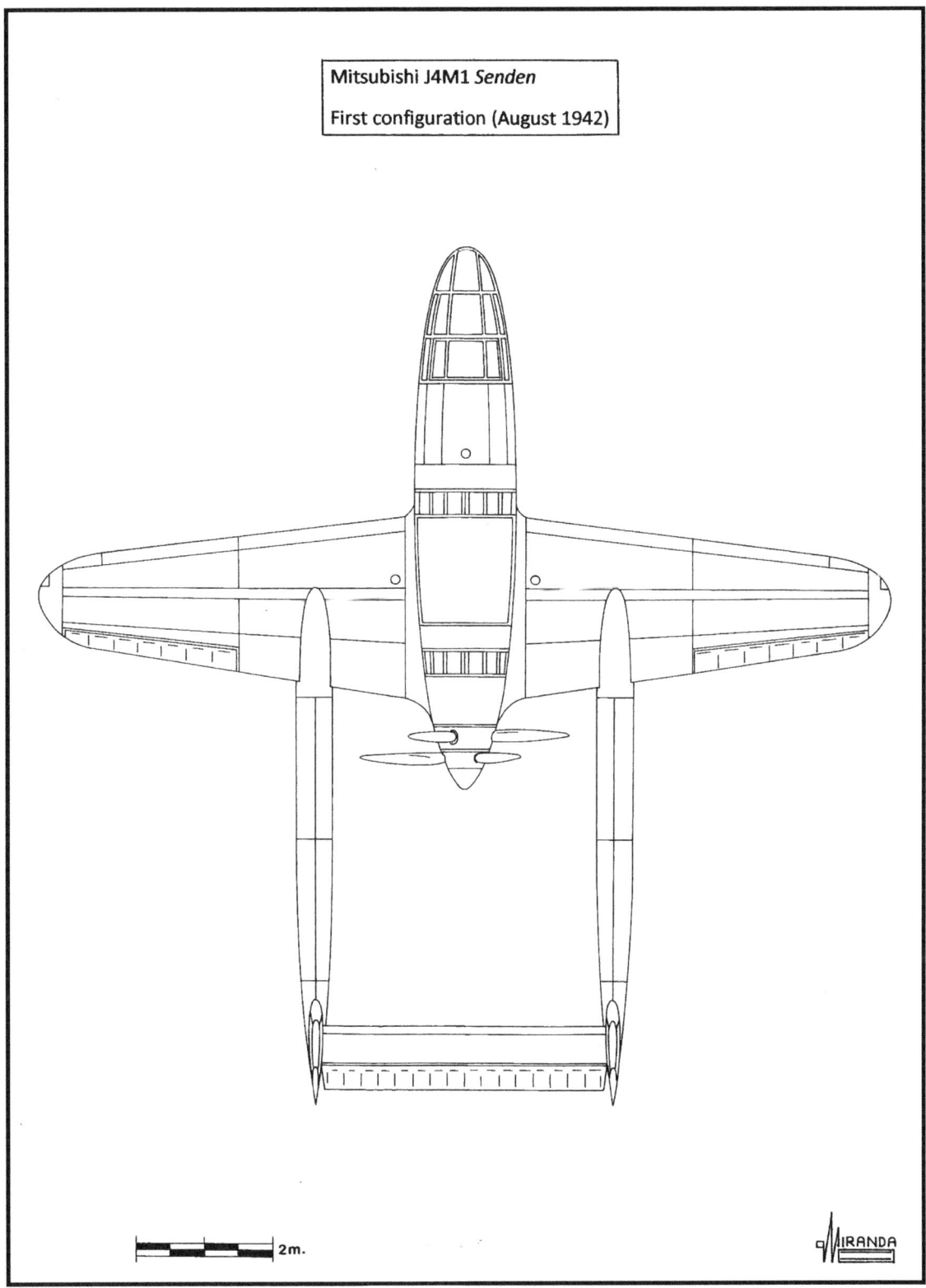

Mitsubishi J4M1 *Senden*

First configuration (August 1942)

2m.

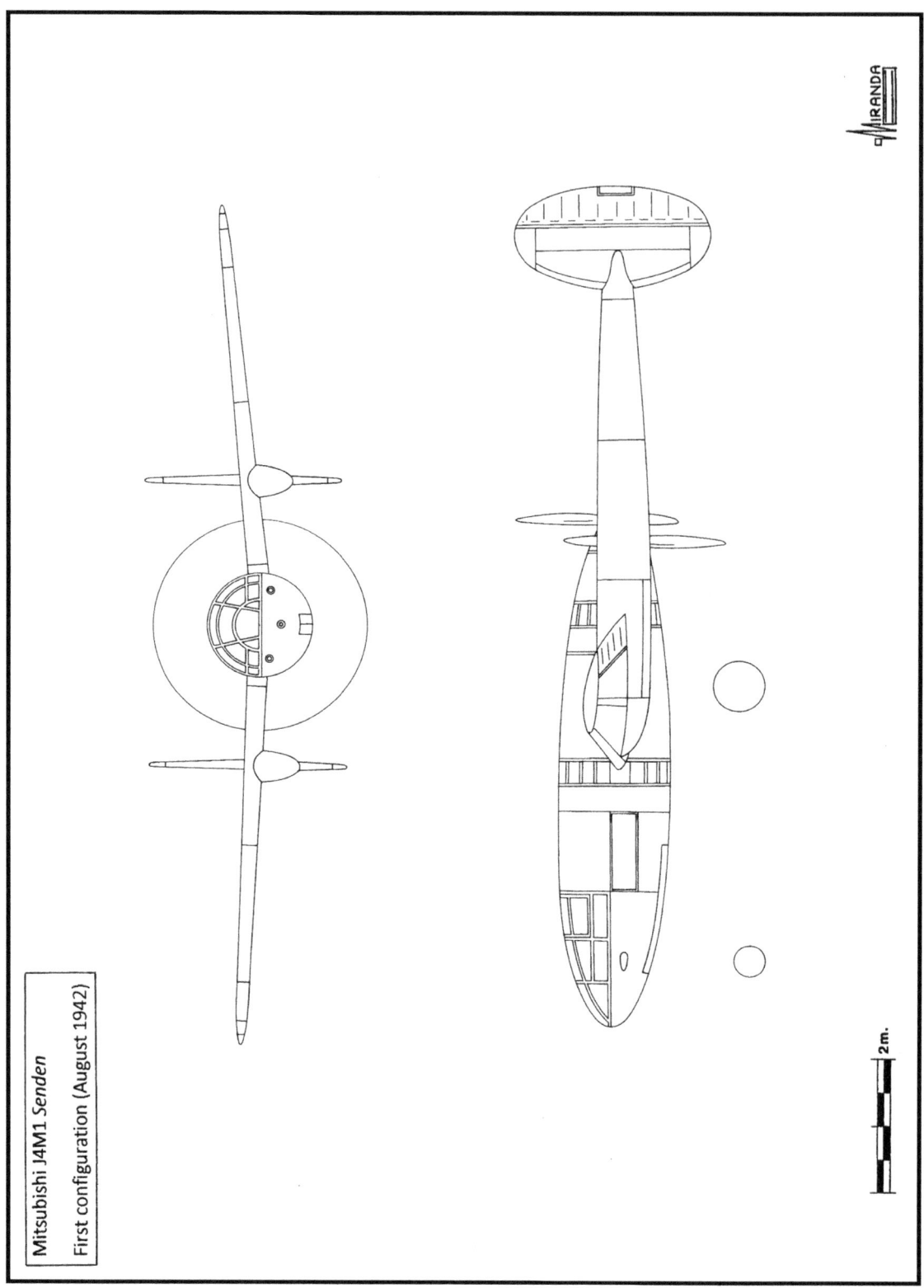

Mitsubishi J4M1 *Senden*

First configuration (August 1942)

2 m.

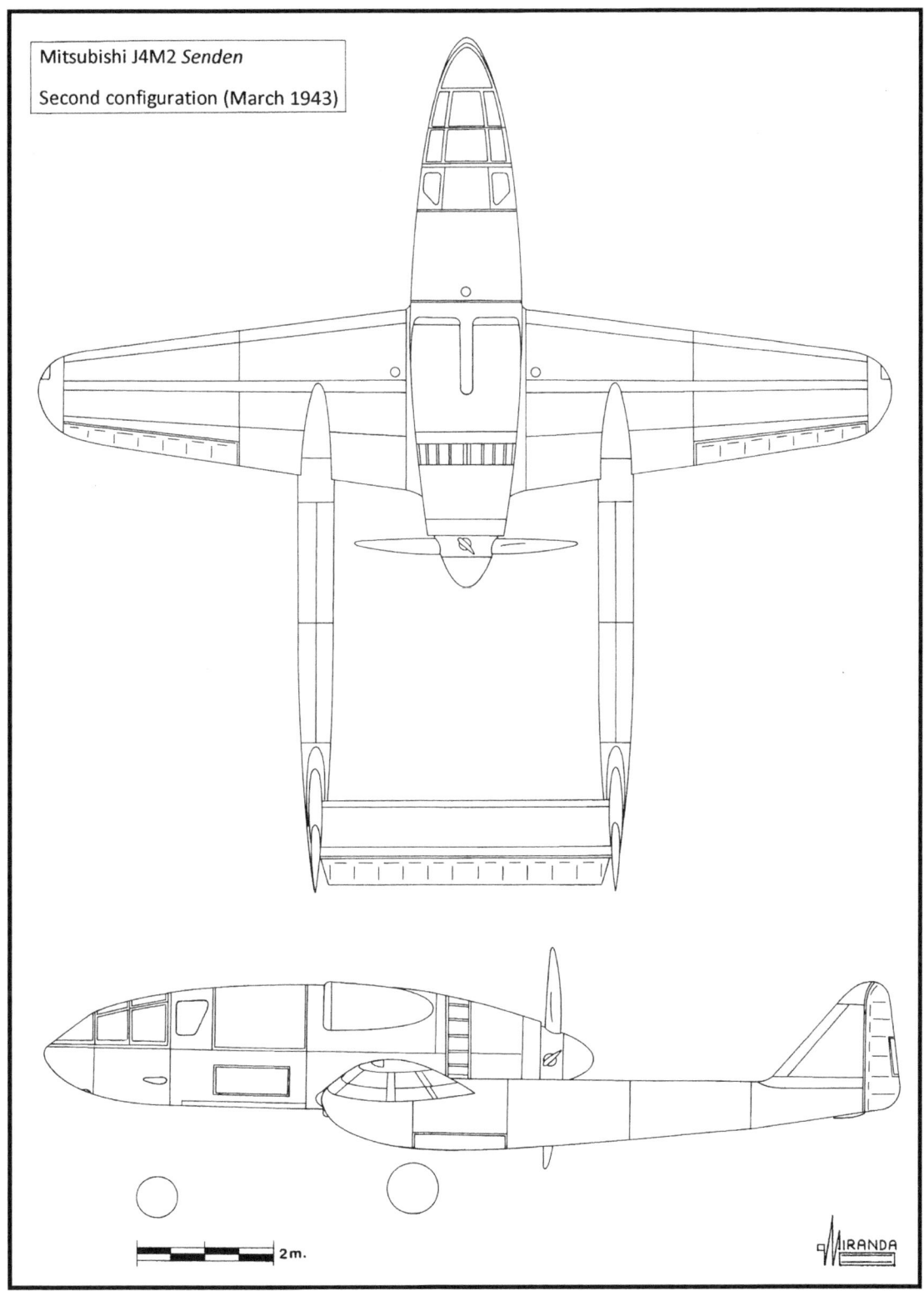

Mitsubishi J4M2 *Senden*

Second configuration (March 1943)

2 m.

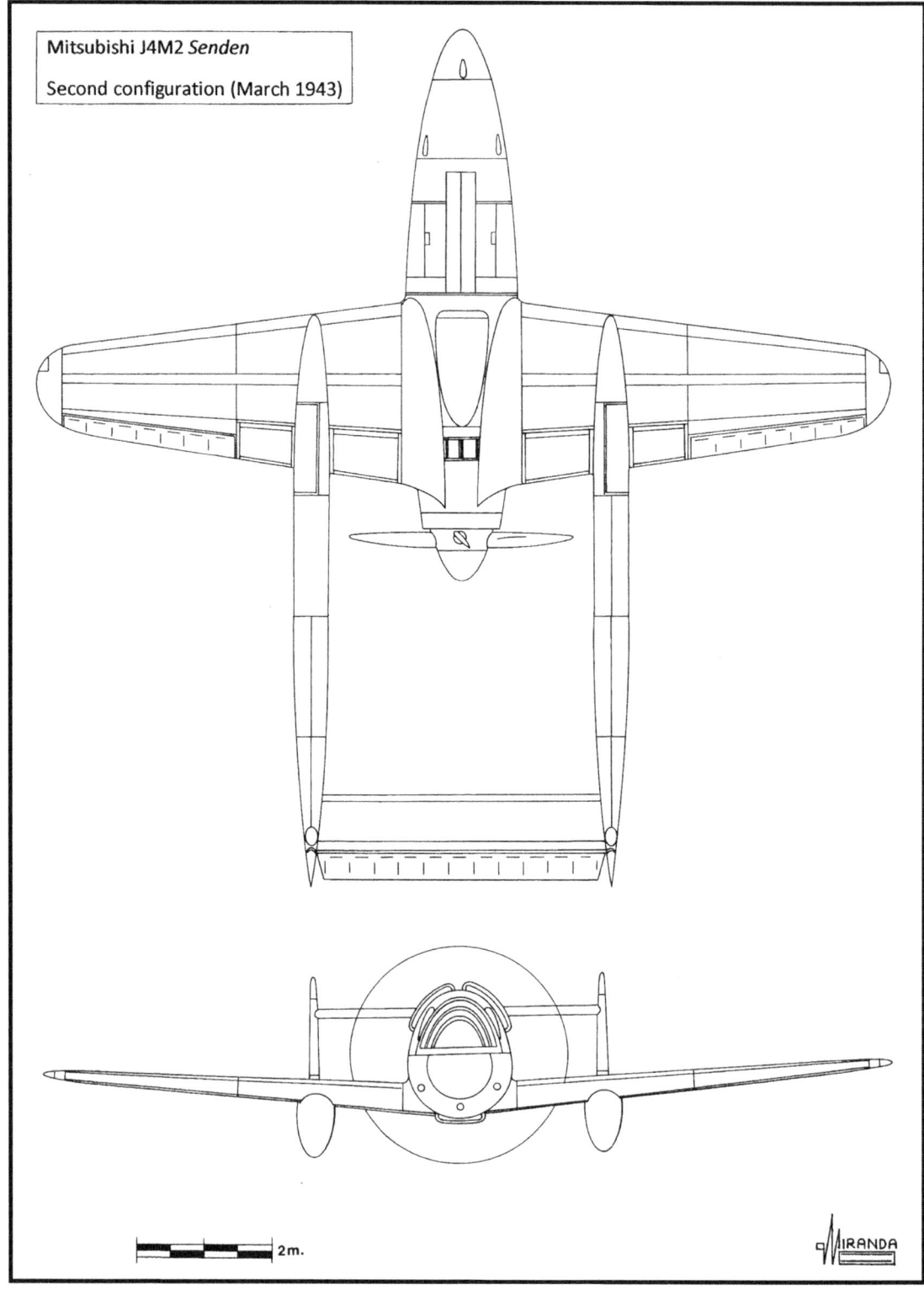

Mitsubishi J4M2 *Senden*

Second configuration (March 1943)

2m.

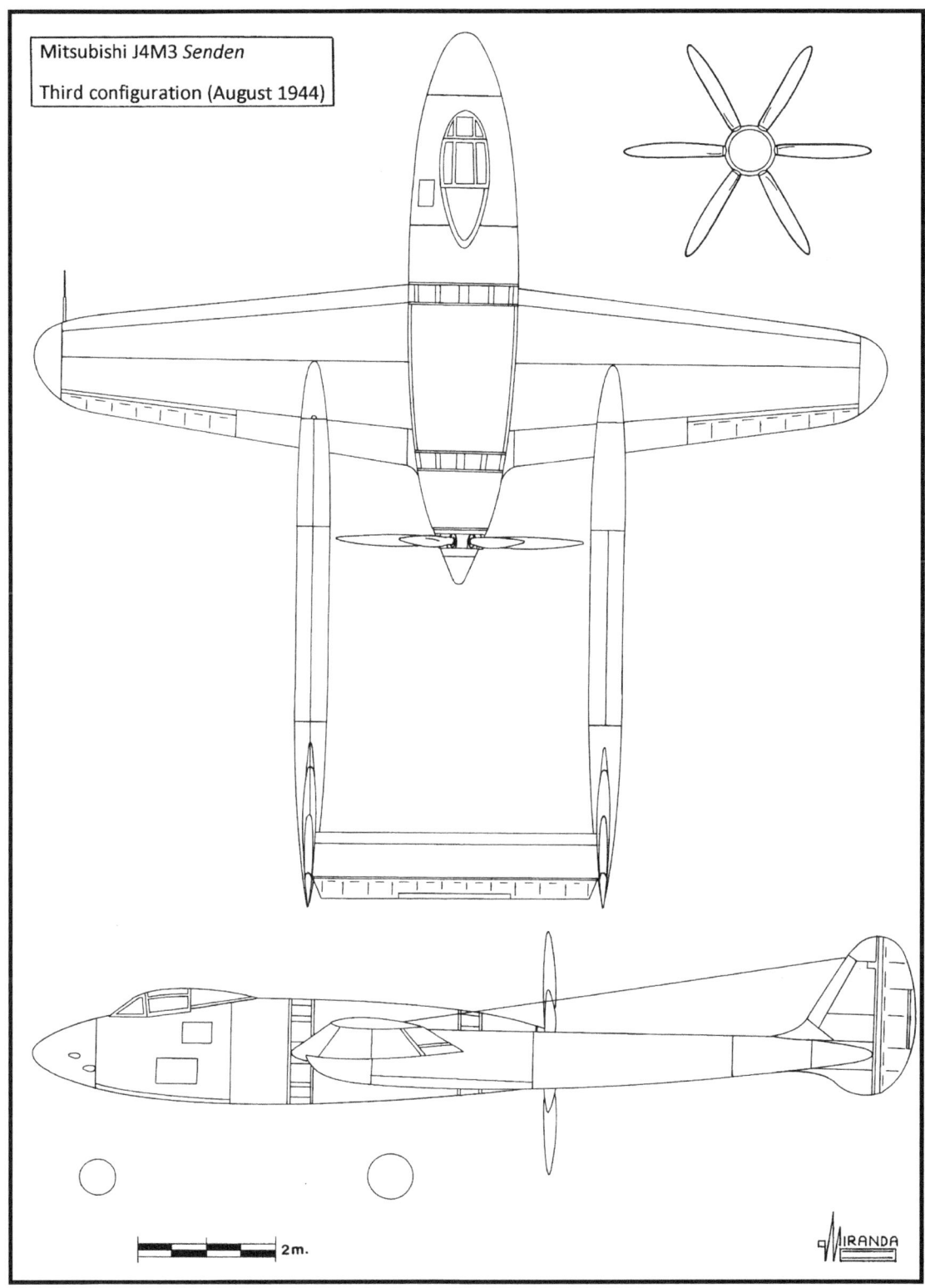

Mitsubishi J4M3 *Senden*

Third configuration (August 1944)

2m.

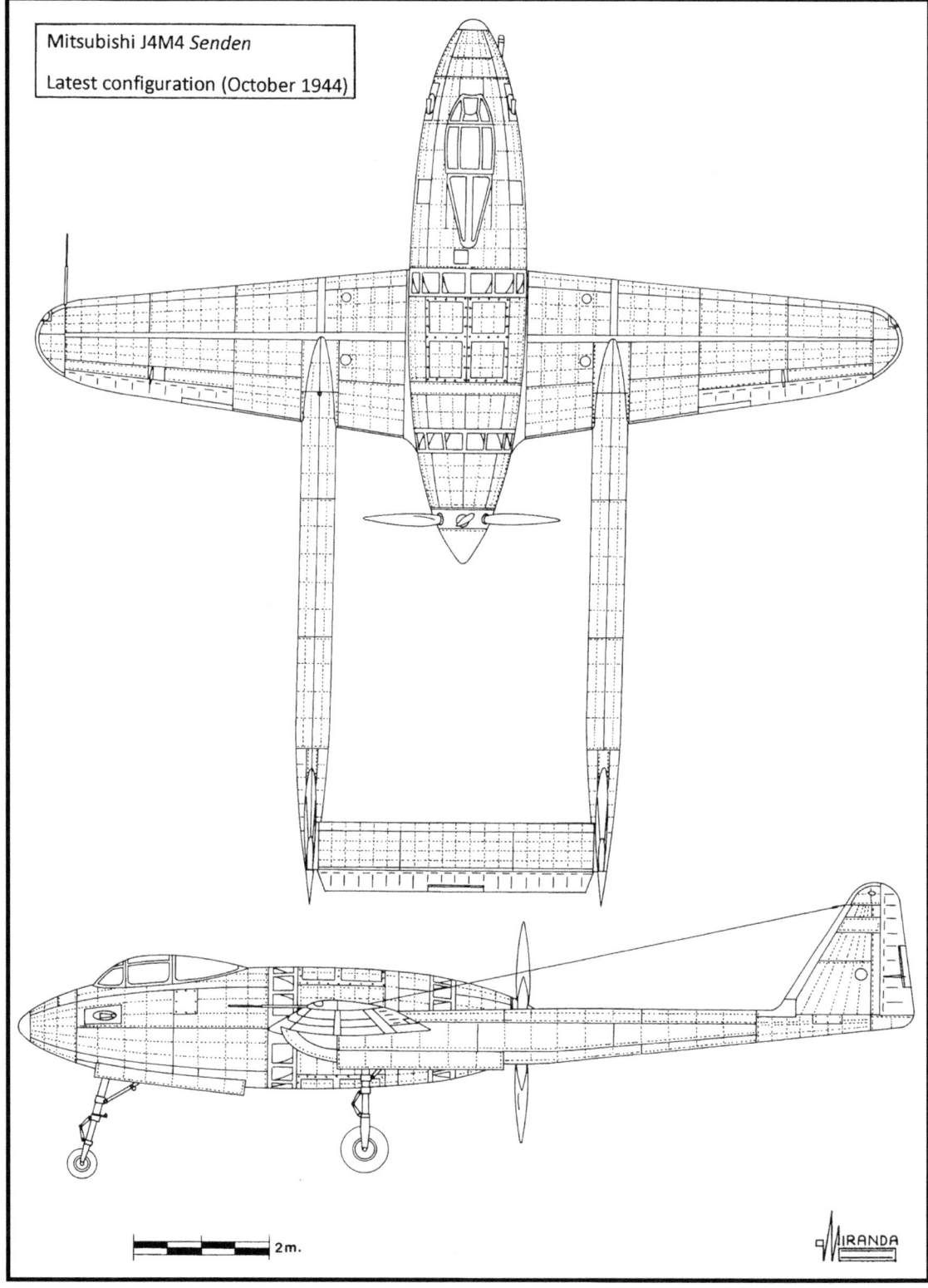

Mitsubishi J4M4 *Senden*

Latest configuration (October 1944)

2 m.

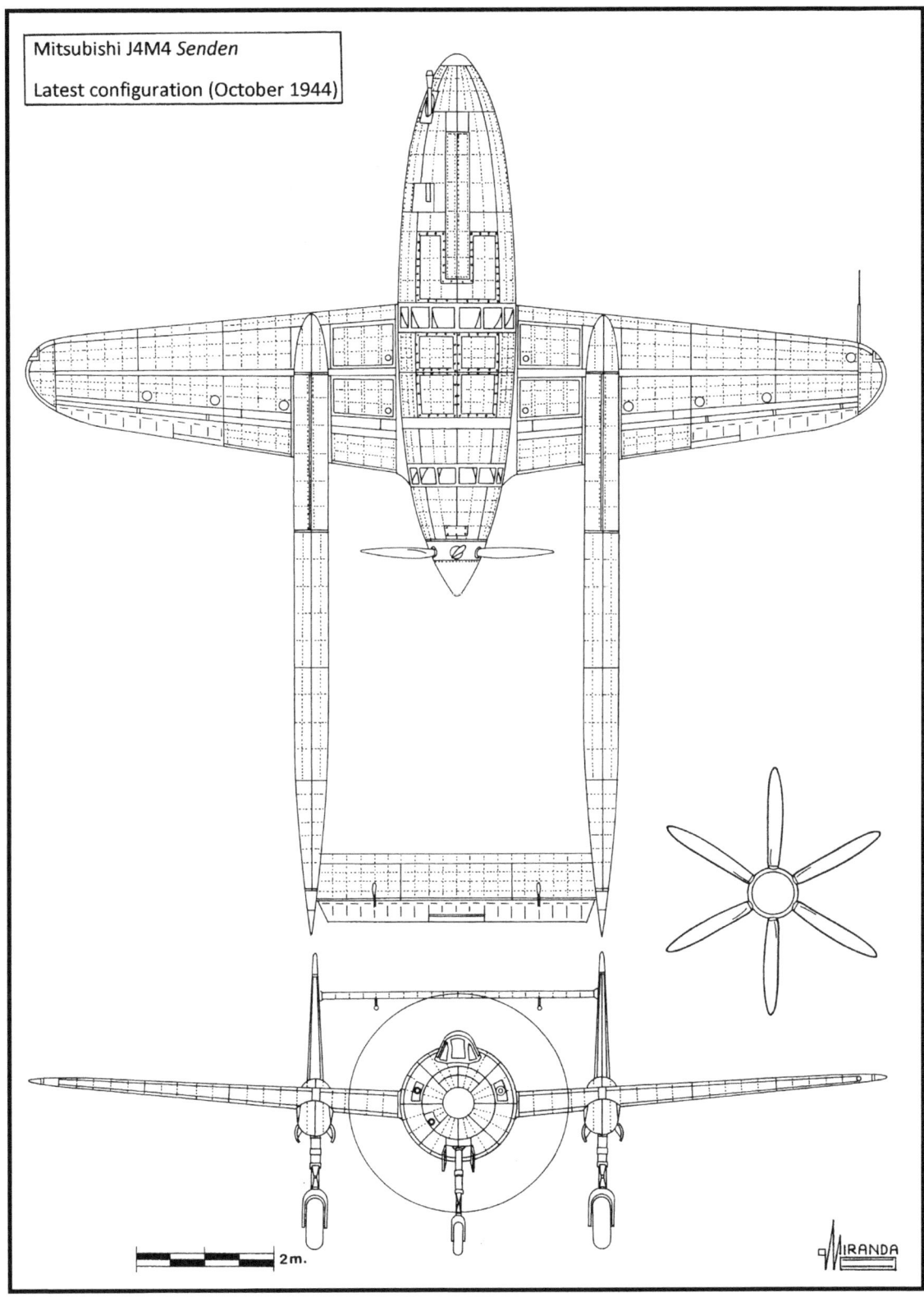

Mitsubishi J4M4 *Senden*

Latest configuration (October 1944)

2 m.

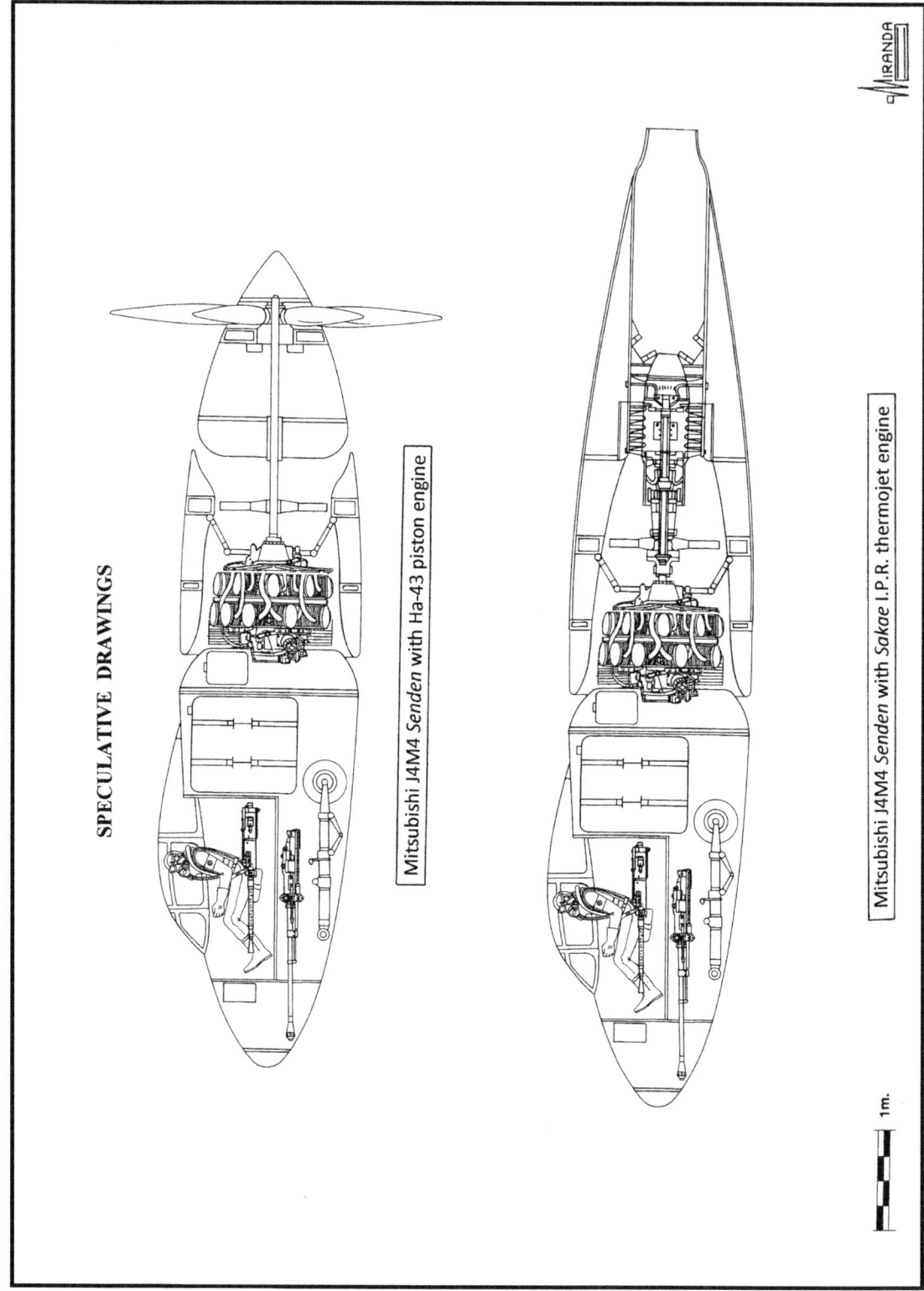

SPECULATIVE DRAWINGS

Mitsubishi J4M4 *Senden* with Ha-43 piston engine

Mitsubishi J4M4 *Senden* with *Sakae* I.P.R. thermojet engine

1 m.

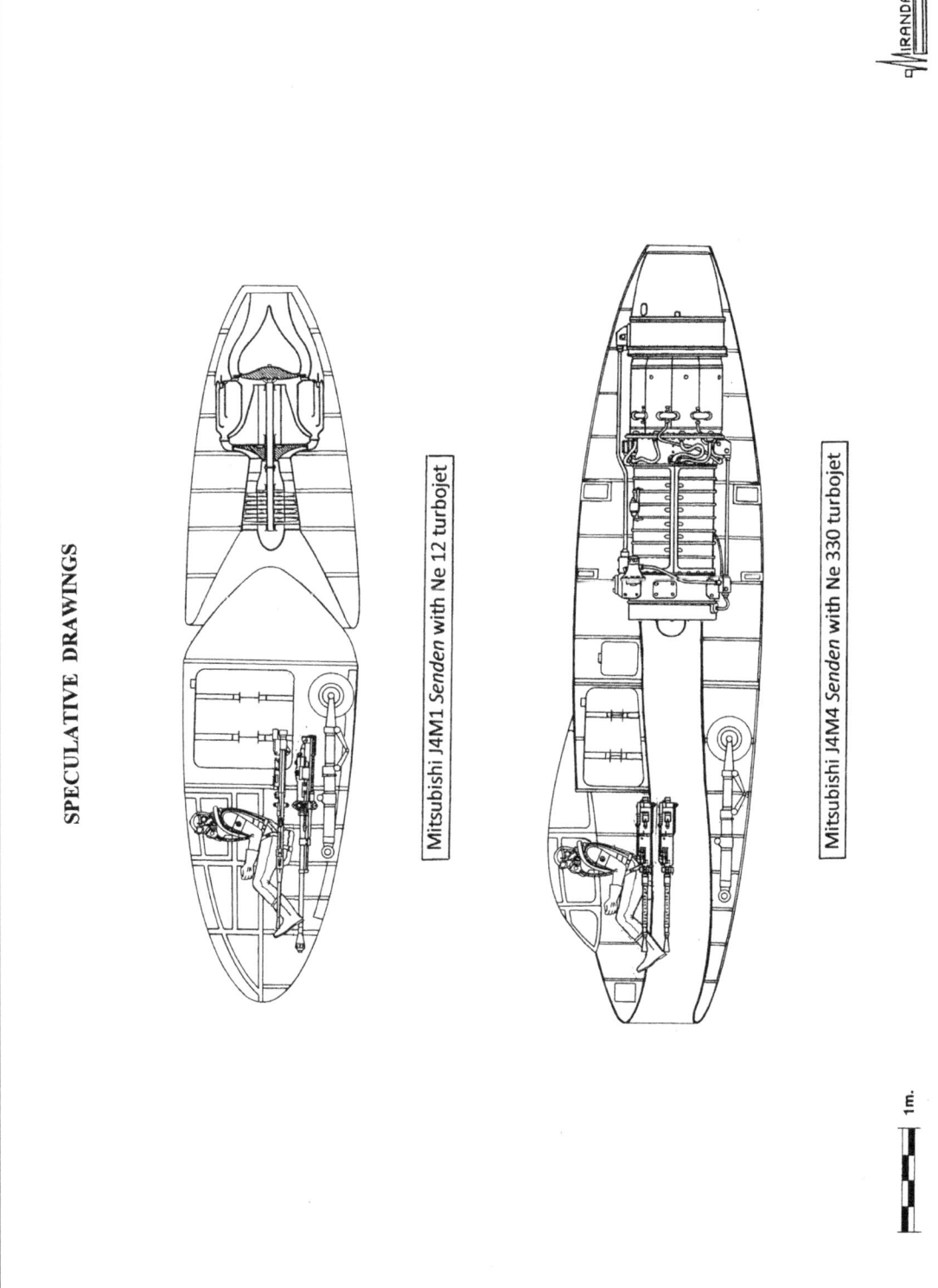

SPECULATIVE DRAWINGS

Mitsubishi J4M1 *Senden* with Ne 12 turbojet

Mitsubishi J4M4 *Senden* with Ne 330 turbojet

1 m.

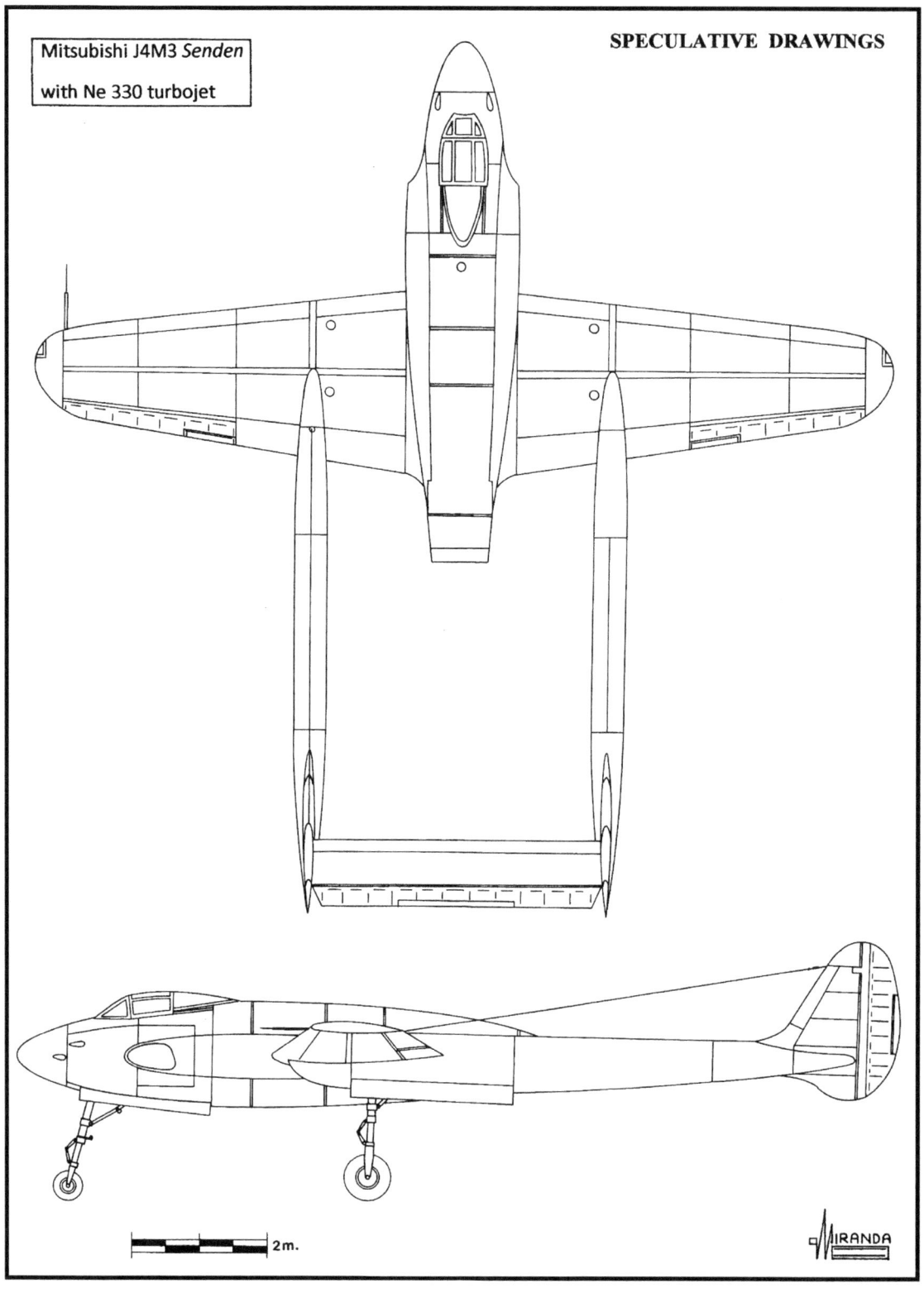

Mitsubishi J4M3 *Senden*

with Ne 330 turbojet

2m.

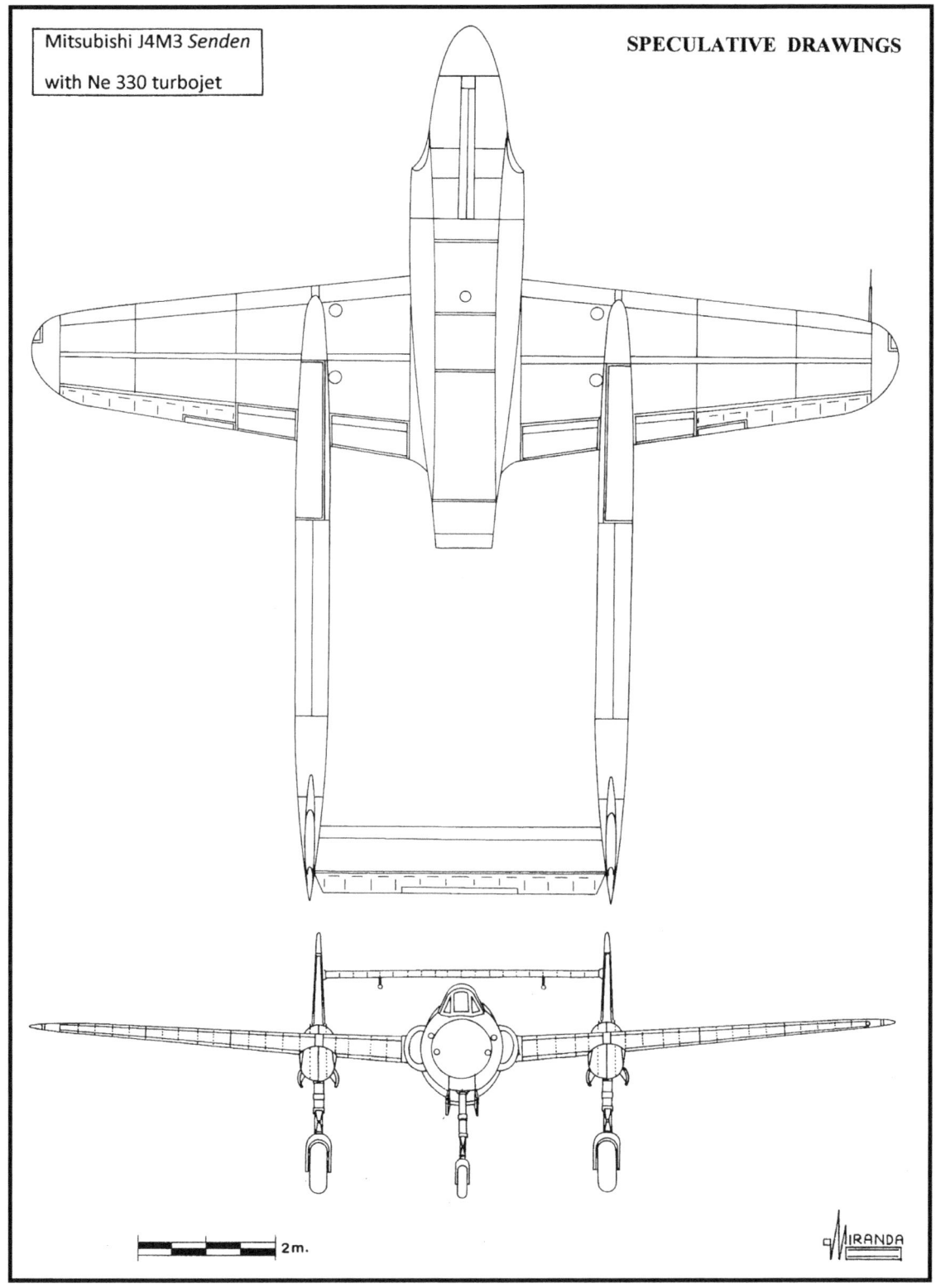

Mitsubishi J4M3 *Senden*
with Ne 330 turbojet

SPECULATIVE DRAWINGS

2 m.

MIRANDA

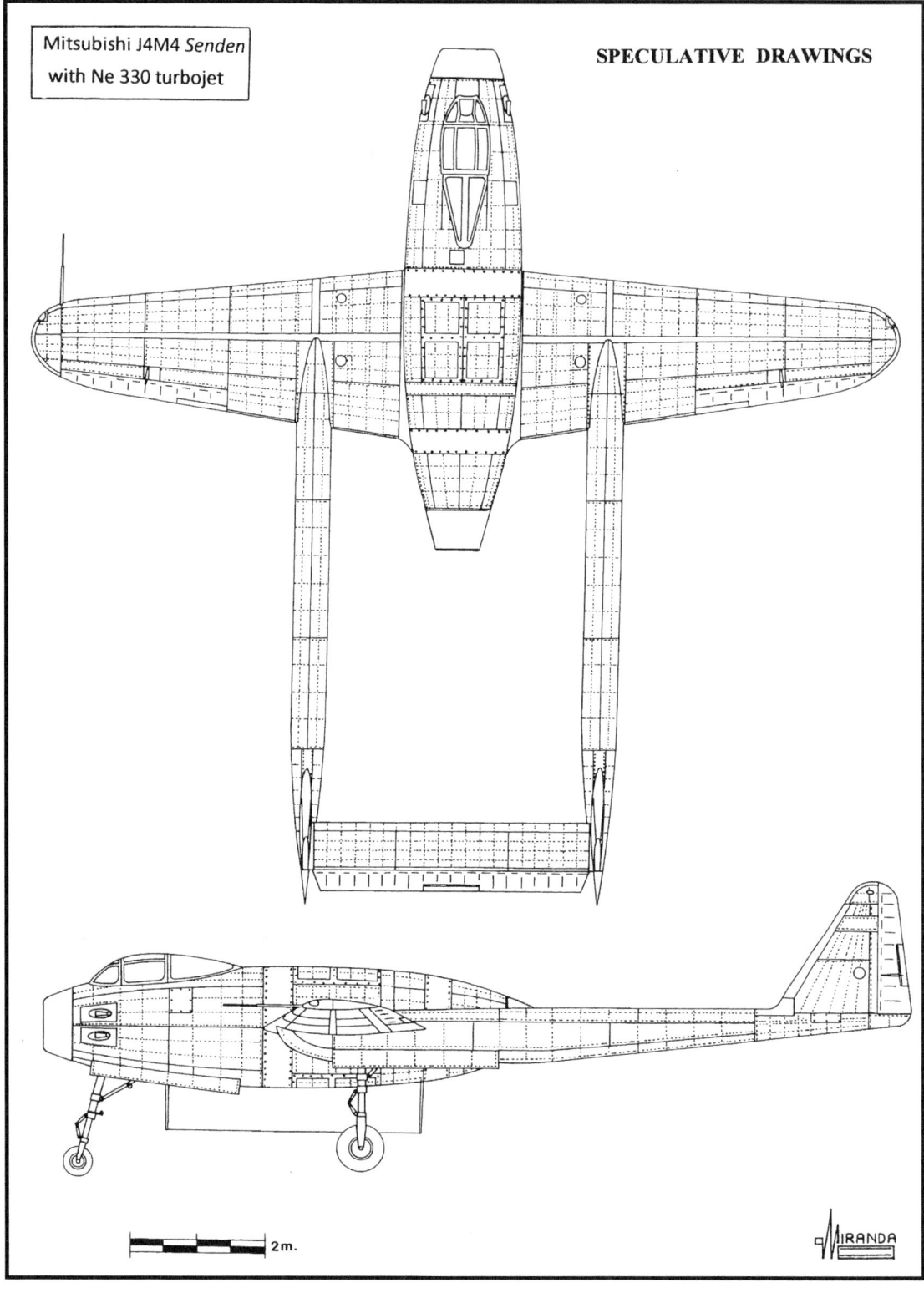

Mitsubishi J4M4 *Senden*
with Ne 330 turbojet

SPECULATIVE DRAWINGS

2 m.

MIRANDA

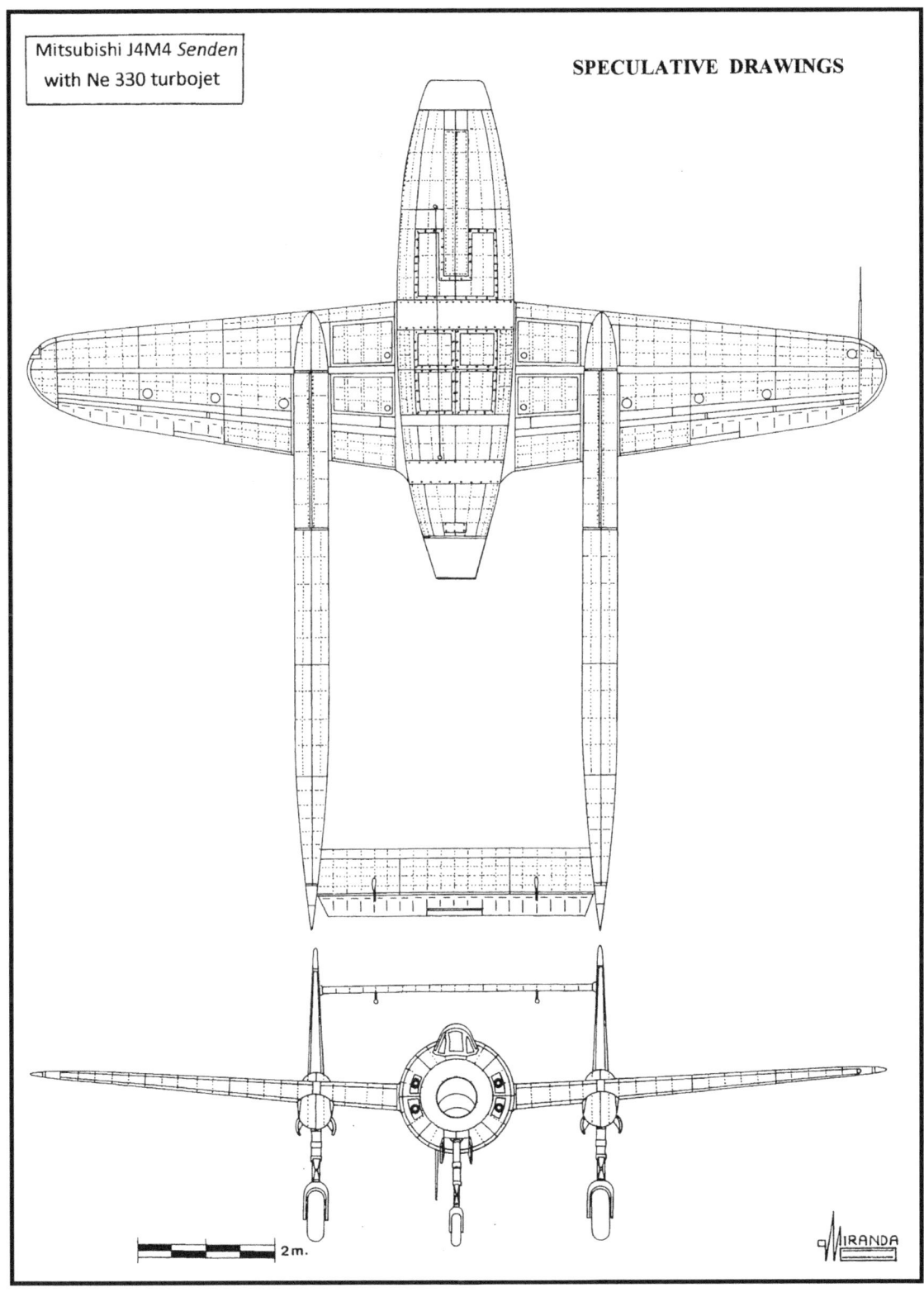

Mitsubishi J4M4 *Senden*
with Ne 330 turbojet

SPECULATIVE DRAWINGS

2 m.

SAAB J 21 RB

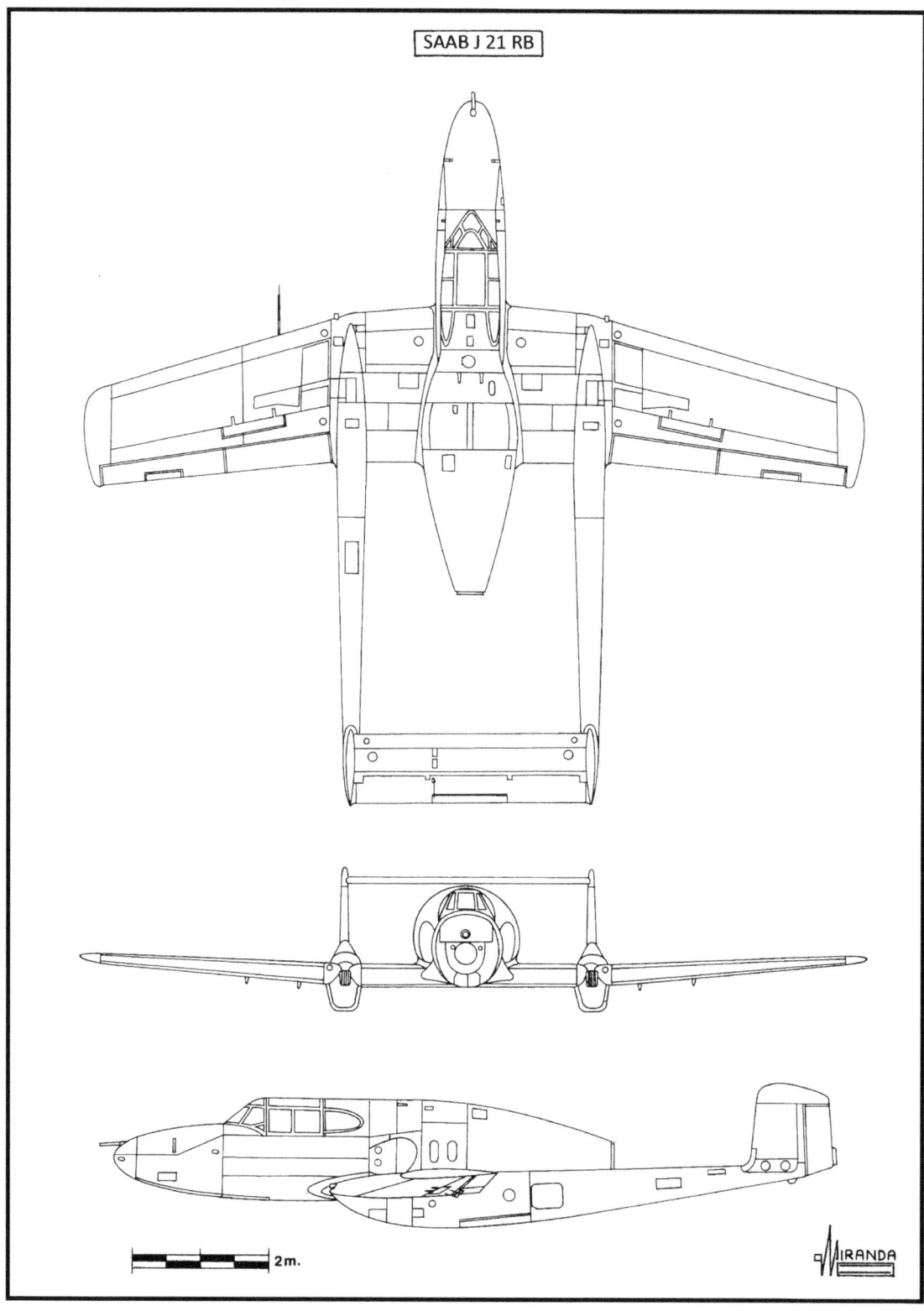

2m.

MIRANDA

Kyushu J7W1 Shinden

Throughout aviation history, there have been designs of the 'canard' or 'tail first' types as an alternative to the conventional 'engine first' configuration. However, despite the creativity of designers, manufacturers have systematically left aside the mass production of such solutions. When the second generation of fighters designed during the Second World War started to experience serious aerodynamic problems, due to the transonic flux, they made several attempts to solve them using the 'canard' configuration to eliminate airscrew slipstream effects on aircraft drag.

The British firm Miles built and tested the M.35 and M.39B prototypes as technical demonstrators of the M.39 bomber. The German Henschel designed the heavy fighter named P.75 that was propelled by a DB 613 A/B coupled engine, though mass production was abandoned in favour of the Dornier Do 335. Several prototypes of 'canard' fighters were built in Italy and the USA.

The 'canard' formula had many advantages for the design of fighters: the armament could be grouped around the nose without any hindrance by either the engine or the propeller; it was easily accessible for maintenance; ground visibility was considerably improved; and it was easier to install a tricycle type undercarriage. The engine, located behind the pilot, acted as protection against the rear impacts, and in the event of a fire, flames did not go to the cockpit as used to happen with the classical designs. Besides, being joined to the main spar meant less weight and stronger structural sturdiness.

In combat, an enemy pilot not familiar with the new configuration could easily mistake the direction to which the canard fighter moved during the deflection aiming. The same tactic is used by some tropical fish that have a spot in the shape of a false eye near the tail to confuse their predators. Only two problems marred all the advantages: the difficulty to refrigerate the engine and the bailing out, due to the position of the pusher airscrews.

At a time when ejector seats did not yet exist, the solution was to install an explosive device to detach the propeller in case of emergency. Early in 1939, the Italians built the Ambrosini SS.4, a 'canard' prototype fighter powered by one 960-hp Isotta Fraschini Asso XI RC.40 engine. The aircraft was destroyed in 1941 due to a vibration problem in the engine mount, and the project was cancelled.

On 21 December 1941, the 'canard' prototype Curtiss CW-24B made its first flight at Muroc airbase, powered by a 275-hp Menasco C-6S-5 engine. Despite the strong security measures, the intelligence services of the IJN obtained enough information about the project to believe that it was the successor of the Curtiss P-40 fighter. In fact, the definitive Curtiss XP-55 version was not selected by the USAAC for production, and only three prototypes were built, two of which were destroyed in accidents.

Americans were not lucky with the Curtiss XP-55. After four years of flight testing, they had not achieved an aeroplane sufficiently stable to take part in combat operations. Although it was less sensitive to the compressibility buffeting than conventional aircraft, thanks to a NACA 0015-type wing profile, it was also too heavy and slower than the P-47 and P-51 in service.

Before cancelling the project, Curtiss proposed the production of a jet version based on the original P 249-C project, known in the specialised literature as P 286-17 or CW

24-C. It would have been propelled by a centrifugal de Havilland H-1B Goblin turbojet with a 1,059-l fuel tank located behind the pilot and armed with four 0.50-calibre M2 machine guns. Its mass production was abandoned in favour of the Lockheed P-80.

To meet the 1943 IJN requirements (18-shi-Otsu non-official specification) calling for a land-based, high-performance interceptor able to counter the new Allied fighters, Nakajima proposed the twin-engined J5N1 Tenrai and Kawasaki the J6K1 Jinpu. Early in 1943, Lieutenant Commander Masaoki Tsuruno of the First Naval Air Technical Arsenal proposed the construction of an 18-shi-Otsu 'canard' fighter based on the information obtained on the XP-55.

The *Kaigun Koku Hombu* ordered the firm Chigasaki Seizo KK to construct three wooden experimental gliders—MXY6—with 'canard' lifting surfaces to prove the feasibility of the concept. Glider tests, towed by one Nakajima B5N bomber, began at Yokosuka in autumn 1943, demonstrating good flight characteristics. One of the prototypes was finally fitted with a 22-hp Nihon Semi Ha-90/11 four-cylinder-boxer, air-cooled engine, driving a two-bladed wooden airscrew from a Kugisho MXY4 anti-aircraft target.

In 1945, the MXY6 was proposed to the IJN as a prototype suicide plane, but the project was not carried out because of the priority given to the construction of the Showa Toka bomber.

MXY6 3rd Prototype Technical Data

Wingspan: 9.14 m
Length: 7.3 m
Height: 2.95 m
Wing area: 17 sq. m
Max. weight: 500 kg
Max. speed: 320 kph

After promising MXY6 tests, the *Kaigun Koku Hombu* ordered the Kyushu Hikoki KK (Watanabe Tekkosho) to design a high-performance 'canard' interceptor. An one-sixth-scale wind tunnel model was tested by September 1944. Construction of the X-18/J7W1 prototype, equipped with laminar flow wings with a 45 per cent maximum thickness of the chord, had already begun on 4 June and was completed in April 1945. The engine selected by the IJN was a 2,130-hp Mitsubishi MK9D (Ha-43-42) radial engine (without the torque converter of the Ha-43-21) with a two-speed mechanical first stage and Vulkan coupling second stage turbocharger, methanol injection and forced cooling fan. The Sumitomo/VDM six-bladed, constant-speed pusher propeller had a diameter of 3.4 m.

It was decided that the production version would be armed with four Type 5, 30-mm cannons with 60 rpg and two Type 100, 7.92-mm machine guns. Pilot protection would consist of one 70-mm-thick armoured glass windshield and one 16-mm-thick anti-bullet board armour plate. The first flight of the prototype took place on 3 August 1945.

During testing, the plane suffered cooling problems while running the engine still on the ground, the powerful MK9D generated a great deal of torque and the aircraft pulled hard starboard at take off. Small retractable wheels were added to the base of each fin to prevent tail damage upon landing. In flight, the prototype showed strong vibrations in the propeller and its extended drive shaft. The IJN expected production of 150 aircraft per month during 1946, built by Kyushu and Nakajima, but the construction of the second prototype was not completed.

J7W1 Technical Data

Wingspan: 11.114 m
Length: 9.76 m
Height: 3.555 m
Wing area: 22.9 sq. m
Max. weight: 4,928 kg
Max. speed: 750 kph
Service ceiling: 12,000 m

When the first jet engines were available, the designers realised that the new power plant was ideal for the 'canard' fighters (less heavy than the twin booms of the Vampire type, SAAB J-21, and Vultee XP-54 and more stable than the Northrop XP-56 flying wing). Given time, the refrigeration conducts designed for the piston engine were converted into air intakes for the jet engine.

The Kyushu firm designed a jet version of the J7W1 Shinden known as J7W2 Shinden-KAI (not official name), propelled by one Ne 130 axial flux turbojet with 900 kp of thrust. The second prototype would have been possibly completed with a Ne 20 turbojet, the only one available, for flight testing. Removing the propeller would have made the use of a large landing gear unnecessary and the J7W2 would have used a smaller landing gear. Had the Second World War not ended, it could have been a formidable adversary for the B-29s.

J7W2 Technical Data

Wingspan: 11.114 m
Length: 9.76 m
Wing area: 22.9 sq. m
Max. weight: 4,930 kg
Max. speed: 800 kph

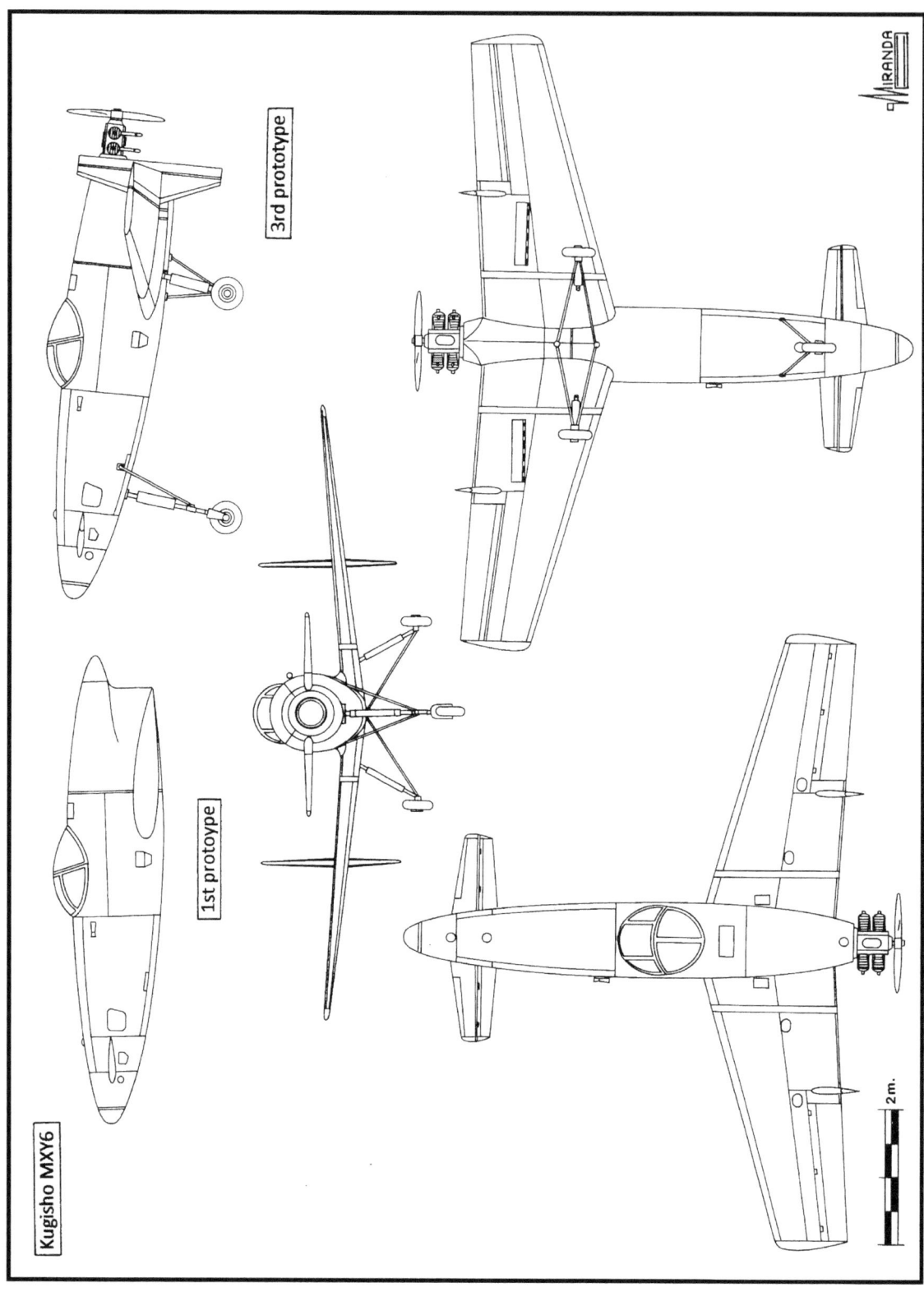

3rd prototype

1st protoype

Kugisho MXY6

2 m.

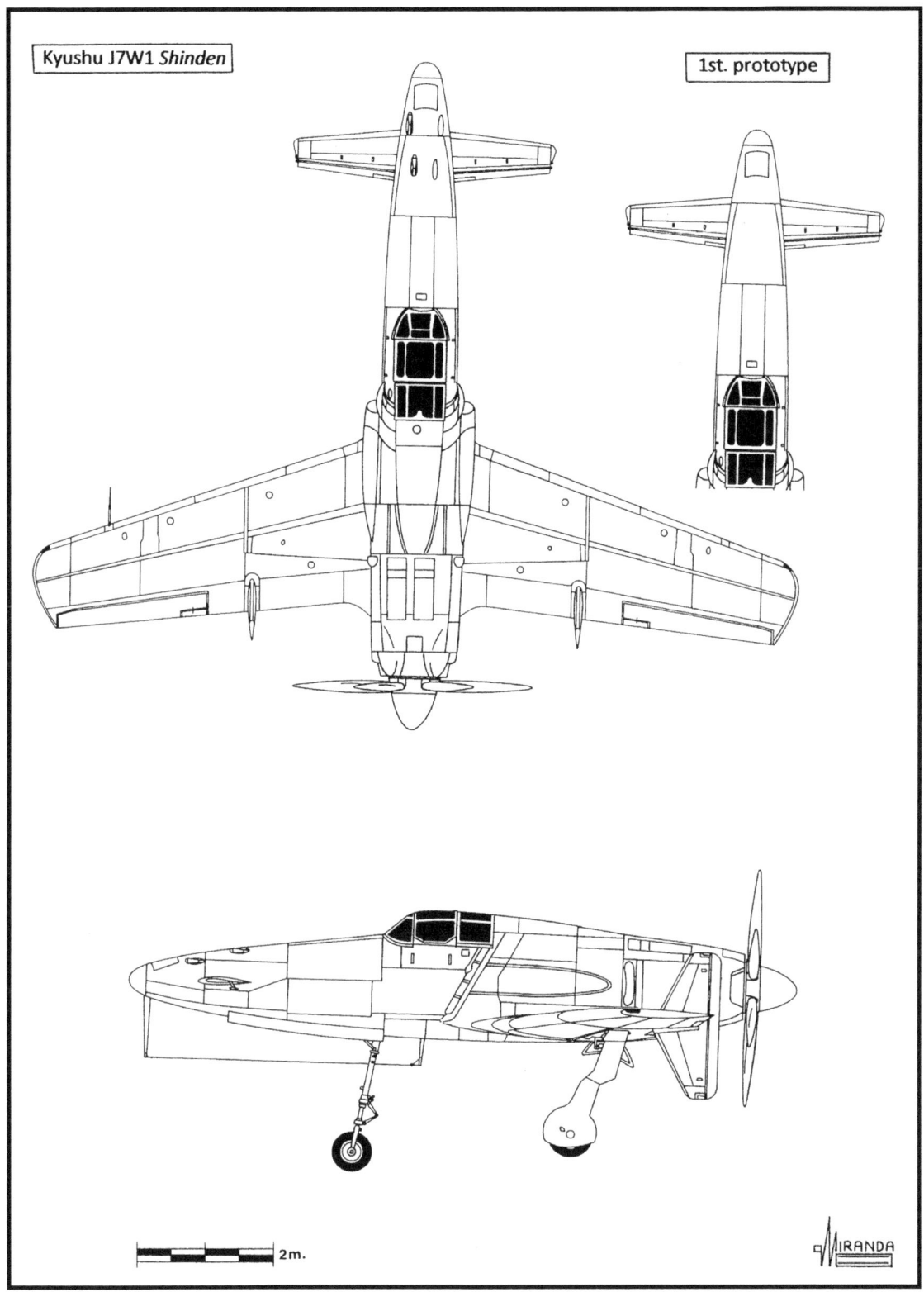

Kyushu J7W1 *Shinden*

1st. prototype

2m.

Kyushu J7W1 *Shinden*

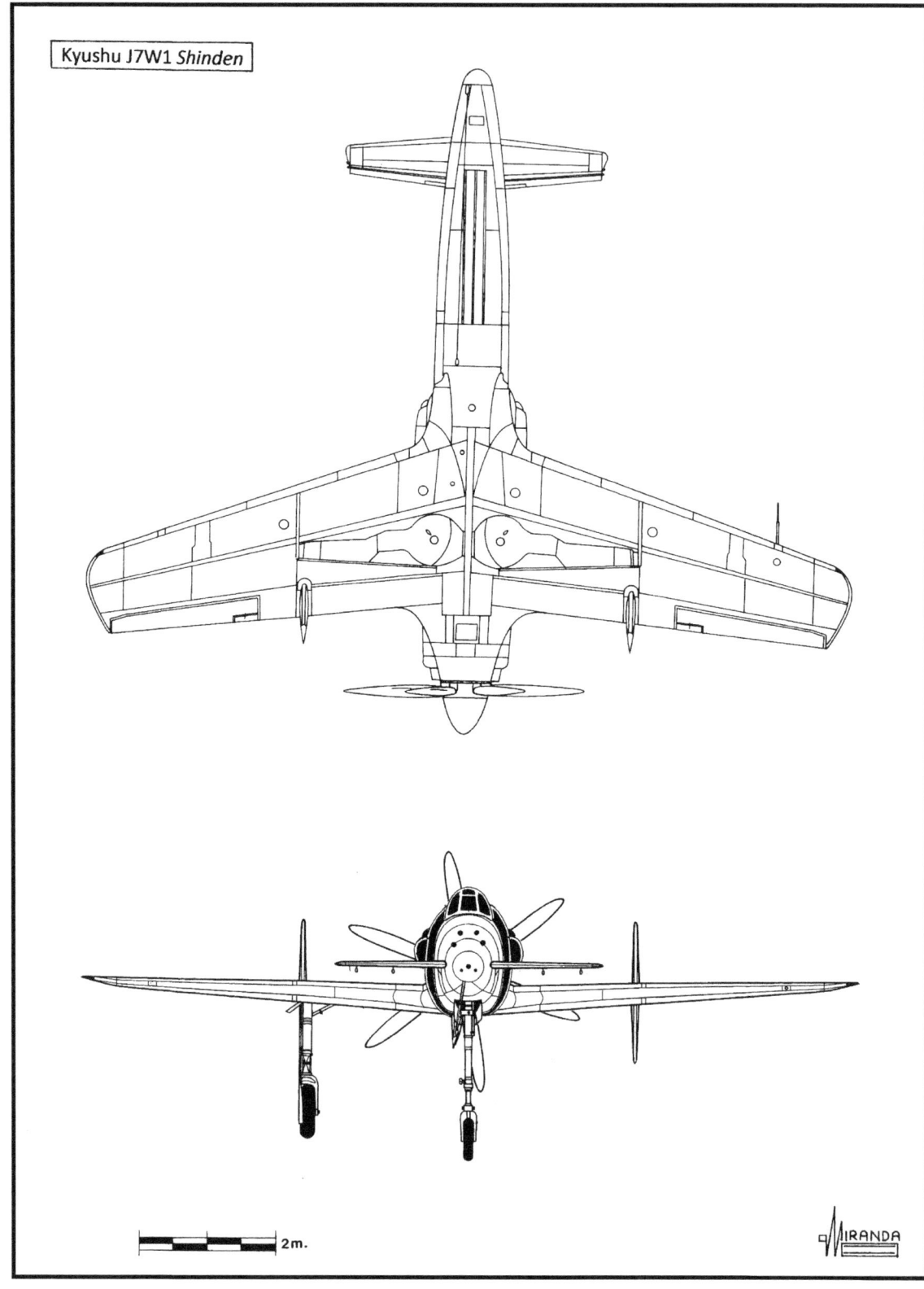

2m.

MIRANDA

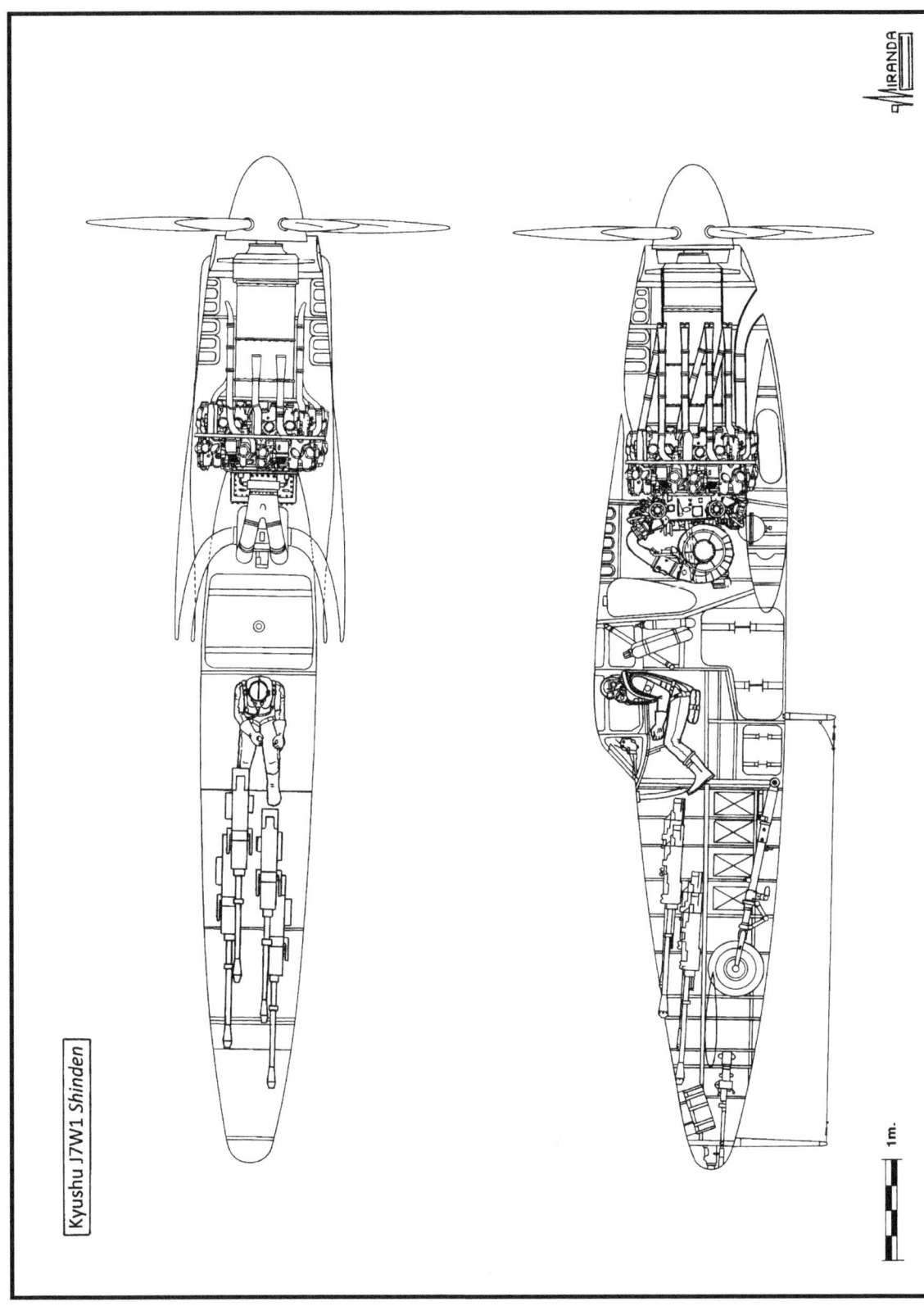

Kyushu J7W1 Shinden

1 m.

SPECULATIVE DRAWINGS

Kyushu J7W1 second prototype

Ne 20 turbojet

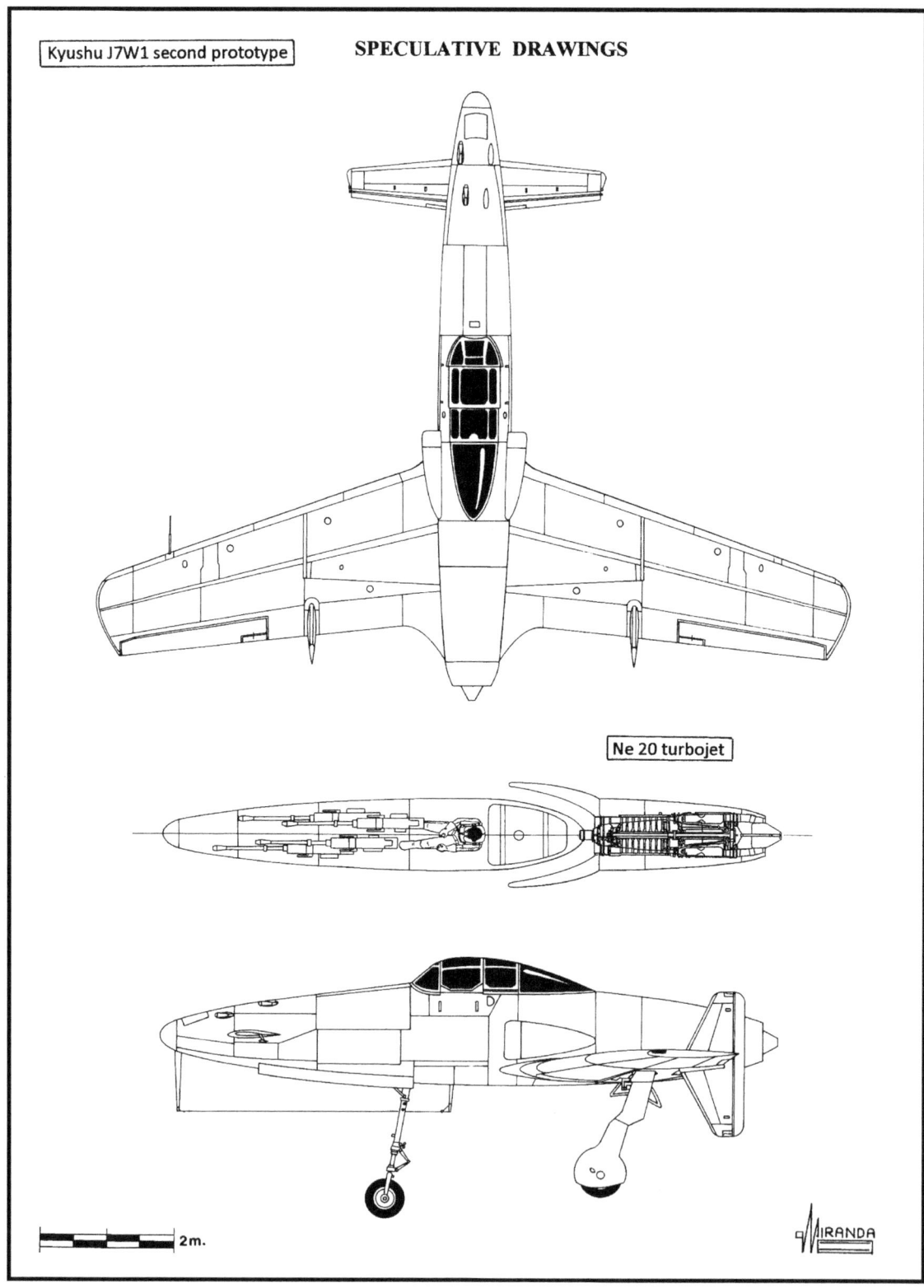

2m.

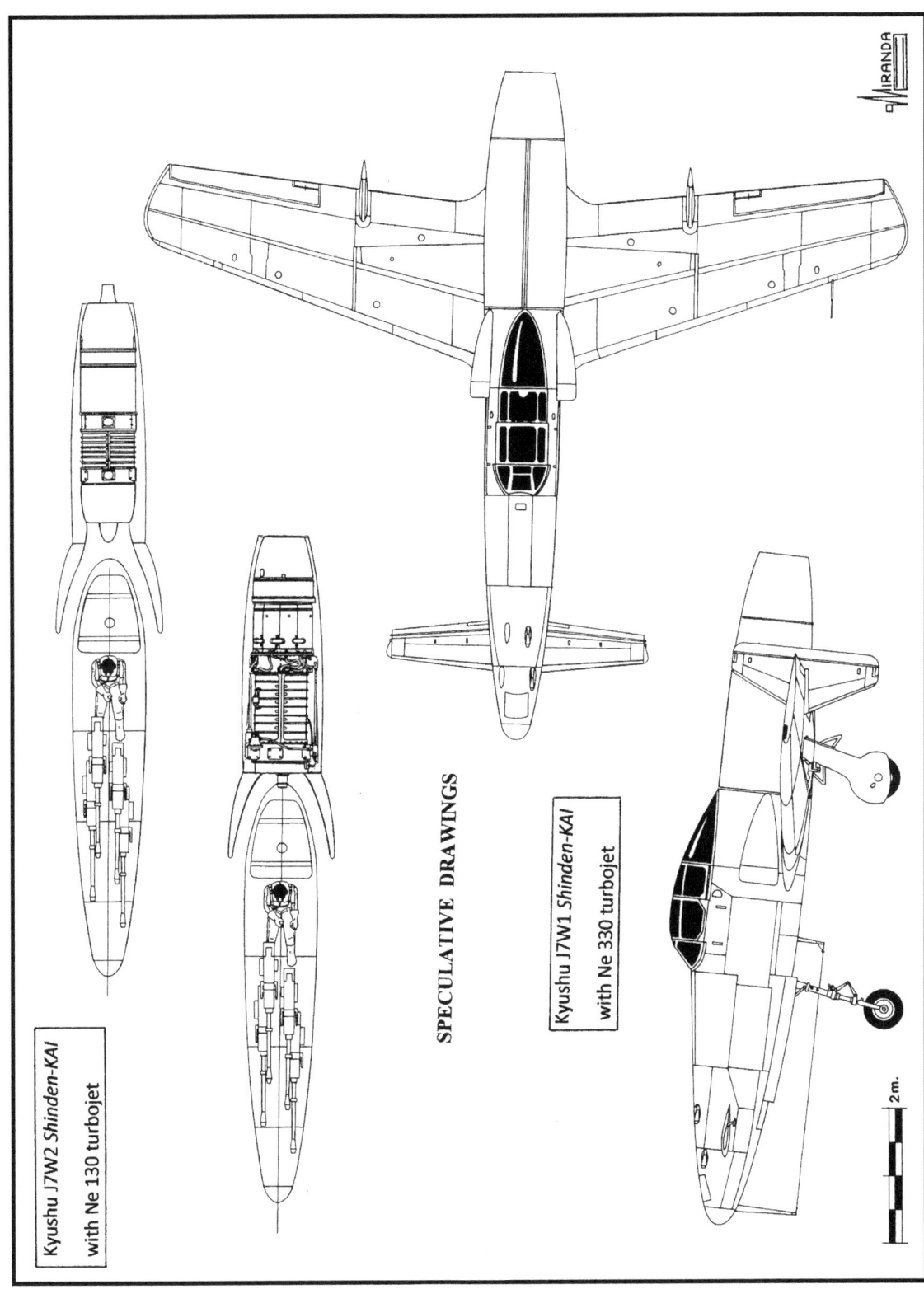

Kyushu J7W2 *Shinden-KAI*
with Ne 130 turbojet

SPECULATIVE DRAWINGS

Kyushu J7W1 *Shinden-KAI*
with Ne 330 turbojet

2 m.

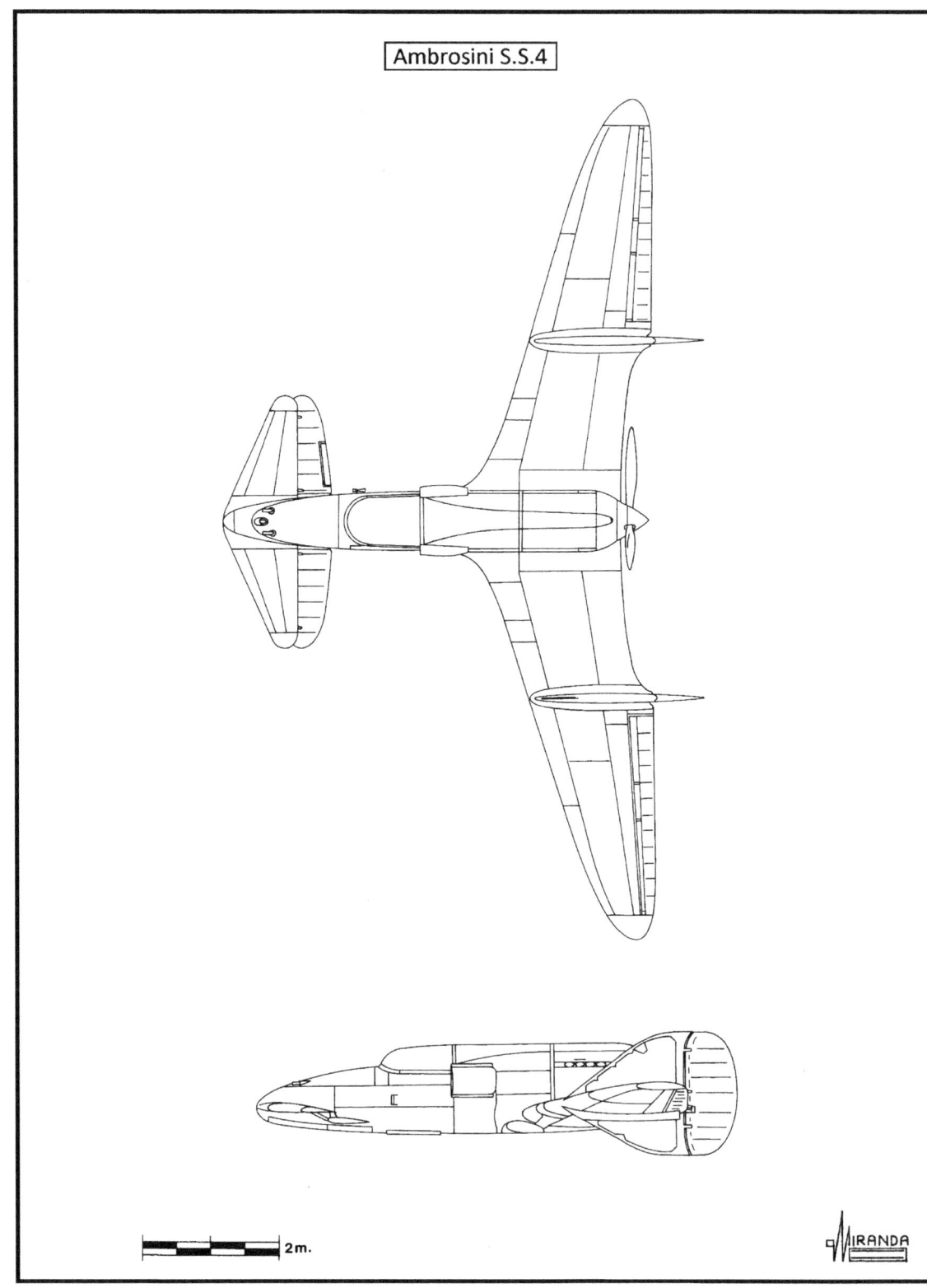

Ambrosini S.S.4

2m.

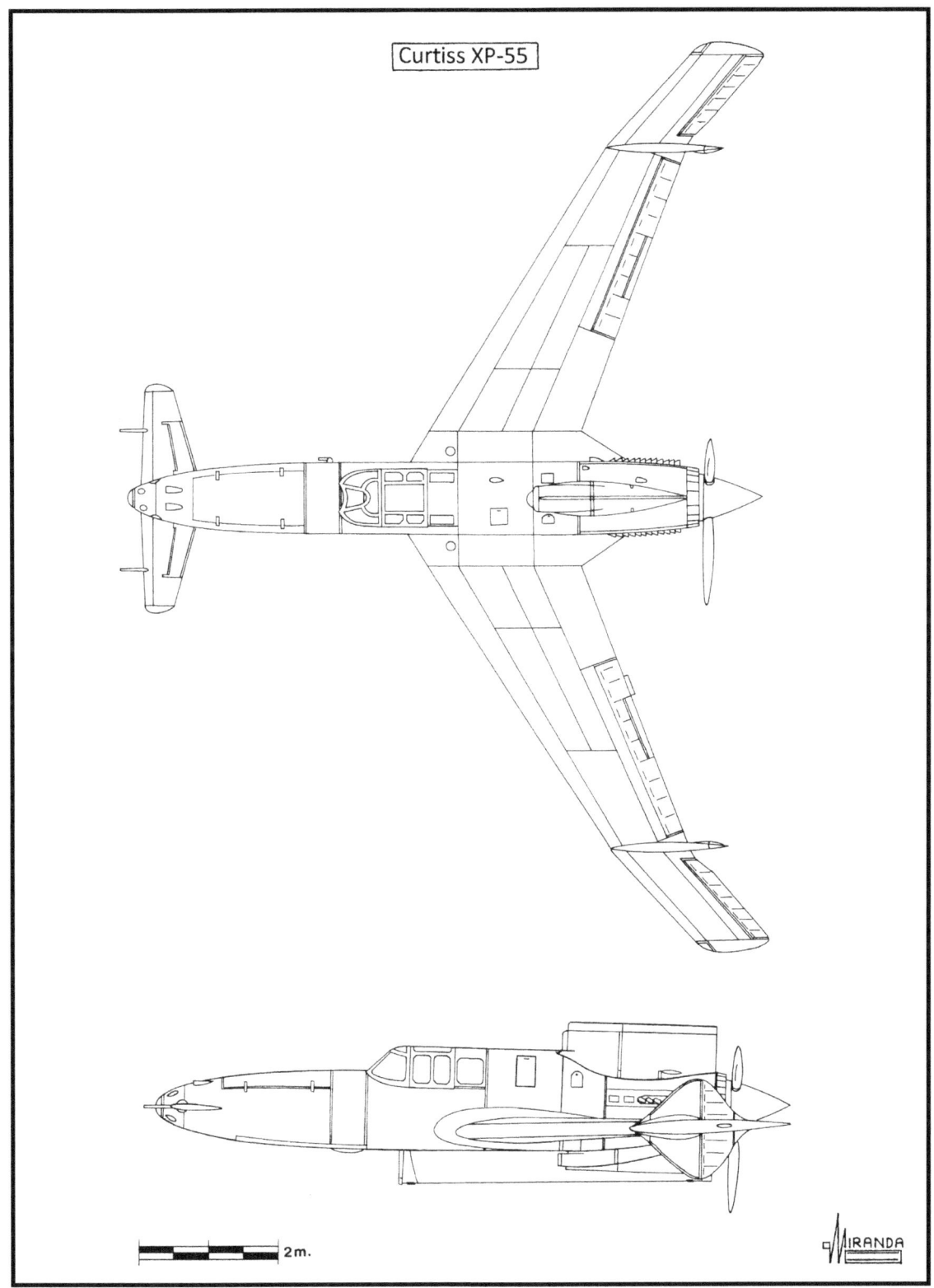

Curtiss XP-55

2 m.

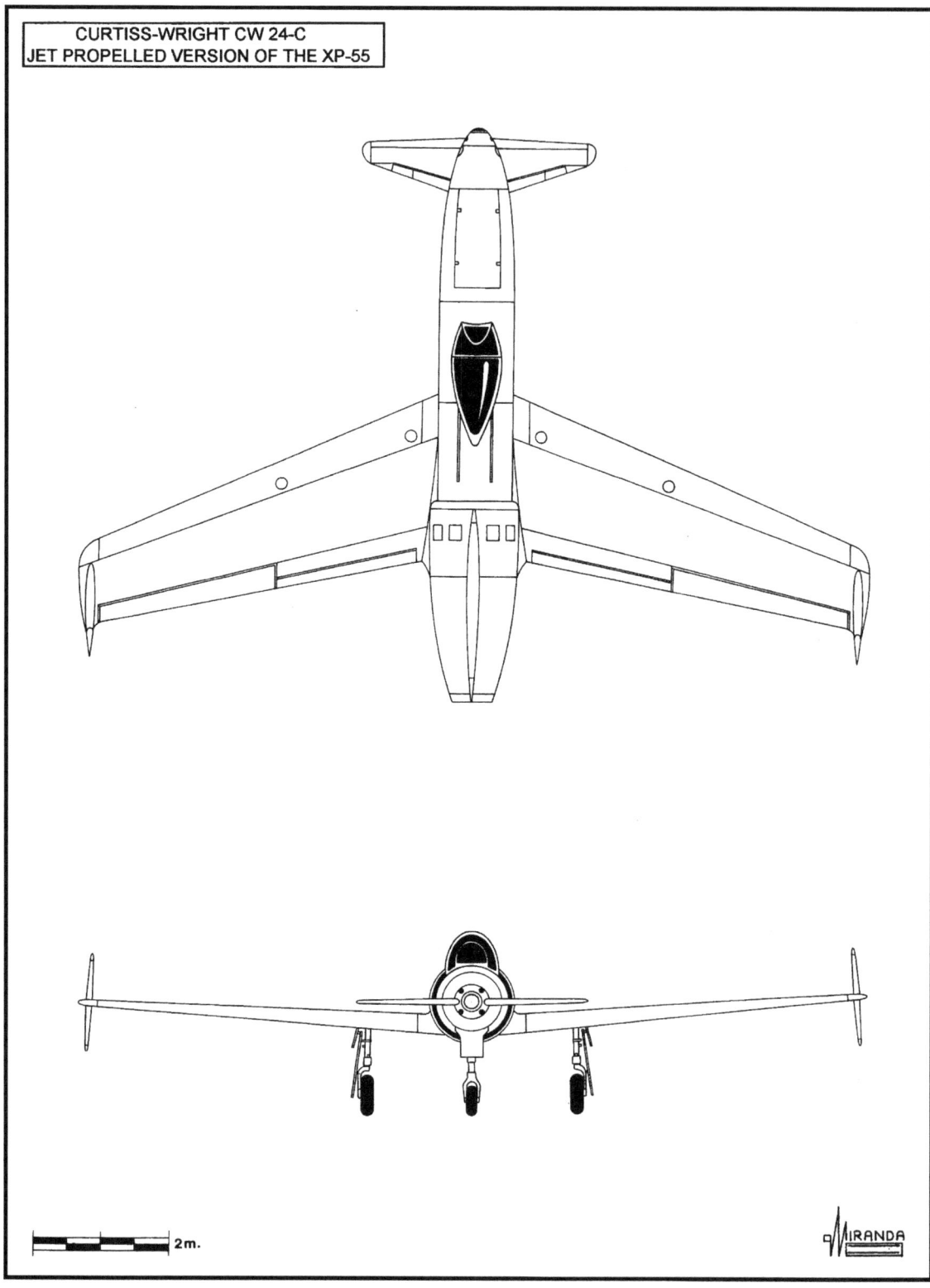

CURTISS-WRIGHT CW 24-C
JET PROPELLED VERSION OF THE XP-55

2m.

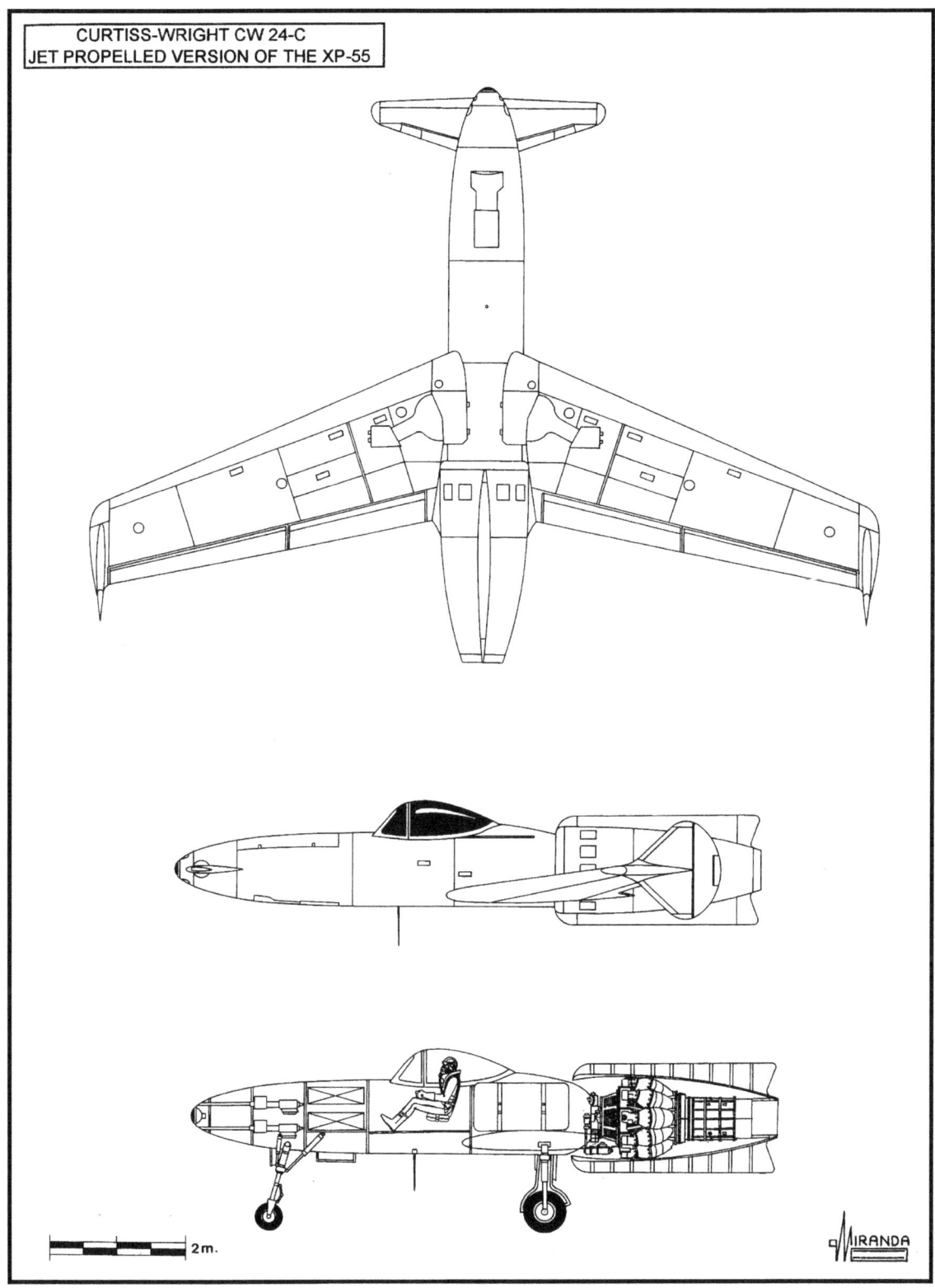

CURTISS-WRIGHT CW 24-C
JET PROPELLED VERSION OF THE XP-55

2m.

Henschel P.75

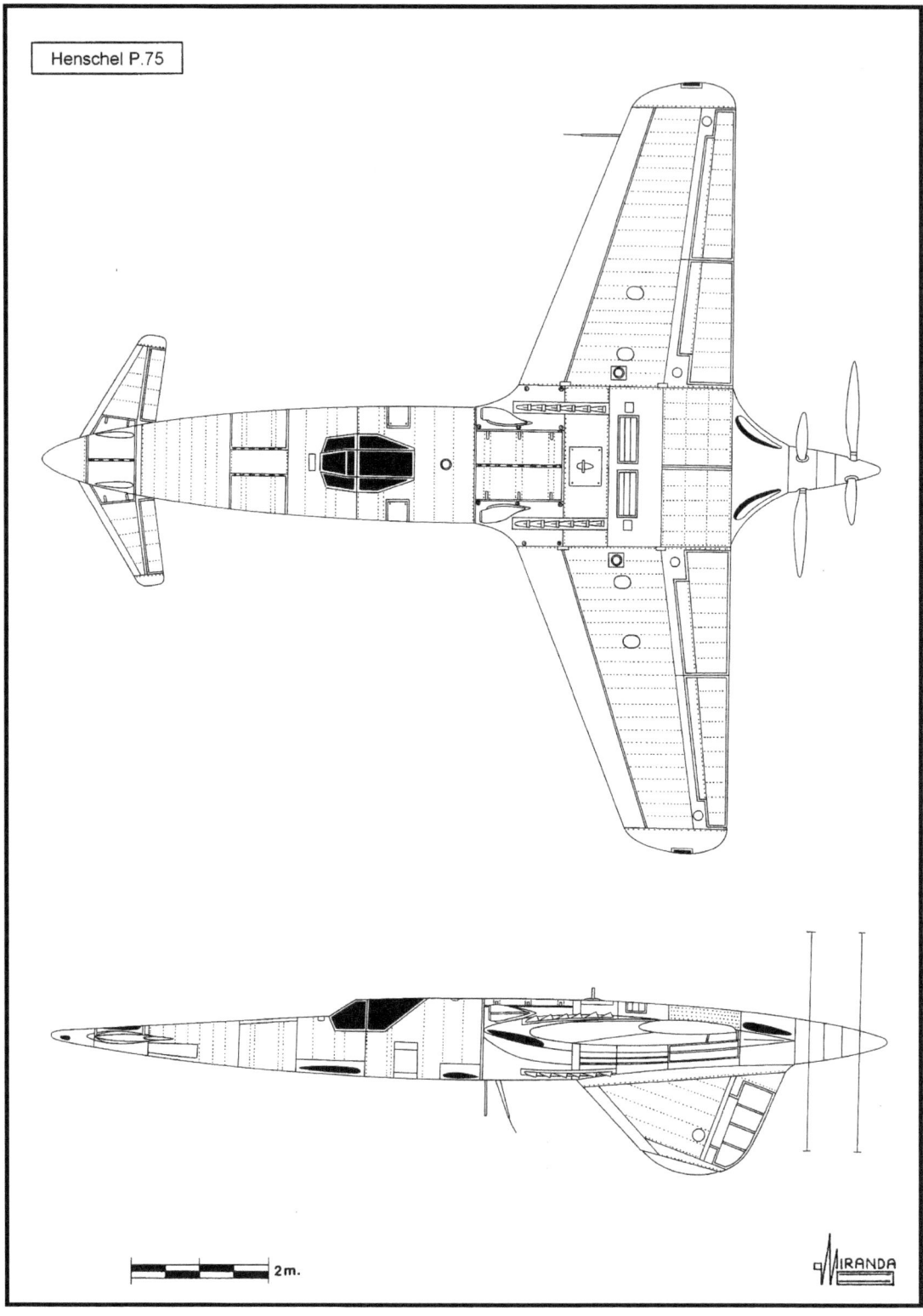

2m.

Nakajima Kikka

Presented to the *Kaigun Koku Hombu* on 14 September 1944, as a candidate to the *Kokoku Heiki No.2* project, the J9N1/MXN1 (speculative designations) Maru-Ten was a suicide bomber armed with one (fixed) 807.5-kg Number 80 Model 2 bomb. Lacking an undercarriage, it took off from a cart propelled by two Toku-Ro.1 Type 2 rockets, running over 200 m of rails.

As with the projected Ohka 43-Otsu of Kugisho, the Maru-Ten was armed with two 13-mm Type 3 machine guns to defend from the Allied fighters. It also had foldable wings that could be hidden in caves and railroad tunnels. In September 1944, the IJN issued the '19-shi specification' calling for a special attack bomber with a 693-kph max. speed and 350-kgf take-off run when using two 450-kgf RATOG bottles.

In November 1944, after a series of tests made with a Betty bomber, it was concluded that the Ne-12B centrifugal turbojet, with only 320 kgf static thrust, did not produce anywhere near the power required to propel this aircraft, which had a range of just 204 km due to its high rate of fuel consumption: 510 kg/h.

On 9 December, *Kaigun Koku Hombu* decided to modify the project '19-shi special attack bomber' into the 620-kph 'anti-invasion' fast bomber J9N2/MXN2 (speculative designations), propelled by two Yokosuka/Kugisho Ne-20 axial turbojets with 475–490 kgf static thrust, tricycle type landing gear, armoured windshield, automatic extinguisher devices, and two Type 99, 20-mm cannons, but the weight of the (launchable) bomb had to be reduced to 500 kg.

With the possibility of using the Ne 20 axial turbojet (only 62 cm in diameter), Nakajima proposed to *Kaigun Koku Hombu* three possible configurations for the 'anti-invasion' fast bomber. The first proposal consisted of a twin-boom airframe with two Ne 20 turbojets mounted on the upper and lower sides of the fuselage. In the second proposal, they were located under the wing roots; the third proposal was a variant of the Maru-Ten with the engines mounted under the wings. The mock-up was presented to the IJN on 28 January 1945, receiving the official designation Kikka/Kitsuka.

The first Nakajima/Yokosuka Kikka (J9Y1 speculative designation) prototype was based upon the third proposal and flew for the first time on 7 August 1945. To gain some time, it was built with the main landing gear of an A6M5 Zero-Sen and the tailwheel of a P1Y Ginga as a nosewheel.

First Prototype Technical Data

Wingspan: 10 m
Length: 9.25 m
Height: 3.05 m
Wing area: 13.2 sq. m
Max. weight: 3,950 kg
Max. speed: 677 kph
Service ceiling: 10,700 m

The prototype was used as the basis for an emergency fighter project (J9Y2 Kikka-KAI speculative designation) powered by two Ne 20-KAI turbojets with 570–650 kgf static thrust and armed with a Type 5, 30-mm cannon. The wing area was extended to 14.51 sq. m for a 12,300 m service ceiling and a time to climb to 10,000 m of twenty minutes. The estimated maximum weight for this version was 4,152 kg and the maximum speed was 785 kph.

The possibility of using the new Ishikawajima-Shibaura Ne 130 turbojets, with 900 kgf static thrust, allowed the design of an air-superiority fighter (J9Y3 speculative designation) with combat flaps and leading-edge slots to improve manoeuvrability, armed with four Type 5, 30-mm cannons. The protection for the pilot consisted of one 70-mm-thick armoured windshield and 12-mm steel plates at the back of the seat. The two fuselage fuel tanks of 330 and 425 l were protected with 22-mm-thick leakproof rubber. The estimated maximum weight for this version was 4,232 kg and the max. speed was 713 kph.

On 13 June 1945, *Kaigun Koku Hombu* decided on the mass production of the special attack bomber and the emergency fighter. At the time of Japanese surrender, a second prototype was completed and eighteen pre-production aircraft were in various stages of assembly. The third prototype Kikka-K was a two-seat trainer/reconnaissance variant (J9K speculative designation) with an estimated max. speed of 721 kph.

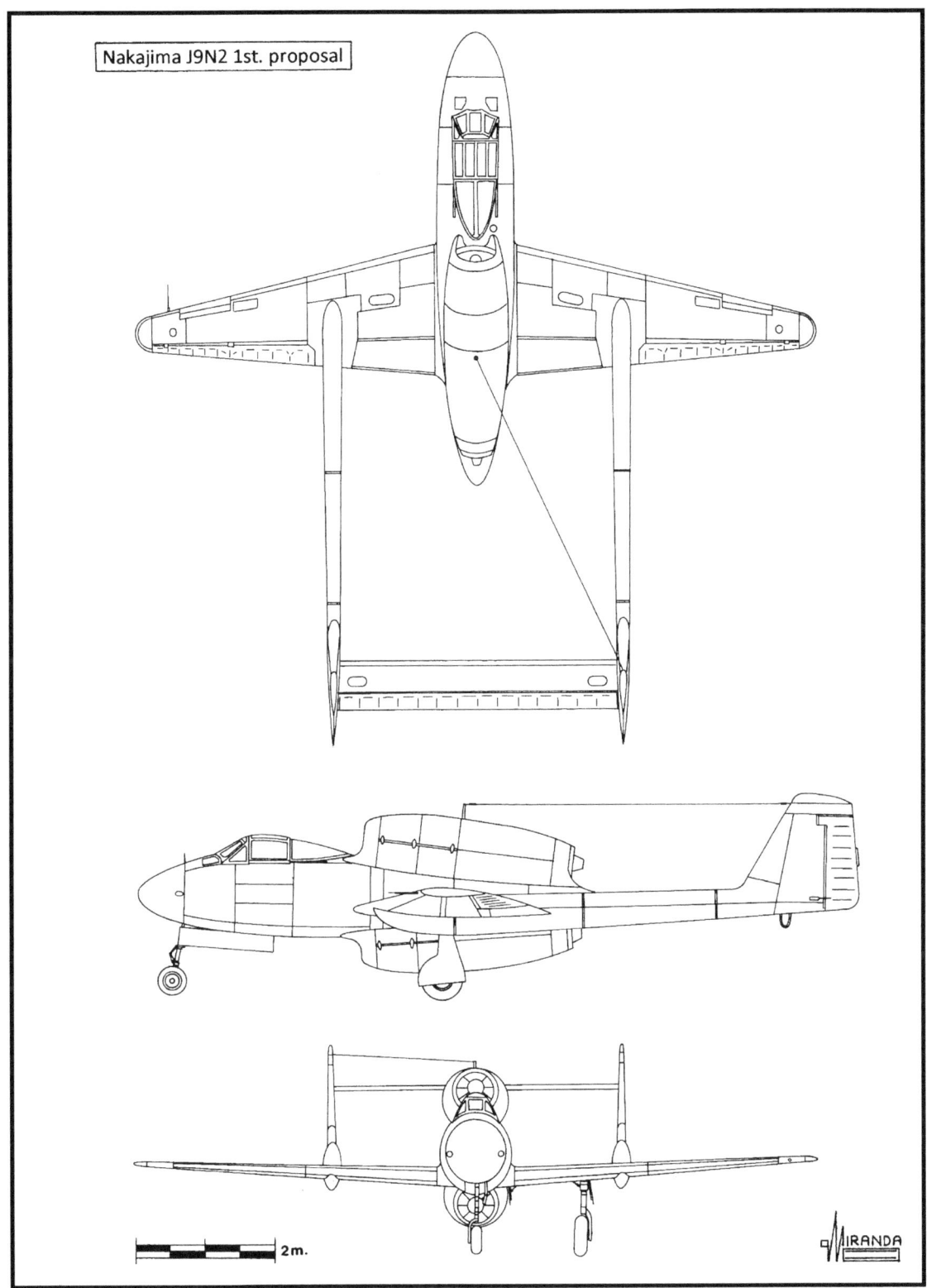

Nakajima J9N2 1st. proposal

2m.

Nakajima J9N2 2nd. proposal

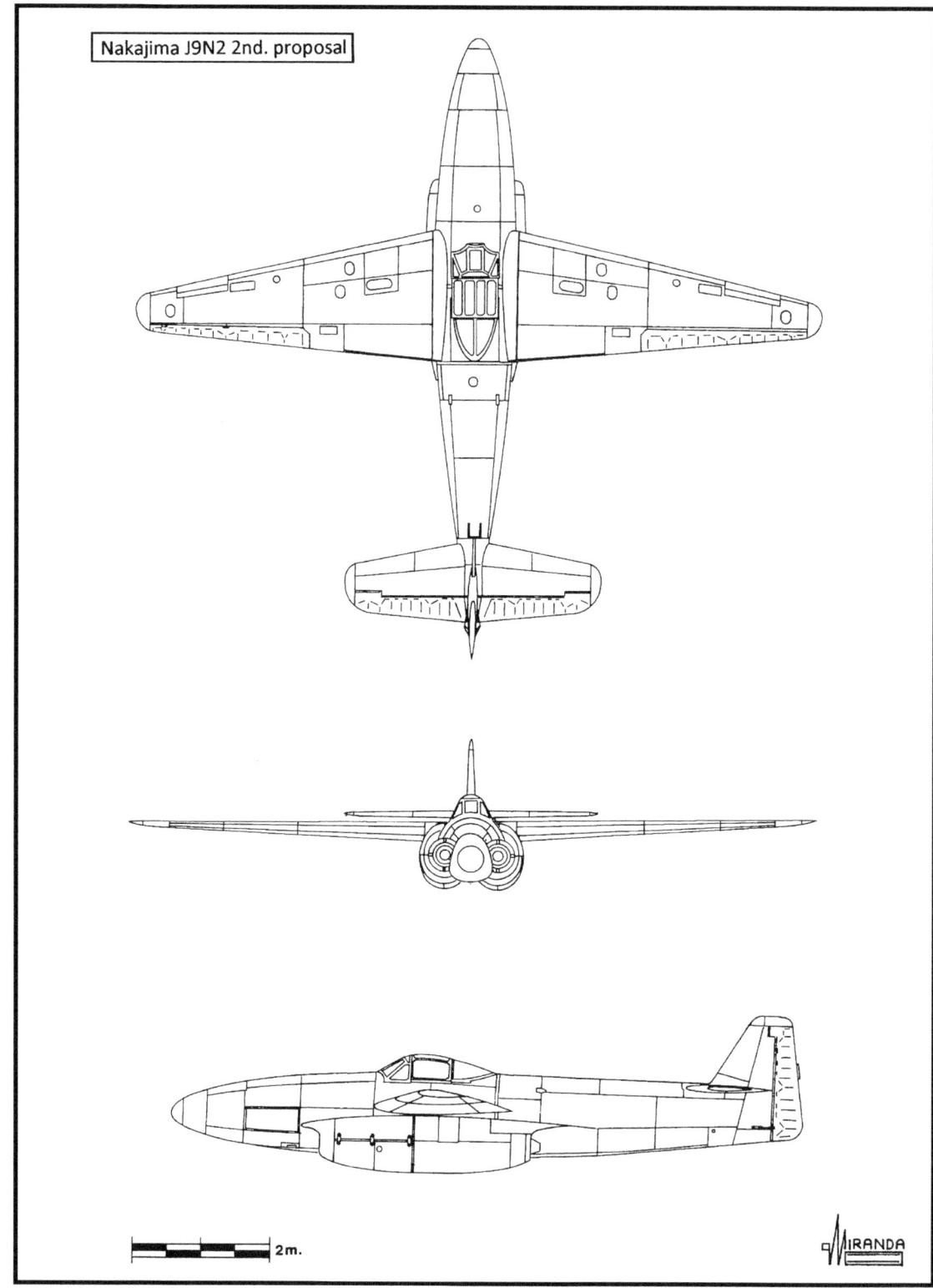

2m.

MIRANDA

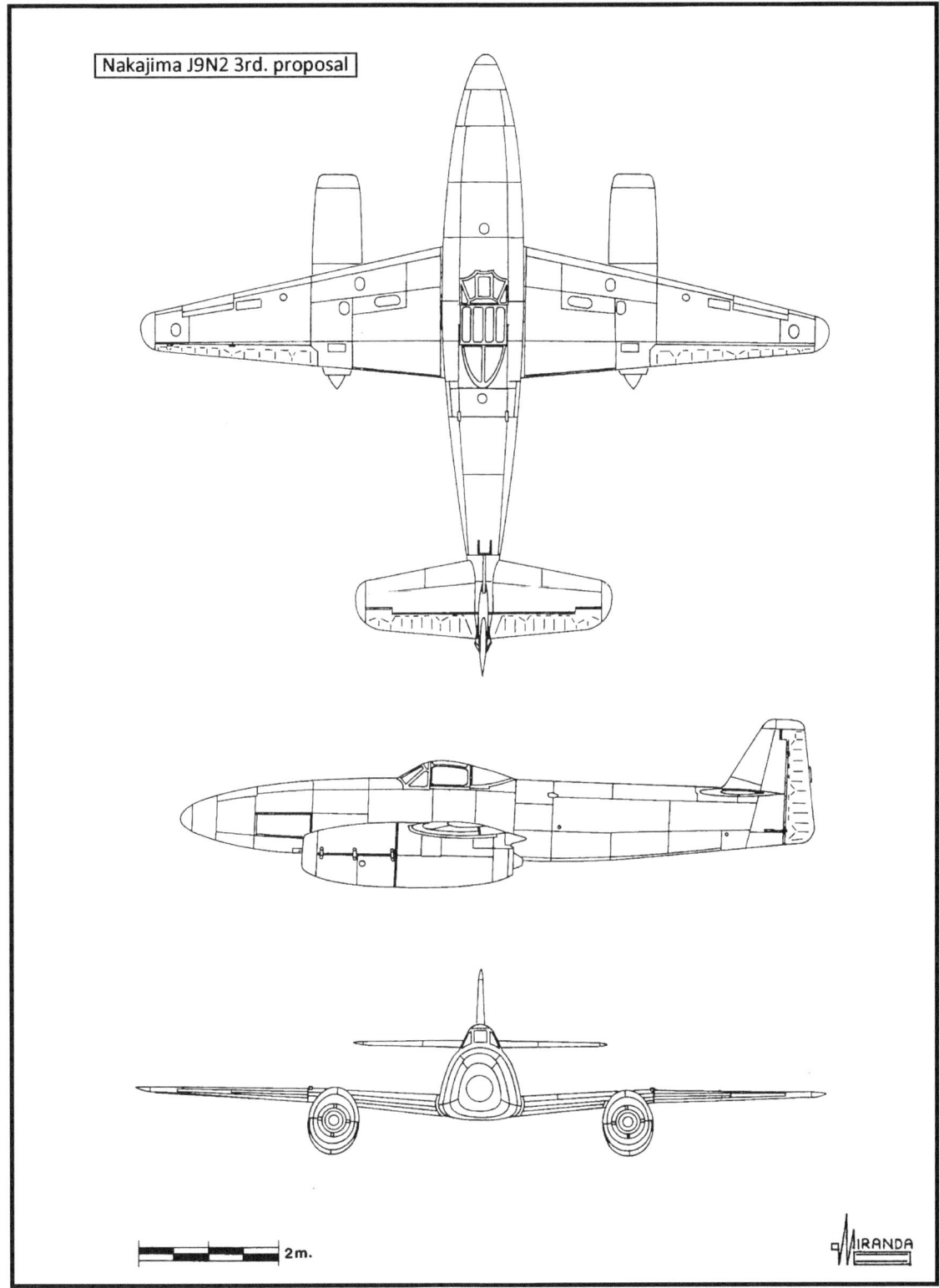

Nakajima J9N2 3rd. proposal

2 m.

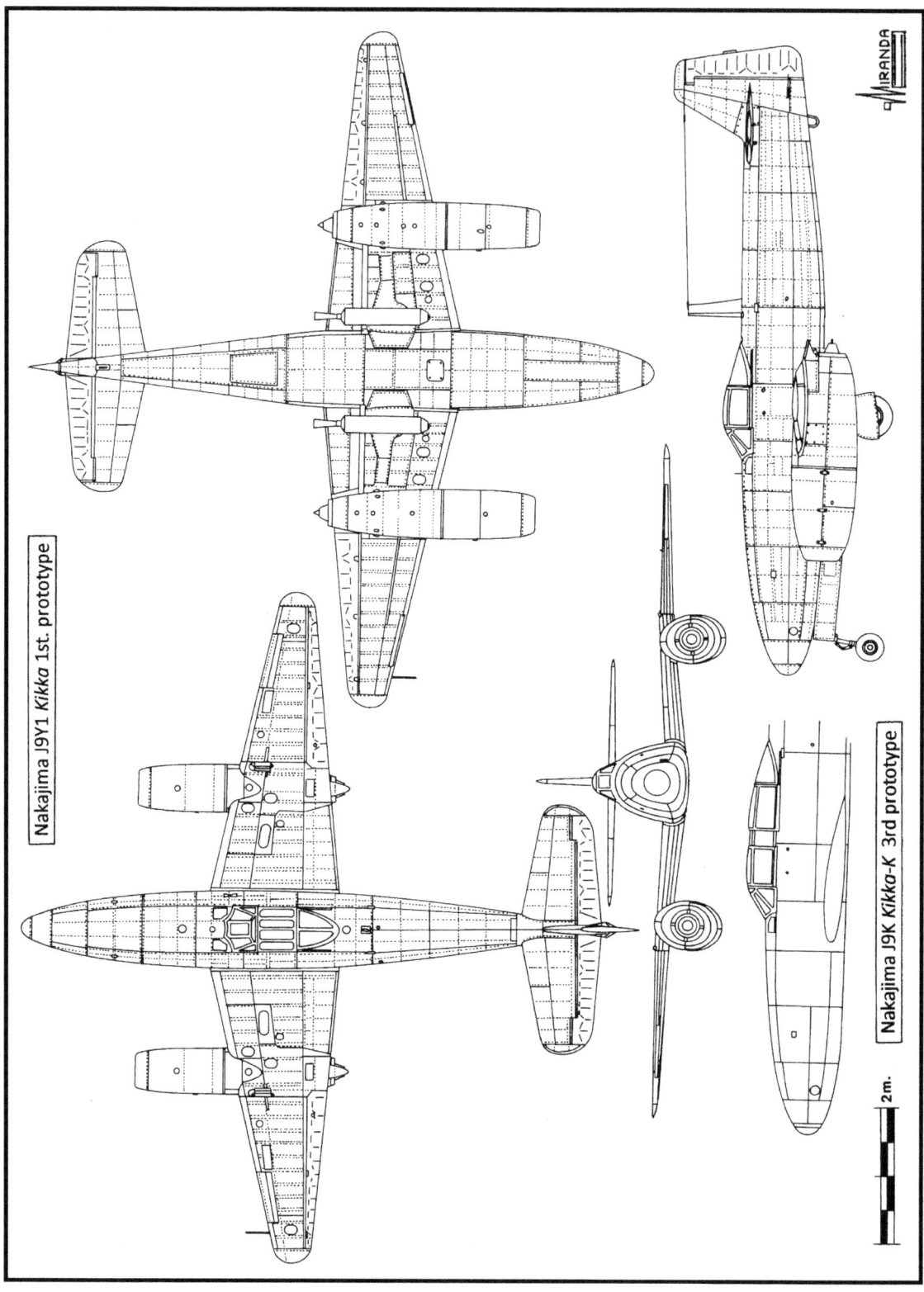

Nakajima J9Y1 *Kikka* 1st. prototype

Nakajima J9K *Kikka-K* 3rd prototype

2 m.

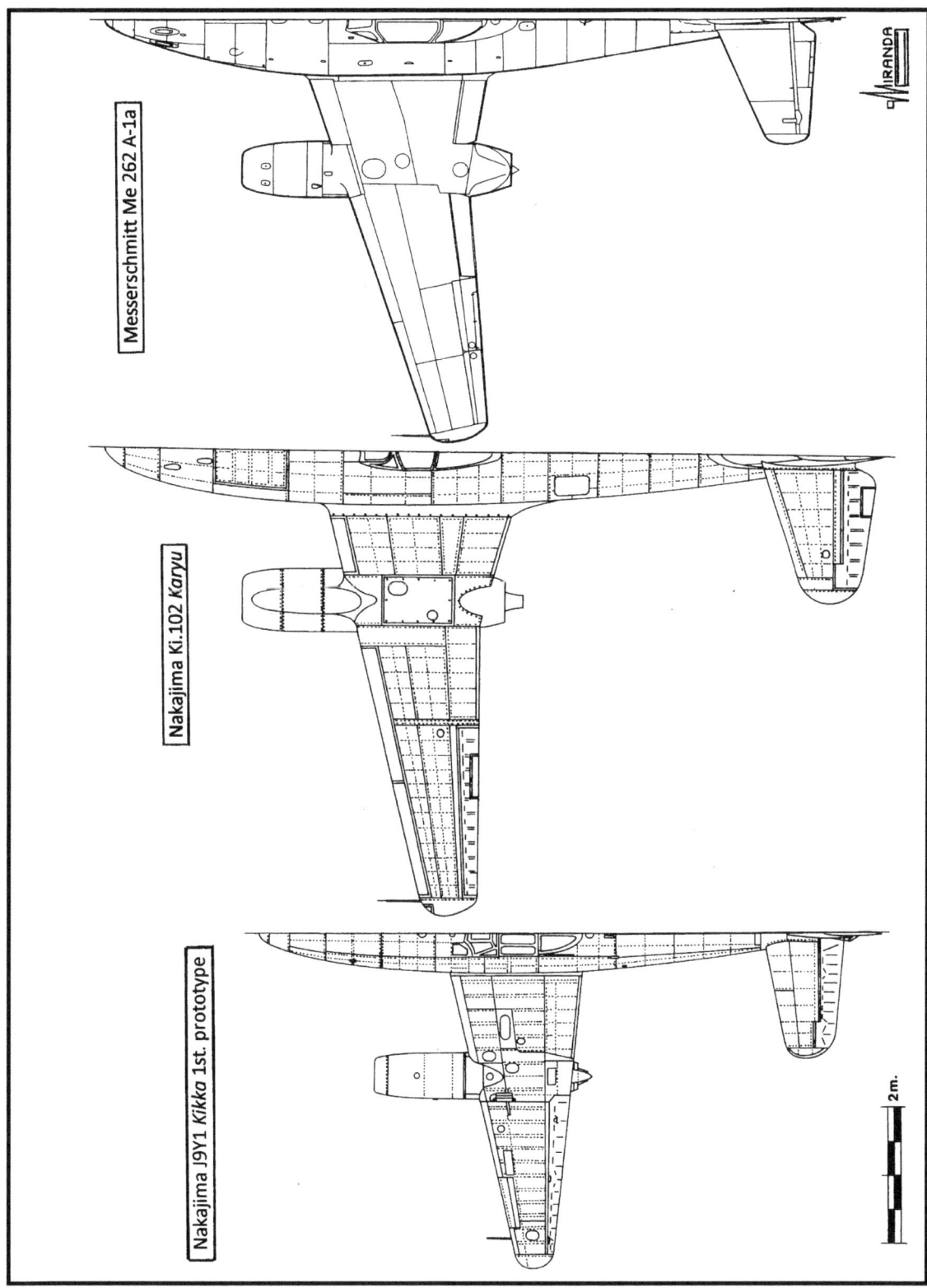

Messerschmitt Me 262 A-1a

Nakajima Ki.102 *Karyu*

Nakajima J9Y1 *Kikka* 1st. prototype

2m.

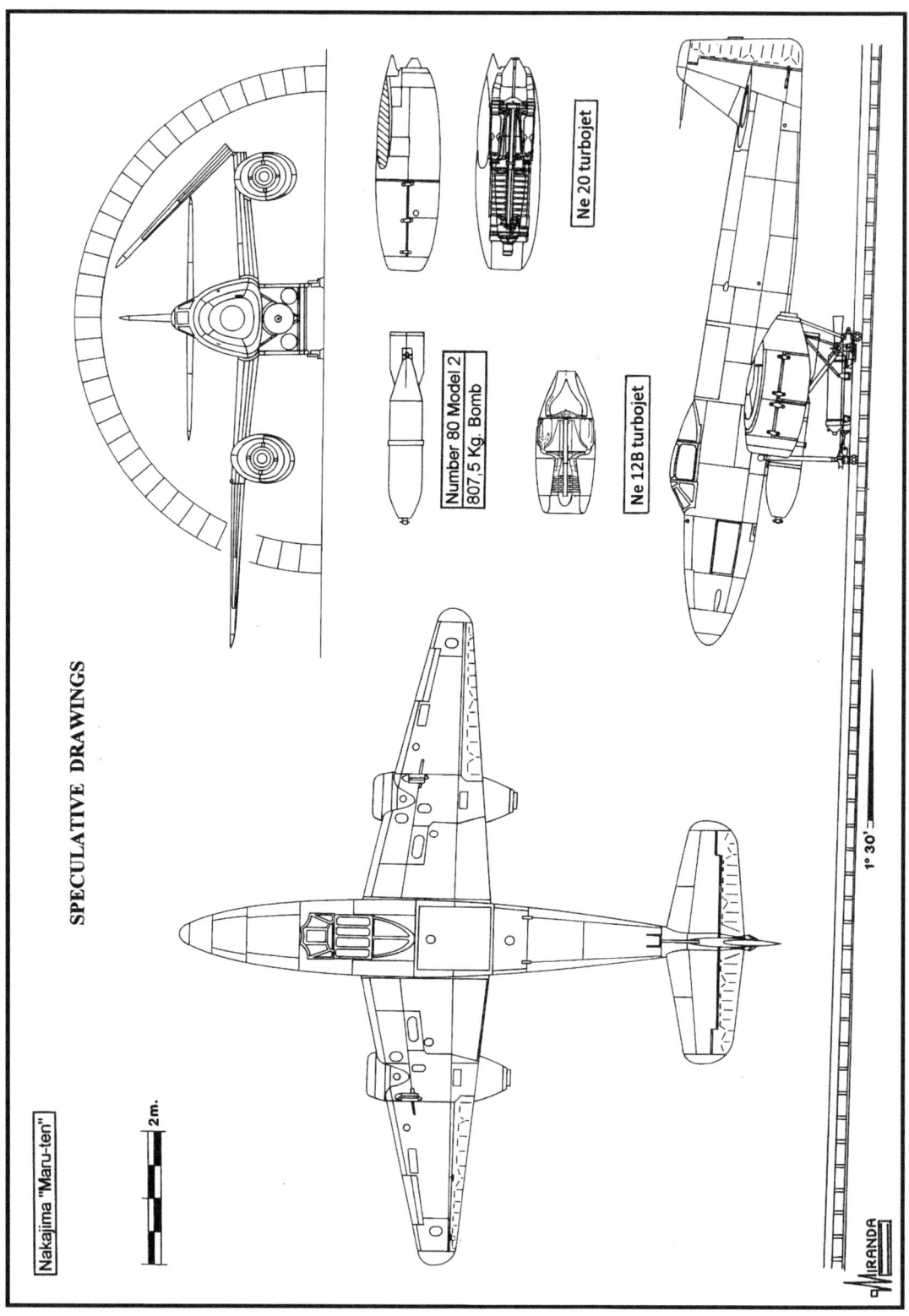

SPECULATIVE DRAWINGS

Nakajima "Maru-ten"

2 m.

Ne 20 turbojet

Number 80 Model 2
807,5 Kg. Bomb

Ne 12B turbojet

1° 30'

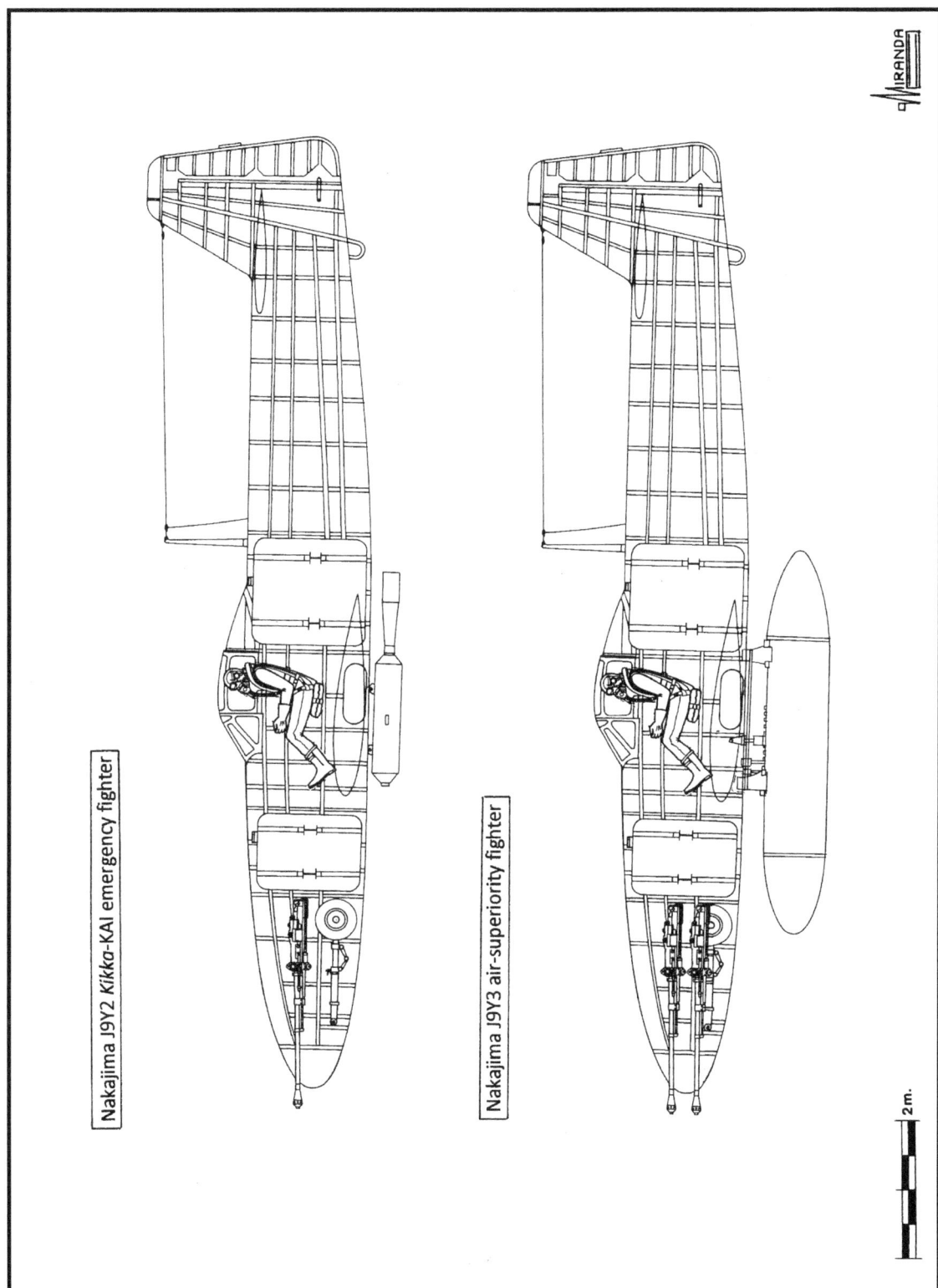

Nakajima J9Y2 *Kikka*-KAI emergency fighter

Nakajima J9Y3 air-superiority fighter

2 m.

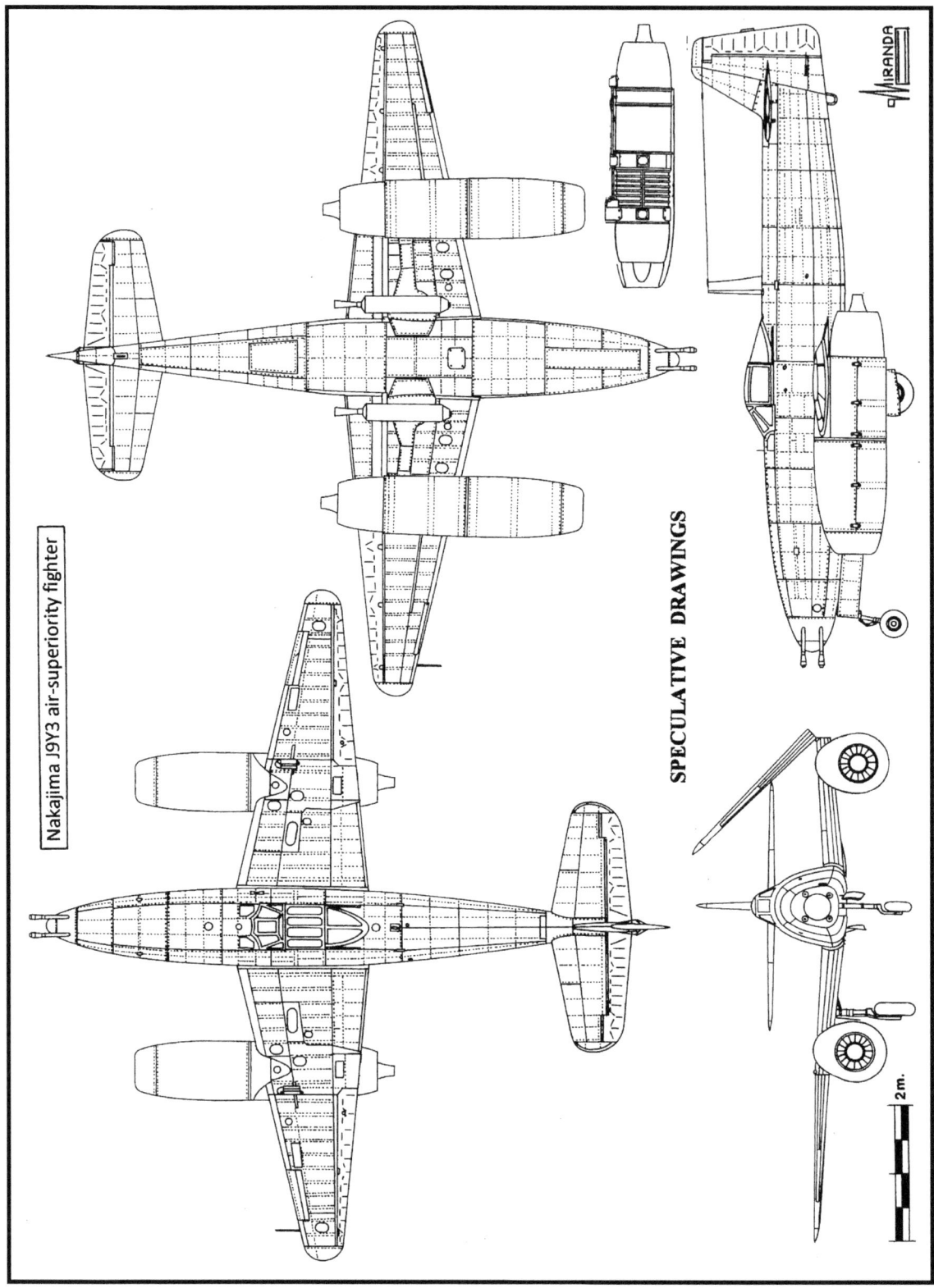

Nakajima J9Y3 air-superiority fighter

SPECULATIVE DRAWINGS

2 m.

Yokosuka R2Y Keiun

The extraordinary expansion of the Japanese empire during the winter of 1941–1942 changed the priorities of the IJN at every level. One of the most important was the localisation of the fleet of the Allies in the vastness of the world oceans, from Alaska to the oriental coast of Africa.

After the bitter experiences with the Focke-Wulf Kondor during the Atlantic Battle, all task forces of some strategic importance included aircraft carriers. Their fighters quickly and efficiently removed from combat the huge and slow Kawanishi H6K flying boats that the IJN had been using in reconnaissance missions.

With the subsequent appearance of the new Corsairs, Thunderbolts, and Mustangs in the theatre of operations, the Gekkos and Gingas could escape by operating by night only. The technological gap between both sides turned out to be practically impossible to overcome.

The single-engined *Saiun* was very fast but also had an insufficient range for most of the missions and occasionally had to be disassembled and carried by a submarine to the operational area. As a transitional solution, the IJN acquired some Ki.46 recce aeroplanes from the IJA.

The only other alternative was to turn to German technology, and the designers of Yokosuka believed to have found the answer with the prototype of the Heinkel 119 V4, acquired in 1940. It was a *Schnellbomber* propelled by two in-line engines positioned side by side within its fuselage. By 1942, the Germans had put aside the concept due to refrigeration problems, excessive vibrations, and loss of power associated with the extreme length of the power shaft. Yet the Japanese ignored that and started building the Y-40 (later known as R2Y1) in the Naval Technical Arsenal of Yokosuka (Kugisho) during the summer of 1944.

During the tests of the propulsion system, using two Atsuta 30 engines in parallel position and a 4-m-long extension shaft, the same issues arose as those observed by Heinkel. The project was put on hold during the building of the prototype until the end of 1944 when the features and technical data of the Ne-12 were published. The design team of Yokosuka proposed the transformation of the R2Y1 to a suicide bomber to the IJN, under the name R2Y2, propelled by two Ne-30 turbojets with 850 kgf of static thrust—an engine that was a scaled-up version of the Ne-12 still under research. It was agreed that the prototype would be finished for flight tests until the production variant of the engine was available.

The first Japanese turbojets were centrifugal engines based on the German Heinkel HeS 8A of 1939. They burnt a great amount of fuel and could only increase its power by augmenting the central section's diameter. In the case of the Ne-30, to reach the 850 kgf pledged by the manufacturer, it required a diameter of 103 cm. Yet such large engines positioned in the underwing nacelles would have generated too much drag. Therefore, the engines were finally, and with great difficulty, positioned within the fuselage airframe in a staggered position.

In its initial configuration, the R2Y2 had a solid nose replacing the propeller hub and two triangular air intakes in the wing roots. It was a rational solution that required minimal modifications to the R2Y1 fuselage. A problem arose in the wings as the installation of the 'S' ducts interfered with the main spar, weakening its structure. To solve that, the air ducts had to be replaced by others in 'Y' positions within the fuselage and a new air intake in the extreme nose. It was not a good solution as the air ducts system interfered with the housing of the undercarriage nose leg, using much of the volume assigned to the fuel tanks in the original project.

Besides, the results of the experiments made with air ducts of different lengths, connected to the turbojets of the Me 262 V1 W.Nr. 130015, were unknown in Japan in November 1944. The Messerschmitt technicians had determined that the turbulence and resonance phenomenon that the air experienced within the air duct alarmingly diminished the performance of the turbojets and recommended that the new designs of aircraft used short ducts.

At any rate, only one prototype of the Ne-30 was built for evaluation. Its manufacturing was cancelled in favour of the new axial type turbojets Ne-130 and Ne-330 that were more efficient and could be positioned under the wing without generating too much drag. The possibility of having the advanced Ne-130 of 900 kgf static thrust in the medium term led to the last modification of the project: a heavy interceptor armed with cannons (possibly four Type 5 of 30 mm or two Ho-301 of 37 mm in the nose) with two turbojets in the underwing nacelles. The final design, named R2Y2-KAI (R2Y2-G according to some authors), had an estimated maximum speed of 800 kph and a service ceiling of 10,500 m. It would have been the answer to the B-29, had the length of the war adapted to Japanese estimations.

Technical Data

R2Y2 First Suicide Variant Solid Nose, Lateral Air Intakes, Mid-Tailplane
Wingspan: 14 m
Length: 13.08 m
Engines: 2 × Ne-30 turbojets with 850-kgf peak thrust each
Armament: 2 × Type 3 13-mm machine guns and 1 × Number 80 Model 2 807.5-kg bombs

R2Y2 Second Suicide Variant, Nose Air Intake, Mid-Tailplane
Wingspan: 14 m
Length: 12.31 m
Engines: 2 × Ne-30 turbojets with 850-kgf peak thrust each
Armament: 2 × Type 3 13-mm machine guns and 1 × Number 80 Model 2 807.5-kg bomb

R2Y2-KAI Interceptor Low Tailplane
Wingspan: 14 m
Length: 13.8 m
Height: 4.24 m
Wing surface: 34 sq. m
Weight empty: 5,700 kg
Weight loaded: 8,850 kg
Max. speed: 800 kph
Service ceiling: 10,500 m
Range: 1,270 km
Engines: 2 × Ne-130 turbojets with 900-kgf peak thrust each
Armament: cannons in the nose

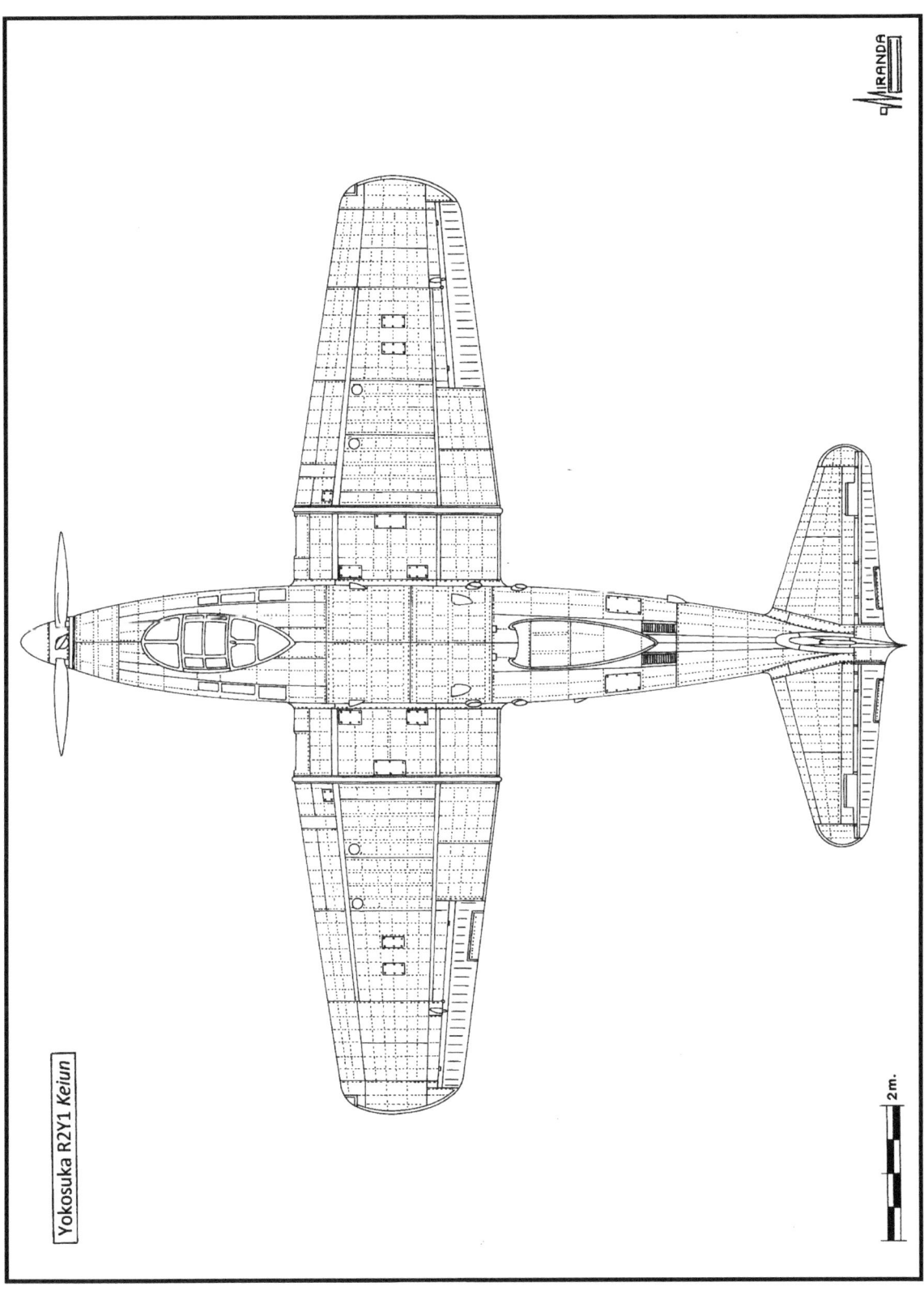

Yokosuka R2Y1 *Keiun*

2 m.

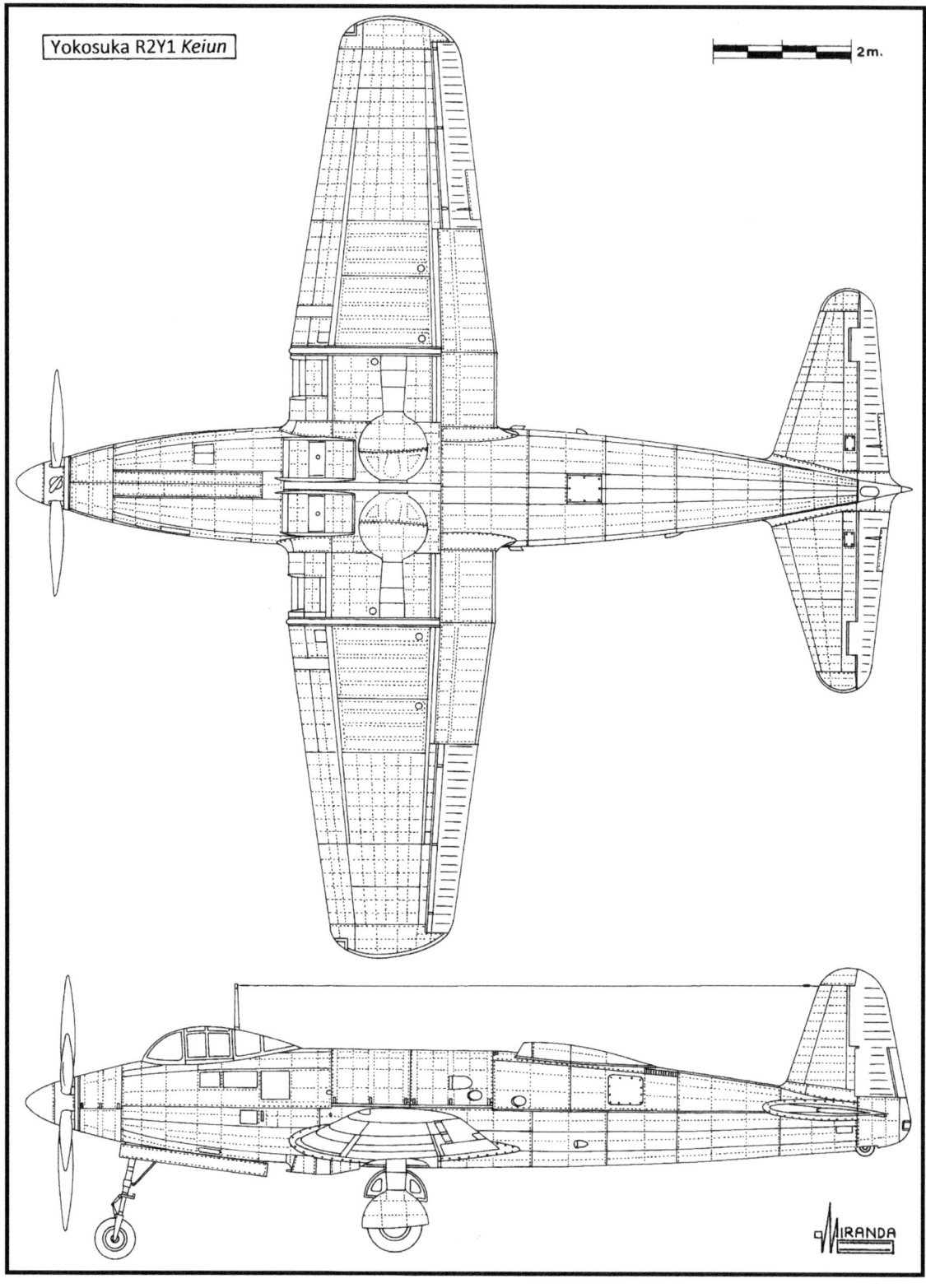

Yokosuka R2Y1 *Keiun*

2 m.

MIRANDA

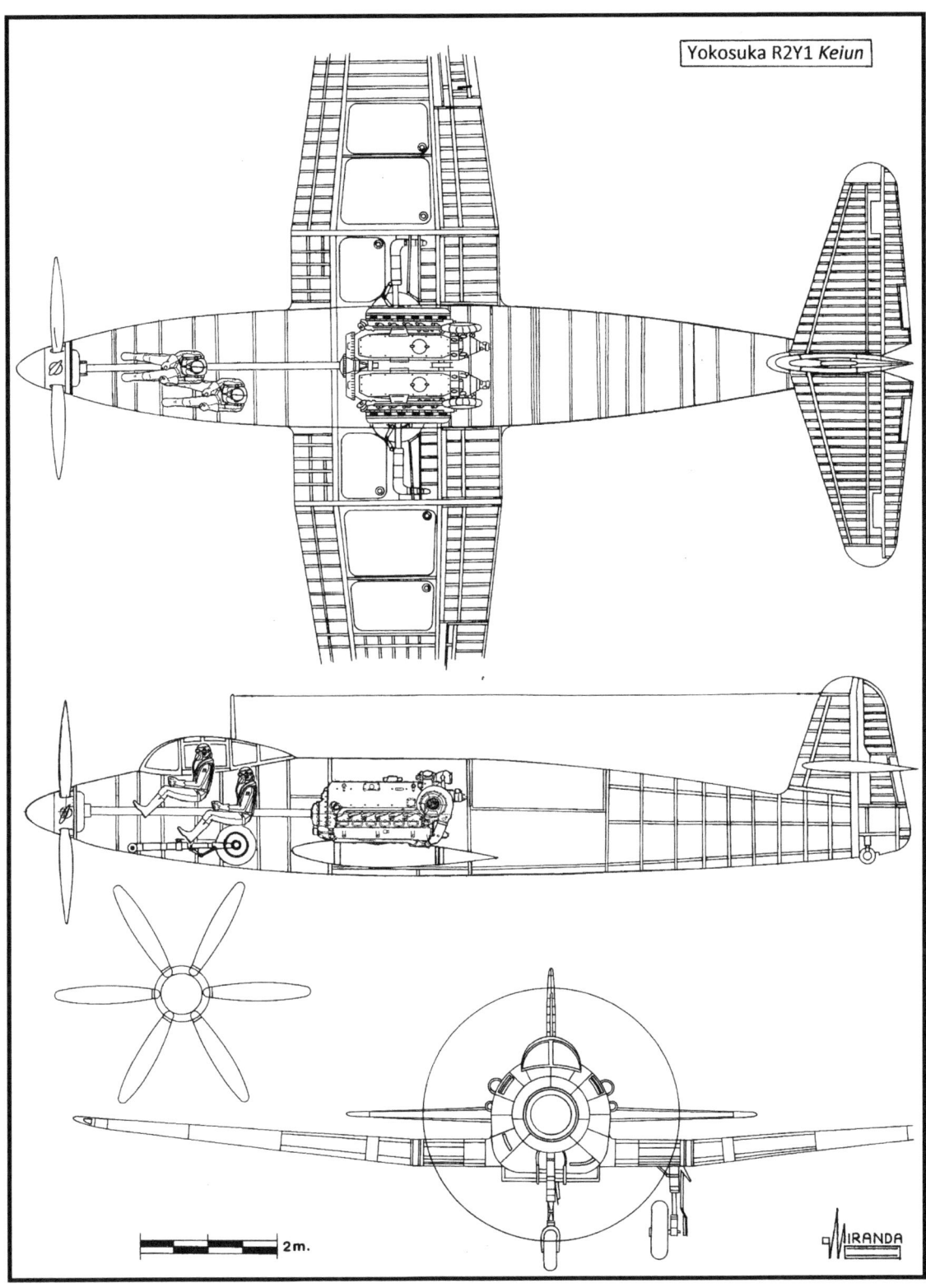

Yokosuka R2Y1 *Keiun*

2m.

MIRANDA

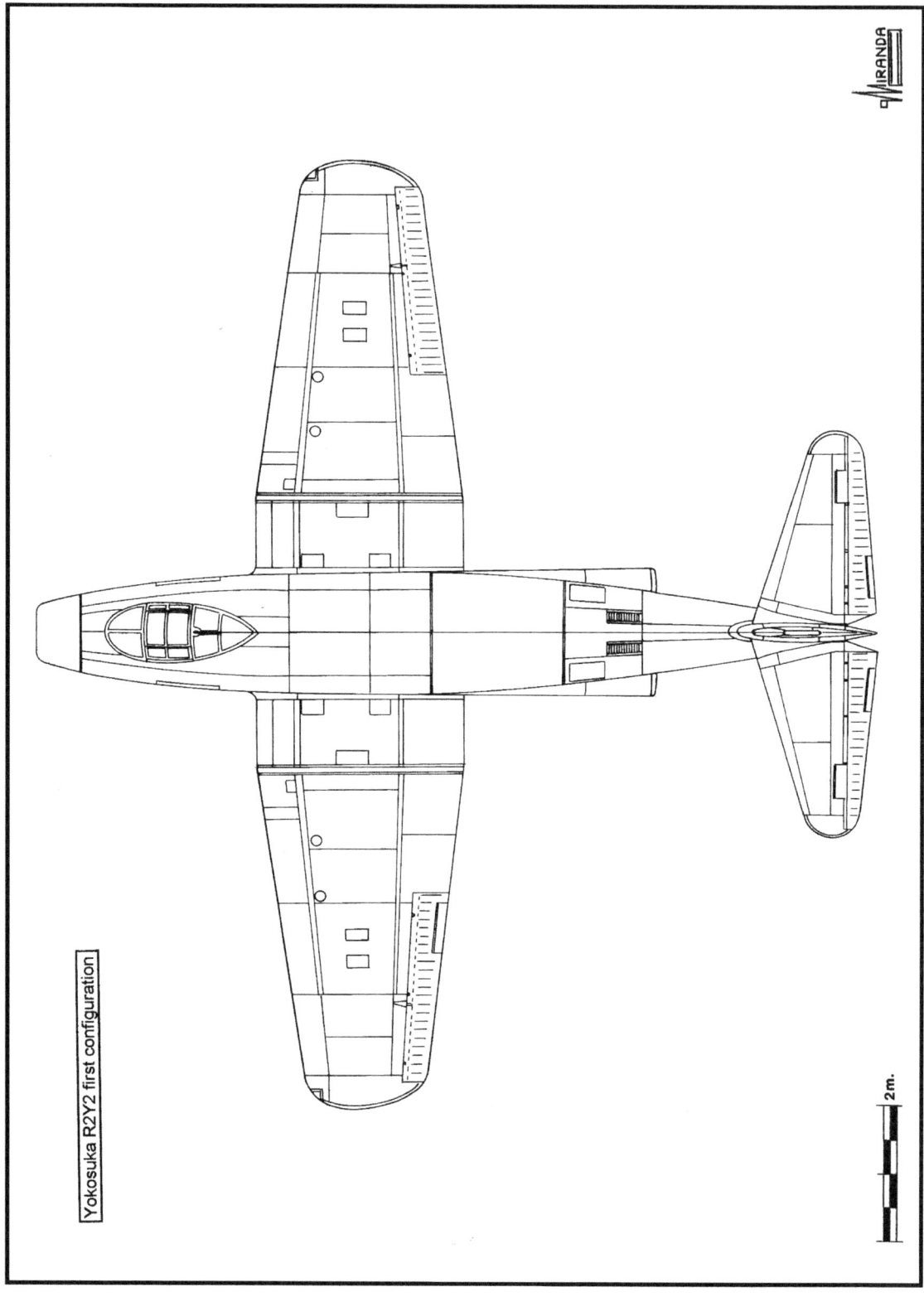

Yokosuka R2Y2 first configuration

2 m.

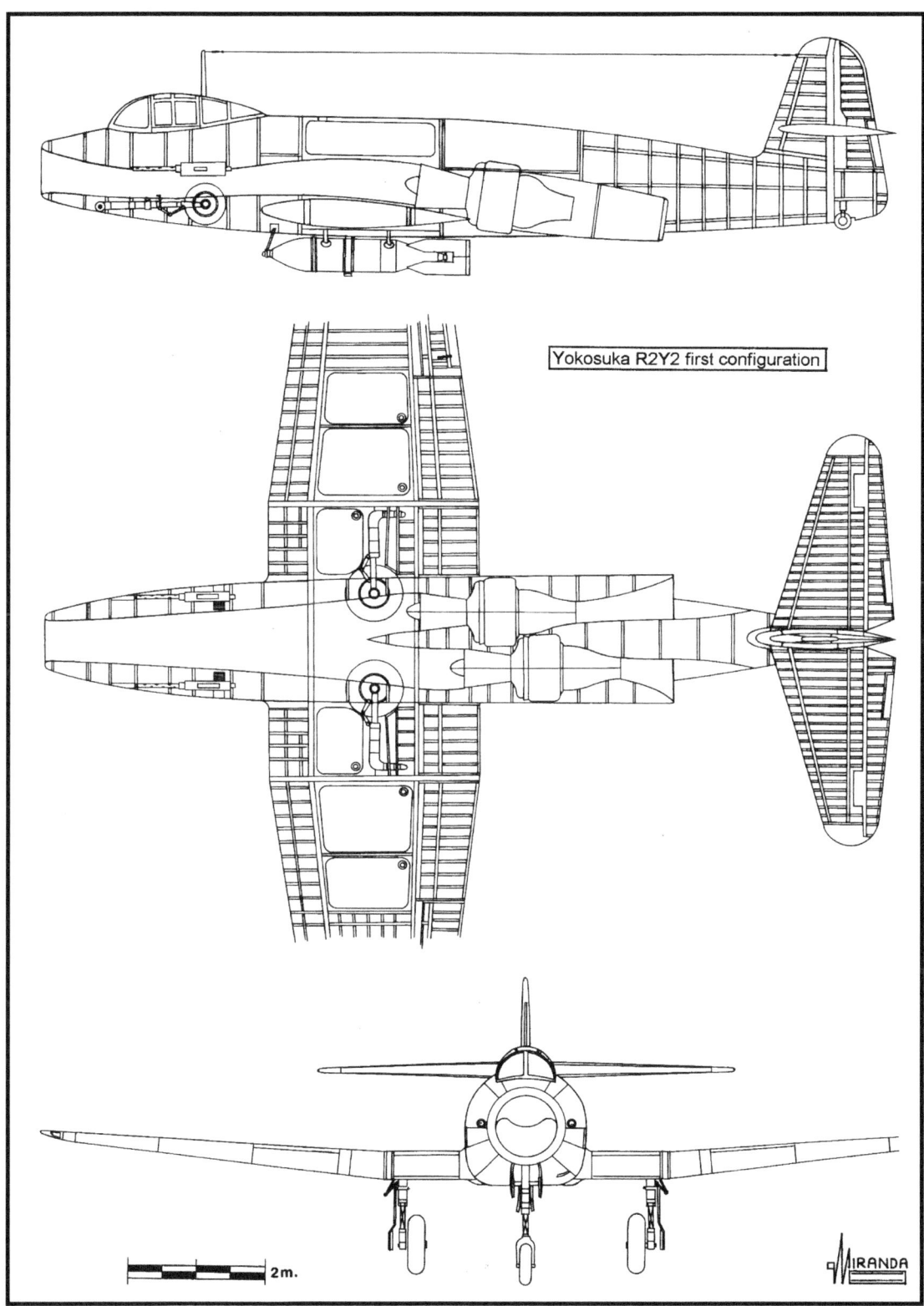

Yokosuka R2Y2 first configuration

2 m.

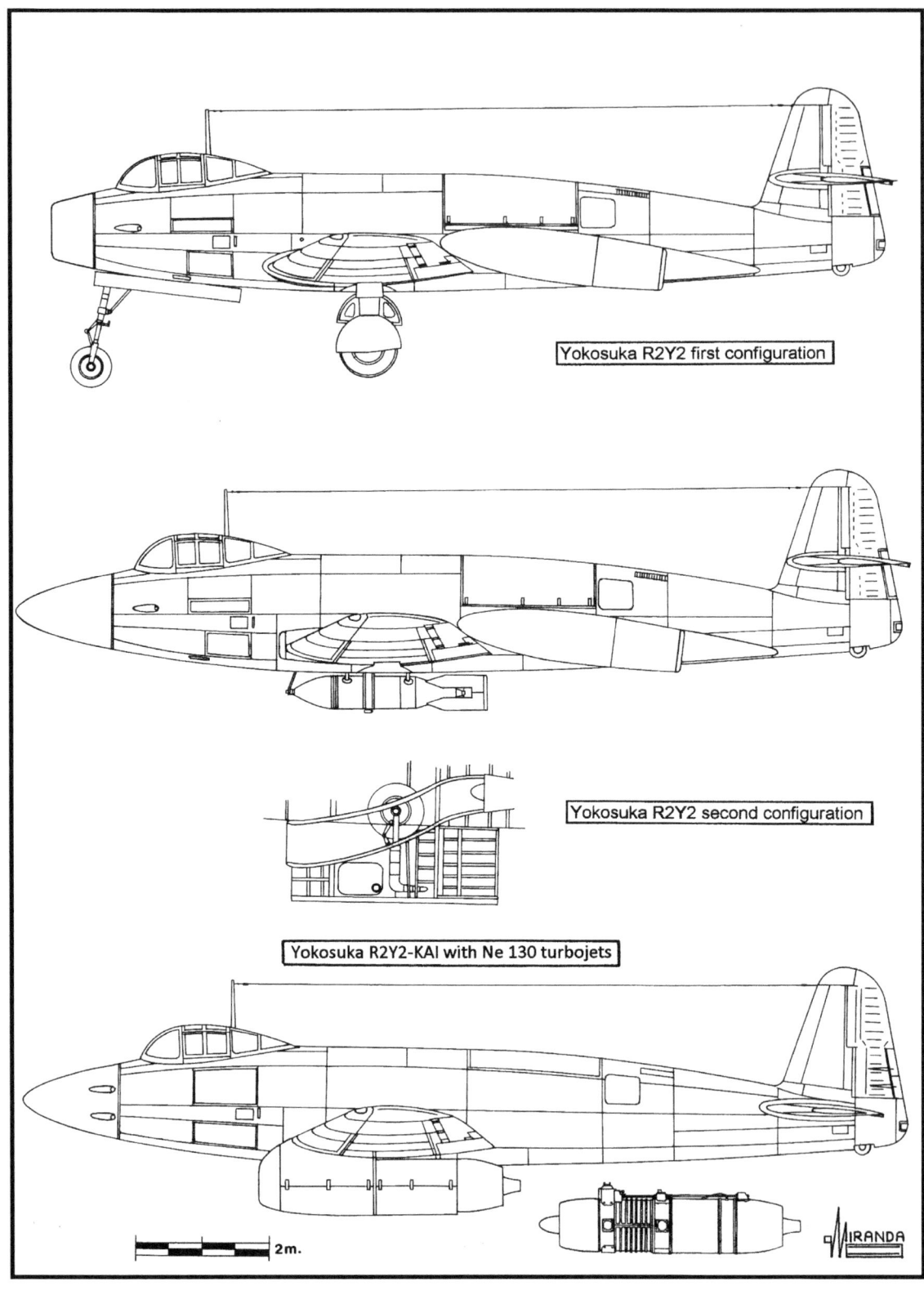

Yokosuka R2Y2 first configuration

Yokosuka R2Y2 second configuration

Yokosuka R2Y2-KAI with Ne 130 turbojets

2m.

MIRANDA

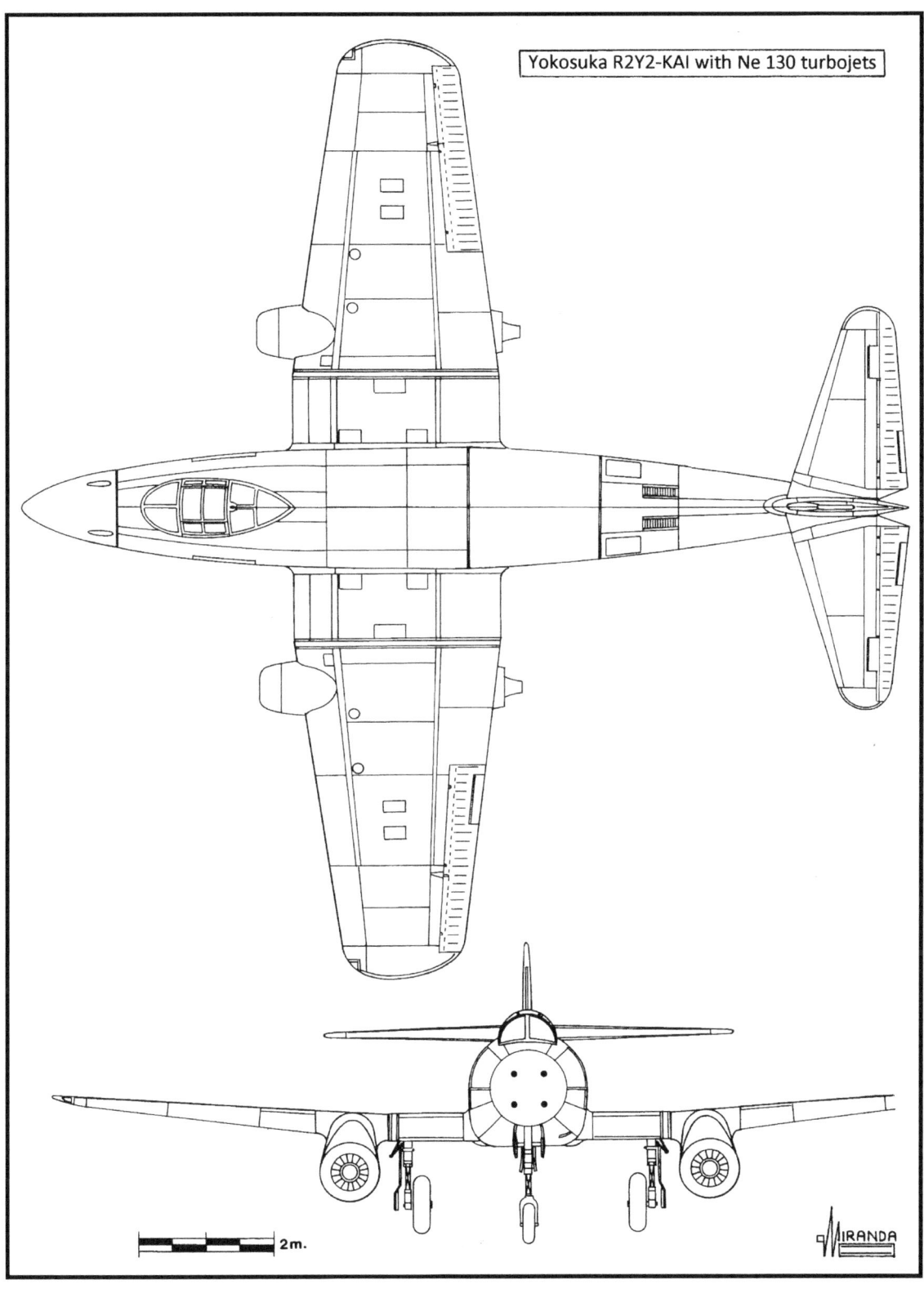

Yokosuka R2Y2-KAI with Ne 130 turbojets

2m.

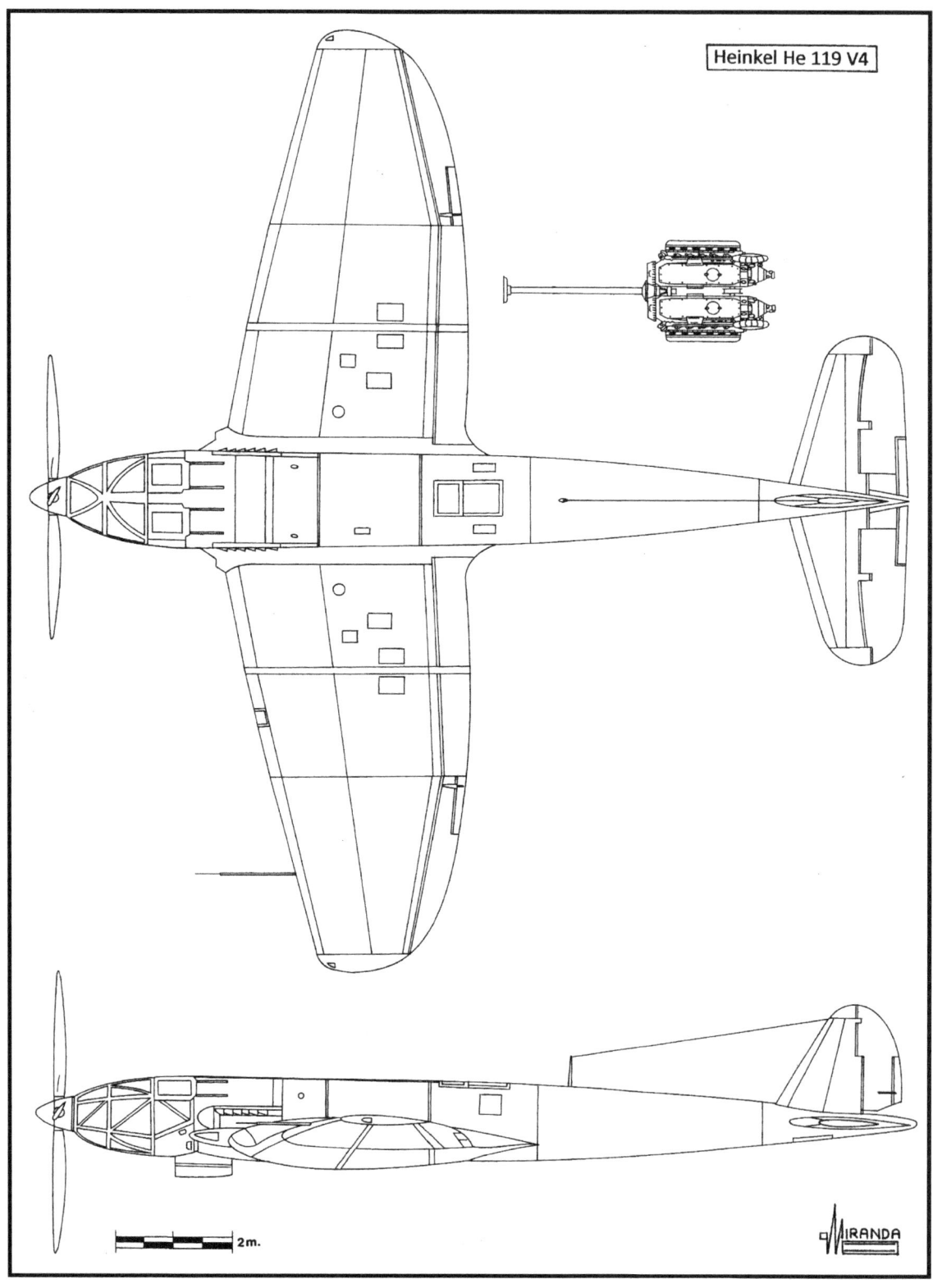

Heinkel He 119 V4

2m.

MIRANDA

Mizuno Shinryu II

Grabbing the opportunity of having the new rocket engines developed by the IJN to propel the Ohka, the engineers of Mizuno decided to develop their own rocket glider.

It had an unusual 'canard' configuration to facilitate the short take-off and it was built of wood, plywood, and iron plate, with four Type 2 rocket engines at the rear of the fuselage. Three different versions were manufactured: *kamikaze*, anti-tank, and interceptor. The suicide version had no undercarriage, using the same rails and rocket cart system as the Ohka 43-Otsu for take-off. It would have been able to carry a 250-kg bomb in the fuselage, behind the pilot.

Like the D4Y4 Suisei suicide bombers and the Type 5 Shinyo motorboats, the Shinryu II would have possibly been equipped with two or four 12-cm barrage ISR rockets that would have made it more difficult for the enemy gunners to reach the target during the terminal dive.

The anti-tank version took off by its own means over a primitive landing gear of skids, helped by a Type 1 ventral rocket that was detachable. It is assumed that it had the four rocket engines in the fuselage to maintain its flight altitude during the attack. It used eight 8-cm anti-armour hollow-charge ROTSU rockets, housed in iron tubes welded to the undercarriage, with a -7-degree pitch so that they could be shot without losing any altitude or speed. The aircraft had spoilers and it was expected to survive to be able to land and refuel for the next attack.

Although this version has been described as anti-tank, as it used that type of armament, it seems more realistic to assume that it would have been used to attack the LCA. The interior of the island would have had thousands of suicide commands waiting for the Sherman tanks with 10-kg magnetic demolition charges of the 'lung mine' type.

The interceptor was equipped with oxygen, pressurised cockpit and reflex gunsight. It was towed by a conventional piston fighter that took it off above 8,000 m releasing it over the stream of bombers. It was armed with eight Ro.3 rockets that exploded by means of a time fuse at a predetermined distance, releasing shrapnel and incendiary pellets in a conical pattern.

Like its German counterpart W.Gr 21, the Ro.3 was not very accurate and lost altitude very fast. For that reason, the launching tubes were fixed at a 7-degree pitch, calculated so that the parabolic path of the rocket would be compatible with the performance of the reflector gunsight.

All versions of the Shinryu II had machine guns with ammo tracer to help the correction of the attack trajectories. These would also be of use to the interceptor to defend from the escort fighters, evade them thanks to its manoeuvrability and return to base on a gliding flight. The four rocket engines, started sequentially, would help it to regain altitude after an attack over the formation of B-29s or to distance away from the escort fighters.

Technical Data

Airframe: wood, fabric and iron plate
Wingspan: 10 m
Length 7.80 m in the interceptor version
Height: 2.70 m
Wing area: 19 sq. m
Max. speed: 500 kph in the *kamikaze* version
Ceiling: over 8,000 m in the interceptor version
Range: 15 km in the *kamikaze* version
Engines: 4 × Toku-Ro.1 Type 2 with 600-kg peak thrust during thirty seconds. In the anti-tank and *kamikaze* version another Toku-Ro.1 Type 1 was used with 300-kg peak thrust during ten seconds, in ventral position, to provide additional boost during take-off
Armament: 4 × Type 89, 7.7-mm guns that were reduced to two in the *kamikaze* version. Eight Ro.San Dan (Ro.3) 10-cm SCR AA rockets in the interceptor version, eight ROTSU 8 cm S.C.R. hollow charge rockets in the ant ship/antitank version, two or four RAK 12-cm I.S.R. barrage rockets and one 248.7-kg Type 99 Number 25 Model 1 bomb in the *kamikaze* version.

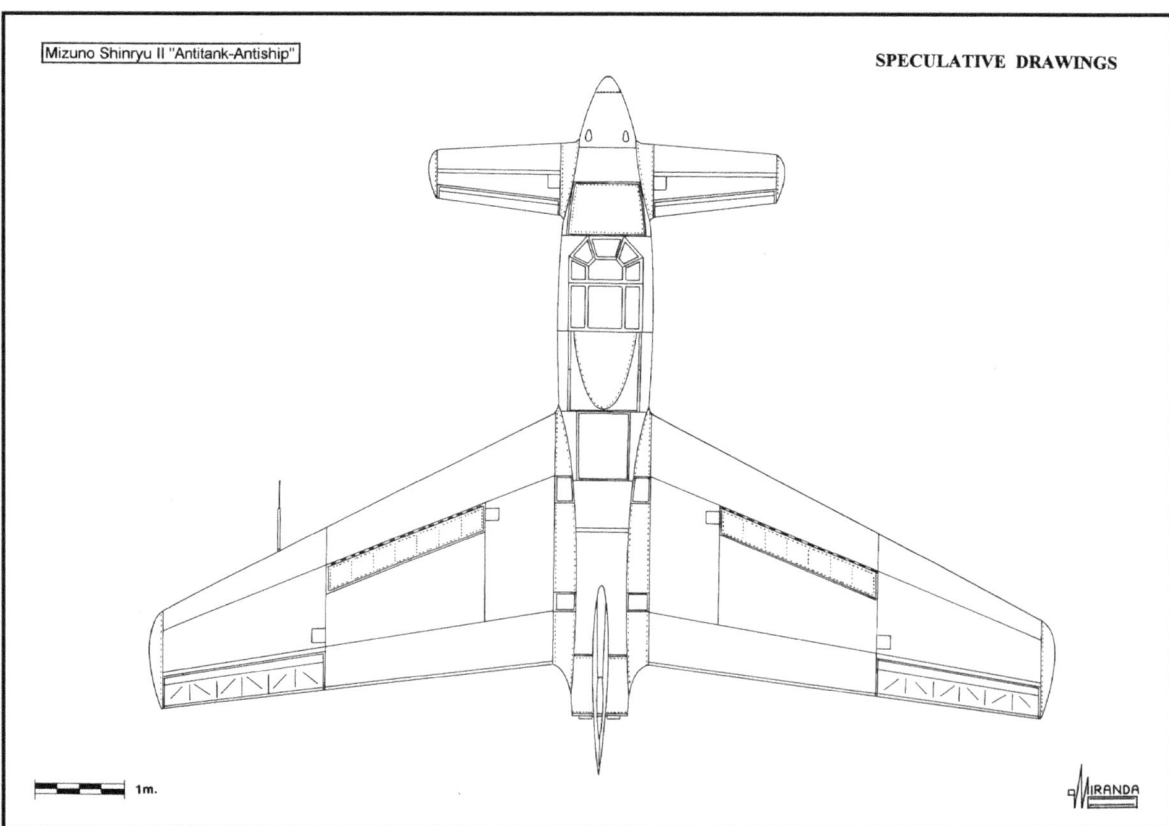

Mizuno Shinryu II "Antitank-Antiship"

SPECULATIVE DRAWINGS

1m.

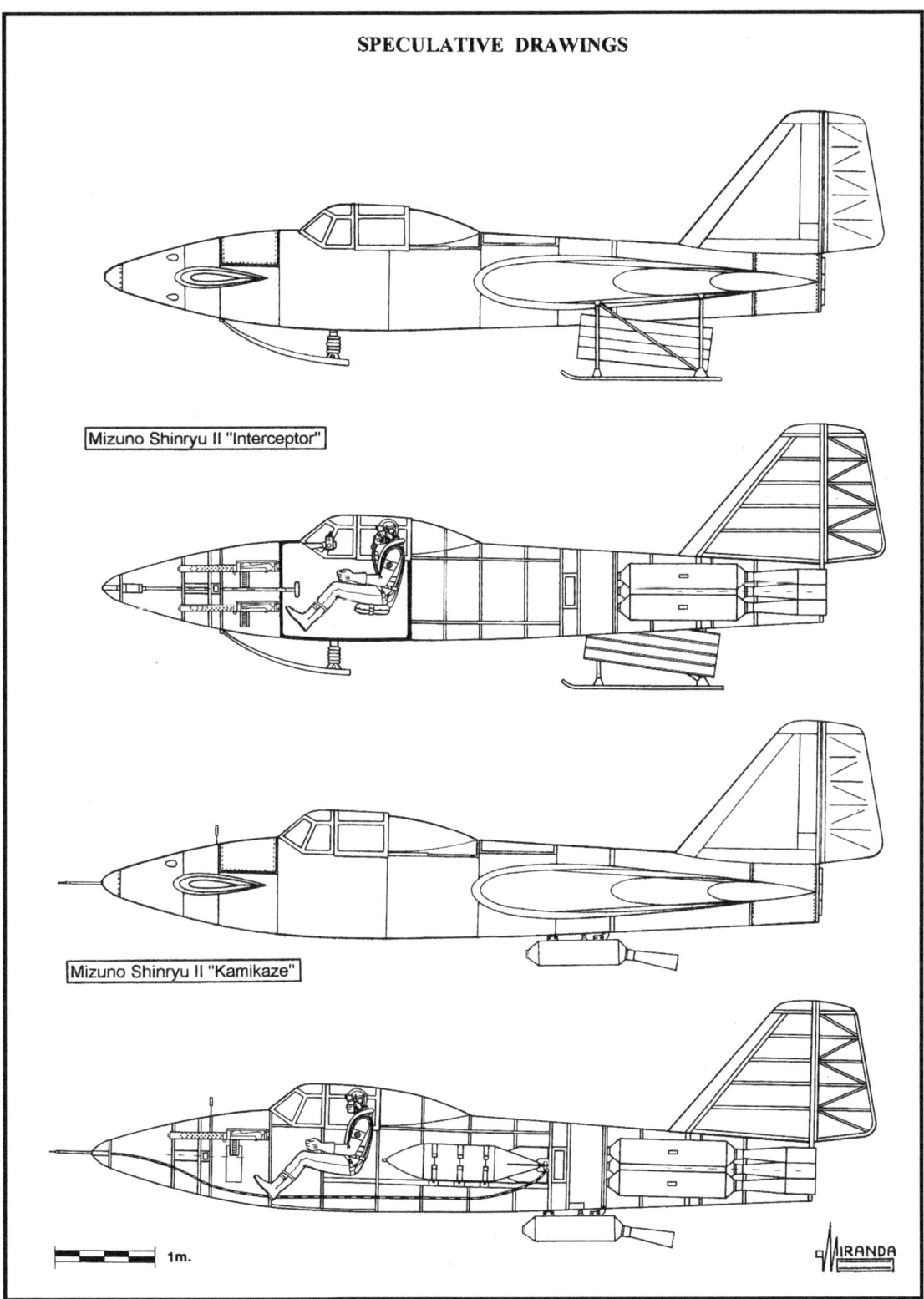

SPECULATIVE DRAWINGS

Mizuno Shinryu II "Interceptor"

Mizuno Shinryu II "Kamikaze"

1m.

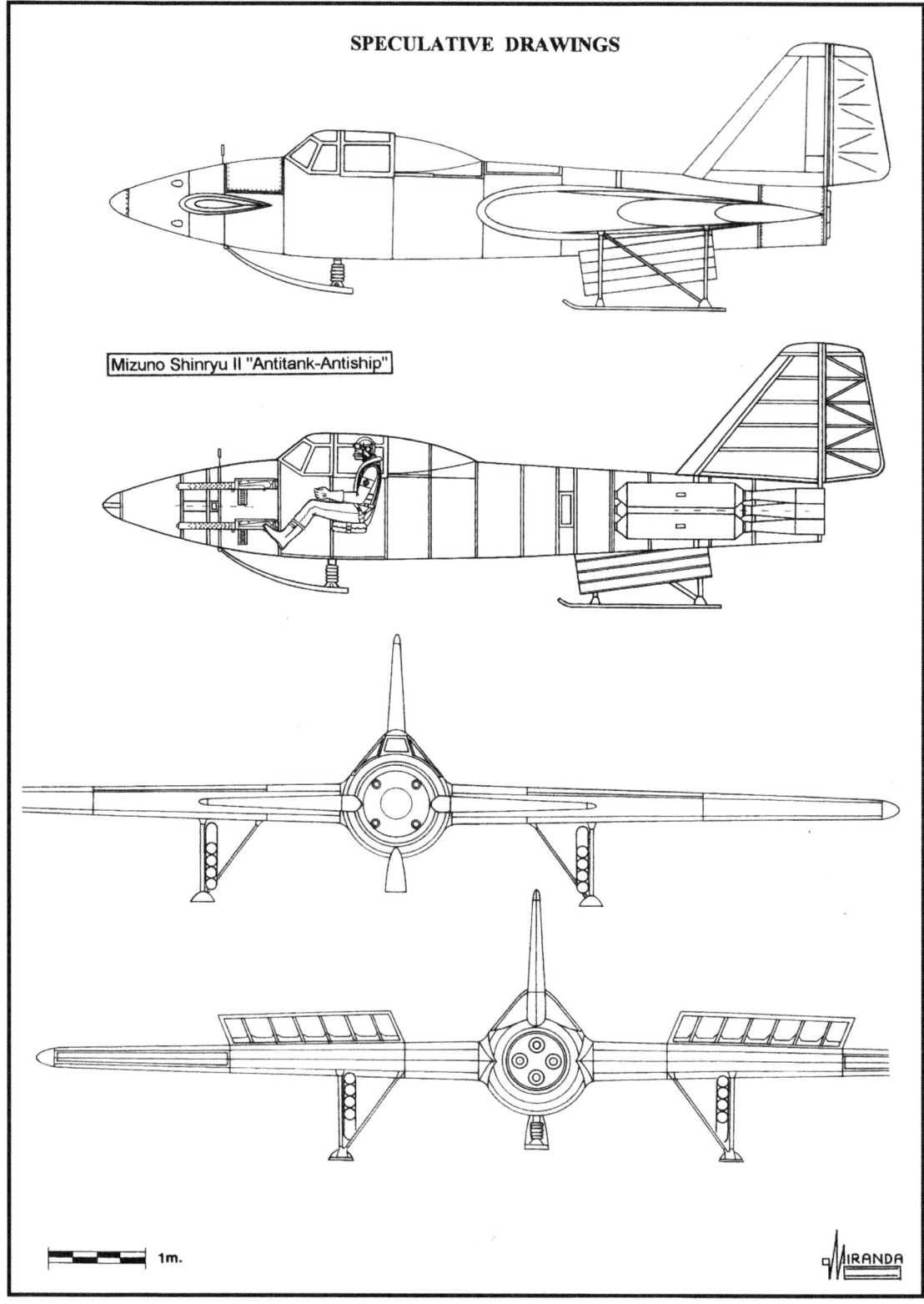

SPECULATIVE DRAWINGS

Mizuno Shinryu II "Antitank-Antiship"

1m.

MIRANDA

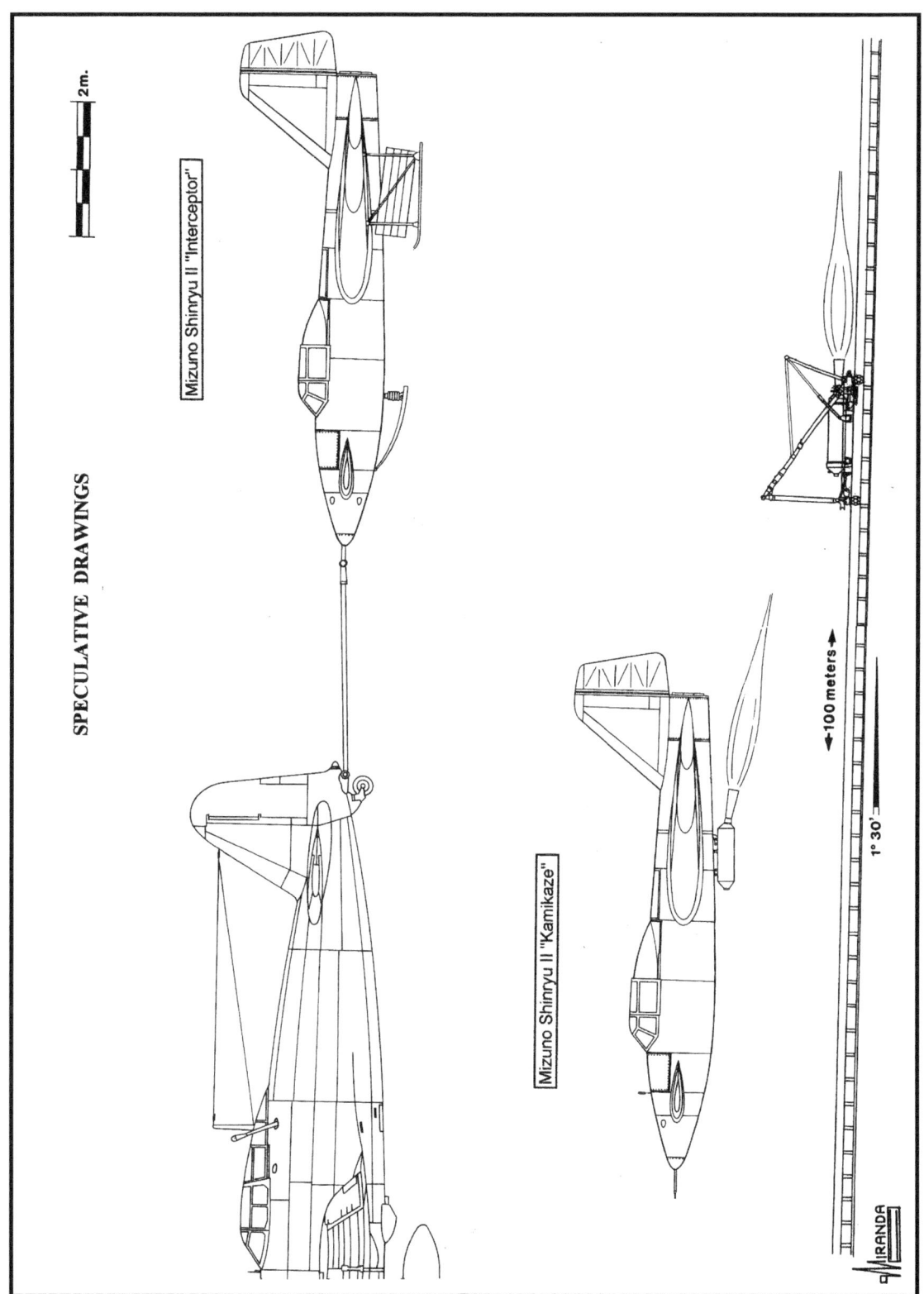

SPECULATIVE DRAWINGS

2 m.

Mizuno Shinryu II "Interceptor"

Mizuno Shinryu II "Kamikaze"

100 meters

1° 30'

MIRANDA

Kakukyoku Rammer

The Kakukyoku Rammer was a radio-guided, anti-aircraft, vertically launched ramming missile designed by Yujiro Murakami in March 1945, following a requirement of the IJN. It was exclusively propelled by solid fuel rockets and could reach 9,000 m in altitude in 100 seconds.

The absence of an explosive warhead required a degree of accurateness that was impossible to achieve with the primitive guidance systems of the time. Therefore, the missile was reconverted into a piloted rammer, a project shared between the IJN and the IJA to be handed over to the Kawasaki Company.

The vertical take-off was discarded as the g-forces would have been excessive and rendered the pilot unconscious. The rammer would be towered by a high-altitude interceptor up to 10,000 m and released near the bomber stream. The pilot would then fire the four rockets until reaching Mach 0.91 in six seconds and fly in a collision path towards the B.29 without any possibility of surviving.

Technical Data

Airframe: steel and wood. Cockpit pressurised, with oxygen system and telephonic link with the towing plane. It had no control panel, just the controls of a glider plus a handle to detach the trolley after take-off and another to get detached from the towing plane
Engines: 4 × solid fuel rockets Toku-Ro.1 Type 1 with 300-kg thrust each for ten seconds.
Wingspan: 4.44 m
Length: 3.45 m
Height: 1.80 m
Wing area: 5 sq. m
Max. weight: 800 kg
Max. speed: Mach 0.91
Ceiling: 10,000 m
Climb rate: 312 m/s

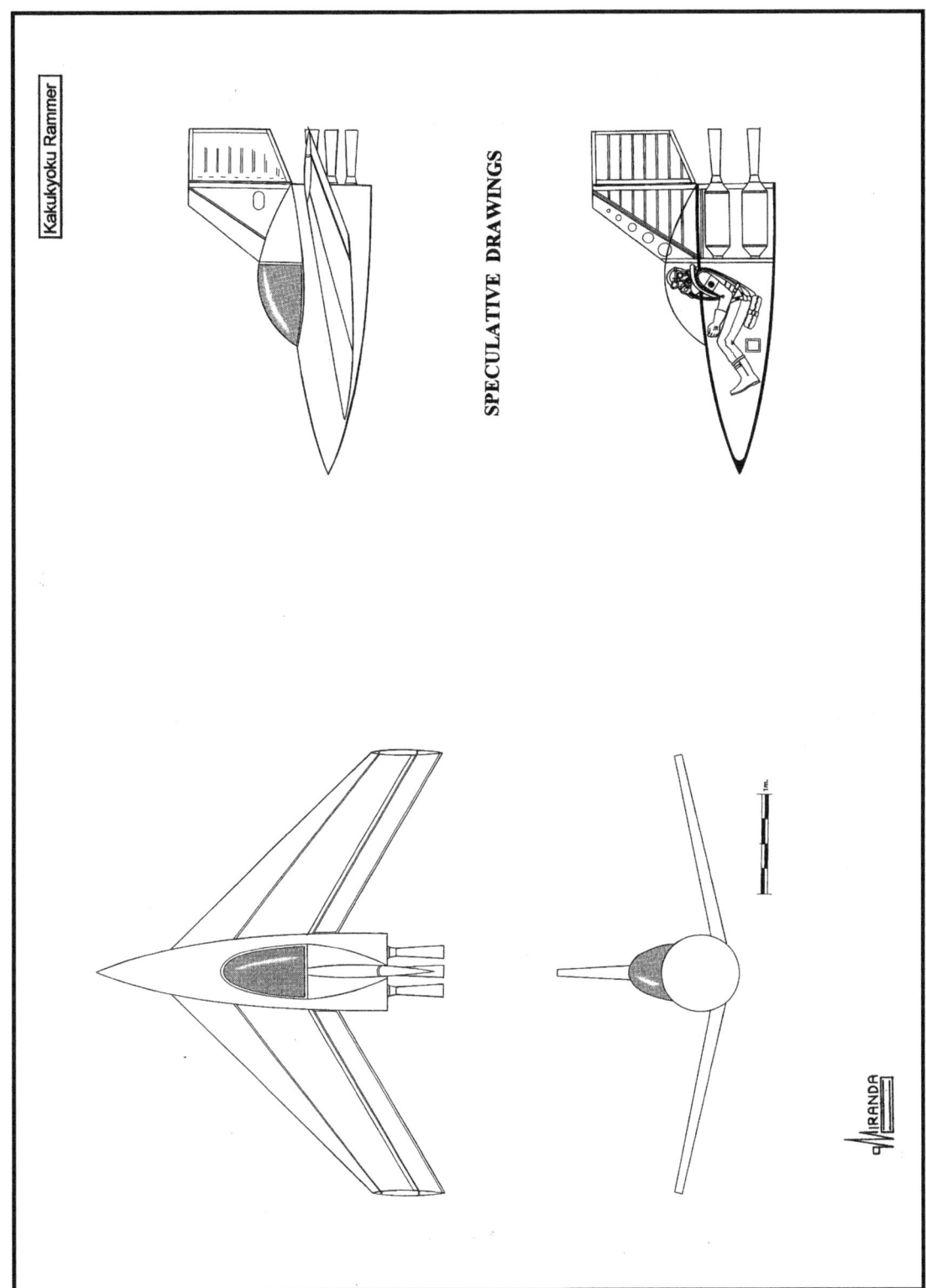

Kakukyoku Rammer

SPECULATIVE DRAWINGS

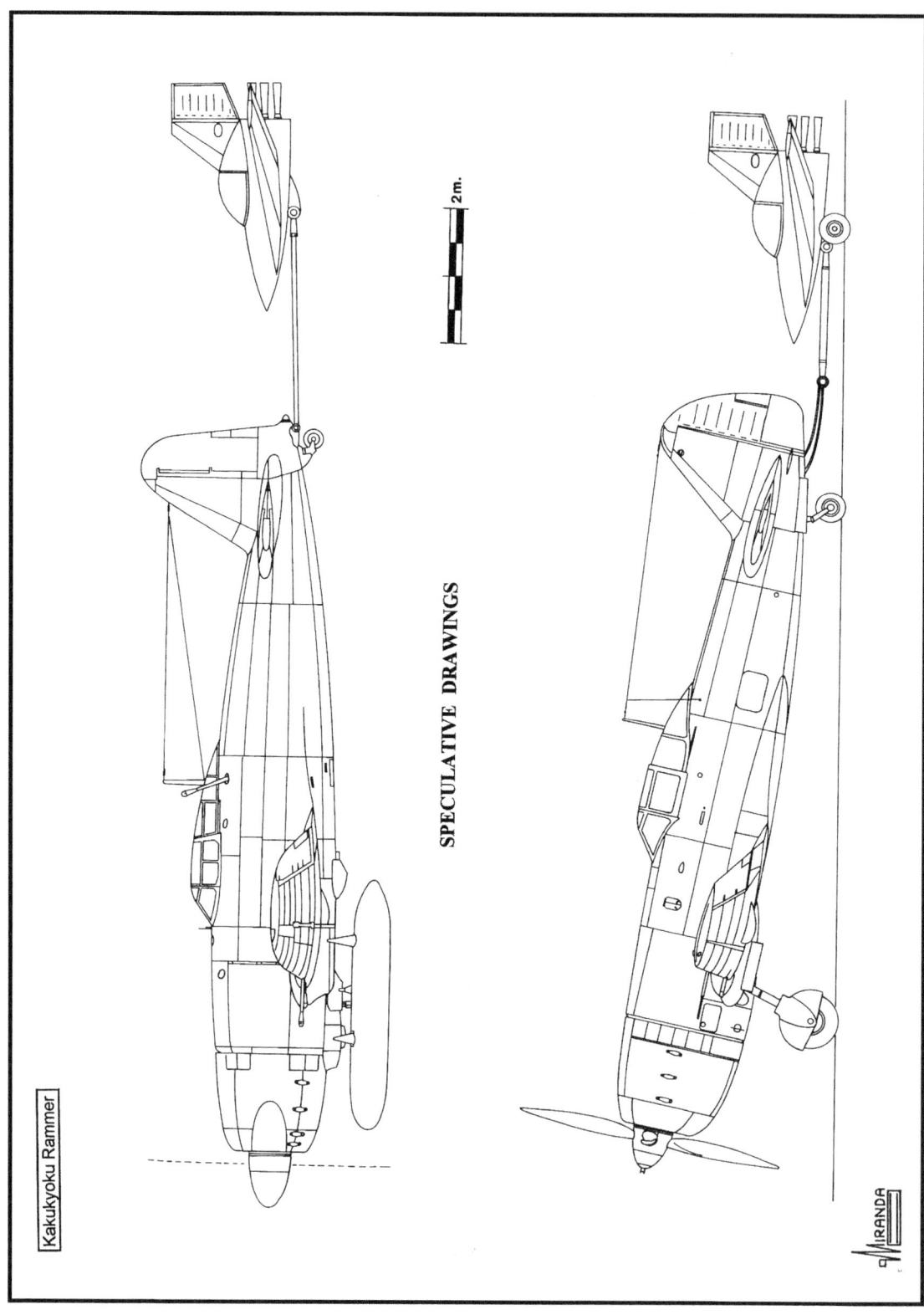

Kakukyoku Rammer

SPECULATIVE DRAWINGS

2m.

Kayaba Katsuodori

Despite their appearances, the short range of the aircraft powered by rockets seriously hindered its military use. The logical alternative was to favour the development of the turbojet to achieve more reliable and powerful engines. Unfortunately, the Japanese industry was not able to produce the required metallic alloys, which were especially resistant to heat and stress. They lacked metals like chromium and molybdenum that were essential to harden the steel.

Yet the advanced materials for the compressor blades of the turbojets would not be ready on time and everyone was aware of it. The Maru Ka-10 pulsejet did not have enough power, and it was soon made evident that they were a dead end. The vibrations they generated were destructive to the aircraft's structure. The situation demanded a new type of engine capable of running on any fuel and easy to build with cheap metals, so the Japanese aircraft industry was forced to consider the use of ramjets.

The theory elaborated by René Lorin in 1913 established that this type of engine produced the maximum thrust at Mach 2, but the theoretical work carried out in Germany by Dr Eugen Sänger in 1940 showed that a ramjet built with a length:diameter ratio of 5:1 could work in the high subsonic speed range, with a lower specific fuel consumption than a rocket and higher thrust than a turbojet.

In the forward conical portion of the engine, the airflow would be decelerated with a simultaneous pressure increase to approximately one-sixth of the flight speed. In the cylindrical combustion chamber, the fuel is injected according to the throttling and mixed with the flowing air. At a speed above 200 kph, the air inlet pressure is enough to start ignition using a ring of spark plugs, with the gases ejected from the jet pipe at a superior speed than that of flying. The first tests carried out in 1941 in the LFA-Volkenrode produced very long flames, discouraging wind tunnel tests with ramjets. Ground tests began in autumn 1941 with a prototype mounted above the Opel-Blitz truck.

In March 1942, a Sänger ramjet with a diameter of 500 mm was tested in flight, mounted above a Dornier Do 17 Z bomber, provided by the DFS *Institut* in Ainring. In December, a second test was carried out with a ramjet of 1,500 mm mounted above a Dornier Do 217 E-2. In the summer of 1944, the same aircraft was used to test the final version of 1,000 mm. The ramjet worked correctly every time, although with low thrust due to the low speed of the bomber.

In theory, the Sänger 1000 had a nominal output of 17,400 hp, the Sänger 1500 of 22,000 hp, and the Sänger 2000 of 61,000 hp, but this could only be demonstrated by installing them on an aircraft capable of flying at Mach 0.8 and an altitude of 15,000 m. In January 1945, the DFS *Institut* issued a report suggesting the mounting of two Sänger 1000 above the wings of a Me 262 A-1. An increase of 200 kph in maximum speed, an increase of 4,000 m absolute ceiling, and the reduction of the climbing time to 10,000 m from twenty-six to six minutes were expected. The plan was thereby frustrated by the shortage of J2 fuel available for flying tests.

On 30 November 1944, the RLM requested the design of a ramjet propelled fighter. In December, the Oberammergau project bureau started working on a version of the Messerschmitt P.1101 powered by a Sänger 1000 in anticipation that the HeS 011 turbojet would not be ready on time. The modifications consisted of increasing the diameter of the fuselage, installing three fuel tanks of 1,500, 500, and 120 litres, and designing a new landing gear whose main wheels would retract in tandem under the engine. The take-off was effected with the help of eight detachable RATO rockets of the Schmidding type 109-533, with 1,000-kp peak thrust each, which accelerated the aircraft to 120 m/sec. The new version was called Messerschmitt P.1101 L (*Lorinantrieb*).

In December 1944, Professor Sänger designed the Überschall-Staustrahljäger (supersonic ramjet fighter), a high-altitude interceptor of 7 tons propelled by a ramjet of 60,000 hp, but the DFS Institut lacked the facilities for its construction. In February 1945, the firm Skoda-Kauba Flugzeugbau-Cakowitz, who had carried out some discouraging experiments with foam coal ramjets, issued an order to the RLM for the design of an interceptor with ramjet propulsion based on the theoretical work of Sänger.

On 25 February 1945, the company produced the SK P14-01 design, a Mach 0.815 fighter powered by a Sänger 1500 with 22,000 hp nominal thrust, 1,000 litres of fuel, the pilot in a prone position, one MK 103/30 heavy cannon, a landing skid, and an estimated absolute ceiling of 10,000 m. The definitive design dated in April was the seven-tone SK P12-02, powered by a Sänger 2500 with 60,000 hp nominal thrust, 1,400 litres of fuel, and a maximum speed of 850 kph. Take-off acceleration was provided by four Schmidding 109-533, mounted above a detachable tricycle trolley.

In March 1945, a Heinkel design team under the leadership of the *Dipl.-Ing.* Siegfried Günter designed a high-altitude tailless interceptor named He P.1080, with a 15,100-hp Sänger 900 in each wing root, an armament of two MK 108/30 cannons, and a maximum take-off weight of 3.325 kg. The P.1080 could fly for ninety minutes with 1,100 kg of fuel at an estimated maximum speed of 980 kph. The take-off was carried out from a detachable trolley propelled by four RATOG Schmidding 109-533 rockets. The P.1080 was the last project developed by the firm during the Second World War.

In 1938, the Kayaba-Seisakusho Works Corporation was sponsored by the IJA Aero-Technical Research Institute (*Rikugun*) to investigate the feasibility of tailless aircraft. In January 1939, the HK-1 flew for the first time—a tailless glider with a 25-degree swept wing. The following prototype, the K2, had wingtips fins and flew by early November 1940. The K3 had a cranked rear swept flying wing with three pairs of control surfaces on the trailing edge. It was destroyed in 1941, unable to recover stability during a flat spin.

At that time, Japan was already preparing for war and the IA cancelled the Kayaba programme to concentrate its efforts on the production of the Ki.43 and Ki.44 conventional fighters. In 1943, the IJA No. 2 Aeronautical Technology Research Institute, in collaboration with Kawasaki, built the Ne 0 ramjet engine based on the designs of the Sänger. The Ne 0 was 2.10 m long with a combustion chamber of 60 cm in diameter.

During ground tests conducted in July, the ramjet produced 60 kgf static thrust and at the end of that year was tested in suspended flight under the fuselage of a Kawasaki Ki.48-II bomber. Early in 1944, the IJA ordered to Kayaba the design of the Katsuodori, a ramjet point interceptor powered by an advanced version of the Ne 0 with 750 kgf thrust.

The new engine, called Kayaba Model 1, had a combustion chamber 1 m in diameter and could run with heavy kerosene or crude pine root oil that the local chemical industry produced as ersatz fuel. The Katsuodori would have had a very similar airframe to that of the Heinkel P.1078 C German project of February 1944, with 35-degree rear-swept wings built with wood and plywood, with vertical fins in the wingtips, containing 2,000 litres of fuel. The circular fuselage would be built using steel and contain the ramjet and cockpit with the pilot in a prone position.

The take-off was made with detachable landing gear and the help of four Toku-Ro.1 Type 3 RATOG detachable rockets, with 600 kgf peak thrust and twenty seconds of life. The ramjet started at 367 kph and could run for thirty minutes. When the fuel ran out, the Katsuodori landed like a glider on a retractable skid and a tailwheel. Kayaba had planned to manufacture its own version of the Ho-301, a 40-mm recoilless rocket-gun, modifying it to fire 30-mm rounds.

In July 1944, the IJA decided to cancel the Katsuodori to concentrate on the manufacture of the Mitsubishi Ki.200 rocket fighter. To salvage the project, Kayaba adapted its design to accept the Ne 20 turbojet. The prototype was expected to be completed by the end of 1944, but the award of Ne 20 to the Kikka programme forced its final cancellation.

Kayaba Katsuodori Technical Data

Wingspan: 8.99 m
Length: 4.48 m
Height: 1.85 m
Wing area: 12.57 sq. m
Max. weight: 3,000 kg
Max. speed: 900 kph
Service ceiling: 15,000 m

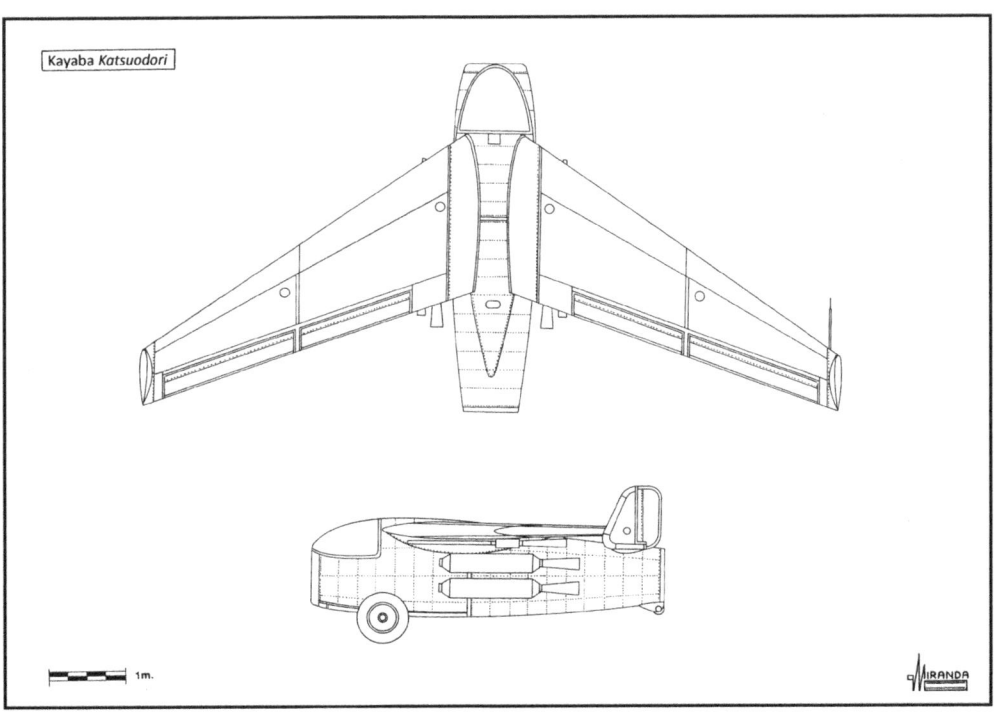

Kayaba *Katsuodori*

1m.

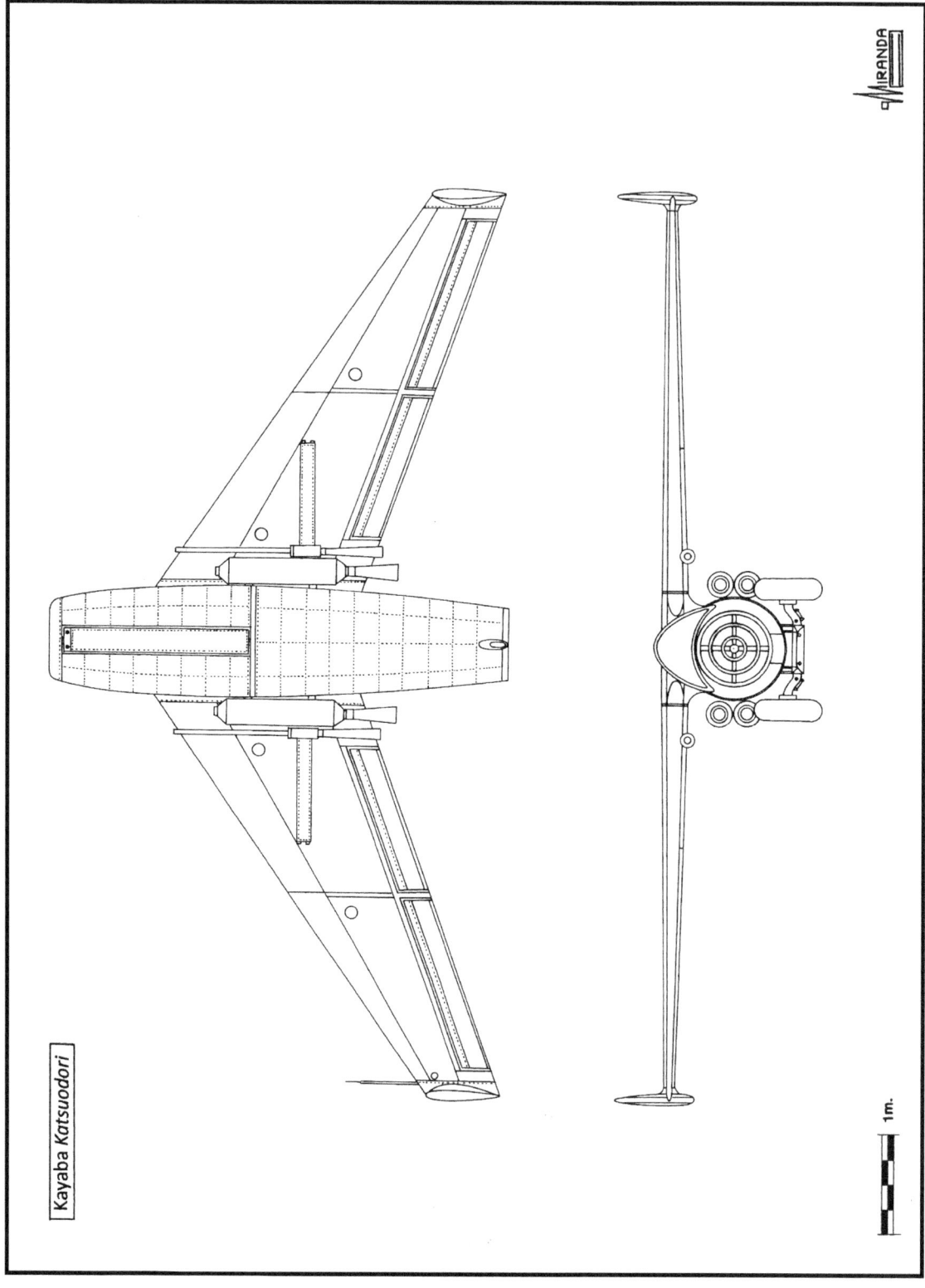

Kayaba *Katsuodori*

1m.

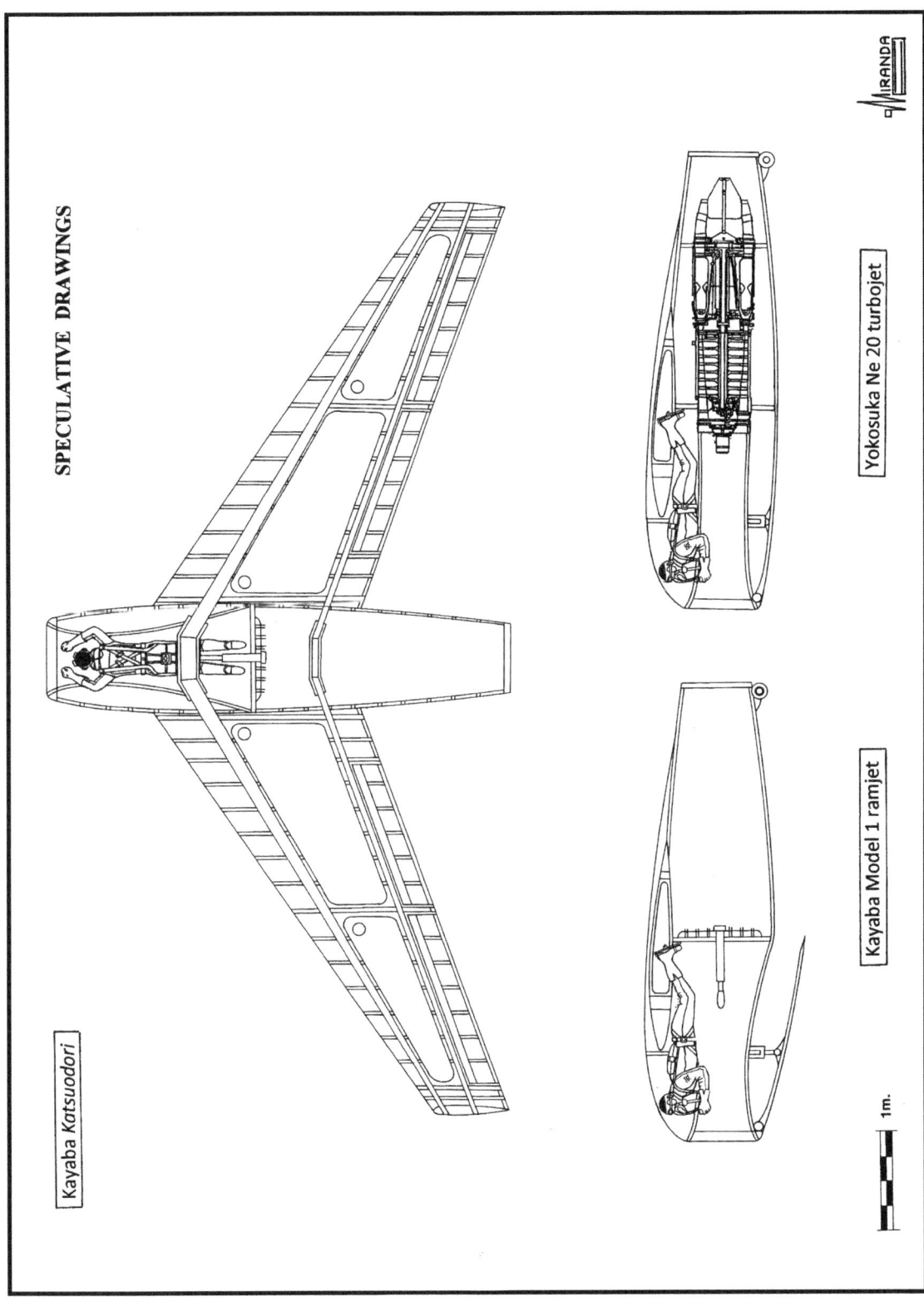

SPECULATIVE DRAWINGS

Kayaba *Katsuodori*

Yokosuka Ne 20 turbojet

Kayaba Model 1 ramjet

1 m.

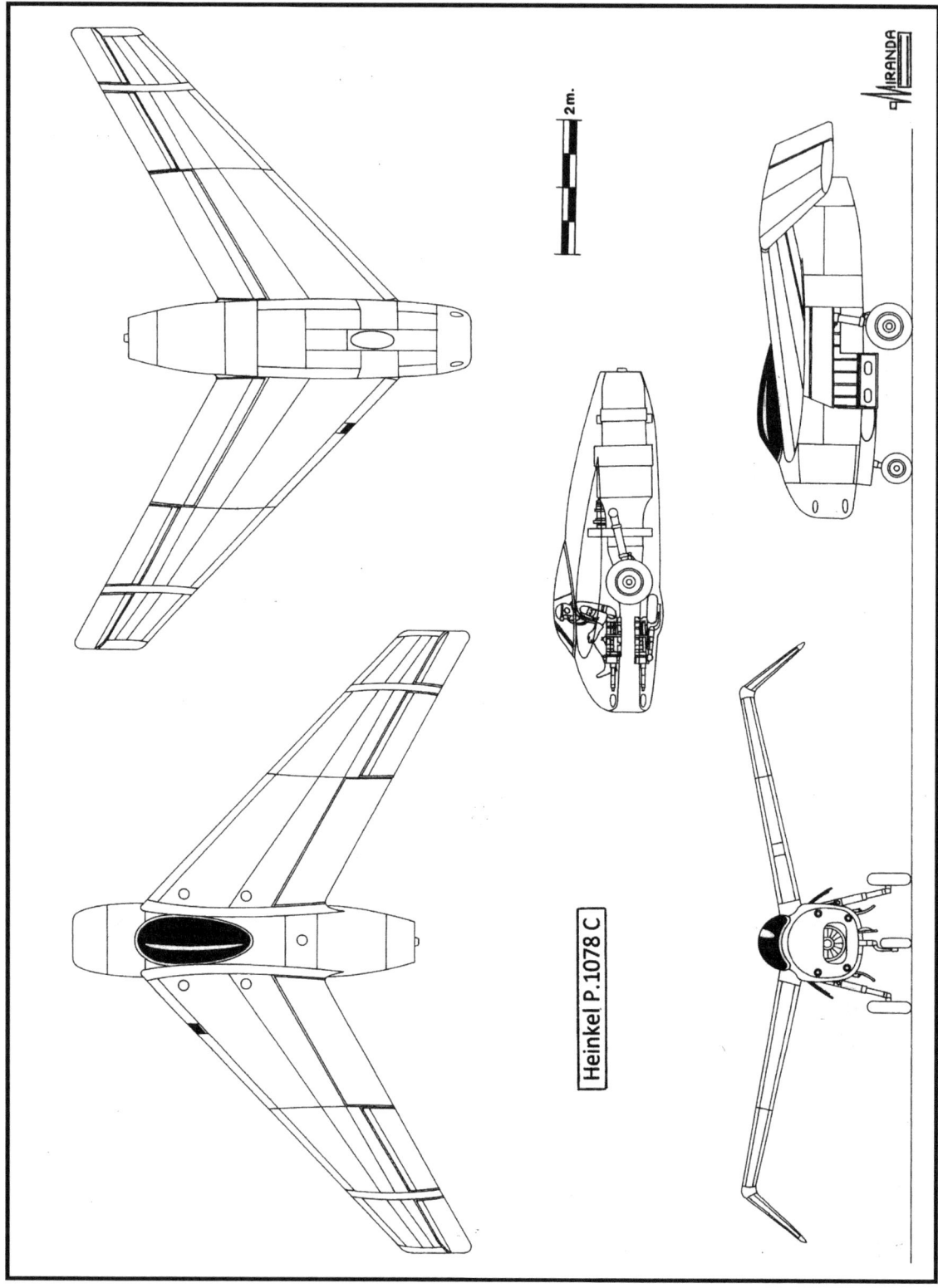

2 m.

Heinkel P.1078 C

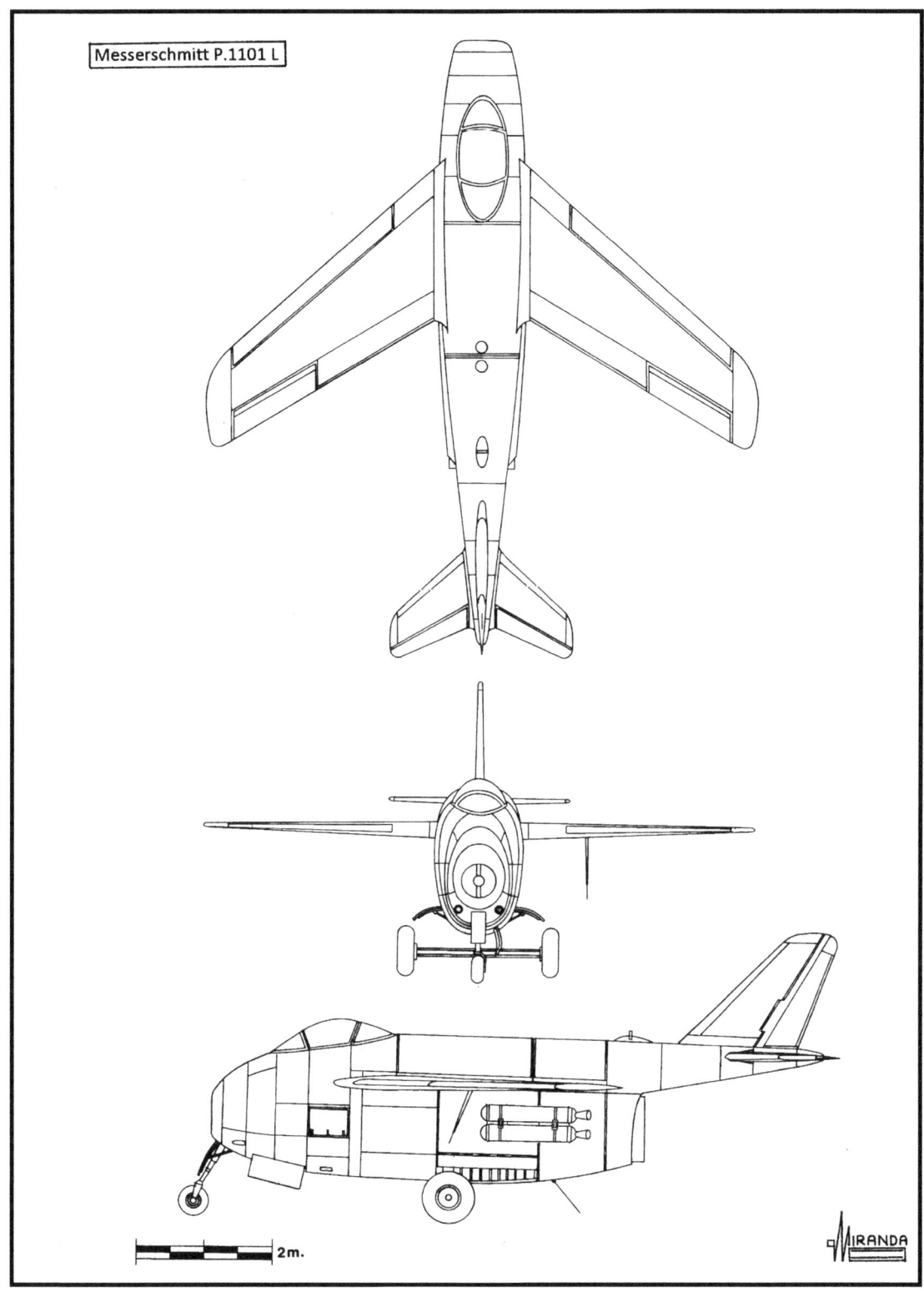

Messerschmitt P.1101 L

2m.

Fighters of the Dying Sun

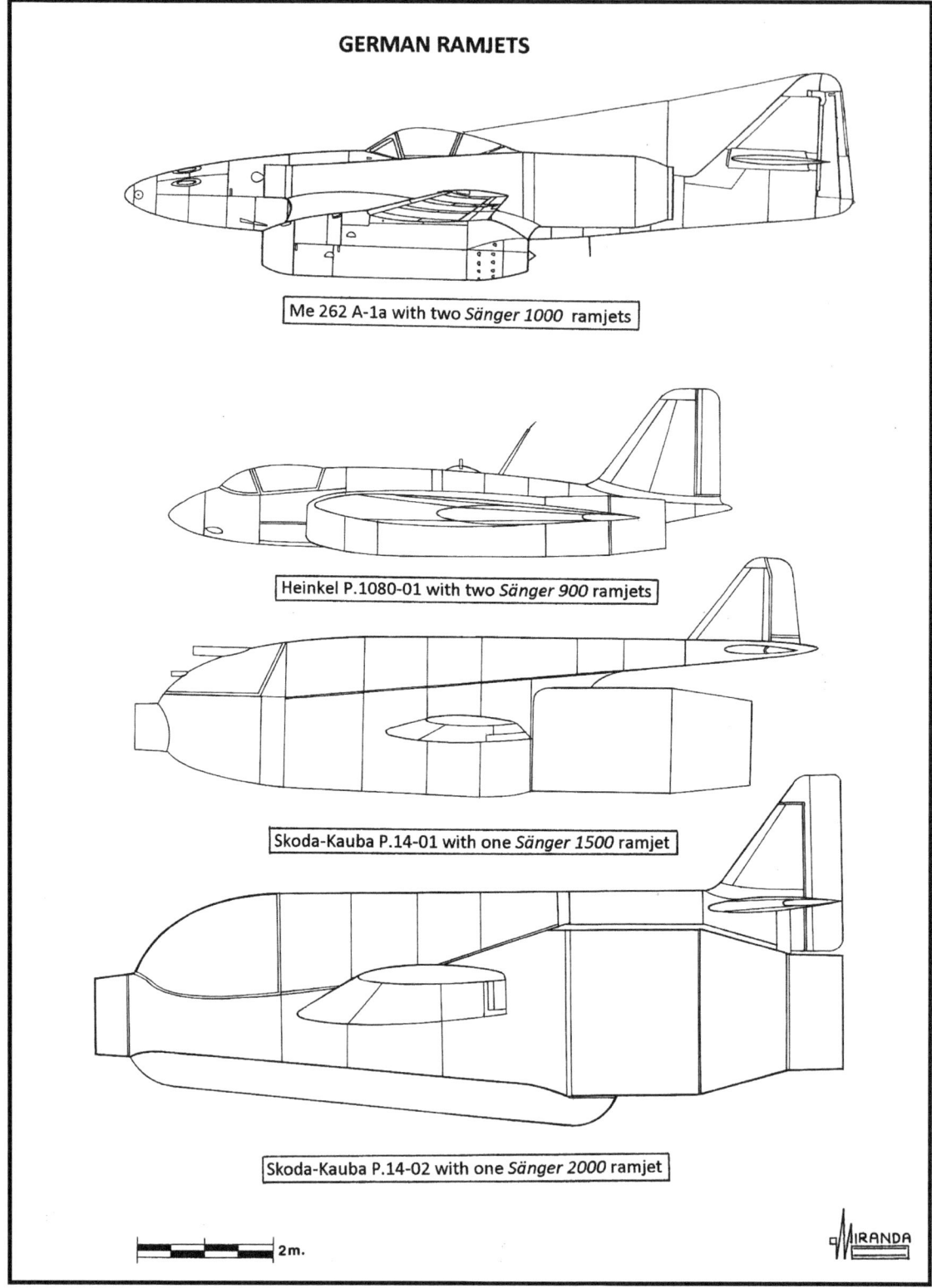

GERMAN RAMJETS

Me 262 A-1a with two *Sänger 1000* ramjets

Heinkel P.1080-01 with two *Sänger 900* ramjets

Skoda-Kauba P.14-01 with one *Sänger 1500* ramjet

Skoda-Kauba P.14-02 with one *Sänger 2000* ramjet

2 m.

MIRANDA

4

Rocket Fighters

For many years, Alexander M. Lippisch was one of the most audacious aeronautical designers in the world. Always ahead of his time and seldom understood for his technological innovation, he obtained some official support thanks only to the exceptional circumstances created during the Second World War.

During the 1920s and '30s, he methodically followed his dream of building a tailless aircraft that would be stable and safe enough for civil use. His working method consisted of testing the new ideas, first as a flying balsa model, then as a manned glider, and finally as a powered aircraft. The results achieved with his sport aircraft—Ente, Storch, and Delta—were not very good. They were machines that were difficult to fly and often required seasoned pilots.

The 'Delta IV c' developed in 1936, with the support of the *Deutsche Forschungsanstalt für Segelflug*, was the first Lippisch design to obtain a full certificate of airworthiness as DFS 39. The development of liquid-fuel rockets in Germany had reached the level of practical results in 1936. Wernher von Braun worked on a 300-kg thrust engine in Kummersdorf and Helmut Walter on the 400-kg HWK RI. In 1937, Heinkel performed tests with both engines, which were still very unstable, with a tendency to explode. The von Braun engine promised to reach 900 kg and Walter engine intended to reach 600 kg before a year.

After the He 176 flight, the new power system could not be ignored anymore, although it attracted the RLM attention in the worst sense. The Luftwaffe had not forgiven the Heinkel He 51 fiasco during the Spanish Civil War and had already decided that the main fighter provider onwards would be Messerschmitt and that the new rocket engine was ideal to power a high-altitude interceptor. The authorisation to build the He 176 V2 was denied and the V1 was sent to the Berlin Air Museum.

Dr Lorenz of the *Technische Amt* (Research Department of the Air Ministry of the Reich), which was sponsoring the Walter developments, was convinced that the conventional aircraft were not fitted to use the new powering system, as confirmed with the He 176. In his opinion, the tailless/swept-wing design would be right to reach the high speeds that were desired.

As Lippisch was the most experienced German designer in this field, Dr Lorenz contacted him to propose the development of a DFS 39 version—able to fly at 500 km/h—as a technological demonstrator of the Walter HWK RI-203 rocket that promised enormous power for its weight. The engine used compressed air to force a weak concentration of hydrogen peroxide into a reaction chamber, lined with a paste catalyst, which instantly changed it into water and oxygen. The reaction is so violent that the water emerges as superheated steam, able to provide power after accelerating in the Venturi nozzle.

By the beginning of 1937, the RLM signed a contract with the DFS for the construction of the aircraft, classified as Projekt X under great security measures. Lippisch was only informed of the size, weight, and engine thrust, but he was not provided with blueprints. The first tests performed with wind tunnel models, in the AVA Göttingen, proved that the DFS 39 airframe was not fitted either to support the rocket thrust or fly at high altitude.

To that purpose, a completely new aircraft known as Delta VI d or DFS 194 was designed. Two different variants were considered: *Ausführung I* with anhedral wingtips and reduced tailfin and *Ausführung II* with straight wingtips and a higher tailfin. On 7 July 1938, it was decided to proceed with the development of the *Ausführung II* as it was more stable at high speed. To research behaviour at low speed, a wooden prototype powered by a conventional engine with a pusher airscrew was constructed, to complement the theoretical work, by the end of 1938.

The OKL, worried by the research made by the Soviets on this same field, vetoed its construction to avoid potential leaks, as well as any contact between DFS and Heinkel. This was to be a problem because Lippisch had just discovered that the highly volatile rocket fuel could react with wood causing fires. The DFS lacked the technical means to build a metallic fuselage and so, they contacted Heinkel for that, given its experience with the RI-203.

The official criterion finally imposed and the whole *Projekt X* team moved to the Messerschmitt complex of Augsburg where it was integrated as *Abteilung L* on 1 January 1939. The DFS 194 fuselage with steel tube and Electron (magnesium) sheet skinning was built there. Projekt X was then named Messerschmitt Me 163.

Using the facilities offered by Messerschmitt, it was possible to integrate a Walter RI-203 'cold' rocket engine with 400 kg thrust in the metallic fuselage. Yet the power plant assemblies were integrated with the aircraft airframe, with only the fuel and compressed air lines being removable. As a result, all static tests had to be carried out in the airframe, and the wooden wings were not installed to avoid corrosion problems.

Problems of accessibility and low serviceability advised the design of the Messerschmitt Me 163 A in a way that the rocket was easily removable. In August 1940, the DFS 194 made several test flights in Peenemünde, reaching 550 km/h in one of them. After the good results achieved, the construction of the Me 163 A prototype received the highest priority.

It was conceived as a transitional experimental model, to obtain information applicable to a future fighter version. The Me 163 A had a wooden wing that was 78 cm shorter than the one in the DFS 194 and the trailing edge swept increased from 7 to 10 degrees to improve the pitch moment arm of the elevons at Mach 0.8 critical number. The aircraft was aerodynamically very clean and tended to float in ground effect, which caused some accidents during the first test flights.

To improve the stalling characteristics, 'Type C' leading-edge slots, designed by J. Hubert, were installed in the 40 per cent span with drag landing flaps under the inboard half of the wings. They had the hinge line well forward of the trailing edge so that the pitching moment was not affected. The fuselage was modified to facilitate access to the engine, a 'cold' HWK RII-203 with 750 kg pneumatic controllable thrust and operational temperature of 500 degrees C. The canopy improved its aerodynamics and the tailfin increased its height to 22 cm.

The Me 163 A V1 made its first flight without an engine on 13 February 1941, reaching a speed of 850 km/h in a dive, during its test program. On 13 August, a Me 163 A, powered by a 750-kg variable thrust Walter R II-203 b, flew for the first time. In a subsequent test, it reached 805 km/h in level flight.

The fuel rocket burnt so fast during take-off that the fuel tanks were empty before the end of the tests. To find out the limits, the Me 163 A V4 was towed up to 13,000 feet by a Messerschmitt Bf 110 over Peenemünde West, with a full load of fuel, on 2 October. After the rockets ignited, the aircraft reached Mach 0.84 before suffering the compressibility effects.

The shockwave caused the airflow over the outer wing to separate suddenly, and the aircraft pitched nose down at 11g, plunging into a dive following a shock stall. Shutting the engine, the pilot recovered control, landing normally. It was afterwards ascertained that it had flown at 1,004.5 km/h. The record was kept secret for security reasons, and the construction of eight additional prototypes was ordered to serve as trainers of the Me 163 B, the fighter version.

On 22 October, the OKL approved the construction of seventy airframes of the 'B' series in the Regensburg plant. Production started on 1 December 1941. At that time, the delivery of the RII-211 engines started to suffer delays, putting at risk the whole program. Officially known as HWK 109-509 A, it was a 'hot' double combustion engine, able to operate at 1,750 degrees C with 1,500 kg in the A-O version, 1,600 kg in the A-1 version, and 1,700 kg in the A-2 version. The new engine burnt two types of hypergolic propellants: T-Stoff hydrogen peroxide at a highly concentrated solution and a C-Stoff mixture of methanol (57 per cent), hydrazine hydrate catalyst (30 per cent), and a watery solution of potassium cuprocyanide (13 per cent).

Its production was slow as it represented an excessive technological jump for its time. It was not until August 1943 that the Me 163B V2 made its first flight, powered by the RII-211. At the beginning of 1943, the OKL had serious doubts about the viability of the operational version of the Me 163 Komet. Alongside various clashes that occurred during flight tests, there was a delay in the availability of the HWK RII-211 rocket engine; its first approved units for flying—still far from being safe—would not arrive at Peenemünde until July.

With the appearance of Boeing B-29 bombers in Japanese skies, the IJN leadership decided to copy the Me 163 rocket fighter using the German-supplied manuals as well as a Walter HWK 109-509 rocket engine. On 27 July 1944, a joint IJN-IJA commission formally ordered Mitsubishi to develop their own version of the Komet, named 19-shi-Experimental Interceptor Fighter, using reverse-engineered solutions. The final project was presented to the IJN in August 1944, and the mock-up was subsequently inspected in September.

The prototype, named J8M1 Shusui, flew for the first time on 8 January 1945, with water ballast, towed aloft by a Nakajima B6N1 Tenzan bomber. The first powered flight test took place on 7 July 1945, with the prototype being destroyed because of an engine malfunction.

J8M1 Model 19 Technical Data

Wingspan: 9.5 m
Length: 6.05 m
Height: 2.7 m
Wing area: 17.73 sq. m
Max. weight: 3,870 kg
Max. speed: 888 kph
Service ceiling: 12,000 m
Climb rate: 230 sec. to 10,000 m
Armament: 2 × Type 5 30-mm cannons with 400 rpm and fifty-three rounds per gun

The version of the IJA received the *kitai* number Ki.200 and differed from the J8M1 in having a shorter fuselage with no side windows behind the cockpit. The trolley attachment was moved 30 cm forward to improve stability during take-off. Internally, the hydraulic system and propellant piping were modified to make them safer. The armament was replaced by two Ho-155-II cannons.

Ki.200 Technical Data

Wingspan: 9.5 m
Length: 5.95 m
Height: 2.7 m
Wing area: 17.73 sq. m
Max. weight: 3,000 kg
Max. speed: 800 kph
Armament: 2 × Ho-105-II 30-mm cannons with 450 rpm and fifty-three rounds per gun

Both versions were powered by a Yamakita-Matsumoto Toku-Ro.2 (KR 10) 'hot' bi-propellant rocket engine, with 1,500 Kgf peak thrust. In Japan, the T-Stoff propellant was called Ko-Stoff and the C-Stoff was Otsu-Stoff. Both were colourless liquids that were easy to confuse, which was the cause of several accidents. It was manufactured at the Edogawa Kagaku and Mitsubishi Kasei facilities.

The Shusui fuselage was built with light alloy and steel. It contained a cockpit (with armoured glass screen and seat steel plates, radio and oxygen equipment), 106 ammunition rounds, five propellants tanks with 1,159 litres of Ko-Stoff, one 2.48-m-long Toku-Ro.2 rocket engine, one 1.8-m-long retractable skid, one retractable 200 × 75 mm tailwheel, the detachable undercarriage dolly with two 700 × 200 mm wheels, and attachment points for two detachable Toku-Ro.1 Type 3 RATOG rockets, with 600 kgf peak thrust and twenty seconds of life.

The 27-degree rear swept-wings were built in wood and plywood, with fixed leading-edge slots in its 40 per cent span, flaps, and ailerons with metallic structure and fabric covering, metallic drag flaps, four propellants tanks with 536 litres of Otsu-Stoff and two 30-mm cannons. The tailfin was built in wood and plywood, and the rudder with metallic structure and fabric covering.

Before the end of the Second World War, Mitsubishi manufactured six J8M1 prototypes and one Ki.200. The full-scale production was commissioned by Mitsubishi, Fuji Hikoki and Nissan Jidosha—a joint manufacture of 155 aircraft by March 1945, 1,300 by September, and 3,600 by March 1946. These fighters would then be used to activate ten IJA *Hikosentais* based in Tokio, Nagoya-Osaka, and Manchuria. The 312th *Kōkūtai* would be the first unit of the IJN to use the Shusui.

The design of the J8M2 Shusui-KAI Model 21 was finished in July 1945. It was a modified version of the J8M1 with one of the ammunition tanks being replaced by two propellant tanks to extend the engine endurance from 5.5 to seven minutes. The J8M2 was a dead-end design as the Japanese lacked the operational experience acquired by the Luftwaffe with the Komet.

At attack speed, the Me 163 could only make three shots with each cannon, despite its notable rate of fire of 600 rpm, superior to that of the Japanese cannons. The MK 108/30 was not considered effective against B-17 bombers at a range of 400 m.

J8M2 Shusui-KAI Model 21 Technical Data

Wingspan: 9.5 m
Length: 6.05 m
Height: 2.7 m
Wing area: 17.73 sq. m
Armament: 1 × Type 5 30-mm cannon with 400 rpm and fifty-three rounds

The J8M2 was modified again as Model 22, widening the fuselage diameter from 120 to 130 cm, which allowed an increase of the number of propellants by 8 per cent and the use of two cannons. The wingspan and overall length were also slightly increased.

J8M2 Model 22 Technical Data

Wingspan: 10 m
Length: 6.428 m
Height: 2.7 m
Wing area: 18.66 sq. m
Armament: 2 × Type 5 30-mm cannons with 400 rpm and fifty-three rounds per gun

The Messerschmitt Me 163 C was designed to increase the engine endurance of the Me 163 B using one HWK 109-509 C-1 rocket engine, with a auxiliary cruise combustion chamber that provided great operational flexibility. The fighter could use both chambers for take-off, climb, and combat, saving propellants while cruising with the auxiliary, but the OKL decided that the small increase in propellant capacities of the Me 163 C-0 did not justify its construction.

The Luftwaffe estimated that a rocket fighter should have at least fifteen minutes of powered endurance to be effective and instructed Messerschmitt to redesign the Me 163 with an enlarged fuselage, increased propellant tankage, and retractable tricycle undercarriage. The new aircraft, named Me 263 V1, was powered by a HWK 109-509 C-4 bi-propellant rocket engine with 1,700 kgf peak thrust from the main chamber and 300 kgf from the auxiliary chamber. The prototype was completed by Junkers at Dessau in August 1944. Data of the HWK 109-509 C was provided to the Japanese who used the information to build their own version: the Toku-Ro.3 (KR 20) with 1,600 kgf from the main chamber and 400 kgf from the auxiliary chamber.

Early in 1945, the IJA Rikugun Institute started the design of the Ki.202, a rocket fighter with enough propellant capacity for ten minutes and twenty-eight seconds of powered flight. The final design was projected for February and the prototype completion was scheduled for August. To save fuel, the Ki.202 was to be launched by a rocket cart system, as the Ohka 43-Otsu. The semi-recessed landing gear was not detachable.

Ki.202 Technical Data

Wingspan: 9.75 m
Length: 7.71 m
Height: 2.74 m
Wing area: 18.39 sq. m
Max. weight: 5,015 kg
Max. speed: 900 kph
Climb rate: 207 sec. to 10,000 m
Armament: 2 × 30-mm Ho-155-II cannons with 400 rpm and eighty rounds per gun

The Yokosuka MXY8 Akigusa was a tailless training glider developed by the First Naval Air Technical Arsenal (Kugisho) for the future pilots of the Shusui. The MXY8 was an unpowered version of the J8M1 entirely built of wood/plywood with a loaded weight of just 1,037 kg.

During the first flight tests, performed in December 1944, the prototype was towed to altitude by a Kyushu K10W1 trainer, proving satisfactory handling characteristics.

Two other prototypes were built by Kugisho, one of which was delivered to the Army Aerotechnical Research Institute (Rikugun) for evaluation and served as the basis for the development of its own training glider—Yokoi Kokuki Ku.13—with the same dimensions as the MXY8. The other served as a model for the construction at the Maeda Aircraft Institute, a series of sixty Akigusa units for the IJN. This version was provided with water ballast tanks, which simulated the weight of rocket propellants to achieve more realistic training, and was operated by the 312th *Kōkūtai*.

To avoid the rapid loss of altitude and increasing the flight time, a version of the Akigusa was designed, powered by a 105-hp Hirth/Hitachi Ha-11 Hatsukaze II pusher engine, driving a two-bladed wooden propeller. Yet its construction was rejected in favour of the more advanced MXY9 Shuka.

MXY8 Technical Data

Wingspan: 9.5 m
Length: 6.06 m
Height: 2.7 m
Wing area: 17.37 sq. m
Max. weight: 1,037 kg

The MXY9 Shuka was the Akigusa airframe powered by a Tsu-11 Campini type thermojet developed for Kugisho. The Tsu-11 consisted of a conventional reciprocating engine, a single-stage compressor wheel, and a combustion chamber (containing an annular fuel-injection system and two igniter plugs) that burned the air–fuel mixture creating a thrust of 250 kg.

The reciprocating engine was a 105-hp four-cylinder in-line, air-cooled Hitachi Ha-11 (Japanese version of the German Hirth HM 504-A2). The thermojet had a length of 220 cm, a diameter of 64 cm, and a weight of 200 kg. At full throttle, the Ha-11 reached 3,000 rpm and the compressor 9,000 rpm. The Tsu-11 was flight tested under the bomb bay of a Ginga by the end of 1944.

In November 1944, the construction of a prototype began, but the full-scale production was cancelled after the destruction of the Maeda-Ohe plant by a bombardment on 18 December 1944. The Tsu-11s were used in the construction of the Ohka Model 22 suicide bombers in the Ichigisho plant.

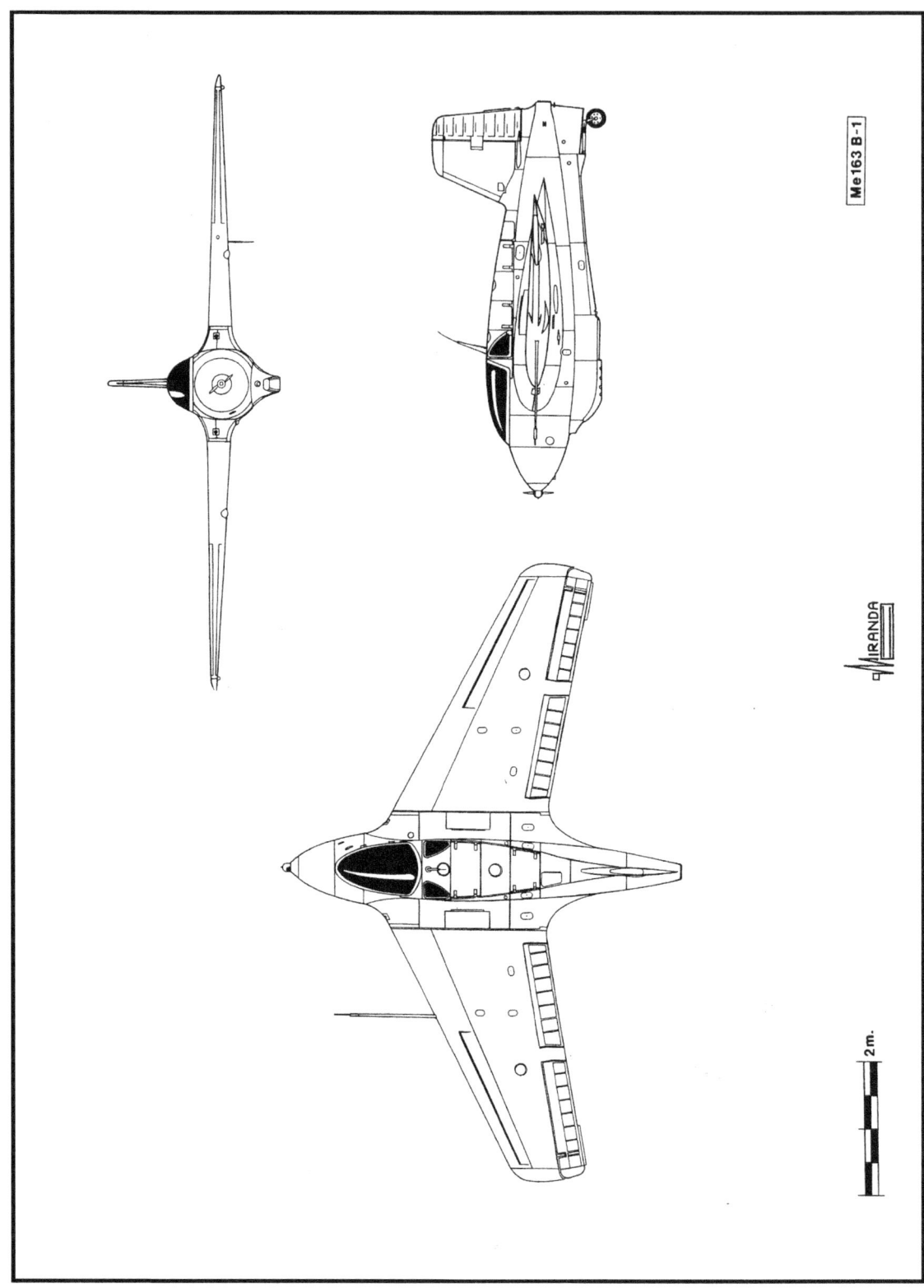

Me163 B-1

2 m.

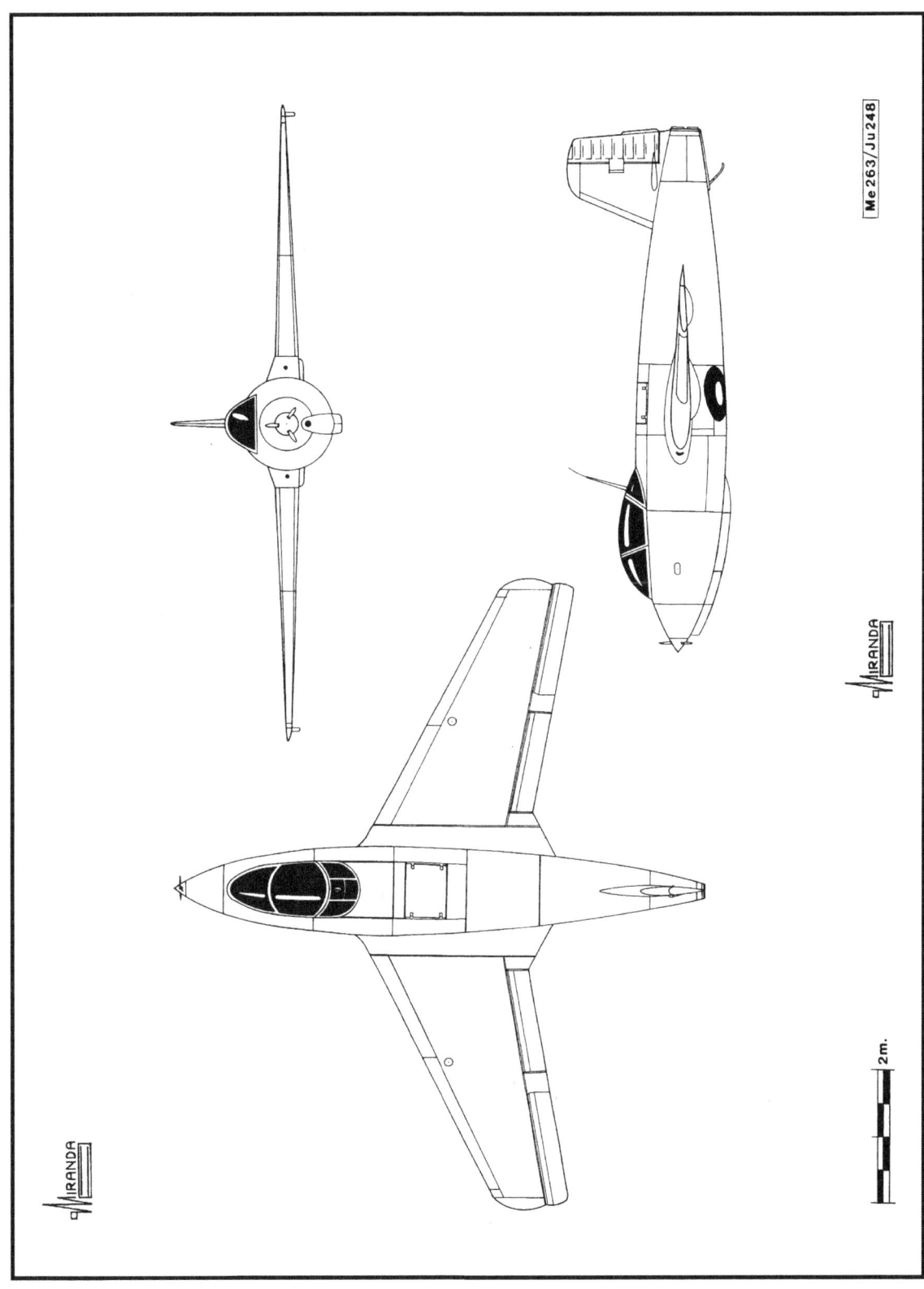

2m.

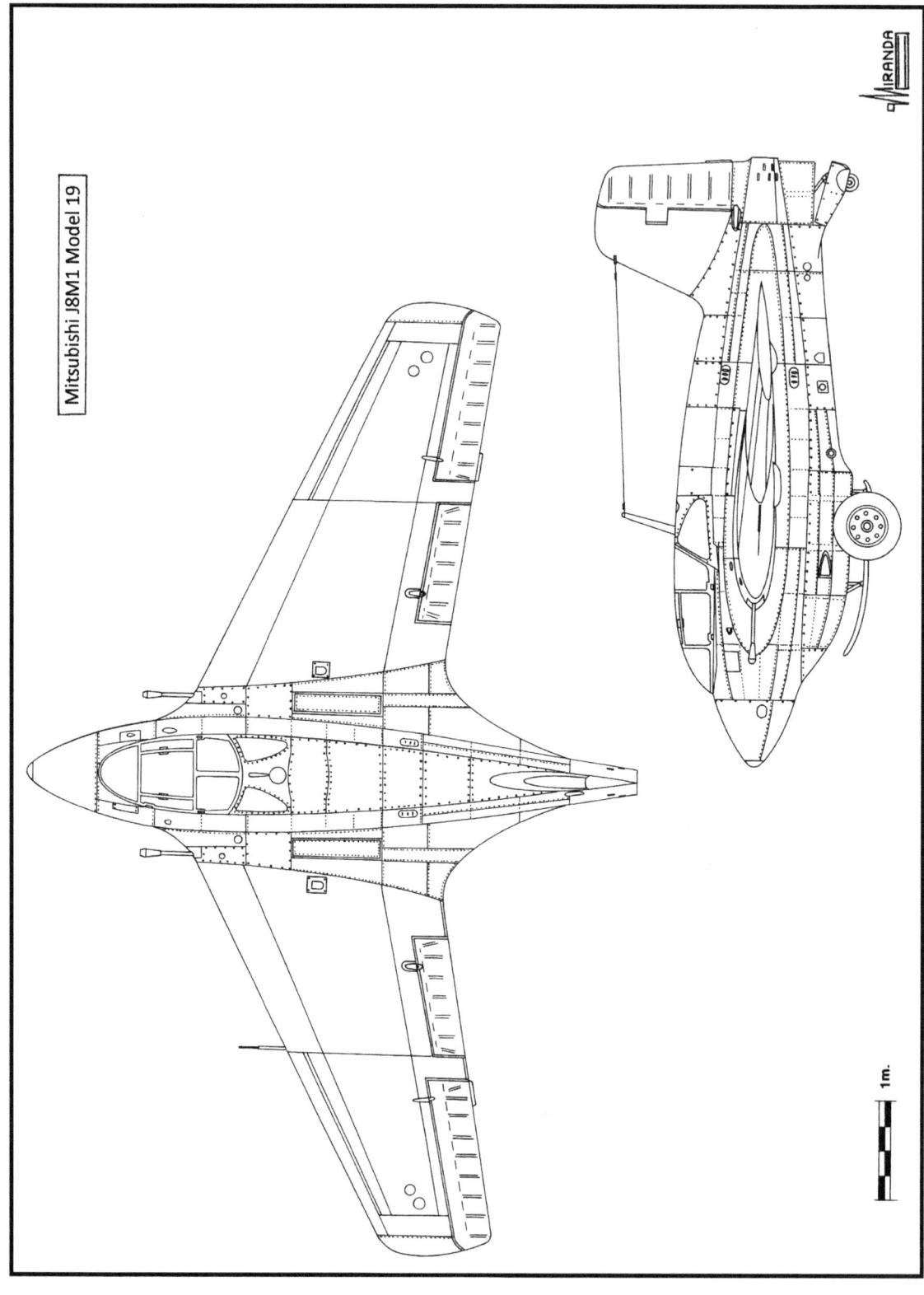

Mitsubishi J8M1 Model 19

1 m.

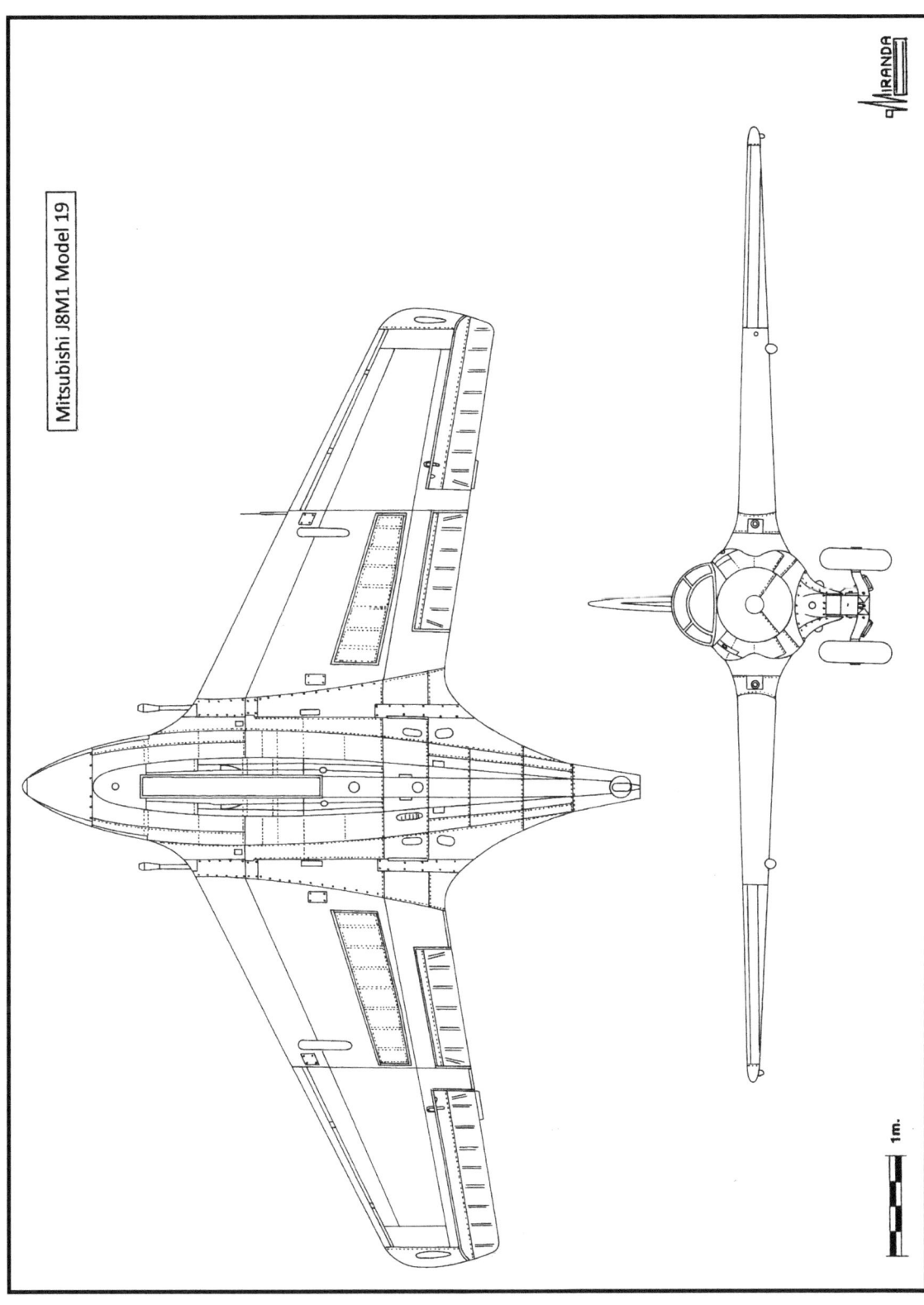

Mitsubishi J8M1 Model 19

1 m.

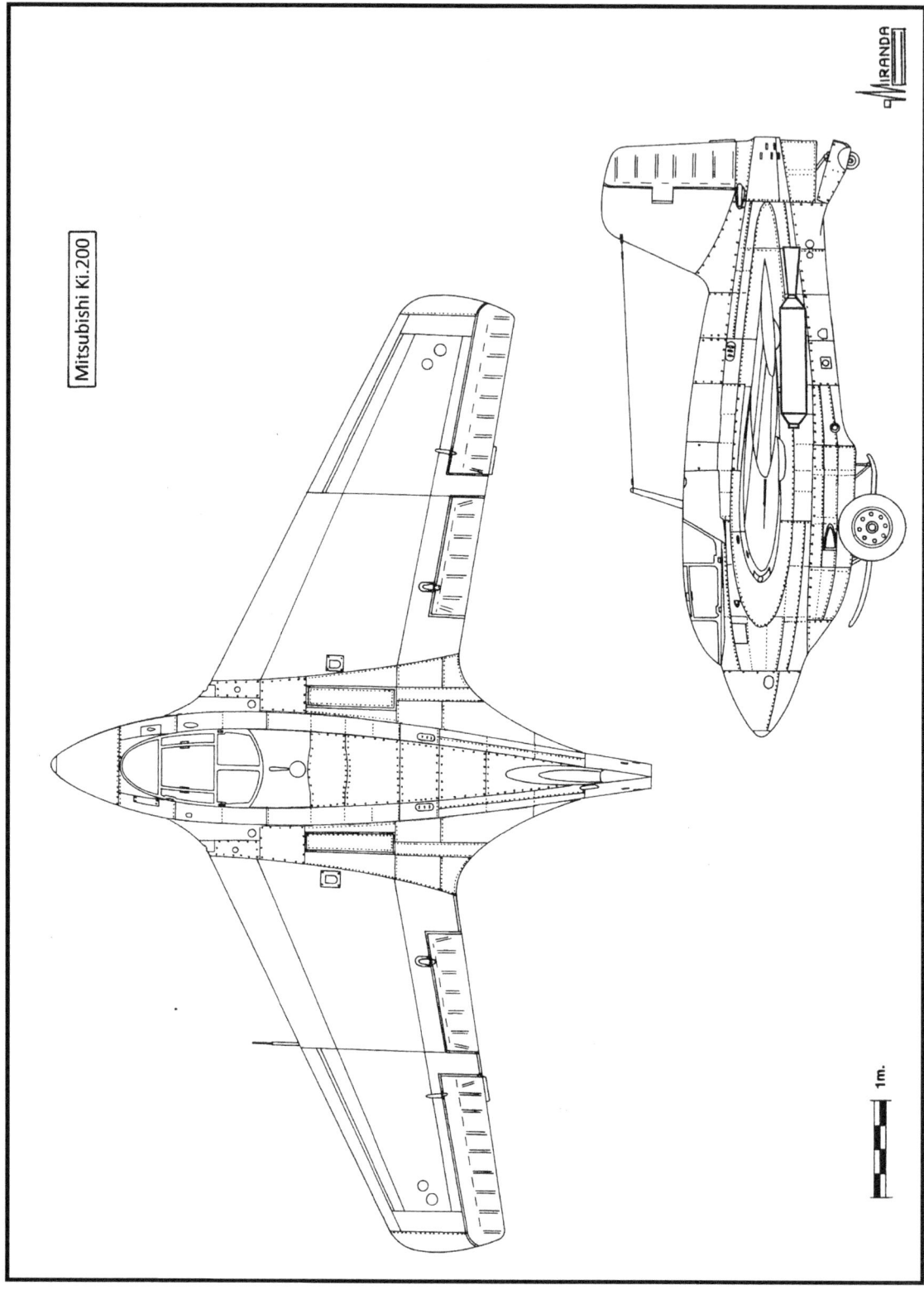

Mitsubishi Ki.200

1 m.

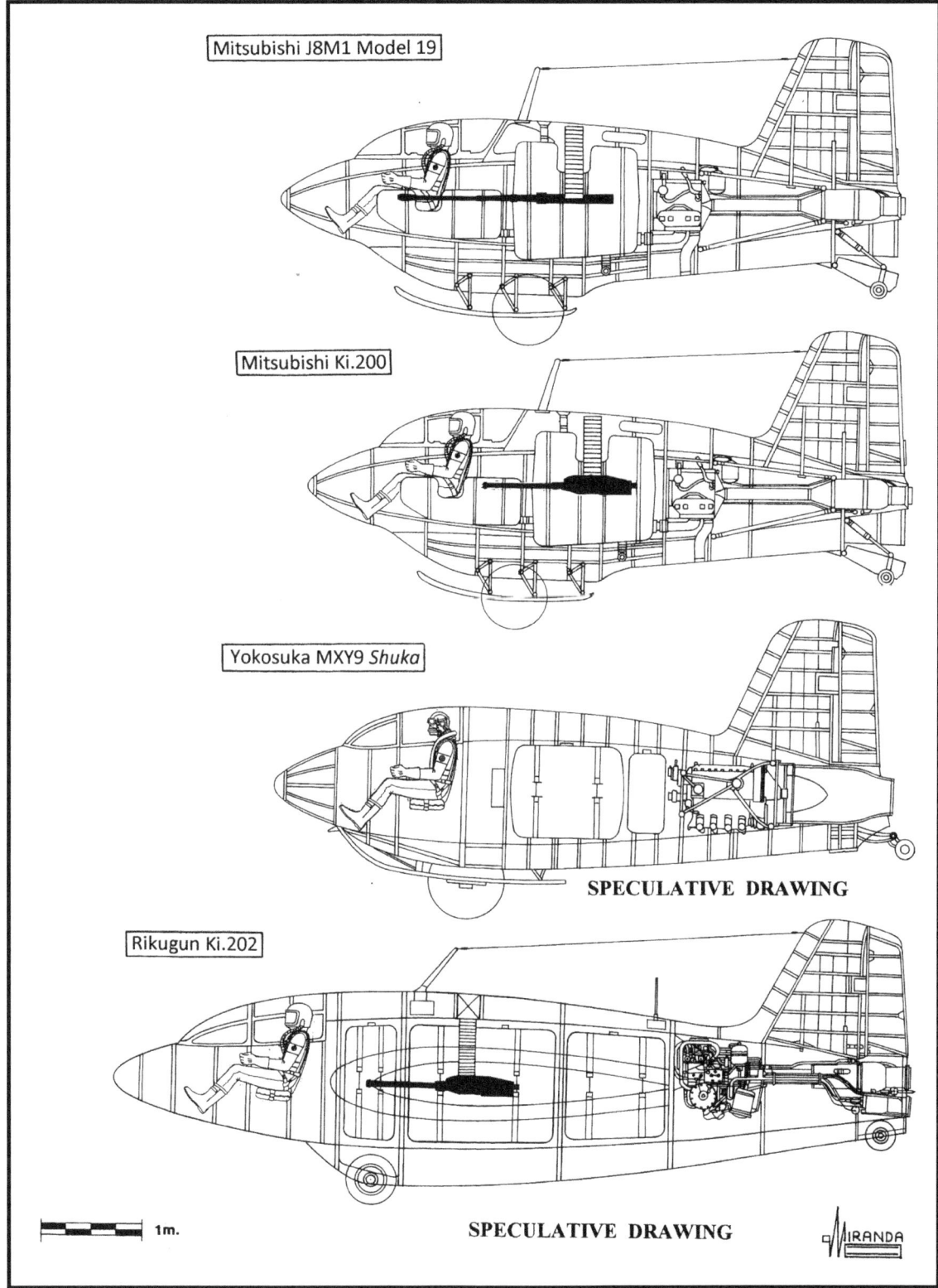

Mitsubishi J8M1 Model 19

Mitsubishi Ki.200

Yokosuka MXY9 *Shuka*

SPECULATIVE DRAWING

Rikugun Ki.202

1m.

SPECULATIVE DRAWING

MIRANDA

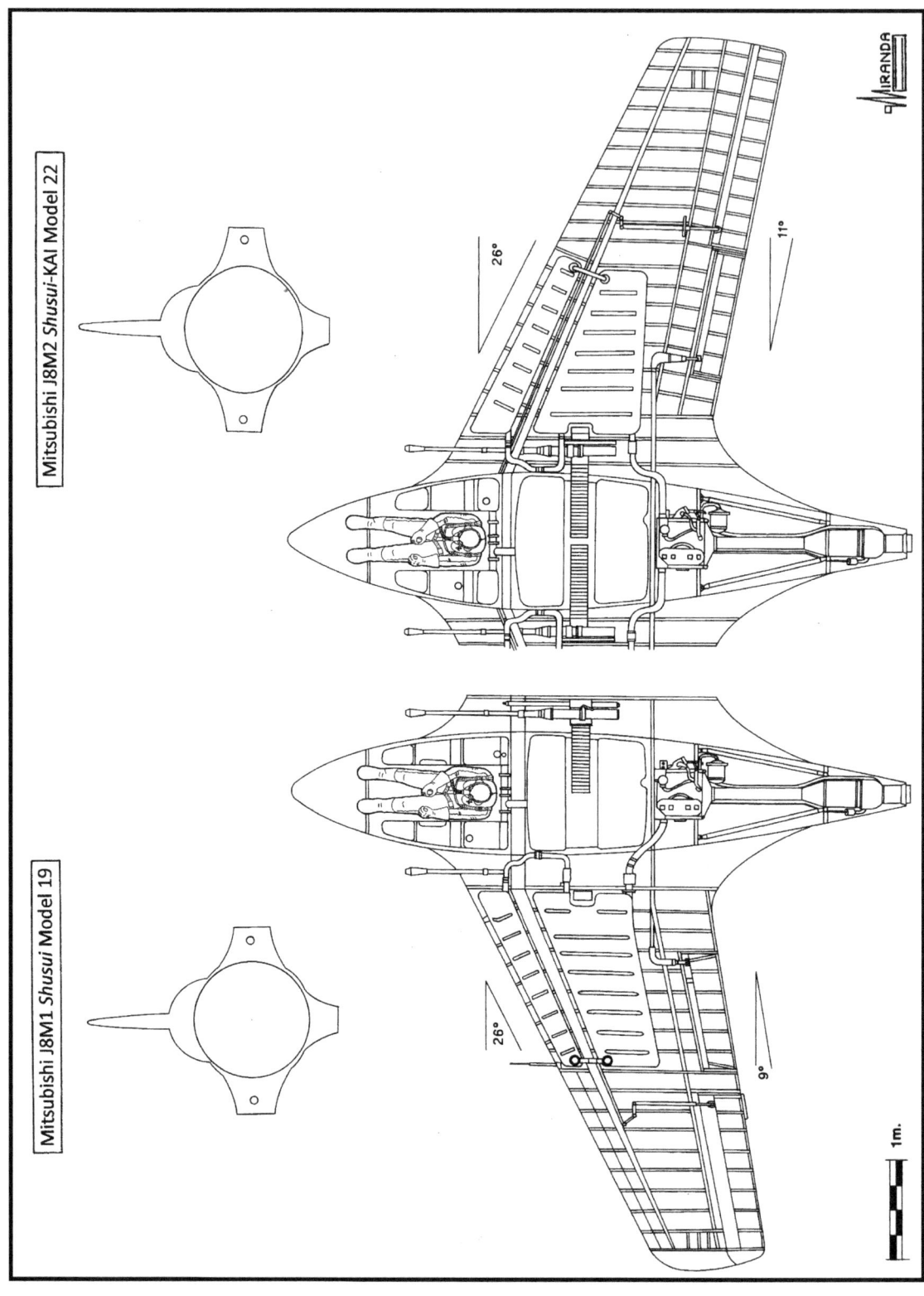

Mitsubishi J8M2 *Shusui*-KAI Model 22

Mitsubishi J8M1 *Shusui* Model 19

26°

11°

26°

9°

1 m.

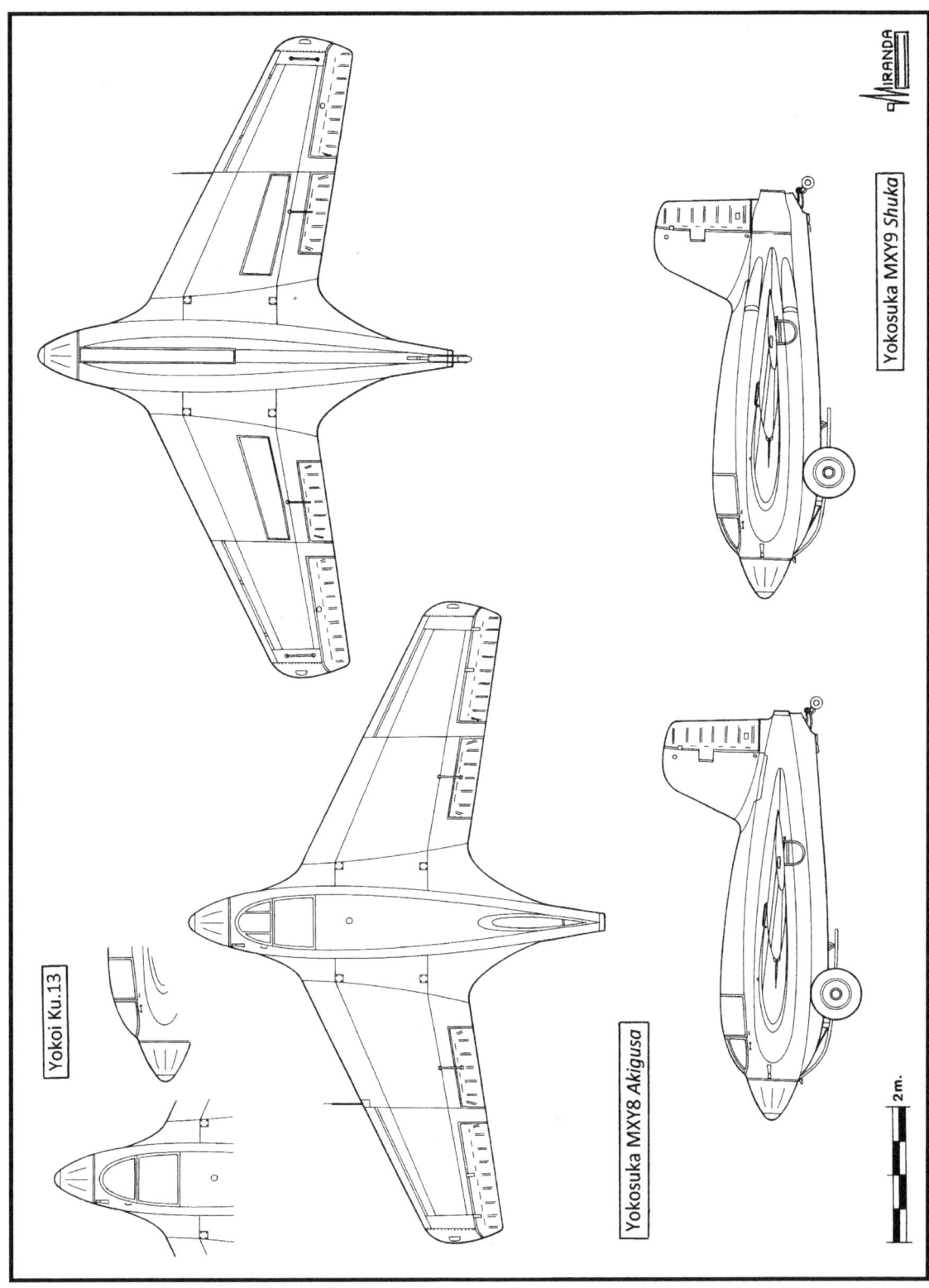

Yokosuka MXY9 *Shuka*

Yokoi Ku.13

Yokosuka MXY8 *Akigusa*

2 m.

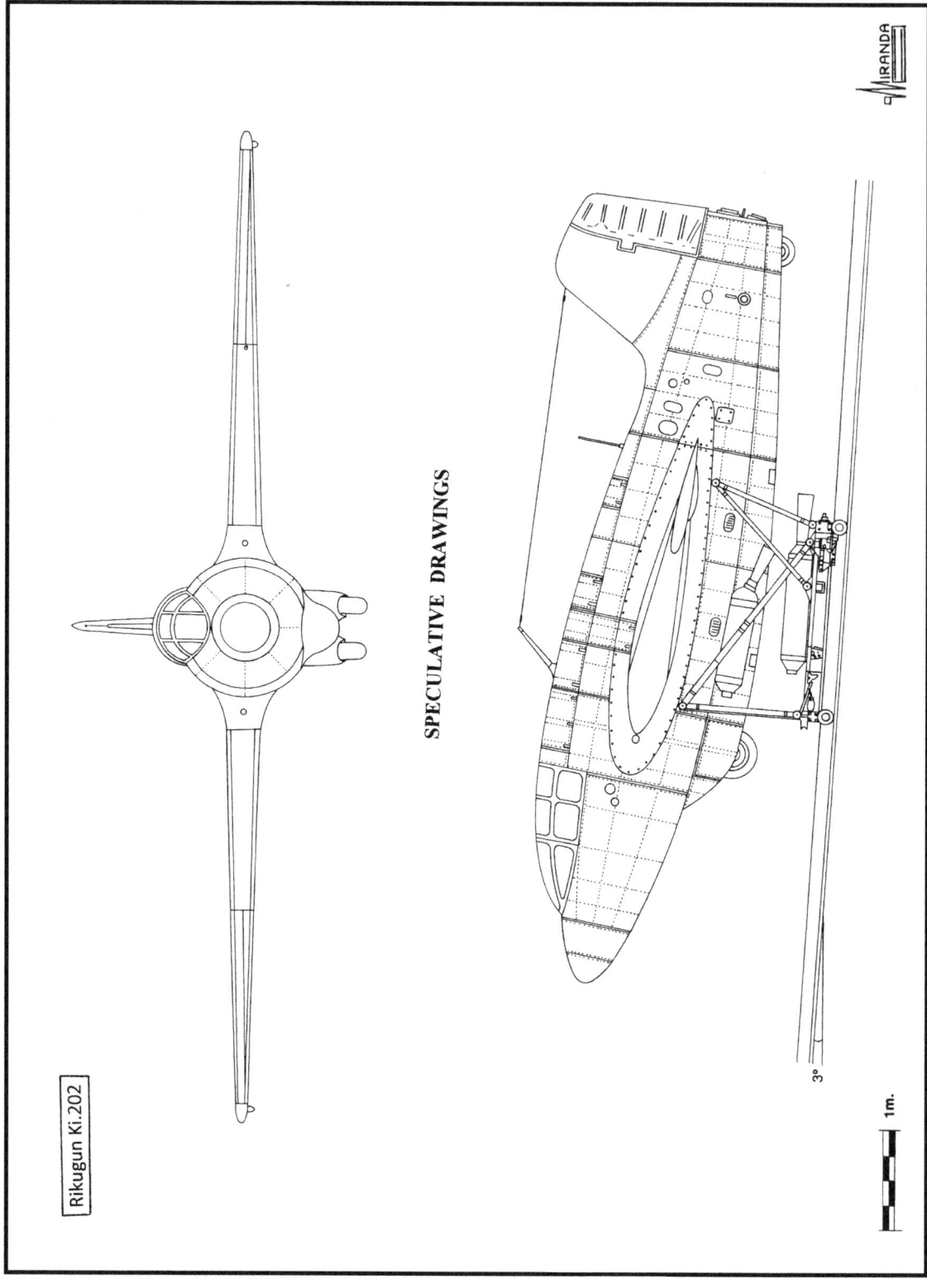

SPECULATIVE DRAWINGS

Rikugun Ki.202

3°

1m.

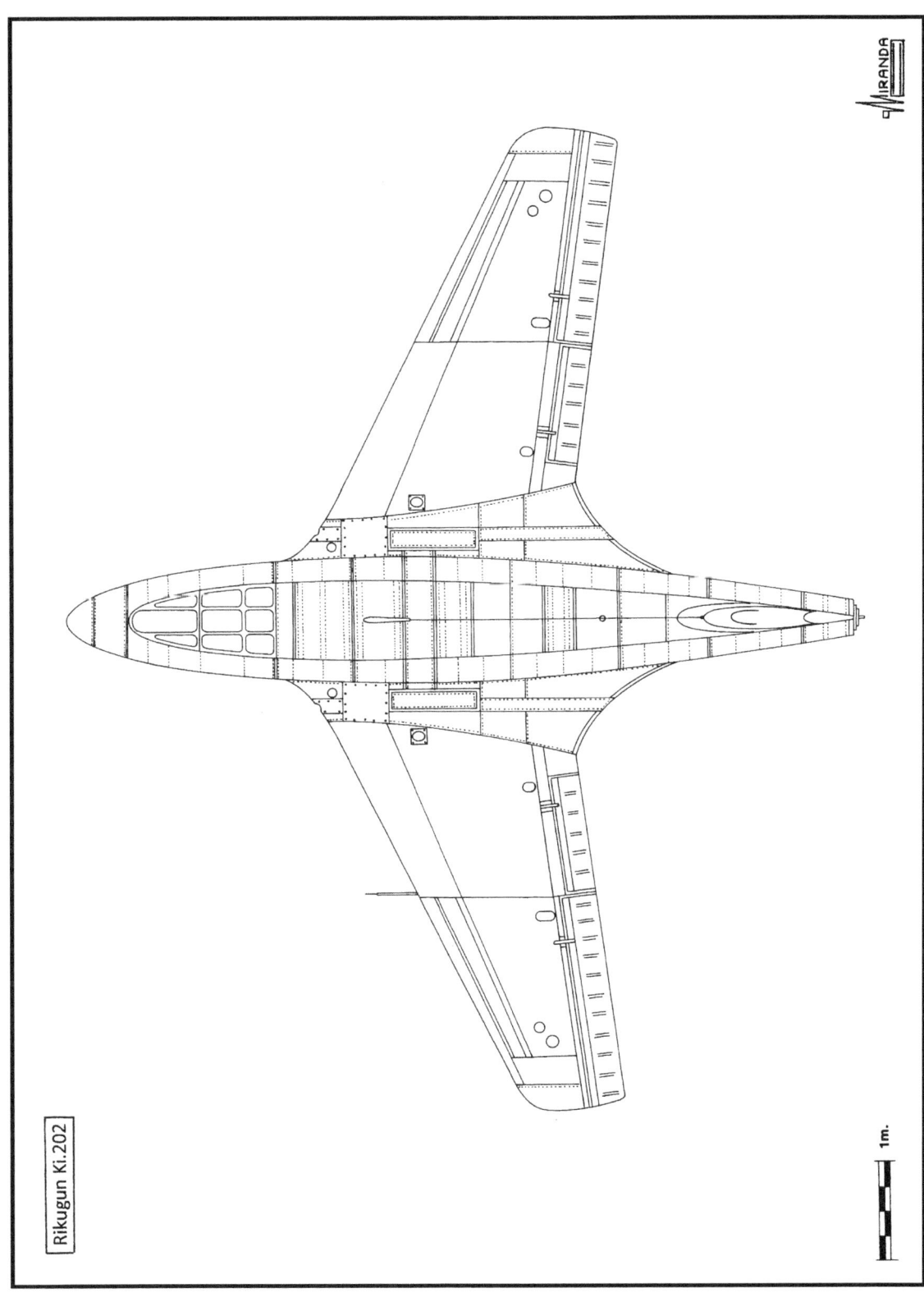

Rikugun Ki.202

1m.

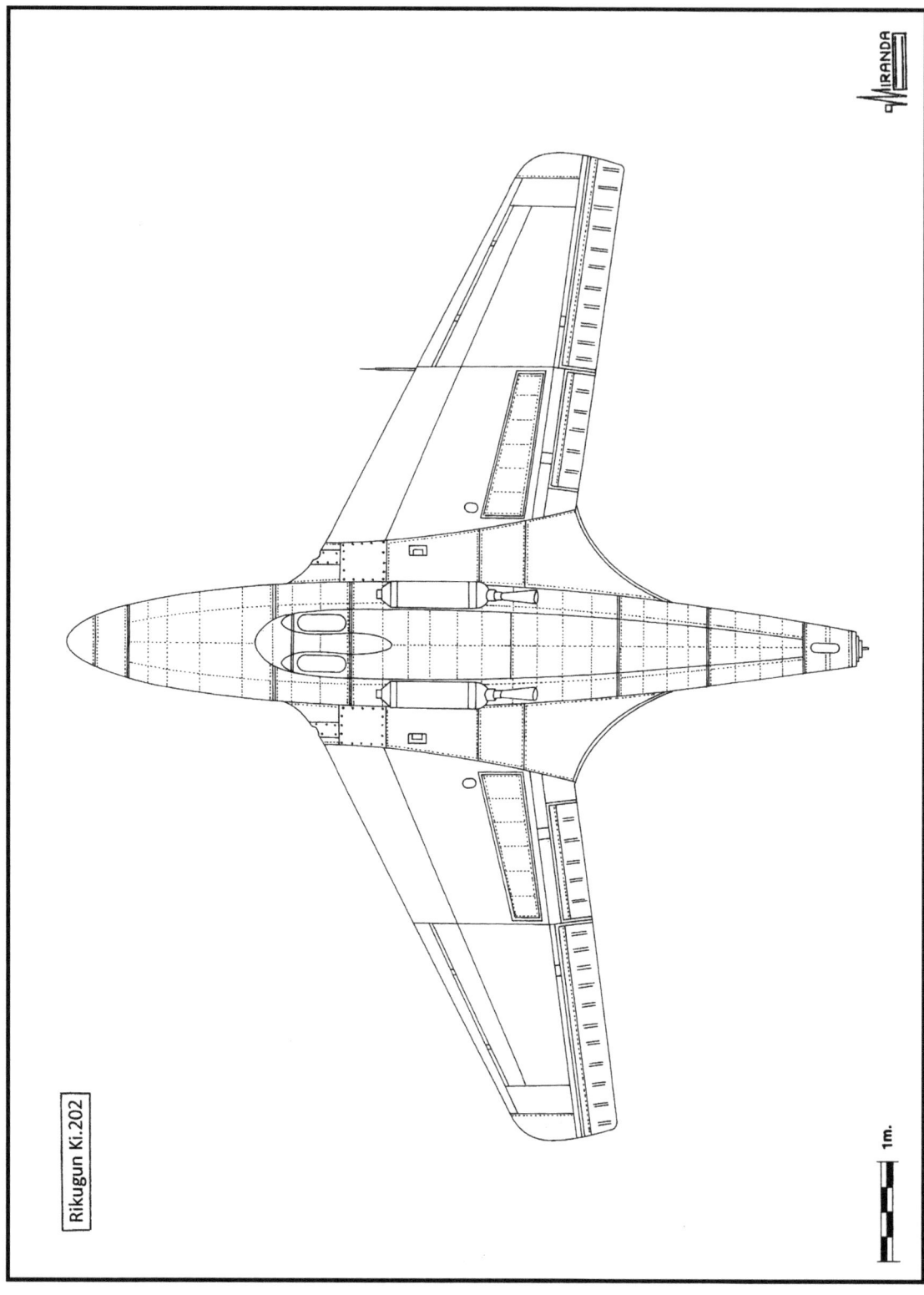

Rikugun Ki.202

1m.

5
Night Fighters

Nakajima J1N1 Gekko

The Nakajima J1N1 was designed in 1939 as a 13-shi three-seat, long-range escort fighter to operate jointly with G3M bombers. Yet the prototype was not adequate for the task, demonstrating little manoeuvrability during flight tests.

In 1941, the IJN authorised the production of the two-seat reconnaissance version named J1N1-Hei with a range of 3,780 km. It was used in Rabaul, Guadalcanal, and the Solomon Islands between July 1942 and spring 1943, being misidentified as Focke-Wulf Fw 187 by American pilots of the VF-5 fighter squadron.

In 1943, the Allied fighters were too fast for the J1N1, and the Japanese pilots preferred to use the Ki.46. Some J1N1 of the 251st *Kōkūtai* were field modified as night fighters by installing a nose searchlight, two Type 99-2 20-mm cannons in 30-degree *Schräge Musik* configuration, and two more that could shoot 30 degrees down obliquely. The modification was tentatively called J1N1-Hei-KAI, obtaining good results in combat with the downing of six B-17s, six B-24s, one Hudson, and one Ventura.

The Allies ignored the existence of Japanese night fighters until November 1943. The IJN ordered the conversion of other aircraft into night fighters, under the official name of J1N1-S Gekko Type 11. Between February and October 1944, the J1N1-S of the 321st *Kōkūtai*, fitted with H-6 ASV radars, conducted antisubmarine patrols and attacks against torpedo boats in Leyte Gulf, operating from Tinian. Other Gekko units proved very useful in strafing missions, firing their ventral cannons. They were used for night raids over Morotai, equipped with two 62.8-kg Type 97, No. 6, Mk II bombs. Since August 1944, most Gekkos flew in defence of the homeland but lacked the speed and ceiling necessary to engage the B-29 bombers.

Some units were modified by removing the ventral barrels to save weight. Tests were also carried out with two types of AI radars—the H-5, a version of the ASV A-6, and the FD-1, with Yagi low drag antennas of just two dipoles.

When the Americans changed the method of attack of their night bombers at low altitude, the J1N1-Sa Gekkos Type 11-Ko of the 302nd *Kōkūtai* that had already been equipped with a FD-2 AI radar had their chance to destroy eleven Superfortresses, shooting with three Type 99-2 dorsal cannons from 100–150 m and with 50–70 m difference in altitude. In early 1945, the 332nd and 210th *Kōkūtais* were also equipped with J1N1-Sa fighters. On 5 September, a Gekko made a *tai-atari* attack against a B-24 south of Samar Island, with both aircraft being destroyed.

On 2 January 1945, a Gekko acted as the lead plane for the suicide Zeros of the Kongo Unit No. 30 in the Surigao Straits. In late 1944, the suicide Gekko unit was formed with aircraft and pilots from the 153rd and 765th *Kōkūtais*. On 28 December, a J1N1-Hei of the Gekko unit, equipped with two 248.7-kg Type 99, No. 25, Model I bombs, made a *tokko* attack against Allied ships in the Bohol Sea.

J1N1-Sa Type 11-Ko Technical Data

Wingspan: 16.98 m
Length: 12.68 m
Height: 4.56 m
Wing area: 40 sq. m
Max. weight: 6,900 kg
Max. speed: 500 kph
Estimated service ceiling: 9,500 m

Kawasaki Ki.45 Toryu

By early March 1945, the B-29s began a series of devastating low-altitude night raids against the sixty-seven major cities in Japan. Despite what happened in Germany, the IJA had not foreseen the need to build specialised night fighters. Taken by surprise by the strategy change by the Americans, the pilots of the Ki.45 improvised some night technical interception techniques, coordinating their attacks with the ground searchlights regiments. They also used a B-17 caught in Bandung for nocturnal visual localisation practices. Some Ki.45-KAI-Hei aircraft underwent field transformations for night fighting, fitting them with two 20-mm Ho-5 guns in a 35-degree *Schräge Musik* configuration and one 37-mm Ho-203 cannon in the nose.

The fires lit the undersides of the B-29s, making them visible to the pilots of the Toryus, Gekkos, Raidens, and Zeros that awaited the opportunity to destroy them at a low altitude, firing at their belly from close range. This version was called Ki.45-KAI-Bo and was armed with a non-standard 40-mm Ho-301 cannon in the ventral tunnel and two 20-mm Ho-5 guns at a 70-degree angle *Schräge Musik* configuration. In 1945, at least twelve Toryus were equipped with one TAMA Taki-2, Model II AI radar, with the antennas installed in a transparent nose cone, operating in an 80-cm wavelength. This version was called Ki.45-KAI-Bo and was armed with a non-standard 40-mm Ho-301 cannon in the ventral tunnel and two 20-mm Ho-5 guns at a 70-degree *Schräge Musik* configuration.

Ki.45-KAI-Bo Technical Data

Wingspan: 15.02 m
Length: 10.51 m
Height: 3.70 m
Wing area: 32 sq. m
Max. weight: 5,500 kg
Max. speed: 547 kph
Estimated service ceiling: 10,000 m

Mitsubishi Ki.46 Shin Shitei

With a top speed of 604 kph and a ceiling of 10,700 m, the Shin Shitei was immune to interception until the arrival of the new P-38-F and Spitfire Mk V fighters to the Far East. Flying at a cruising speed of 425 kph, they could remain aloft for nearly six hours. Impressed by their performance, the IJA made several attempts to obtain variants of Ki.46 suitable for air-to-air combat.

By early 1943, seventeen Ki.46-II were modified by fitting to their nose one 37-mm Type 94 cannon—a very heavy weapon taken from an army medium tank. The Type 94 was to be loaded manually by the pilot and had a rate of fire lower than three rounds per minute. In February 1943, six modified Ki.46 were sent to Rabaul, to fight against the B-17 and B-24. Operating with the 13th *Sentai*, they proved that the excessive weight made the aircraft nose-heavy and difficult to manoeuvre.

On 24 November, six additional Ki.46s were modified as Hyakushiki Shitei III (Air Defense Fighter) with the installation of a Type 94 in a 57-degree *Schräge Musik* configuration activated by the radio operator. Integrated into the 17th Independent *Chutai*, they were used to defend the Nakajima-Tokyo factories against the B-29 of the 73rd BW. Fifteen aircraft of the Ki.46-Hei version were manufactured in July 1944. They had two Ho-5 cannons in the nose and one Ho-204 automatic cannon of 37 mm in *Schräge Musik* configuration. In the autumn, some tests were conducted at the Hitachi Training Centre using a 'Hei' experimentally armed with a Type 94 cannon in a dorsal position. The plane achieved an altitude of 12,300 m using 95-octane fuel, but it was proved that its flight was too unstable to properly aim the cannon. It was also too heavy and took over twenty minutes to reach the level of flight of the B-29.

Some of these aircraft were experimentally used as night fighters by the 16th *Dokuritsu Hikotai* and the 17th Independent *Chutai*. It turned out that they lacked stability for sustained shooting using the Ho-204 cannons because the fuselage structure was too light and could not absorb the recoil. The Ki.46-III-Ko version entered service in August 1944. It was faster (650 kph), with new engines Ha-112-II, direct fuel injection, rear armour plating, and an improved oxygen supply system. It could also transport a 600-l fuel tank under the fuselage that provided an extended range of 4,000 km. During the autumn, tests were performed at the Hitachi Training Centre using a 'Ko' experimentally armed with a Type 94 in the dorsal position. The plane could attain an altitude of 12,300 m, using 95-octane fuel, but again, its flight at that altitude was too unstable to properly aim the cannon.

The IJA then ordered the manufacturer to transform ninety units of the Ki.46-III-Ko into fighters. The first seventy-five machines became the 'Otsu' model, with a flat windscreen, two staggered 20-mm Ho-5 cannons, and attachments under the wing roots to carry two 60-kg Type 2, Number 6, Mk 21 *Ta-Dan* air-to-air bombs. Fifteen more units were transformed into the Ki.46-III-Hei version, with two Ho-5s in the nose and one 37-mm Ho-204 in a 57-degree *Schräge Musik* configuration.

The Otsu was used against the B-29 by two *Sentais*, six *Chutais,* and one *Hikotai,* proving that its armament was too light to destroy the giants.

Ki.46-III-Hei Technical Data

Wingspan: 14.7 m
Length: 11.16 m
Height: 3.88 m
Wing area: 32 sq. m
Max. weight: 5.05 kg
Max. speed: 620 kph
Estimated service ceiling: 10,700 m

Nakajima Ki.84 Hayate

In July 1942, the IJA issued a requirement for a night fighter to defend Rabaul's base against B-17 attacks. In August 1944, Nakajima modified a Ki.84-I-Ko by installing a single 20-mm Ho-5 cannon, with 300 rounds, at a 45-degree *Schräge Musik* configuration behind the cockpit. The 13-mm bulletproof steel plate was removed, an aerodynamic cover tube was installed to protect the rear canopy from the blast, and a cut-out was made on the moving side so that it could slide backwards about 60 per cent of the opening before remodelling.

In October, the second prototype was built by modifying a Ki.84-I-Otsu, and both aircraft performed test flights at Fusa airfield. It is believed that at least twelve aircraft were converted to this configuration.

In some documents written by Major Iwamiya, technical director of IJA General Affairs Division, and Lieutenant Commander Noboru Kimura of the Technical Department of the IJA Headquarters, installing a Taki-2 AI radar on the version Ki.84-I-Tei production was considered. According to other authors, the Ki.84-I-Tei would be armed with two Ho-5 cannons firing at 45 degrees and the USAF Report 1946 describes a plane that has three cannons.

Ki.84-I-Tei Technical Data

Wingspan: 11.24 m
Length: 9.92 m
Height: 3.38 m
Wing area: 21 sq. m
Max. weight: 3,700 kg
Max. speed: 670 kph
Estimated service ceiling: 11,700 m

Yokosuka D4Y Suisei

When the Japanese government acquired the manufacturing licence of the in-line Daimler-Benz DB 601A engine in 1940, the main manufacturers of fighters made plans to create an interceptor that was faster and had a higher ceiling. The IJN was not initially interested in the possibilities offered by the German engine, as the Zero was superior to all the Allied fighters operating in the Far East.

Future combat to defend the fleet were expected to take place at medium and low altitude, against slow Swordfish and Devastator torpedo aircraft, with a pathetic escort of Buffaloes. Yet the Val dive bomber was also getting out of date and the new in-line engines of the Atsuta series offered aircraft carriers the possibility to use reconnaissance and dive bomber aircraft that were faster than the Fulmars and Wildcats that defended the Allied fleets.

Therefore, Aichi was commissioned to build two versions of the D4Y1 Suisei—reconnaissance and dive bomber—powered by a 1,100-hp Atsuta 12, to be replaced by the 1,400-hp Atsuta 32 in the second series, the D4Y2. The design of the Suisei was based on the combat experiences of the Ju 87 Stuka in Europe and on its failure against the British fighters when used in strategic missions.

Japanese engineers concluded that the robust airframe and little refined aerodynamics of the German dive bombers were not compatible with local manufacturing systems. The new aeroplane manufactured by Aichi had a bomb bay to internally transport bombs and both the undercarriage and airbrakes were fully retractable within the wing. Faster than the Zeros and the Allied fighters of the time, the aircraft was expected to operate without any escort.

Unfortunately for Japan, the adaptation of German technology, the development of new engines, and their integration with the airframe required more time than had been foreseen, and Suiseis were not sent into combat until mid-1944, sent against Hellcats and Seafires guided by the interception radar of the powerful Allied Task Forces.

German technology did not adapt well to the complex systems of Japanese manufacturing. The in-line engines of the Atsuta series were built in such a way that proved to be lighter than their Daimler-Benz counterparts, but also more fragile and difficult to maintain. The D4Y programme aimed to achieve a fast reconnaissance carrier-based aircraft, and it was never considered during the first phases that it might generate any issues because it involved a reduced number of very sophisticated machines that operated in good maintenance conditions from the best ships of the IJN.

When the mass manufacturing of the dive-bomber version was decided, the airframe proved to be too light. Its longitudinal resistance had to be increased and its engine mount reinforced. After the loss of almost all their aircraft carriers in the Battle of Leyte Gulf, the D4Y2 started operating from ground bases under very rudimentary conditions and using fuel of very low quality. The problems of the Atsuta aggravated, considerably reducing the number of available aircraft.

As it happened with the Ki.61 fighter of the IJA, the solution was to use the much more reliable and powerful Kinsei 62 radial engine for the new version D4Y3 Mod.33. Albeit a bit slower than its predecessor but without any problems operating from ground airfields, it proved to be the ideal aeroplane for *tokko* missions.

By mid-1944, around a dozen of D4Y2s were transformed into two-seat D4Y2-S night fighters to fight against B-29s. The night fighter conversions were made at the 11th Naval Aviation Arsenal at Hiro. They had a 20-mm Type 99 Mod 2 cannon at a 30-degree angle, *Schräge Musik* configuration and two 60-kg Type 3 Mk 27 rocket bombs under the wings.

This lighter version of the Suisei was also the fastest, with a speed of 580 kph and a ceiling of 10,700 m; it was expected to achieve success in combat. Yet one 20-mm cannon was not enough to face the gigantic Boeing bomber. The Luftwaffe statistics show that they needed to make at least thirty-six impacts in vital points to bring down a B-29. It would have been necessary to shoot 200 rounds with a Type 99 cannon from a distance of 1,000 m to make it, staying several minutes under the formation of bombers and flying in their same direction, instead of performing a unique frontal attack, as the IJA had recommended.

After the technical valuation of the Yokosuka *Kōkutai*, at the beginning of 1945, nine aircraft were sent to the 302nd *Kōkutai* of Atsugi for combat testing, and another three to the 131st of Kanoya by mid-April. At least two pilots of the 302nd *Kōkutai*—Yoshimitsu Naka and Takaji Inumaru—claimed B-29s shot down thanks to lucky impacts of the rarely accurate Mk 27 bomb-rockets, possibly on 14 and 25 May 1945.

The D4Y3-S was a project-only variant powered by a Kinsei 62.

The D4Y2-S's performances were not considered enough by the IJN, and one Suisei Type 12 was modified, as high-altitude experimental aircraft, at the Engine Department of Kugisho. One Hitachi 92 turbocharger was mounted under the bomb bay and connected from the engine exhaust pipes by two 'S' ducts. The Japanese defeat was received during the experiment preparations at Oppama airfield.

D4Y2-S Model 12 Technical Data

Wingspan: 11.5 m
Length: 10.22 m
Height: 3.63 m
Wing area: 23.6 sq. m
Max. weight: 4,750 kg
Estimated max. speed: 580 kph
Estimated service ceiling: 10,700 m

Nakajima C6N Saiun

The Nakajima C6N was designed as the successor of the Aichi D4Y. The Saiun was a fast carrier-based, long-range reconnaissance aircraft, almost immune to Allied interception. The airframe structure was very light, with six unprotected fuel tanks located inside the wings—features that made it very vulnerable to battle damage.

With the same maximum speed as the Hellcat and an absolute ceiling of 12,500 m, the Saiun could travel 3,000 nautical miles with a ventral fuel tank of 762 litres, eluding all Allied fighters except for the Mustang. The C6N was too valuable for the IJN intelligence services due to its ability to locate Allied fleets and only intervened in the *kamikaze* offensive marginally.

The structural weakness of the aircraft did not allow the installation of a bomb under the fuselage and had to be renovated according to the existing plans for the future version of bombardment C6N1-Ko Mod.21. The wings were probably strengthened, eliminating the 1,921-l external tanks and installing one 800-kg bomb that was bolted under the centre section of the wing.

Two C6N were also modified as C6N1-S night fighters, with a Type 5, 30-mm cannon mounted at a 30-degree *Schräge Musik* configuration, installed behind the pilot.

In July–August 1945, the two prototypes performed operational tests with the 302 *Kōkūtai*-3rd *Hikotai* based in Atsugi. On the night of 1 August 1945, one of the aeroplanes intercepted a B-29 without shooting it down. The IJN concluded that the maximum speed and ceiling of the C6N1-S was insufficient to fight the B-29s.

Nakajima decided to improve the performances of the Saiun using a NK9K-2 Homare 24 Ru engine, with a Hitachi 92 (Ru 212) turbocharger, driving a four-bladed, constant-speed, VDM C6P10 propeller. The prototype, which was known as C6N2 Model 12, proved capable of flying at 12,500 m, but its maximum speed was not considered to be high enough.

The C6N3-KAI Model 22 was a night fighter project powered by a Mitsubishi Ha-43-11 radial engine, with Hitachi Model 10 turbocharger and two Type 99-2, 20-mm cannons mounted at a 30-degree *Schräge Musik* configuration.

C6N1-S Technical Data

Wingspan: 12.5 m
Length: 11.15 m
Height: 3.96 m
Wing area: 25.5 sq. m
Max. weight: 4,500 kg
Estimated max. speed: 600 kph
Estimated service ceiling: 10,800 m

Yokosuka Ginga, Kawanishi Kyokko, Nakajima Byakko, and Kugisho Tenga

The Yokosuka P1Y1 Ginga was designed in 1940, following a specification of the IJN (clearly inspired by the Junkers Ju 88) requiring a fast bomber that would be suitable for dive-bombing and low-altitude torpedo attack.

In March 1945, some units of the P1Y1 Model 11 of the 762nd *Kōkutai* were equipped with an H-6 ASV radar to perform night attacks against US Navy ships. The P1Y was tested in alternative roles.

Early in 1944, the Kawanishi Company was instructed by *Kaigun Koku Hombu* to produce a night fighter variant under the designation P1Y2-S Kyokko Model 26. The new planes would be powered by two 1,850-hp Mitsubishi MK4T-A Kasei 25a radial engines, that were considered safer than the Homare 12 Ginga, and armed with a Type 5, 30-mm cannon angled at 35 degrees in a *Schräge Musik* configuration. The prototype flew in June 1944 and Kawanishi modified a total of ninety-six Ginga airframes.

Between March and November of 1944, a certain number of Kyokko entered into service with *Kōkutais* Nos 302 and 321, but they were not successful against B-29s. The low speed of 523 kph and the service ceiling of 9,400 m only proved disappointing. The plan was to install the FD-2 AI radar in the series version.

Kakajima also built the P1Y1-S Byakko night fighter, a Ginga armed with two Type 99-2, 20-mm cannons, angled at 30 degrees in a *Schräge Musik* configuration. In the summer of 1945, the P1Y1-S performed operational tests with the 302nd *Kōkutai* based in Atsugi. Byakko performed better than Kyokko, but it also did not enter service. At least one P1Y1-S was equipped with a H-5/FD-1 AI radar, an experimental version of the H-6 ASV with Yagi antenna, that had been specially designed to generate less drag in the nose.

In July 1945, the first flight tests of the Mukade conversion were conducted in the Yokosuka Arsenal. The Mukade was a modification of the Ginga that specialised in a long-range strafing role against the US B-29 bases. The project was inspired by the ventral armament of the Gekko and consisted of twelve 20-mm cannons angled at 30 degrees downwards and fired from an altitude of 200 m over the rows of refuelled and bombed-up B-29s. They hoped a fireball effect would take place with entire ranks of Superfortress, blowing each other up.

The Mukade tactics were part of Operation Ken-Go consisting of attempting an attack against the USAAF base at Iwo Jima using thirty-six Gingas of the Mitate Unit No. 6, thirty-six Mukade and thirty G4M bombers that had been modified for transporting suicide commands. There was also the project of the P1Y3 Mod.33, a Ginga with an enlarged fuselage and extended wingspan specially modified as a mothership for the Ohka Mod. 22 jet bomber Model 33 did not go beyond the drawing board.

After the Battle of the Coral Sea in May 1942, the IJN admitted the need to have a ground-based fast reconnaissance aircraft. Little afterwards, the Naval Air Arsenal at Yokosuka received the specification 17-Shi to design an aircraft that could fly at 666 kph at an altitude of 6,000 m. Under the project name Y-30, it was assigned to two teams that would study the different possibilities of a single or a twin-engined aircraft.

The R1Y1 Seiun would have had a classic airframe and been propelled by a Mitsubishi 24-cylinder, liquid-cooled, 2,500-hp experimental engine. The R1Y2 Gyoun would be an evolution from the Ginga with two Mitsubishi Mk10A (Ha-214) 2,400-hp radial engines. The Seiun engine did not prove to be acceptable in the medium term, and the estimated performance of the Gyoun showed that it did not comply with the requirements of the 17-Shi. Dr Masao Yamana of Kugisho suggested the use of German in-line engines, paired inside the fuselage, to build the R2Y1 Keiun with a single nose propeller and long power shaft. The formula did not work, and the team of Kugisho proposed its transformation to the IJN into a suicide fast bomber with two Ne-30 turbojets.

The opportunity to have these new engines reactivated the Gyoun, using a Yokosuka P1Y1 Ginga as a prototype, propelled by the two turbojets under the wing nacelles. The final model was known as Tenga and would have probably been propelled by two Ne-130 turbojets with a power equivalent to that of a German Jumo 004. The most important modifications, compared to the Ginga series, included the adoption of a solid nose cone and the installation of the main undercarriage legs between the engines and the fuselage.

Tenga Technical Data

Wingspan: 20 m
Length: 15 m
Height: 4.3 m
Wing area: 55 sq. m
Max. weight: 10,500 kg
Estimated max. speed: 700–750 kph
Estimated service ceiling: over 10,000 m
Engines: 2 × Ne-30 centrifugal turbojets with 850-kgf peak thrust or 2 × Ne-130 axial turbojets with 900-kgf peak thrust

Aichi S1A Denko

Late in 1943, *Kaigun Koku Hombu* issued the 18-shi-Hei specification, calling for a night fighter with a max. speed of 685 kph, an eight-minute climb to 6,000 m, a take-off run of 400 m, and an endurance of five hours.

By November, the Aichi company started the design AM-25 and completed the mock-up in August 1944. The new aircraft was a two-seat heavy fighter called S1A, powered by two 2,000-hp Nakajima NK9K-S Homare 22 radial engines, with an oxygen and water/methanol injection power boost and forced cooling fan, driving four-bladed, constant-speed airscrews. The armament was to be six Type 99-2, 20-mm cannons—two forward-firing in the nose, two in the nose, mounted in a 30-degree *Schräge Musik* configuration, and two in the rear fuselage turret.

In the heavy fighter/destroyer version, the two angled cannons were replaced by a Type 5, 30-mm forward-firing cannon. The night fighter version would be fitted with a Gyoku-3 AI radar, with the radiating antenna enclosed in a nose wooden radome and one Yagi receiver antenna mounted under the nose, a Taki-11 radio altimeter with two inverted 'T' dipoles mounted under the wings, and a Taki-30 IFF device with rod antenna mounted in the back of the rear fuselage. The building of two prototypes was started in 1944, but they were both destroyed during Allied bombing raids.

Denko Technical Data

Wingspan: 17.5 m
Length (with Yagi antenna): 15.1 m
Height: 4.61 m
Wing area: 47 sq. m
Max. weight: 10,180 kg
Estimated max. speed: 588 kph
Estimated service ceiling: 12,000 m

Kawasaki Ki.102

As the Ki.45 Toryu was proving to be a satisfactory heavy fighter, the *Koku Hombu* instructed Kawasaki Kokuki Kogyo KK to develop a successor with the 102 *kitai* number. The construction of the new fighter was to start in June 1944 in three different versions:

The high-altitude interceptor Ki.102-Ko, powered by two 1,400-hp Mitsubishi Ha-112-II Ru supercharged engines, driving three-bladed Hamilton propellers with 3 m of diameter.
The anti-invasion attack aircraft Ki.102-Otsu Type 4, with two 1,400-hp Mitsubishi Ha-112-II non-supercharged engines.
The night fighter Ki.102-Hei, with supercharged engines.

Only the Otsu version reached the series production phase, with 215 aircraft completed, and it was in combat action over Okinawa operating with *Sentais* Nos 3, 28, 45, and 75.

The production of the 'Ko' and 'Hei' versions was delayed because of difficulties with the Ru-102 turbo-superchargers. Only six units of the Ki.102-Ko were built, as well as two prototypes of the Ki.102-Hei.

The night fighter had a longer wingspan, lengthened fuselage, redesigned tail surfaces, and a Taki-2 AI radar. It would carry two forward-firing Ho-5, 20-mm cannons and two Ho-155, 30-mm cannons mounted in a 40-degree *Schräge Musik* configuration.

Ki.102-Hei Technical Data

Wingspan: 17.25 m
Length: 13.05 m
Height: 3.7 m
Wing area: 40 sq. m

Max. weight: 7,600 kg
Estimated max. speed: 600 kph
Estimated service ceiling: 13,500 m

Mitsubishi A6M2, A6M3, A6M5, and A6M5-S Zero Sen

At the outbreak of the Second World War, the IJN lacked specialised aircraft for night warfare. The Mitsubishi A5M and A6M fighters were often used for both day and night fighting, crewed by specially selected pilots for their excellent night vision, which was boosted using a methamphetamine called M-33-N Philopon.

The Zero fighters were extensively used in night missions, defending their airfields against the attacks of the Douglas A-20, North American B-25, and Lockheed PV-3 medium bombers. Sometimes, they attempted interceptions using searchlights for guidance—a tactic that was first used at Rabaul by the Zeros of the 204 *Kōkūtai*.

Some A6M2 of the 203rd *Kōkūtai Shumshu* Detachment, defending the Imaizaki airfield in the Kuriles Islands, were painted in black with no apparent modifications, but that local initiative was not generalised. Most Zeros used for night missions kept their original FS 14077/FS 24201 paint scheme.

By the end of 1944, some A6M5-Ko of the 1st *Hikotai*, 302nd *Kōkūtai*, based in Atsugi, were experimentally fitted with one Type 99-2, Model 4, 20-mm cannon mounted in the fuselage, behind the pilot, at 30 degrees to the aircraft's centreline, protruding through the left-side fuselage skin. It was not a night-fighting device; with that angled cannon, it would have been possible to fire at the enemy fighter, in a dog fight, before the Zero got to his tail. This modification was apparently designed to fight against the Hellcats.

The sideways-angled cannon was very unpopular because an accident killed a maintenance man who was walking on the wing. The system was modified by installing the cannon 30 degrees forward and 10 degrees to the left in a *Schräge Musik* configuration, firing through the rear section of the glazed canopy. When the Americans changed the method of attack of their B-29s from high altitude to night low altitude, the Zeros, Raidens, and Gekkos of the 302nd *Kōkūtai* had their chance to destroy eleven Superfortresses. In October 1943, the needs of the war forced the IJA to create new units specialised in night warfare that were usually integrated by Zeros and Gekkos.

There never was an official version of the Zero night fighter, though the A6M5-S designation was used by some post-war historians referring to the A6M5 and A6M5-Hei with *Schräge Musik* armament. Every *Kōkūtai* made the field modifications that they considered to be necessary.

The 153rd *Kōkūtai*, based in Babo airfield (New Guinea) operated with some A6M3 Model 32, with *Schräge Musik* armament, in July 1944. At the same time, the 201st *Kōkūtai* of Tacloban (the Philippines) had several A6M5 Model 52 that had also been modified. The 252nd *Kōkūtai*, based in Taroa airfield (the Marshall Islands), used the A6M3 Model 22 as modified night fighters at the beginning of 1944. At Rabaul, in March 1944, the *Hikotai* 316 became a night fighter unit equipped with modified A6M3 Model 32 and the 332nd *Kōkūtai* of Iwakuni, used A6M5-Hei Model 52, with *Schräge Musik* armament, in July 1944.

A6M2 Model 21 Technical Data

Wingspan: 12 m
Length: 9.05 m
Height: 3.52 m
Wing area: 22.43 sq. m
Max. weight: 2,421 kg
Max. speed: 533 kph
Service ceiling: 10,300 m

A6M3 Model 32 Technical Data

Wingspan: 11 m
Length: 9.06 m
Height: 3.57 m
Wing area: 21.53 sq. m
Max. weight: 2,884 kg
Max. speed: 545 kph
Service ceiling: 11,050 m

A6M5 Model 52 Technical Data

Wingspan: 11 m
Length: 9.12 m
Height: 3.57 m
Wing area: 21.3 sq. m
Max. weight: 3.083 kg
Max. speed: 565 kph
Service ceiling: 11,740 m

A6M5-Hei Model 52 Technical Data

Wingspan: 11 m
Length: 9.12 m
Height: 3.57 m
Wing area: 21.3 sq. m
Max. weight: 3,400 kg
Max. speed: 541 kph
Service ceiling: 11,050 m

Mitsubishi J2M3 and J2M4 Raiden

The J2M4 Model 34 Raiden prototype flew for the first time in August 1944, powered by a 1,420-hp Kasei 23c engine with one mechanically driven Ru 302 turbocharger and two Type 99-2, Model 4, 20-mm cannons mounted behind the pilot at a 30-degree *Schräge Musik* configuration. Unresolved difficulties with the Ru 302 caused the project to be cancelled.

By November 1944, the 302nd *Kōkūtai* had a force of twenty-seven A6M5 Zeros and ten J2M3 Raidens. At least one of these was experimentally fitted with one Type 99-2, Model 4, 20-mm cannon mounted in the fuselage, behind the pilot, at 30 degrees to the aircraft's centreline, firing through the left-side fuselage skin.

J2M3 Model 32 Technical Data

Wingspan: 10.8 m
Length: 9.7 m
Height: 3.81 m
Wing area: 20 sq. m
Max. weight: 3,211 kg
Max. speed: 671 kph
Service ceiling: 11,430 m

Schräge Musik

The British bombers of the Second World War had two gun turrets, one dorsal and another in the tail, which were very effective against attacks performed from behind.

To avoid its defensive fire, the Germans developed the *Schräge Musik* tactic, which consisted of shooting against the belly of the bombers using upward-firing cannons mounted in the rear cockpit of the Messerschmitt Bf 110 night fighters. The idea was not new as it has been used by British fighters while fighting against the Zeppelins during the First World War, but its advantage was to be able to shoot directly against the engines and wing fuel tanks that in a classical attack from behind would have been protected by the wing's structure.

After the first successes achieved by the Bf 110, the Luftwaffe used the system with the Dornier Do 217, Focke-Wulf Fw 189 and Ta 154, Heinkel He 219, Junkers Ju 88 and Ju 388, and Messerschmitt Me 262 B night fighters. It was also used in Japan with the Ki.45, Ki.46, Ki.84, Ki.102, A6M, C6N, D4Y, J1N, J2M, P1Y, and S1A.

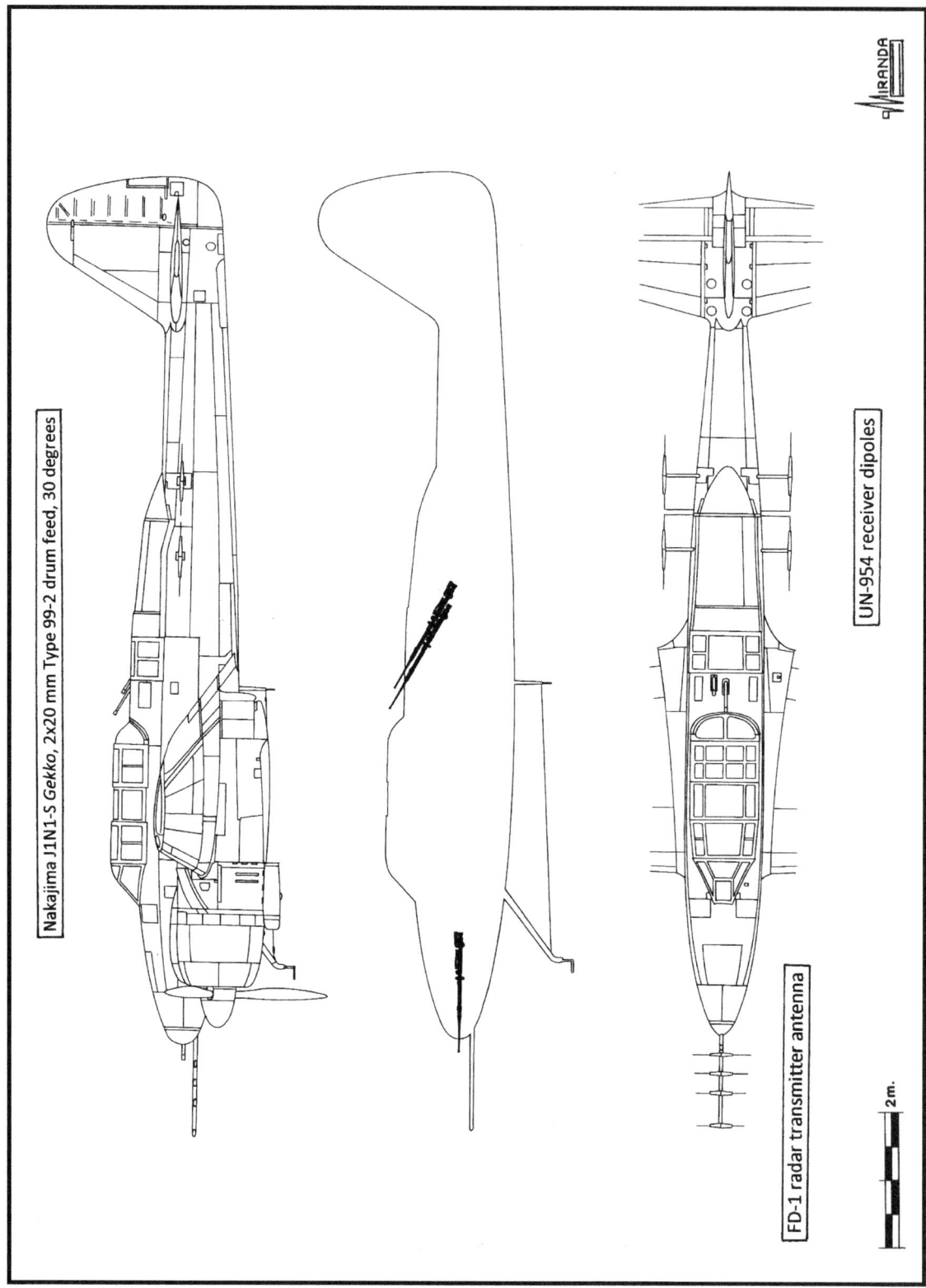

Nakajima J1N1-S Gekko, 2x20 mm Type 99-2 drum feed, 30 degrees

UN-954 receiver dipoles

FD-1 radar transmitter antenna

2 m.

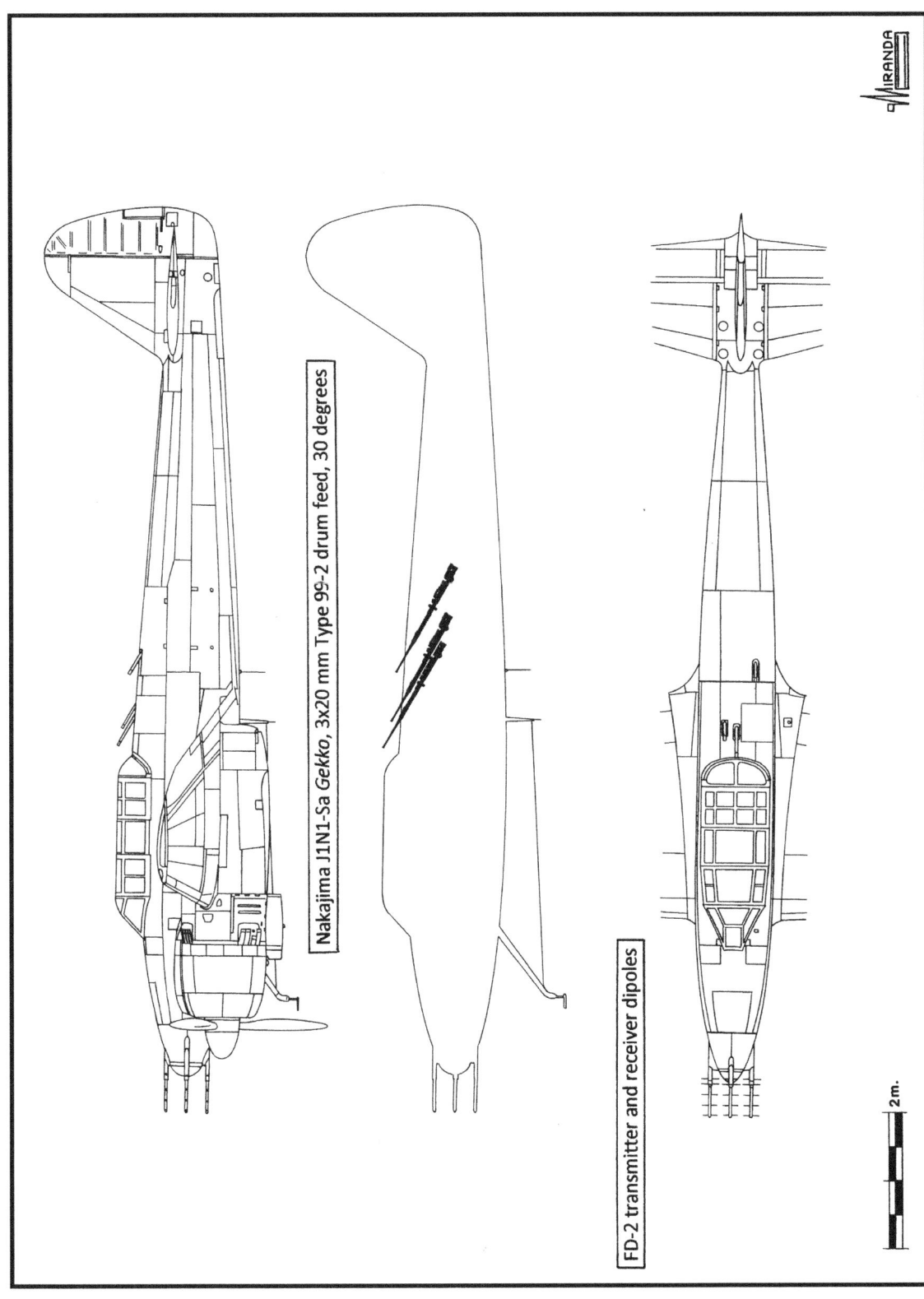

Nakajima J1N1-Sa *Gekko*, 3x20 mm Type 99-2 drum feed, 30 degrees

FD-2 transmitter and receiver dipoles

2 m.

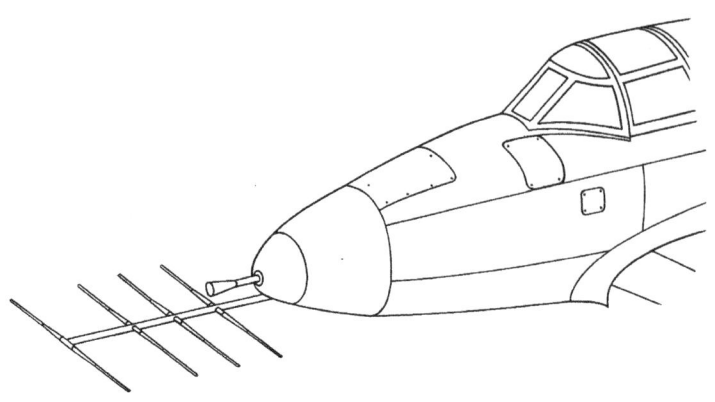

Nakajima J1N1-S *Gekko* with FD-1 radar

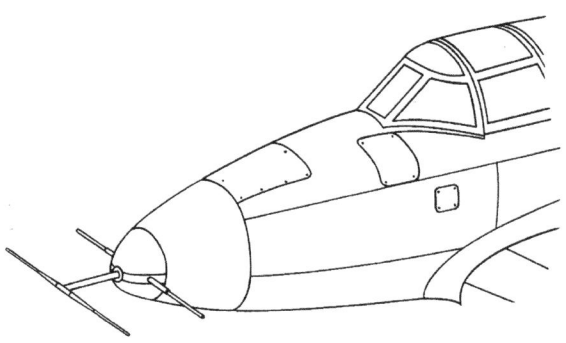

Nakajima J1N1-S *Gekko* with FD-1/H-5 radar

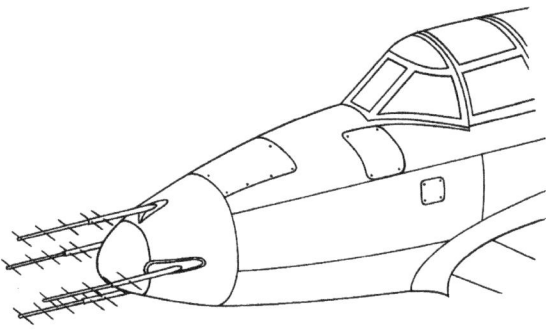

Nakajima J1N1-Sa *Gekko* with FD-2 radar

 2m.

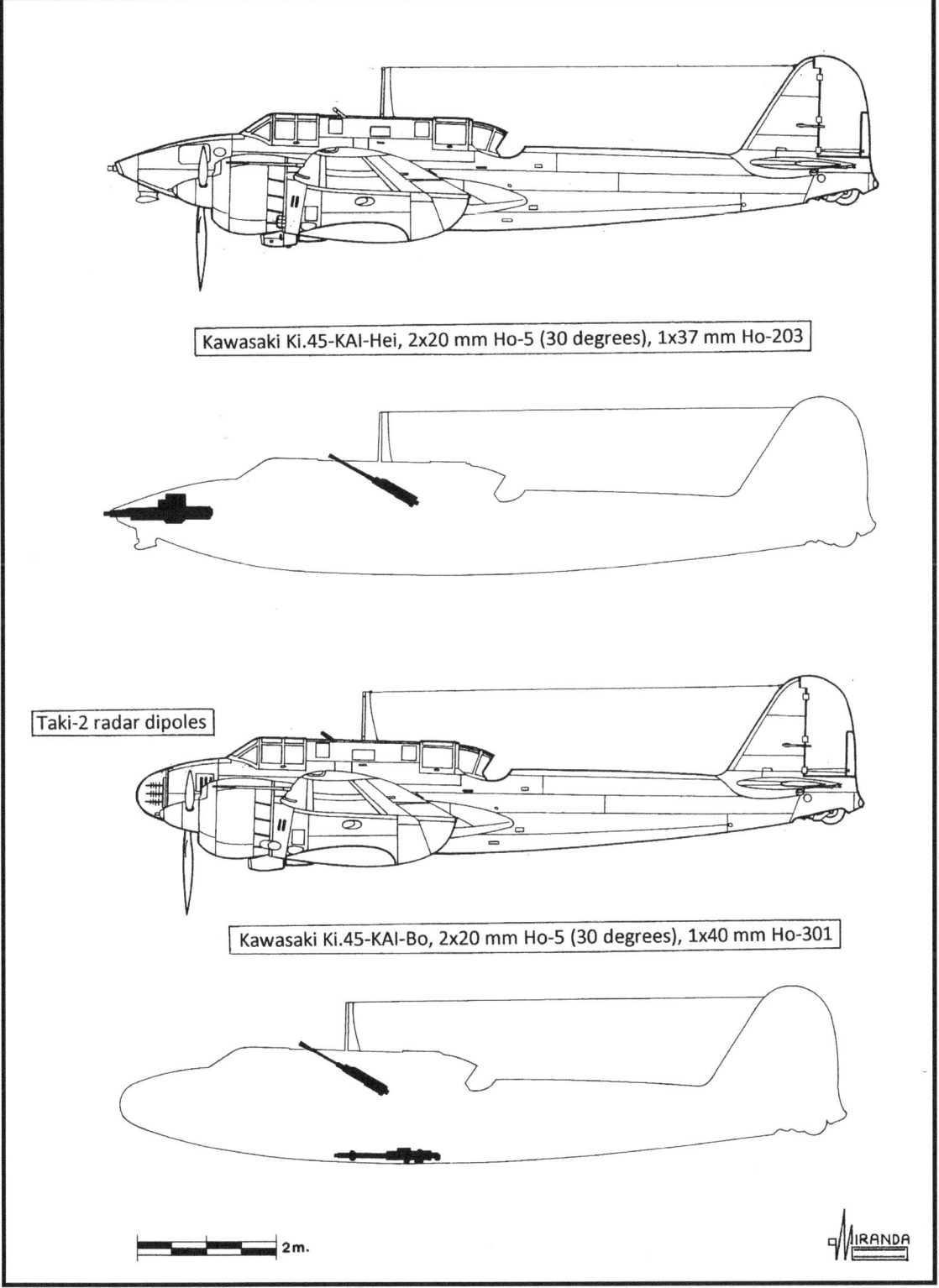

Kawasaki Ki.45-KAI-Hei, 2x20 mm Ho-5 (30 degrees), 1x37 mm Ho-203

Taki-2 radar dipoles

Kawasaki Ki.45-KAI-Bo, 2x20 mm Ho-5 (30 degrees), 1x40 mm Ho-301

2 m.

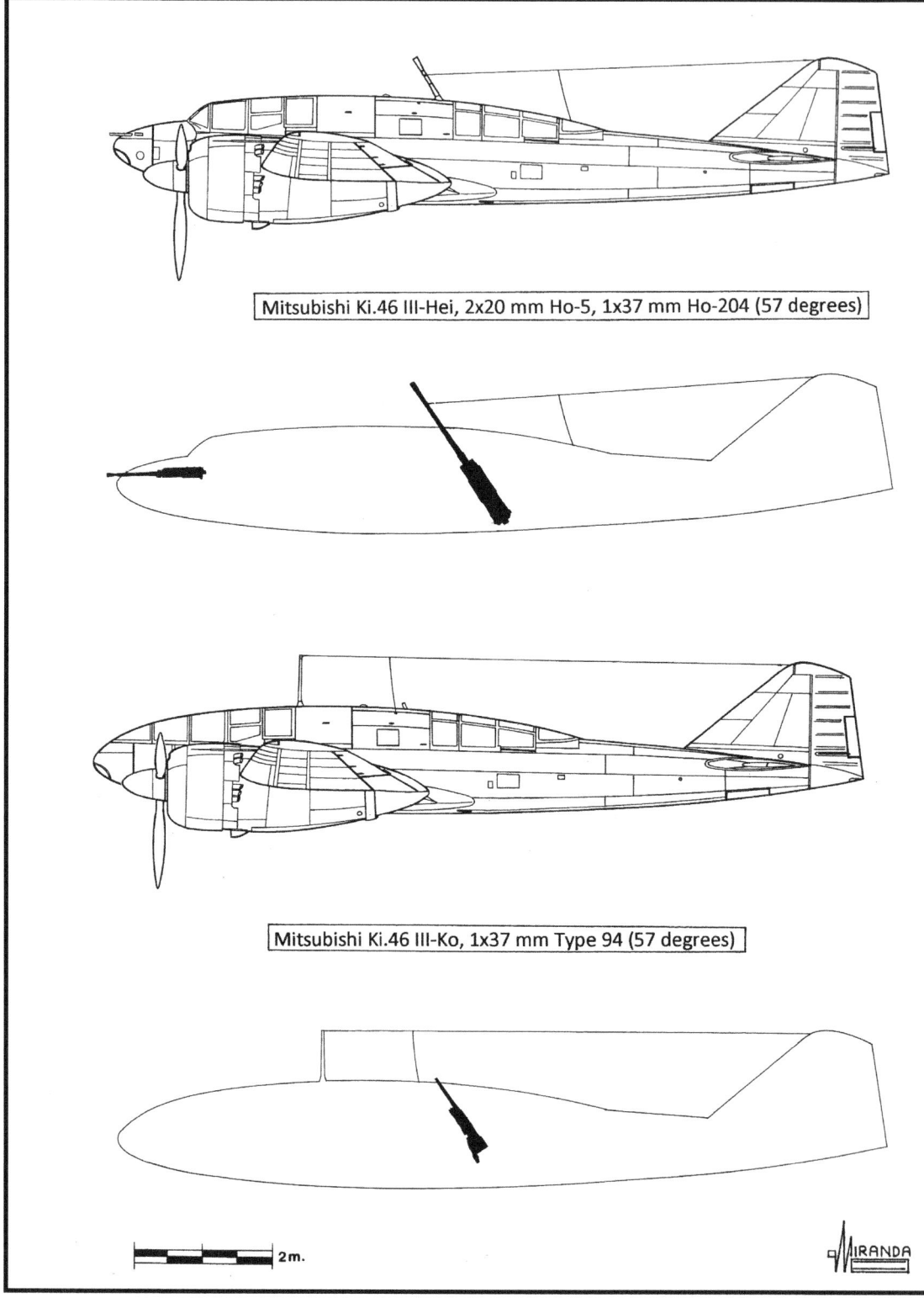

Mitsubishi Ki.46 III-Hei, 2x20 mm Ho-5, 1x37 mm Ho-204 (57 degrees)

Mitsubishi Ki.46 III-Ko, 1x37 mm Type 94 (57 degrees)

2 m.

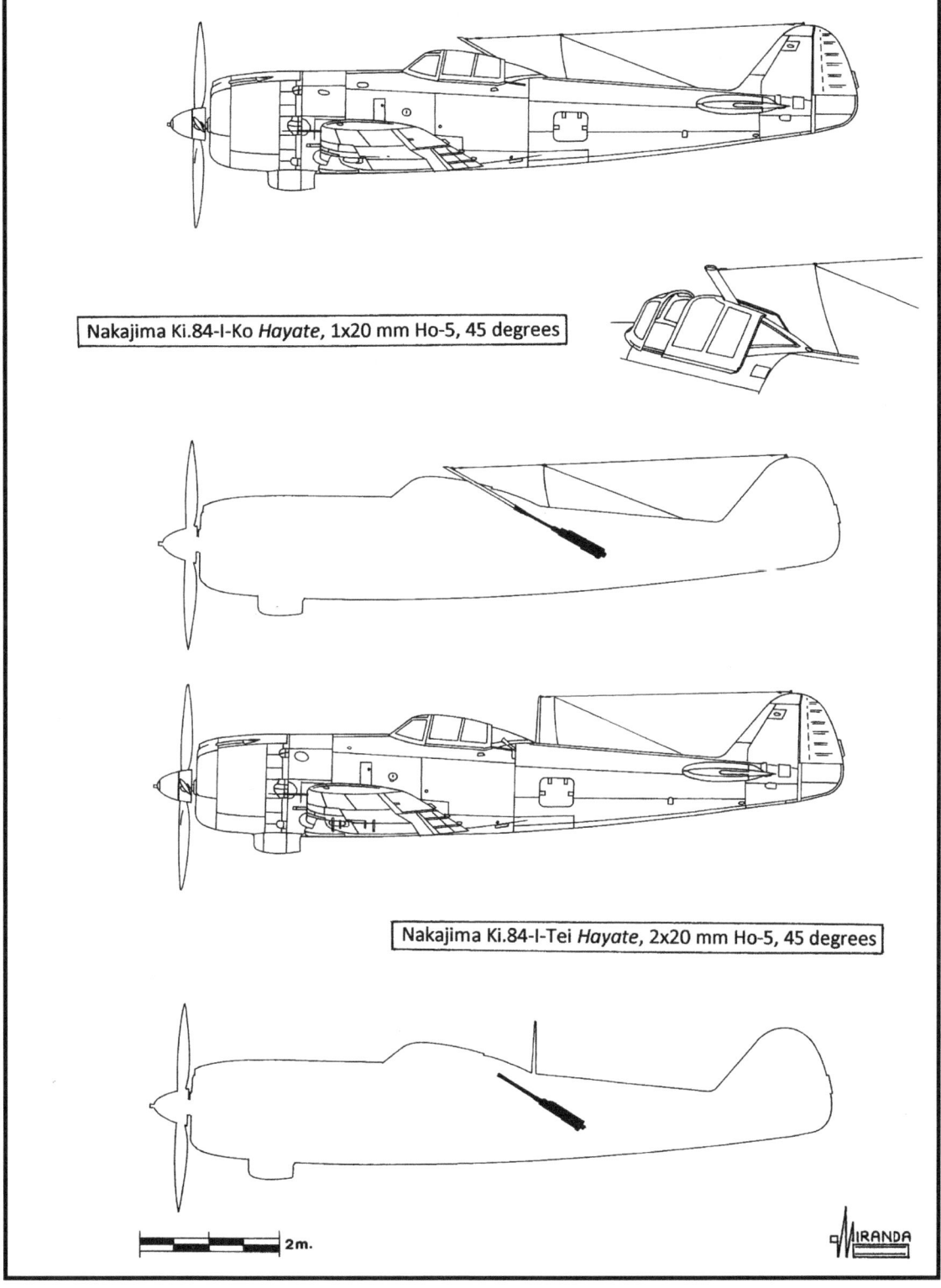

Nakajima Ki.84-I-Ko *Hayate*, 1x20 mm Ho-5, 45 degrees

Nakajima Ki.84-I-Tei *Hayate*, 2x20 mm Ho-5, 45 degrees

2m.

Fighters of the Dying Sun

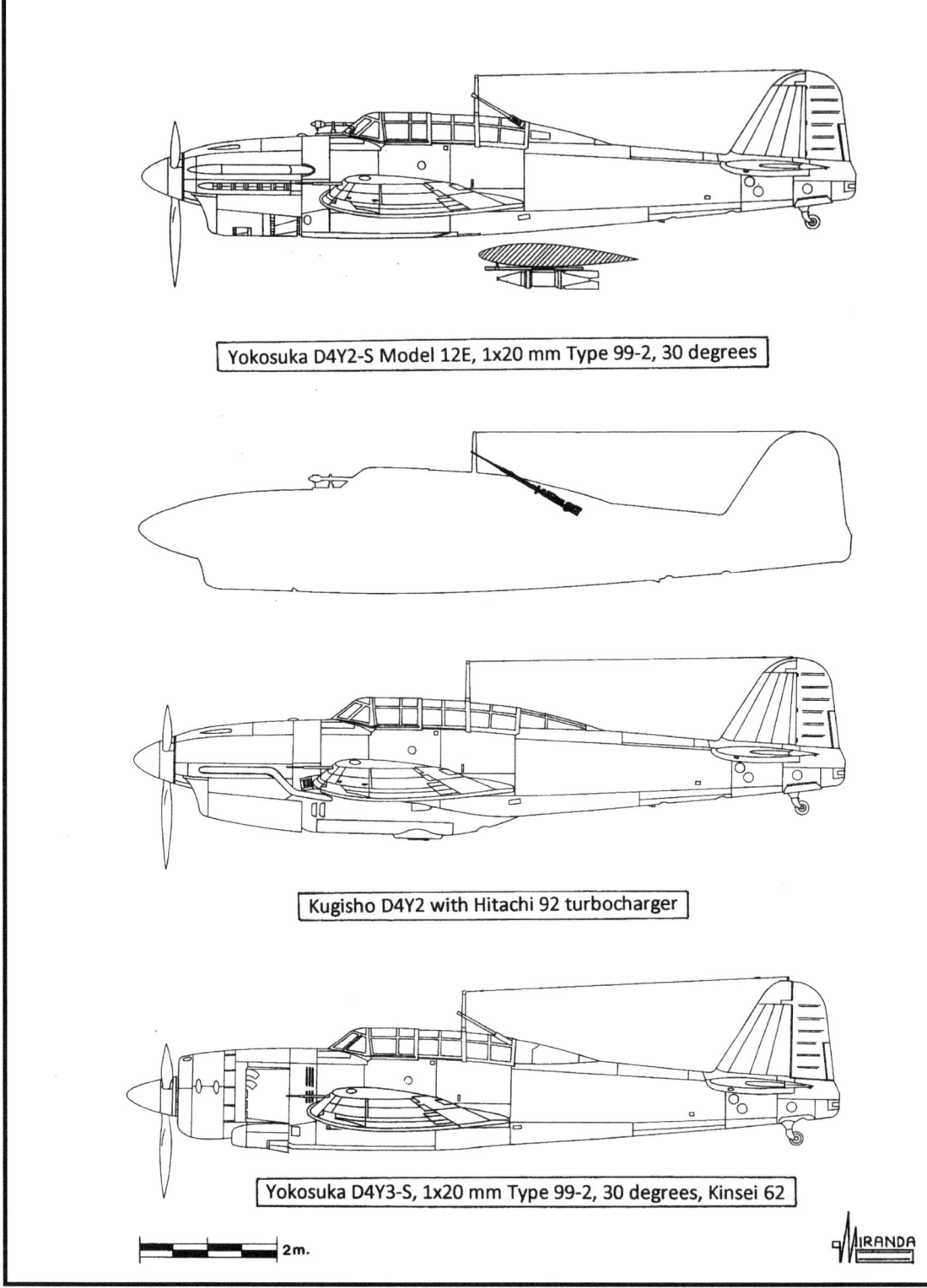

Yokosuka D4Y2-S Model 12E, 1x20 mm Type 99-2, 30 degrees

Kugisho D4Y2 with Hitachi 92 turbocharger

Yokosuka D4Y3-S, 1x20 mm Type 99-2, 30 degrees, Kinsei 62

2m.

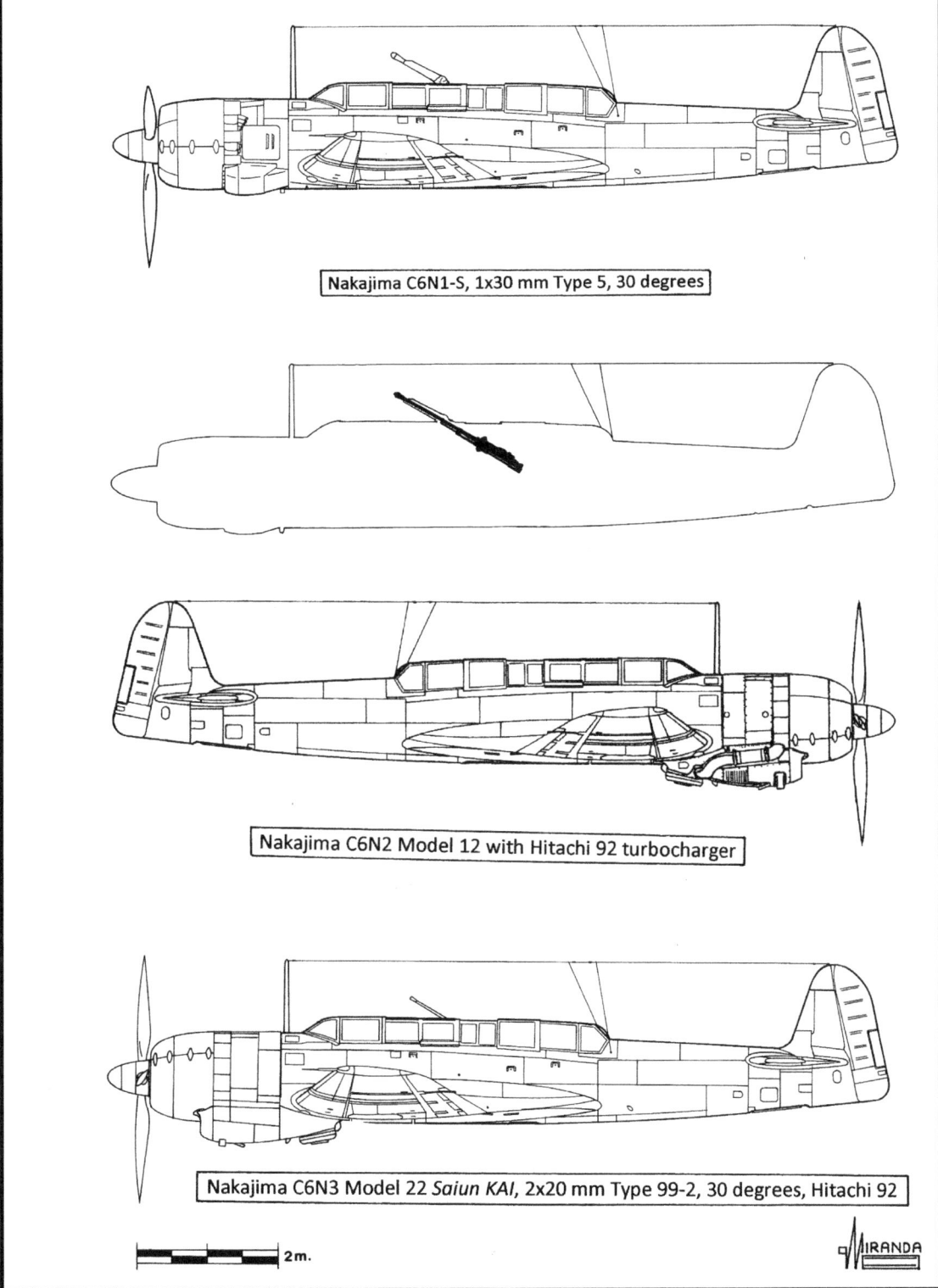

Nakajima C6N1-S, 1x30 mm Type 5, 30 degrees

Nakajima C6N2 Model 12 with Hitachi 92 turbocharger

Nakajima C6N3 Model 22 *Saiun KAI*, 2x20 mm Type 99-2, 30 degrees, Hitachi 92

2m.

MIRANDA

Fighters of the Dying Sun

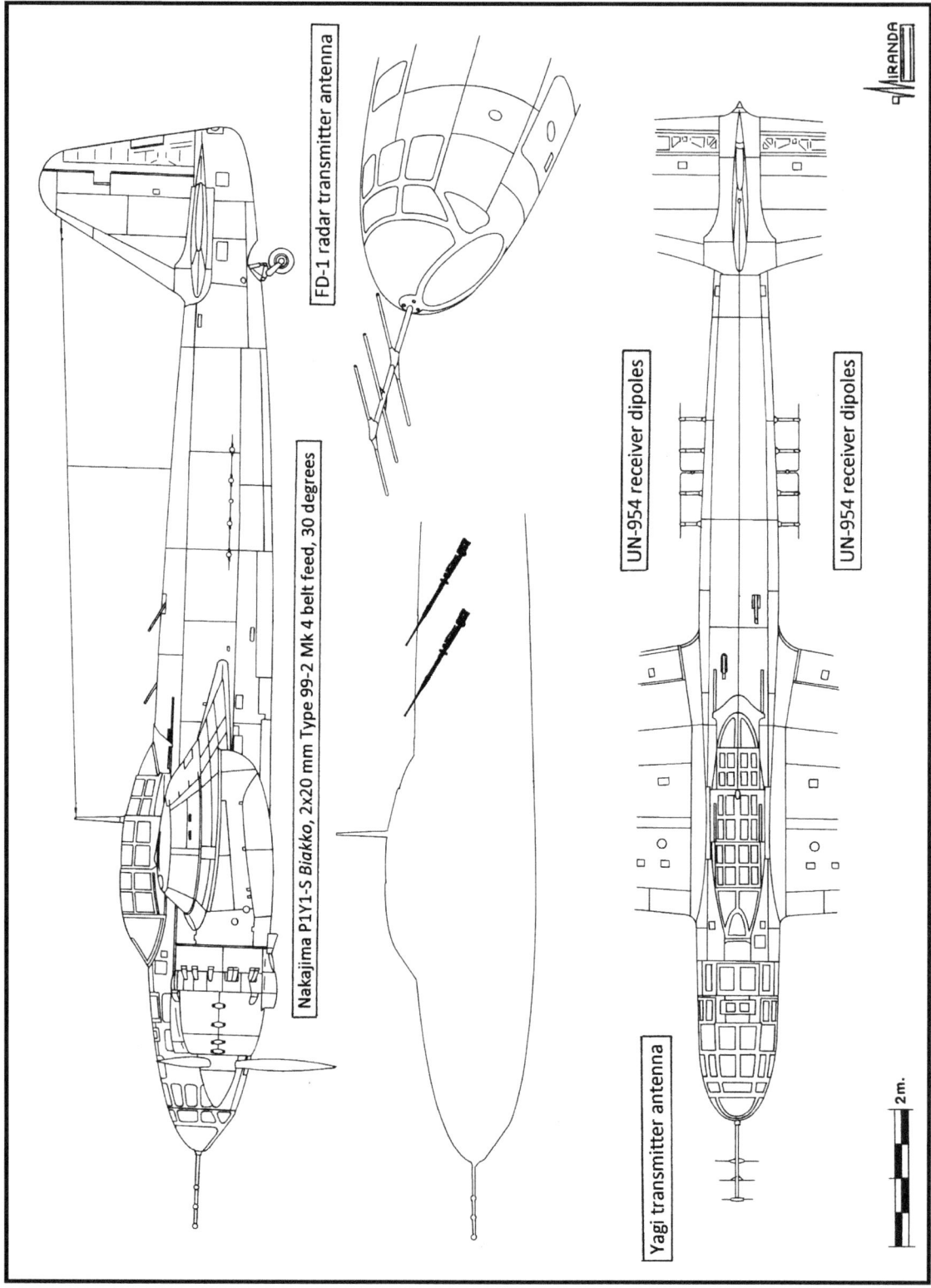

FD-1 radar transmitter antenna

Nakajima P1Y1-S *Biakko*, 2x20 mm Type 99-2 Mk 4 belt feed, 30 degrees

UN-954 receiver dipoles

UN-954 receiver dipoles

Yagi transmitter antenna

2 m.

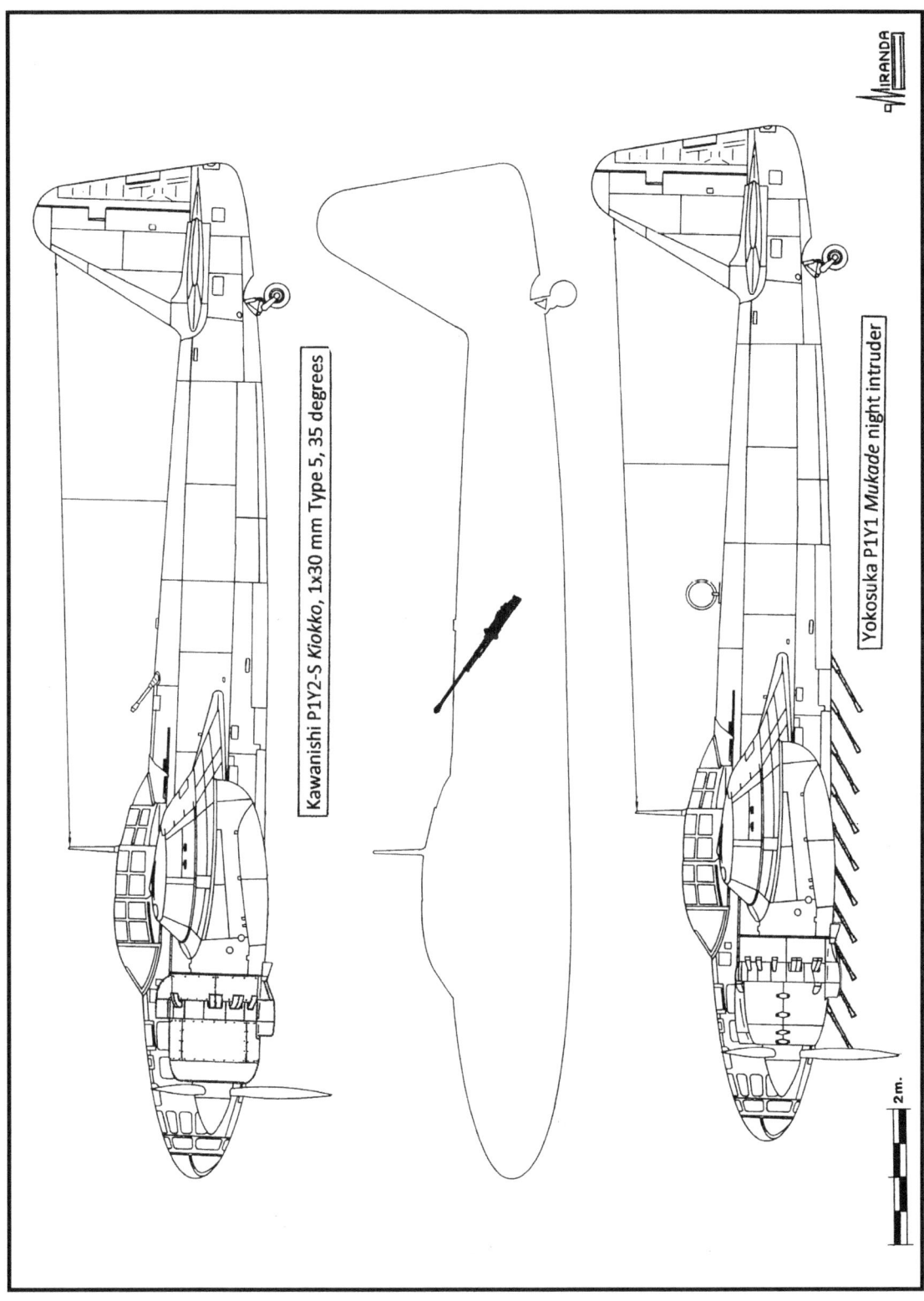

Kawanishi P1Y2-S *Kiokko*, 1x30 mm Type 5, 35 degrees

Yokosuka P1Y1 *Mukade* night intruder

2 m.

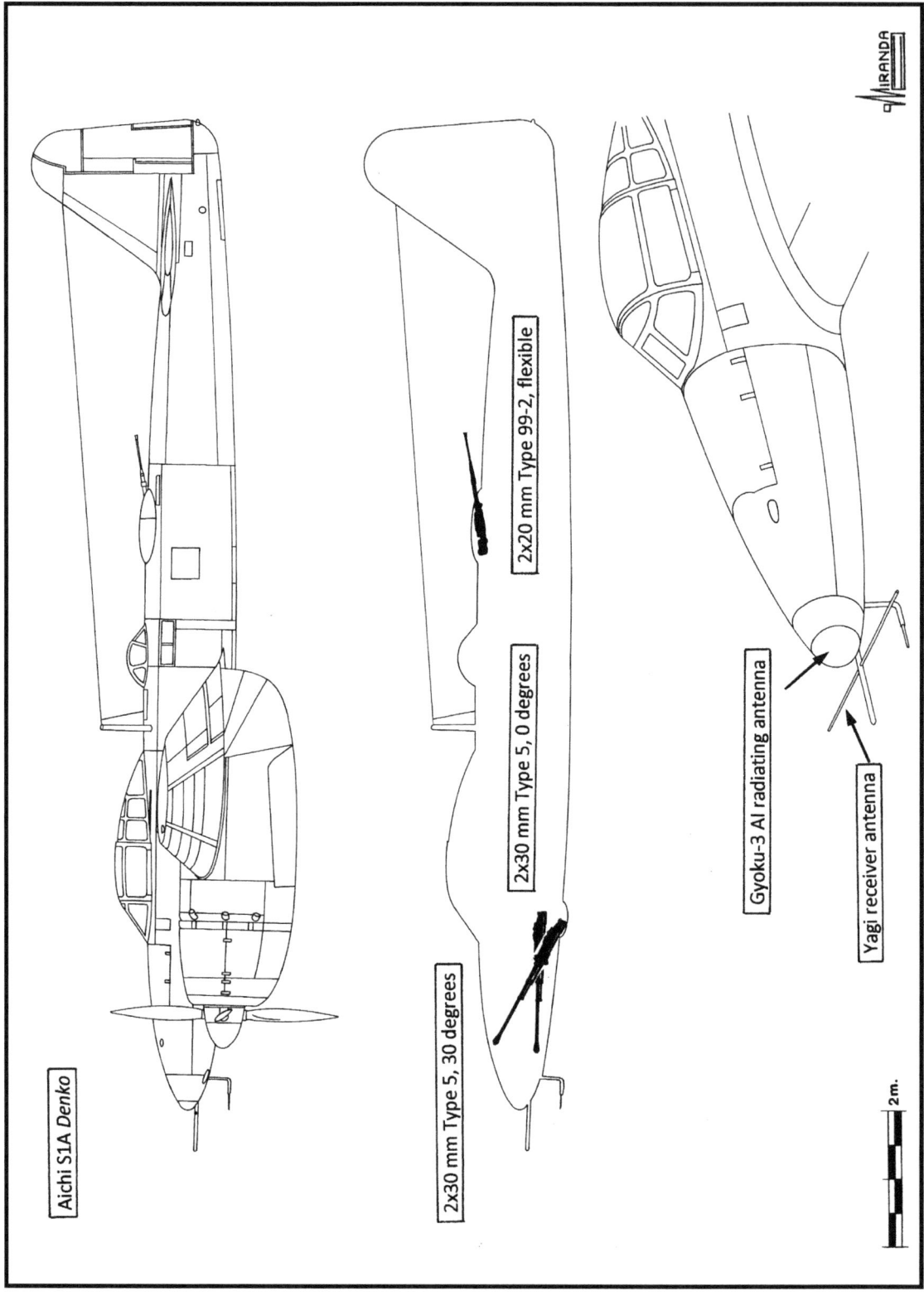

Aichi S1A *Denko*

2x30 mm Type 5, 30 degrees

2x30 mm Type 5, 0 degrees

2x20 mm Type 99-2, flexible

Gyoku-3 AI radiating antenna

Yagi receiver antenna

2 m.

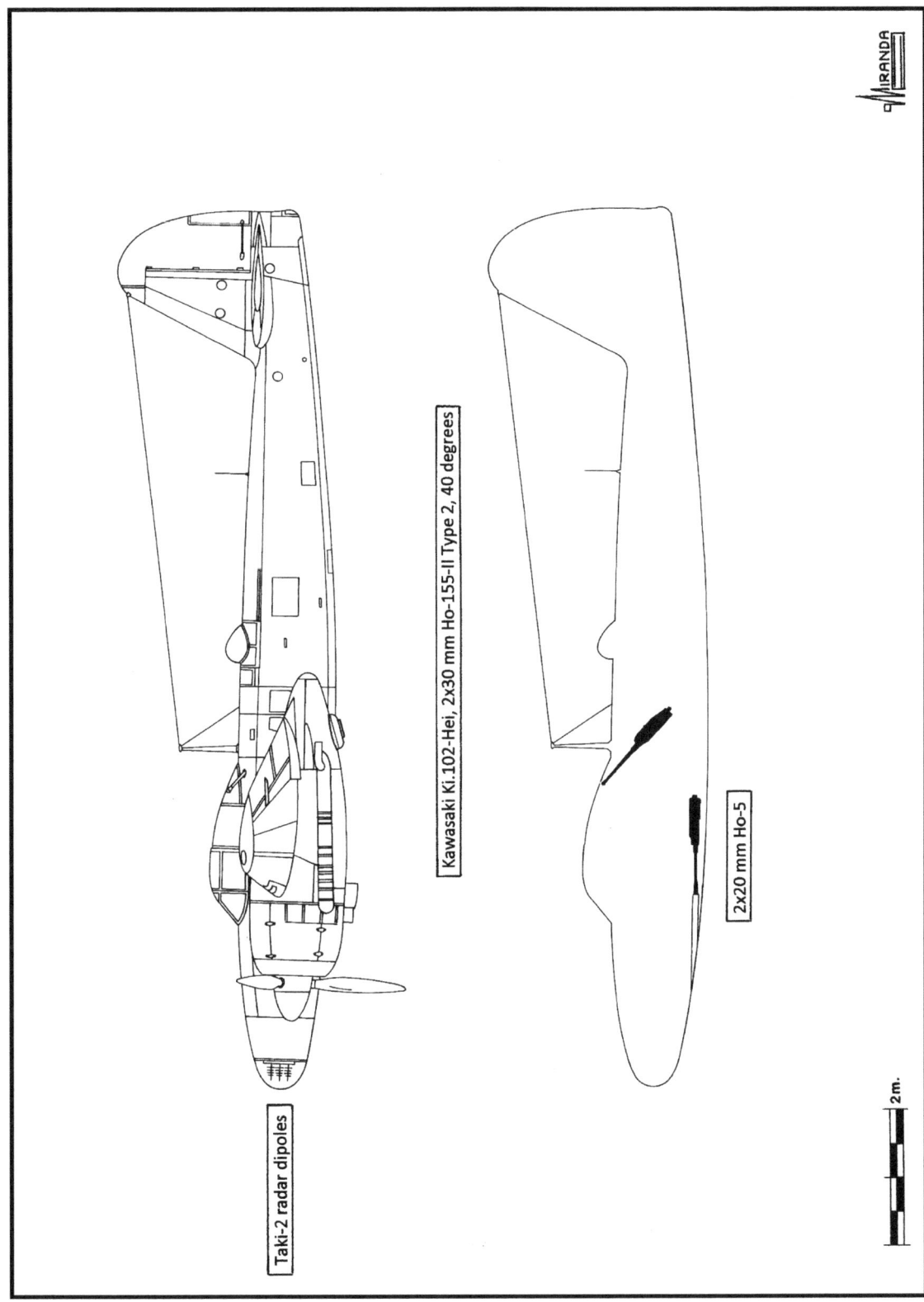

Taki-2 radar dipoles

Kawasaki Ki.102-Hei, 2x30 mm Ho-155-II Type 2, 40 degrees

2x20 mm Ho-5

2 m.

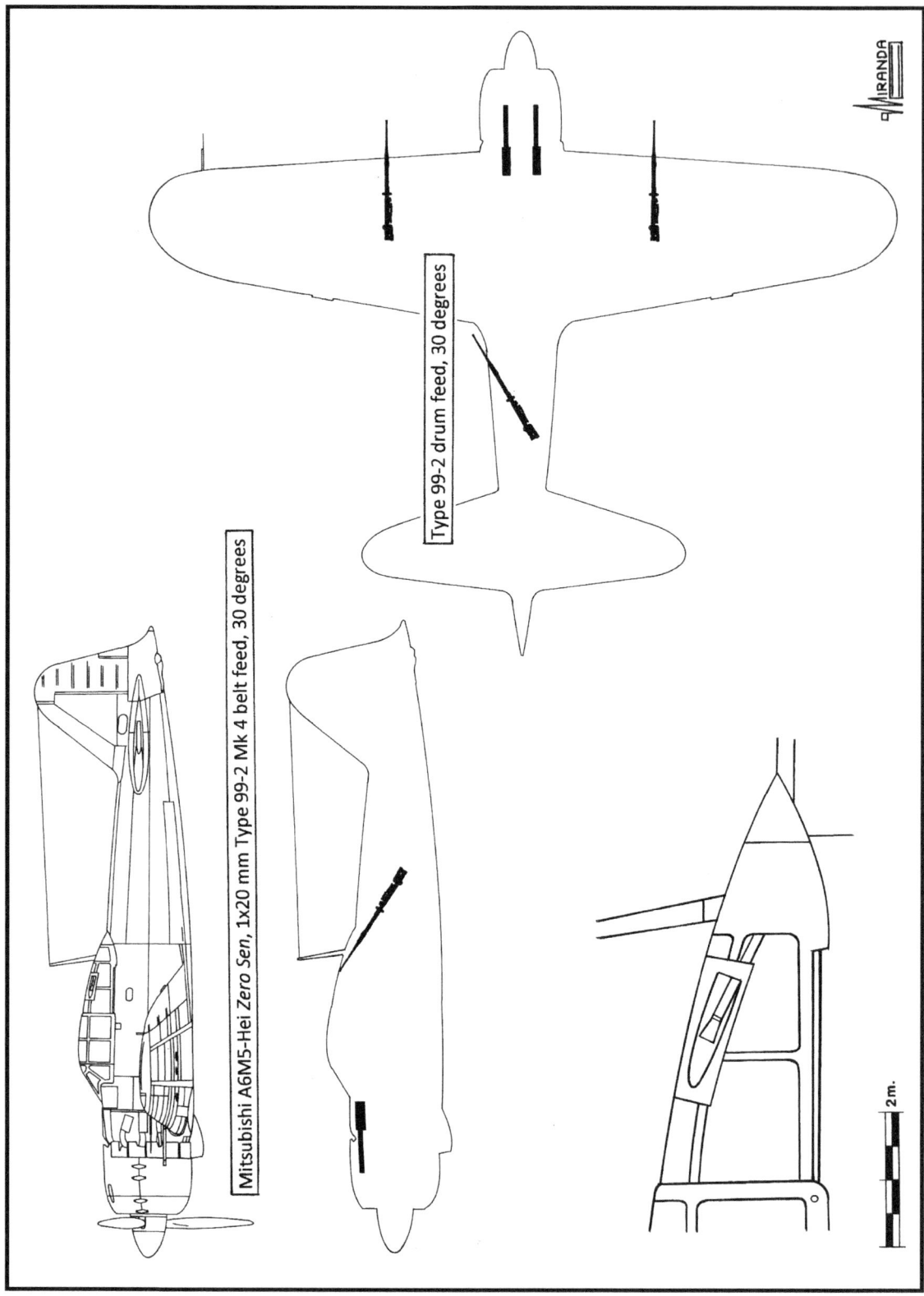

Type 99-2 drum feed, 30 degrees

Mitsubishi A6M5-Hei *Zero Sen*, 1x20 mm Type 99-2 Mk 4 belt feed, 30 degrees

2 m.

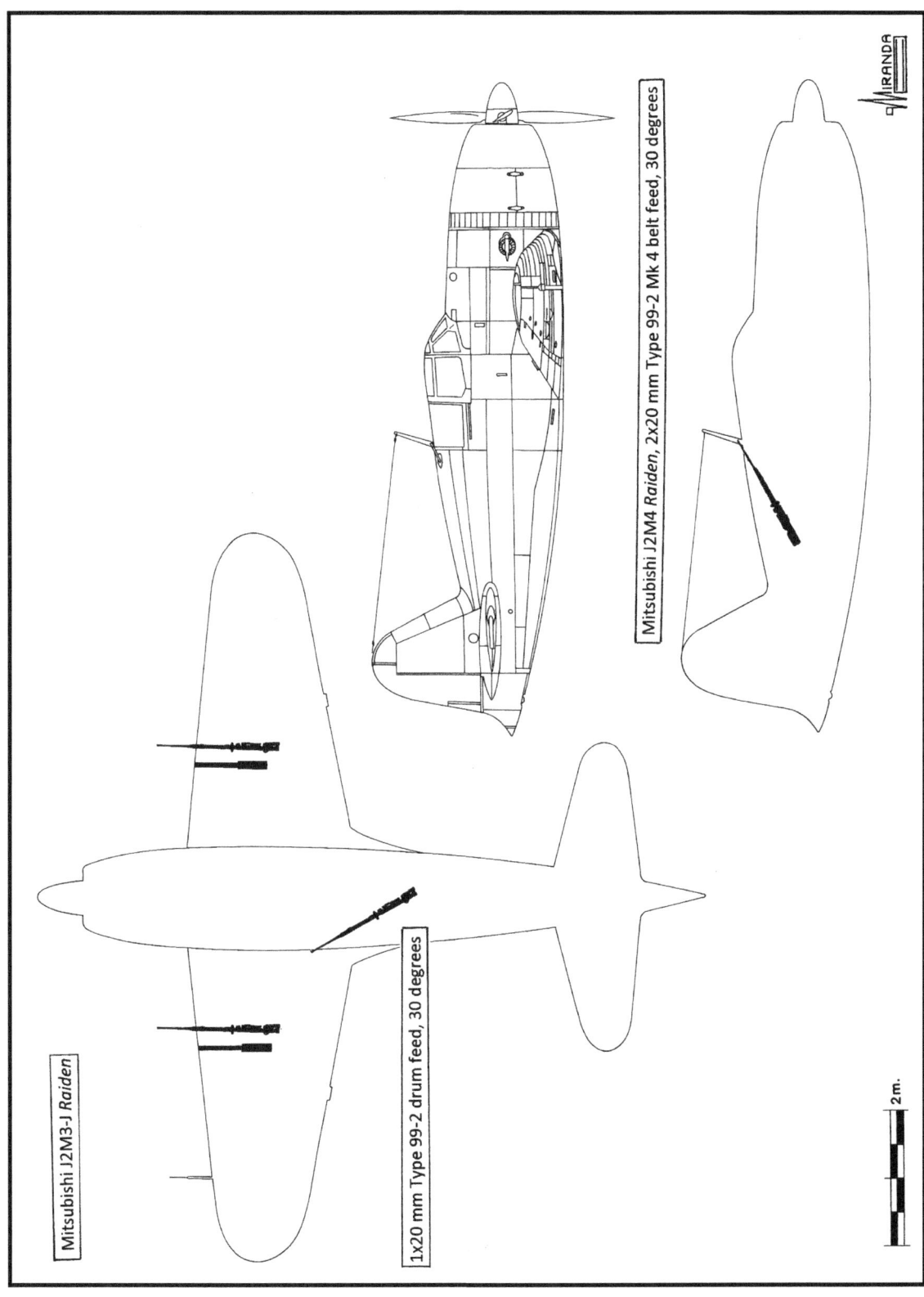

Mitsubishi J2M4 *Raiden*, 2x20 mm Type 99-2 Mk 4 belt feed, 30 degrees

Mitsubishi J2M3-J *Raiden*

1x20 mm Type 99-2 drum feed, 30 degrees

2 m.

6

Radar Warfare

When the Japanese industry was able to manufacture radar equipment light enough to be installed on aircraft, the IJN's main interest was in locating enemy ships using ASV (air-to-surface vessel) equipment.

In August 1942, the H-6 Type 3, Mark 6, Model 4 radar entered service, developed by the Oppama Naval Technical Depot, with a range of 100 km against large surface craft. Between 1942 and 1944, a total of 2,000 units of the H-6 ASV were manufactured by Nihon Musen Co. The H-6, also called Kaze-1, weighed 110 kg and was installed in the four-engined Kawanishi H6K5 and H8K2 flying boats with the mission of locating the US Navy's task forces.

The H-6 radar was also used by the Nakajima B6N2 and Mitsubishi G4M2 torpedo-bombers to carry out nightly torpedo attacks and by the Nakajima J1N1 of the 321st *Kōkūtai* in anti-submarine patrols and night intruder attacks against torpedo boats, with two 250-kg bombs. The Type 3 Model 1 (KMX) magnetic airborne detector was used for anti-submarine patrols by the Aichi E13A1b and Kyushu Q1W1 specialised aircraft.

The antenna's configuration was different for each type of aircraft. The single-engined B6N2 used a Yagi transmitter antenna, with four elements, mounted on the leading edge of the starboard wing, with the four 'T' dipoles of the UN-954 receiver mounted in the fuselage sides. In the multi-engined aircraft, the Yagi antenna was mounted in the nose.

The H-6 operated on a frequency of 150 megacycles, with a 2-m wavelength and 3-kW power output. In September 1944, the IJN carried out some tests with the FM-1, a new ASV radar developed by Tokyo Shibaura Denki with the same performances as the H-6 yet weighing only 70 kg. The prototype was unsuitable for practical use, and production was stopped in favour of the more advanced version called FM-3 that entered service in 1945 with 100 units built. The FM-3 operated with a 2-m wavelength and 2-kW power output, weighed only 60 kg, and could be used by medium-sized anti-submarine plans, but its range was reduced to 70 km.

The N6 was another ASV designed to equip small patrol planes. It operated with a 1.2-m wavelength and 2-kW power output, weighing 60 kg. Only flying tests were conducted with prototypes. Nihon Musen Co. built twenty units in 1944, but it never entered service. Other ASV projects that were not built were the FK-3, a version of the FM-3 developed by Kawasaki for the J6K1 Jinpu, with PPI display and weighing 60 kg, and the FK-4, a more powerful version for large patrol planes, with 20-kW power output and a range of 100 km.

All these radars used the same type of antennas as the H-6 and had limited capabilities to detect aircraft, but the fuselage receiver dipoles could not search the area ahead of the aeroplane. The approach to the target had to be oblique to maintain radar contact, and its use in night fighters was impractical.

The Kasumi-51 was a prototype of cartographic pathfinder radar based on the H2S of a British bomber downed in Rotterdam. In 1944, the Germans sent the Japanese a complete schematic of this equipment, which operated at a 10-cm wavelength with a 5-kW power output, with parabolic rotating antenna and PPI display. Only three prototypes of the Kasumi-51 were built in 1945. During flying tests, it was confirmed that the distance at which it would pick up the shore was only 20 km, which discouraged large-scale production.

As the war progressed, AI (airborne intercept) radars were developed from the H-6 to locate enemy night intruders. Some Nakajima J1N1-S and Kawanishi P1Y2-S Kyokko night fighters were experimentally equipped with H-5/FD-1 radars that did not work well during operational flying tests. The IJN decided to develop specialised AI radars for night fighters.

In August 1944, the FD-2, developed by the 2nd Naval Technical Institute, entered service with the Gekkos of the 302nd *Kōkūtai*. The new AI radar used four nose-mounted Yagi antennas, with five elements each, one pair for sending and one pair for receiving. The FD-2 operated with a 25-cm wavelength, 2.5-kW power output, and a range of 3–10 km. It weighed 70 kg, and a total of 100 units were built.

The FD-2 was used in combat without good results due to the effective countermeasures used by the B-29s. As with the *Hirschgeweih* antennas used by the Luftwaffe, the Japanese discovered that Yagi antennas generated too much drag, penalising the performances of the Gekko.

Between September 1944 and April 1945, the firm Tokyo Shibaura Denki tried to develop, without success, a new type of antenna embedded in the wing's leading edge to save drag. In August 1944, ten prototypes of the Gyoku-3 AI radar were built, using the direction-finding technique to produce a forward conical scan, with the radiating antenna enclosed in a wooden nose radome and one 'T' dipole receiver mounted under the nose. The Gyoku-3 operated on a frequency of 150 megacycles with a 3-kW power output and a range of 4.5 km. It was expected to be used in the new Aichi S1A Denko night fighter but did not get into service. Daytime flight tests were performed at Yokosuka naval base in May 1945.

By the end of 1942, the Tama Technology Research Institute, in cooperation with Toshiba Shibaura Denki and Nippon Electric Co, developed for the IJN an airborne ASV radar named Taki-1, 'Ta' was for Tama and 'Ki' for Kuki (Air). The Taki-1 Model 1 operated at a wavelength of 150 cm with a 10-kW power output and a range of 100 km. During flight tests performed late in 1943, it used two Yagi antennas, with three elements each, mounted on the nose and starboard wing of one Nakajima Ki.49 bomber.

The Model 1 gave a satisfactory search performance, but weighing 150 kg, it was heavy for airborne equipment. The Model 2 was designed in 1944, weighing only 80 kg, for the Mitsubishi Ki.67-I Yasukuni torpedo-bomber.

One Yagi antenna, with five elements, was mounted in the starboard wing, and two 'X' arrays were mounted on either side of the rear fuselage. Each of these antennas could transmit and receive by means of an automatic switch, and all three could be used in rapid rotation or singly to determine relative direction. One A-Type presentation rangefinder provided accurate ranging. Nihon Musen Co. built 1,000 units of the Model 2 in 1944. A lighter Model 3 was developed for fighter bombers, but it was still in the laboratory when the war ended.

The Taki-2 was an AI radar based in the German FuG 202 *Lichtenstein* B/C. It was an 80-cm wavelength 'radio locator', with a 2-kW power output and a range of 3 km, developed in 1944 for the IJA Kawasaki Ki.45-KAI-Bo night fighter. It used four Yagi antennas with five elements and folded driving dipoles mounted in the nose plane, with the antennas installed in a transparent radome. Each of these antennas could transmit and receive. A motor-driven distributor connected each antenna to the receiver in rapid succession, for azimuth, elevation, and range determination. It is believed that at least twelve Toryus were converted to 'Bo' configuration and were undergoing operational tests at the time the war ended. It does not seem likely that this set would have given enough directional accuracy for night-fighting operations. Early in 1945, studies were being made, resulting in the Model III (Tama-3) AI radar, with a wavelength of 20 cm and a weight of 70 kg.

Taki-3 was an airborne ASV sea search radar developed in August 1943 by the radio department of the Aeronautical Laboratory from Tokyo Imperial University. The Tama Institute rejected the set in 1944 due to its poor performance. Taki-8 was a 'wave disturber' jammer designed by the X-band of the B-29. Taki-11 was a high-altitude radio-altimeter (based in the German Siemens FuG 101, with two inverted 'T' dipoles mounted under the wings) with a wavelength of 80 cm and a range between 12,000 and 200 m. It was developed for the Nakajima Ki.201 jet fighter. Taki-13 was the low-altitude version for the Ki.67 torpedo-bomber, with a range of 150 to 20 m. A total of 1,000 units were manufactured.

Taki-14 was a prototype of cartographic pathfinder radar, based on the British H2S with a parabolic rotating antenna and PPI display. It operated at a wavelength of 27 cm, with a 2-kW power output and a range of 2 km, with just one prototype being built by Tokyo Shibaura Denki Co. in 1945. Taki-15 Type I was an airborne IFF transponder, with a range of 150 km, for the emissions of the Tachi-3 ground radar. It was developed for the Ki.201 jet fighter with one rod antenna mounted in the back of the rear fuselage.

Flight tests showed heavy interferences caused by the corona effect at high altitude, a defect that was amended in the Type II refined version using a T-R tube to protect the receiver and one rod antenna mounted under the fuselage belly. Some 120 units were built in 1945.

Taki-23 was a jammer covering wavelengths from 7 m to 80 cm. Taki-24 was a version of the Taki-14 with a 10-cm wavelength. Taki-30 was an IFF device with a rod antenna, carried by the Ki.201 interceptor to indicate to the ground system Tachi-28 its accurate location. Fifty units were built in 1945. Taki-34 was a version of the Taki-24 developed by Sumitomo Co. in November 1944, with a 5-cm wavelength, 10-kW power output, and 80-cm parabolic antenna.

As a result of the raid carried out by Doolittle's bombers in April 1942, the IJA began the construction of a chain of fourteen radar sites covering the south and east of the main Japanese islands, from Ashizurimisaki to Shimoshizu, including the island of Hachijo-jima. This radar warning system, equivalent to the British Chain Home, used Tachi-6 radar sets ('Ta' was for Tama and 'Chi' for ground) with a range of 300 km. When the Saipan-based B-29 heavy bombers made their first raid against Tokyo, in November 1944, they were detected by the Tachi-6 thirty minutes in advance—approximately the time it took for Shoki, Toryu, and Raiden interceptors to climb to 9,000 m (the flight altitude of B-29s).

The problem for the Japanese fighters was that American bombers were flying at more than 700 kph, driven by a strong wind of 220–290 kph. These winter winds, common in the area, had not been foreseen by the Americans and greatly affected the accuracy of the bombardment, which had to use the AN/APQ-7 cartographic radar to locate the targets frequently hidden by clouds. Early in March 1945, the AAF staff decided to change the bombing tactic to a series of low-altitude night attacks with the M-47 and M-69 incendiary bombs.

Until then, the Japanese reaction had not been very effective. Out of the seventy-eight B-29s lost in combat missions between November 1944 and March 1945, fifty-three were due to mechanic failures, mainly in their engines. The Japanese fighters lacked the heavy weapons capable of severely damaging the giants and were forced to fight them through air-to-air bombing and suicide attacks. When the bombers began to be escorted by P-51 day fighters in April, the chances of the twin-engined Ki.45, Ki.46, and J1N1 decreased and were withdrawn from service.

Though the majority of 64 sites of Japanese radars provided an early warning, some gun-laying Sumitomo Tachi-3 sets directed AA guns and searchlights, but rarely managed to coordinate their performance due to the effective Windows and Rope jamming systems used by the B-29s. The design of these countermeasures was based on intelligence reports that revealed that the Tachi-3 operated at 200 megacycles because it was based on a British GL Mk II captured in Singapore.

As a result of these tactics, out of more than 31,300 B-29 sorties over Japan, only seventy-four were downed by interceptors (forty-two of them by ramming) and twenty by the AA guns. Early in 1942, the IJN used two types of ground-based radars—the early warning Mark I Model 1 (3 m, 100 MHz) and the gun-laying Mark IV Model 1 (1.5 m, 200 MHz). A Mark I captured by the US Marines at Guadalcanal in August 1942 allowed the Americans to know firsthand the level achieved by Japanese technology and to design the first countermeasures systems.

In March 1943, a B-24 Ferret, fitted with an APA-24 direction-finding antenna, performed reconnaissance flights over Kiska Island and discovered signatures of two Mark I radars. Some Consolidated PBY flying boats were also configured as Ferrets, but neither of them nor the submarines equipped with SIGINT devices could detect the new typed of Japanese radars in 1943. In February 1944, following the capture of Kwajalein

Atoll, the Americans found information about the Mark II Model 2 shipboard radar (10 centimetres, 3 GHz).

Some B-29s were fitted with SIGINT and jammer countermeasures to pick-up Japanese surface radars and other B-29s specialised in jamming missions, known as Porcupines, accompanied the bomber formations. The Japanese also tried to develop jammers and IFF devices that never got into combat as their performances were considered inferior to those of the American teams that could interfere with them.

Japanese GCI fighter direction was rudimentary, and over Japan, there was often chaotic radio communication, with night fighters left to their own devices. The IJA and the IJN used separate warning systems. In June 1944, the Imperial General Headquarters instructed the integration of the Atsugi, Iwakuni, and Omura IJN *Kōkutais* into the respective IJA district. As late as March 1945, the IJA/IJN cooperation had been made effective only in Kobe, Nagoya, and Kyushu with less than one-fifth of its fighters assigned to home defence.

The Allies were not able to make good use of their transportable radar sets in Dunkirk, Malaya, Java, Ceylon, and Guadalcanal. These teams were only useful when they were part of a complex organisation capable of leading fighters equipped with IFF (identification friend or foe) devices and with well-trained radar operators, such as the one used by the British during the Battle of Britain. In late 1941, the Allies lacked night fighters to counter Japanese raids.

Following the attack on Pearl Harbor, the Hawaii air defence consisted of four Curtiss P-40Cs, eighty-five Curtiss P-40Bs, thirty-seven Curtiss P-36As, six Boeing P-26As, and eight Boeing P-26Cs based at Wheeler Air Field; eight Curtiss P-40Cs and two Curtiss P-36As based at Haleiwa Air Field; two Curtiss P-40Bs based at Bellows Air Field; eleven Grumman F4F-3s based at Ewa Air Station; eight Brewster F2A-3s, five Grumman F4F-3s, and five Grumman F4F-3As based at Ford Island Air Station; and five radar stations with SCR-270B sets. After the Japanese attack, out of the 402 military aircraft in Hawaii, 188 were destroyed and 159 were damaged. On 8 December, only eighteen P-40Bs, two P-40Cs, sixteen P-36As, six P-26As, six P-26Cs, and three F4F-3 fighters were left in flying condition.

Fearing a third attack, the few fighters available in Hawaii were constantly kept in flight, but radar operators could not distinguish them from enemy aircraft because they did not have IFF devices installed. The visual detection depended on one observer corps, consisting mainly of civilian volunteers. Identification errors and continuous alarms raised the attrition rate of the planes and exhausted the pilots. In this situation, the Americans decided to use the obsolete P-26s, armed with one 0.50-inch and one 0.30-inch machine guns, as emergency night fighters. Following the withdrawal of the Japanese Fleet, the P-26Cs, equipped with flaps and painted black, continued in service to protect Pearl Harbor from long-range night intruder flying boats based in the Marshall Islands. On 4 March 1942, three Kawanishi H8K1 flying boats from the Yokohama *Kōkutai*, based on Wotje Island, attempted to bomb Pearl Harbor, refuelling from a submarine at French Frigate Shoals. Finally, the attack was aborted due to the poor visibility over Oahu, and the P-26s did not have the occasion to fight.

In January 1942, thirty Hawker Hurricane Mk IIb (Trop) fighters arrived from the 17th and 135th RAF Squadrons with night fighter experienced pilots. On the 24th of the same month, two of the Hurricanes downed a Ki.21 bomber during a night attack over Mingaladon. In May 1943, three Hawker Hurricane Mk IIcs of the 176 Sqn RAF, based at Dum Dum airfield, were fitted with ex-Defiant AI Mk IV radars for the night defence of Calcutta, being replaced by Beaufighter Mk VIs in January of 1944 and Mosquito NF.30s in June 1945.

In January 1941, the USAAC ordered Northrop to develop the specialised night fighter P-61, but after the Japanese attack, it was necessary to transform the Douglas A-20 bomber to a night fighter as a speedy solution. Sixty conversions were authorised under the designation P-70A-1 Nighthawk, with one SCR-540 (SCR meaning signal corps radio) centimetric radar, the US version of the British AI Mk IV and Yagi antennas. The bent folded director dipole (for transmitting) was installed in the solid nose; two fixed quarter wave dipoles, with directors (for azimuth receiving), were mounted on fuselage sides; and two fixed quarter wave rods (for elevation receiving) were mounted one above and one below the port wing. A ventral pack of four 20-mm cannons was fitted in place of the bomb bay.

The 6th NFS (night fighter squadron), with twenty-five P-70 A-1, reached Hawaii in September 1942 and arrived at Guadalcanal in February 1943. The first confirmed combat kill was one Mitsubishi G4M shot down on 19 April. The Nighthawks were too slow and heavy to be effective as night fighters, and eventually, some unmodified Lockheed P-38G day fighters of the 418th, 421st, and 419th squadrons were used for high-altitude interceptions, working with GCI and searchlights, while the P-70s were restricted to low-level missions below 25,000 feet.

Early in 1943s two P-38F from Henderson Field and Guadalcanal were also locally modified with an SCR-540 AI radar mounted in a drop tank. The antennas were fixed on the wings and to either side of the fuselage. The first nocturnal kill was on 16 June 1943. Two single-seat P-38J of the 547th NFS were fitted with one AN/APS-4 radar pod under the starboard wing and used with some success in the Philippines in late 1944. Seventy-five P-38L were modified as P-38M with the addition of a second cockpit and an AN/APS-4 AI radar pod installed under the nose also late in 1944, but the war ended before they could see combat action. The 418th NFS, based in Wake Island, preferred to use some B-25H as night fighters, armed with one 75-mm cannon, as their long endurance allowed them to fly during most of the night. The B-25 ex-bombers were painted flat black but never received any field modification.

The first Northrop P-61A arrived at the Pacific Front in May 1944, equipped with 2,000-hp supercharged engines, with a good climb rate to hunt the Bettys at any altitude and fast enough to intercept the V-1 German missiles. The new fighter, called Black Widow, used two radars—an AI SCR-720A (with 10-cm wavelength, 150-kW power output, 8-km range, and one parabolic antenna with a diameter of 70 cm) and one SCR-695 tail warning radar designed for night fighting in Europe. The main radar included IFF and beacon/homing device. The P-61 used an FR12 A3 gyroscopic fire-control computer and was armed with four 20-mm cannons and four 12.7-mm heavy machine guns. In August 1945, the Black Widow formed part of eight NFS squadrons in the Pacific Theatre, achieving the destruction of sixty-five Japanese aircraft, including the last one shot down during the war, one Nakajima Ki.44.

The lack of night fighters also affected the US Navy, which had to resort to the transformation of fourteen Lockheed PV-1 patrol bombers into a night-fighting role as an interim solution. The aircraft were fitted with one SCR-540 radar set in the nose, with the azimuth antennas installed of the engine nacelles, VHF radios, IFF equipment, and a blister of three forward-firing 12.7-mm heavy machine guns under the nose. In September 1943, the VMF (N)-531 Squadron, with the modified PV-1 night fighters, arrived in the South Pacific accomplishing their first kill, a Betty off Vella Lavella on 13 October. At the end of 1943, 90 per cent of the Japanese bombing attacks were performed at night. To confuse GCI radar operators, night intruders (wood and fabric biplanes) occasionally dropped chaff-simulating false attacks.

In November 1943, during landings in the Gilbert Islands, the US Navy began its first night operations with Hellcat day fighters vectored by shipboard radar, achieving some success. At that time the USS *Enterprise* already had some TBF-1C Avenger torpedo-bombers fitted with the AN/APS-3 radar, an ASV set with marginal AI performance.

The ASV was too bulky for single-seat fighter installation, but these could be guided by a TBF-1C to visually spot the Japanese intruder's blue exhaust flames. The US Navy tried a somewhat different approach using night combat air patrols that consisted of a radar-equipped Avenger (acting as an airborne controller) accompanied by two conventional Hellcats. The first kill was achieved on the night of 22–23 November, when one Mitsubishi Betty was shot down by the Avenger while the Hellcats avoided a collision, a lesson that the British had learnt in 1941 with their Turbinlite teams.

Early in 1944, the first F4U-2 Corsair naval night fighter, equipped with AI radar, finally arrived on Tarawa with the VF(N)-101 Sqn, embarking aboard the USS *Enterprise*. The F4U-2 was an old F4U-1 Birdcage converted into a night fighter with the installation of one Sperry/Western Electric AN/APS-4 AI radar with beacon function, IFF transponder, and AN/APN-1 radio altimeter with two inverted 'T' dipoles fitted under the fuselage belly. Most of the electronic radars, including the Stromberg Mk II modulator, were mounted behind the pilot seat, but the scanner with the 43-cm-diameter parabolic antenna, was housed in a pod merged into the starboard wing's leading edge. The whole set weighed 110 kg. The installation of the pod made it necessary to remove one of the 12.7-mm heavy machine guns.

The AN/APS-4 operated at 3.2-cm wavelength, 40-kW power output, and 4,000-m range; it provided suitable indication for firing guns. Only thirty-four Birdcages were converted into night fighters. In the Pacific Theatre, the VF(N)-75, VF(N)-101, and VMF(N)-532 Squadrons flew the F4U-2 on New Georgia, Eniwetok Atoll, and Wotje Atoll. They also served on USS *Enterprise*, *Essex*, *Hornet*, and *Intrepid* aircraft carriers. The Corsair's long nose and low canopy restricted the visibility of the pilot, making it very dangerous to be used on carrier operations. By January 1945, the US Navy started replacing them with three Bat Eyes Squadrons of F6F-3N and F6F-5N Hellcats, a type of plane considered safer for night missions. The F6F-3N, 150 of which were built with a modified flat windscreen, also used the AN/APS-4 radar fitted into a radome (radar-dome) on the starboard wing, but in this model, there was no need to sacrifice armament.

On 14 May 1945, the VMF(N)-533 flew the F6F-3N from Yontan airfield in Okinawa, achieving his first kill two days later. Grumman built 1,435 F6F-5Ns with the

Westinghouse Electric AN/APS-6A radar and two 12.7-mm machine guns replaced with 20-mm cannons, fitted with exhaust flame dampers, to increase the probability of a first-pass kill. The AN/APS-6A was essentially a compact version of the AN/APS-4 with the modulator in the nacelle, close to the scanner, 3.2-cm wavelength, 40-kW power output, 9,000-m range, a beacon function, an IFF transponder, and an AN/APN-1 radio altimeter. The new AI radar operated in search and gunsight modes, providing a suitable indication for firing guns.

During the first year of naval night fighter operations in the Pacific Theatre, a total of thirty-nine Japanese planes were shot down. In the autumn of 1940, one British scientific mission was sent to the United States to provide information on the radar technical advances being made by Great Britain: IFF transponder, VHF radio, magnetron microwaves, and LORAN electronic navigation system.

During 1941, the Americans developed the FC Mark 3 fire-control radar against surface targets for the US Navy and the FD Mark 4 for directing anti-aircraft weapons. Both radars operated at P-Band frequencies (30–100 cm) and were used in five night flights off Guadalcanal, but without much success due to a lack of experience using the new detection system. The SCR-520, America's first airborne intercept microwave radar operating on S-Band (8–15 cm), was flight tested in March 1941. The anti-aircraft gun-laying radar SCR-584 and the AN/APS-2 ASV, also operating on S-Band, began service in early 1944.

For the all-weather day and night air defence of the fleet, it was necessary to install a ground control intercept (GCI) aboard each aircraft carrier. In the GCI, the night fighter director (FDO) should choose from three types of interception—curve of pursuit, cut-off vector, or head-on intercept—depending on the available fighters and the number of attacking aircraft. The Japanese soon started to use saturation tactics, performing simultaneous attacks with thirty or forty aircraft. From October 1944, the attacks were carried out with suicide planes more and more frequently, and it became necessary for the US Navy to have some kind of airborne early warning system.

The solution, called Project Cadillac, consisted of equipping an aircraft carrier-based TBF Avenger with an AN/APS-20 radar that, operating on L-Band (15–30 cm), could detect large aircraft at ranges of 180 km using a big (2.44 × 0.91 m) elliptical antenna housed in one ventral radome. The 1,043-kg airborne equipment consisted of an AN/APX-13 IFF transponder, an AN/ART-22 relay radar data transmitter, an AN/ARW-35 remote radio control receiver, and an AN/ARC-18 VHF link with the CIC (combat information center) on the home carrier. The system went into service in March 1945. The AN/APQ-7 *Eagle* was a cartographic radar used by the B-29 heavy bombers to locate ground targets over Japan, operated on X-Band (2.5–4 cm) and was so advanced that the Japanese could not replicate it.

7
Operation Downfall

Had Japan not surrendered after the atomic attacks over Hiroshima and Nagasaki in August 1945, the Allies would have been forced to land on the Japanese home islands.

There were plans to carry out the invasion in two phases. The first step, known as Operation Olympic, aimed to occupy the south of Kyushu Island and was to start on 1 November. The second one, Operation Coronet, would have consisted of landings on Honshu Island to control the Tokyo plain, and it was planned for March 1946. The whole plan, Operation Downfall, required 5,000,000 men, 3,000 ships, sixty-six aircraft carriers, loaded with 2,649 aircraft, and all of the aircraft in the 7th, 8th, and 10th Army Air Forces. Casualties were expected to be extremely heavy. A study requested by the US naval secretary estimated that conquering Japan would cost between 1.7 million and 4 million casualties, including 400,000 to 800,000 fatalities, and the destruction of 800 Allied ships.

Japanese High Command understood that human losses were the Achilles' heel of democracies and decided that, after the failure of the *kamikaze* tactics to stop the invasion of Okinawa, the number of casualties caused to the enemy in Kyushu was quite high. They could still negotiate peace by exhaustion and avoid the cost of a final battle at Honshu. Therefore, they forgot the idea of sinking aircraft carriers and battleships and turned their attention to the humble landing craft vehicles (LCV). At this point, the Japanese were no longer interested in sinking the big, heavily armoured warships. The political circumstances were more favourable to the kind of war that caused a high number of casualties to the Allies. It was better to try and destroy the little protected troop transports with a 250-kg warhead.

During the most critical moments of the amphibious assault, dozens of slow and unstable boats, crammed with troops, vehicles, explosives, and fuel, desperately tried to reach the beach under the enemy fire. Some were hit by the artillery, but most of them survived. The Japanese thought that this pattern could be altered and devised all kind of defensive strategies to convert Kyushu into a swamp of blood. They took advantage of the three-to-two local numeric superiority of the Japanese army and mobilised the civil population to perform *banzai* charges.

At sea, the forty surviving submarines of the IJN waited for their opportunity. Many Shinyo suicide motorboats, loaded with 250 kg of explosive, got ready in caves and coastal refuges. It would have been more than enough to destroy the landing ship tank (LST). Fukuryu divers would wait in submarine shelters built at a depth of 15 m to attack the belly of the LCV with anti-tank hollow charges fixed to the end of long poles.

Having most of the interceptors busy defending the fleet, it was expected that just a few fighter-bombers of the Marines would operate at the landing area, attacking the coastal defences. In that scenario, a suicide attack by light bombers could cause a lot of damage. Many training aircraft from the flying schools were modified to counteract that effect. They were Tachikawa Ki.9 and Yokosuka K5Y1 types with a 100-kg bomb under the fuselage or with a single 200-l drum full of gasoline and phosphorous embedded in the rear seat.

The defensive plan of the Japanese High Command (Operation Ketsu-Go) included the use of the 12,725 aircraft available in one single and uninterrupted attack with the purpose of collapsing the defences of the Allied fleet. A force of 2,000 IJA and IJN Japanese fighters would battle to control the skies over Kyushu Island. While the Allied fleet would still be in open sea and approaching Japan, the warships of the Task Force would be attacked by 330 IJN suicide bombers, then a group of 825 IJA and IJN suicide aircraft would try to sink the troop transports.

Once the invasion ships got close to their proposed anchorages, another 2,000 suicide aircraft would be launched hour after hour in non-stop attacks that the Japanese hoped could be sustained for ten days. Thirty-five camouflaged airfields and nine seaplane bases had been built in Kyushu for that purpose. The Japanese also had twenty suicide take-off strips with underground hangars, from where the Ki.115 Tsurugi and Baika Model 1 suicide bombers could operate.

They were also building twenty suicide take-off strips in Southern Kyushu, with underground hangars for the Baikas and Tsurugis, as well as thirty-five camouflaged airfields for the conventional *tokko* aircrafts and nine seaplane bases. There were 2,500 *kamikaze* aircraft in Korea, Honshu, and Shikoki airfields ready for ten days of non-stop attacks that would exhaust the defensive resources of the invading fleet and the loss of a third of their ships. Yet the decisive battle would be fought on the 2,000 yards of sea between the beach and the great supply vessels.

The Ohka 43-Otsu suicide bombers would use some straight railway sections and rocket-propelled trolleys to operate. It was very effective but had the handicap of using the new Ne-20 turbojet, of which just a few units were available. The Ki.115 could use several types of second-hand conventional engines but it required 80-octane gasoline, which was almost non-existent in Japan due to the naval blockade. On the other hand, the Ne-20 could work with a mixture of wood turpentine and charcoal, although the battered Japanese industry could not manufacture them in high enough numbers on time for *Ketsu-Go*.

The Japanese scientists found the solution to this situation with the mass production of pulsejet engines based on the Argus As 109-014 scale drawings that the I-8 submarine had brought from Germany in 1943. The Japanese version, known as Maru Ka-10, was designed by professors Ichiro Tami and Taichiro Ogawa of the Aeronautical Institute of Tokyo Imperial University in 1944. The *Maru Ka*-10 was 3,750 mm long, 550 mm in diameter, and weighed 153 kg, producing 360 kg of thrust at 740 kph. It used Benzol as fuel during the flying tests, although it could also work with low-quality oil or heavy kerosene. It was expected that the operational version would burn 1,600 l of crude pine root oil that the local chemical industry produced as ersatz fuel.

Japan did never receive the blueprints of the V-1 missile or for their manned variant *Reichenberg* as the German submarine carrying them was sunk. They were forced to design their own version based on a general description of the German model. The result was a small, low-wing monoplane made from wood and steel, given the scarcity of aluminium. By the beginning of 1945, their mass production was ordered by the Kawanishi Kokuki KK firm, under the Baika denomination.

The Kawanishi Baika Model 1 took off from a conventional aerodrome, reaching the ignition speed of the pulsejet (360 kph) thanks to the thrust of its three *Toku-Ro.1* Type 2 rockets with 600 kg of thrust, located in the wing roots and in the fuselage centreline. Its main undercarriage (from a Ki.115) and the rockets (from an *Ohka* 43) were jettisoned after take-off.

The high rate of fuel consumption of the pulsejet allowed a range of just 204 km at the cruise speed of 556 kph at sea level. The Model 1 could only operate against troop transports located near the southern coast of Kyushu. To that purpose, they planned to have a Type 97 warhead with 150 kg of Torpex HE (from a Type 91 mod. 1 airborne torpedo) to impact under the ship waterline. Operation Olympic never happened thanks to the use of the nuclear bombs that put an end to the war, saving a considerable number of lives on both sides.

On 9 October 1945, the typhoon *Louise* passed over the Okinawa Island, with winds of 150–220 kph and heavy seas with 9–11 m waves, causing serious damage to the Allied occupation forces based in Nakagusuku Wan, Amami Oshima, Nagasaki, and Wakayama. A total of twelve ships (including six LST) were sunk, 222 were grounded, thirty-two were damaged beyond economical repair, and over sixty aircraft were damaged. In Okinawa, almost all the food, medical supplies, and 80 per cent of all buildings were destroyed with 183 personal casualties.

Had the war not ended by early September, the tremendous storm would have caused serious damage to the invasion force, forcing the cancellation of Operation Olympic. The war against Japan could have become an early Vietnam.

Bibliography

BOOKS

Brindley, J., *Nakajima Ki.44 Shoki (Tojo)* (Profile Number 255)

Bueschel, R., *Kawasaki Ki.61/ Ki.100 Hien in Japanese Army Air Force Service* (Aircam Aviation Series No. 21, Osprey, 1971)

Bueschel, R., *Mitsubishi A6M1/2/2n Zero-Sen* (Aircam Aviation Series No. 16, Osprey 1970)

Bueschel, R., *Nakajima Ki.44 Shoki Ia,b,c/IIa,b,c in Japanese Army Air Force Service* (Aircam Aviation Series No. 25, Osprey, 1971)

Bueschel, R., *Nakajima Ki.84 a/b Hayate in Japanese Army Air Force Service* (Aircam Aviation Series No. 29, 1971)

Dyer, E., *Japanese Secret Projects* (Midland Publishing, 2009)

Dyer, E., *Japanese Secret Projects-2* (Crécy Publishing, 2014)

Francillon, R., *Japanese Aircraft of the Pacific War* (Putnam, 1970)

Francillon, R., *The Kawasaki Ki.45 Toryu* (Profile Number 105)

Francillon, R., *The Kawasaki Ki.61 Hien* (Profile Number 118)

Francillon, R., *The Mitsubishi A6M2 Zero-Sen* (Profile No. 129)

Francillon, R., *The Mitsubishi Ki.46* (Profile Number 82)

Francillon, R., *The Nakajima Ki.84* (Profile Publications number 70, 1966)

Gakken, *The IJA Warplanes* (Gakken Rekishi Gunzo, 2000)

Green, W., *War Planes of the Second World War, Fighters Volume Three* (Macdonald, 1961)

Gustin, E., *Flying Guns, World War II* (Airlife Publishing, 2003)

Imai, K., *Japanese Imperial Army Aircraft, Koku-Fan No. 4* (Burin-Do, 1987)

Januszewski, T., *Japonskie Samoloty Marynarki 1912–1945* (tom 2, Wydawnictwo Lampart, 2000)

Kazuhiko, I., *Kikka: The Technological Verification of the First Japanese Jet Engine Ne 20* (Miki Press, 2006)

Koei, C., *Japan Project Aircraft* (W.W.II Illustrated, 1997)

Makinio, I., *The Final Weapon Shusui, Memory of the Designer* (Kojinsha, February 2006.)

Matsuba, M., *All the experimental aircraft in Japanese Army* (Kantosha Mook, 2008)

Matsuba, M., *Design with Precision #4: Japanese Army & Navy Experimental Aircraft* (Kantosha pubs. 1997)

Mikesh, R., *Kikka* (Monogram Close-Up Vol. 19, 1979)

Millot, B., *Les Chasseurs Japonais de la Deuxieme Guerre Mondiale* (DOCAVIA No. 7, 1976)

Mitsui, I., *Famous Airplanes of the World, No. 24, Army Experimental Fighters* (Burin-Do, September 1990)

Nohara, S., *A6M Zero in Action* (Squadron/Signal Publications, Aircraft Number 59, 1983)

Peczkowski, R., *Mitsubishi J2M Raiden-Jack* (Mushoroom Model Publications, 2004)

Preisler, J., *Code Name Caesar: The Secret Hunt for U.Boat 864 During World War II* (Dutton Caliber, 2012)
Richards, M., *Mitsubishi A6M5 to A6M8 Zero-Sen, Zeke 52* (Profile No. 236)
Ryusuke, I., *Japanese Special Attack Aircraft & Flying Bombs* (Casemate Publishers, 2009)
Sakaida, H., *Imperial Japanese Navy Aces 1937–45* (Osprey Publishing, 1999)
Sakaida, H., *Japanese Air Force Aces 1937–45* (Osprey, 1997)
Scalia, J., *Germany's Last Mission to Japan: The Failed Voyage of U-234* (Naval Institute Press, 2009)
Takamori, J., *Mitsubishi A6M Reisen Zero* (Les Ailes de Gloire No. 2, Indochine, 2000)
Tanaka, M., *Nakajima Ki.84 'Frank' Hayate* (Aero Detail 24, 1999)
Thorpe, D., *Japanese Army Air Force Camouflage and Markings* (World War II, Aero Publishers, 1968)
Yamashita, T., *Kikka* (Model Art, 1998)

PUBLICATIONS

Aireview, 'Unknown Military Aircraft Development', *Airewiew Magazine Special Edition Vol. (2/2).*
Allward, M., 'Jet Propulsion in Japan', *Air Reserve Gazette*, June 1946.
Baëza, B., 'Les Aigles Sauvages de l'Armée Impériale Japonaise', *Avions*, No. 220.
Cortellini, F., '*Un giapponese dal cuore teutónico*', *Model Time* 73/02.
Green, W., 'Fighter A to Z', *Air International*, November 1994.
Green, W., 'Kawasaki's Steam-Cooled Ki.64 Fighter', *Air International,* February 1978.
Green, W., 'Mitsubishi Ki.46 the Aesthetic Asiatic', *Air International*, November 1980.
Green, W., 'The Asiatic Thunderbolt', *Air Enthusiast*, July 1971.
Huggins, M., 'Setting Sun, Japanese Air Defence of the Philippines 1944–45', *Air Enthusiast,* May/June 1999.
Imagawa, Y., 'Japan's Final Sword Stroke … The Story of Shusui', *Air International*, Volume 10, Number 6, June 1976.
Kazuiko, O., 'Les Yeux de l'Armée Japonaise: Le Mitsubishi Ki.46 Shin Shitei (Dinah)', *Avions* No. 197.
Maloney, E., 'Japanese Aircraft Performance & Characteristics', *TAIC Manual*, 2000.
Military, I., 'Airborne Radar: Operations and Tactics', *Military Analysis* (Rep. No. 493).
Military, I., 'German Technical Aid to Japan (Rep. No. 14217)', *Military Intelligence Service,* Washington, 1945.
Military, I., 'Japanese Army Aircraft Production', *Advanced Echelon FEAF* (Rep. No. 5), Air Technical Intelligence Group, 1945.
Military, I., 'Turbojets and Rocket Engines (JAF)', *Advanced Echelon FEAF* (Rep. No. 52), Air Technical Intelligence Group, 1945.
Military. I., 'Ishikawajima Shibaura Turbine', *Reports of Tokyo-Ishikawajima-Shibaura Turbine Co-Ltd*, 1945.
Millot, B., 'Ki.78, *Les Tiroirs de l'Inconnu*', le Fanatique de l'Aviation No. 12.
Millot, B., '*Le Curieux* Kawasaki Ki.64 (Rob)', *Le Fanatique de l'Aviation No. 157.*
Millot, B., 'Les Avions du Pacifique 1941–1945, Kawasaki Hien', *Le Fanatique de l'Aviation* No. 15 to 17.
Millot, B., 'Mitsubishi Type 100, Ki.46 Shin Shitei (Dinah)', *Le Fanatique de l'Aviation No. 87-88.*
Millot, B., 'Nakajima Ki.44 Shoki', *Le Fanatique de l'Aviation* No. 125–126, 1980.
Millot, B., 'Yokosuka R2Y Keiun', *Le Fanatique de l'Aviation* No. 72.
Nagano, O., 'Interview of Commander Osamu Nagano, IJN', Air Technical Intelligence Review, No. F-IR-57-RE.
Picarella, G., 'Kawasaki Ki.100 Database', *Aeroplane*, November 2005.
Rearden, J., 'Enduring Heritage', *Aviation History*, November 2000.
Redermann, H., 'Kawasaki Ki.78', *Flug Revue* 11/1978.
Sakaida, H., 'Air-to-air kamikaze', *Combat Aircraft*, 654.
Salter R., 'Japanese Power Plants for Jet Propulsion', Power Plant Memorandum No. 18, NAVY Department, Bureau of Aeronautics, Washington.
Thompson, S., 'The Zero one step beyond', *Air & Space, Smithsonian*, February/March 1990.
USAF, R., 'Japanese Aircraft Industry in WW2', USAF report for 1946.
Voaden, D., 'Japanese Jet Aircraft at the end of the Second World War', *Air Pictorial*, August 1954.